Proceedings

16th Conference on Software Engineering Education and Training

CSEE&T 2003

Usability = 16 (roles)

UI Designs, as course module:
    8 (UI Dev.)
    76
    253

D1
reduction of
knowledge transfer
according / with
Maturity Model ?
(from knowledge to action)

of high interest:
    78 Strategy-based eval., value systems lyrs vs SE's
    158 Non-technical skills: communication / interaction
    120   "

Bernard p. 140 ; Udo 216 cards

Proceedings

16th Conference on Software Engineering Education and Training

Madrid, Spain
March 20 – 22, 2003

Sponsored by
IEEE Computer Society Technical Council on Software Engineering (TCSE)

IEEE
COMPUTER
SOCIETY

http://computer.org

Los Alamitos, California

Washington • Brussels • Tokyo

IEEE Computer Society Order Number PR01869
ISBN 0-7695-1869-9
ISSN Number 1093-0175

Additional copies may be ordered from:

IEEE Computer Society	IEEE Service Center	IEEE Computer Society
Customer Service Center	445 Hoes Lane	Asia/Pacific Office
10662 Los Vaqueros Circle	P.O. Box 1331	Watanabe Bldg., 1-4-2
P.O. Box 3014	Piscataway, NJ 08855-1331	Minami-Aoyama
Los Alamitos, CA 90720-1314	Tel: + 1-732-981-0060	Minato-ku, Tokyo 107-0062
Tel: + 1-714-821-8380	Fax: + 1-732-981-9667	JAPAN
Fax: + 1-714-821-4641	http://shop.ieee.org/store/	Tel: + 81-3-3408-3118
E-mail: cs.books@computer.org	customer-service@ieee.org	Fax: + 81-3-3408-3553
		tokyo.ofc@computer.org

Editorial production by Bob Werner
Cover art design and production by Joe Daigle/Studio Productions
Printed in the United States of America by The Printing House

Table of Contents

16th Conference on Software Engineering Education and Training (CSEE&T 2003)

Foreword..**xi**

Conference Organizers ....**xiii**

Program Committee...**xiv**

Additional Reviewers ....**xiv**

Remembering Norm Gibbs
Session Chair: Nancy Mead

Norm Gibbs — A Leader in Software Engineering Education...2

Norm Gibbs and his Contribution to Software Engineering Education through the SEI Curriculum Modules..........3
   D. Budgen and J. Tomayko

The Softer Side of Custom Software Development: Working with the Other Players 14
   W. Poole

Norm's Legacy: A Perspective from the Next Generation 22
   D. Bagert

Norm Gibbs — Department Chair, Facilitator, Motivator and Visionary 27
   W. Zage

Keynotes

Teaching How to Engineer Software..30 ML ✗
   D. Rombach

Abstraction — Is It Teachable ? 'The Devil Is In The Detail'..32 ML ✗
   J. Kramer

Software Engineering in the 21st Century — A View from the Trenches.   *cancelled* 33
   C. Horn

Undergraduate Software Engineering Education Options: Independent Programs,
Specializations or Subjects 34
   N. Juristo

Papers

Software Engineering and Industry 1 (Paper Session A)
Session Chair: Ramanathan Narayanan

Teaching Software Engineering Fundamentals to Practicing Engineers 36
P. Strooper, D. Carrington, S. Newby, and T. Stevenson

Industry/University Software Engineering Collaborations for the Successful
Reeducation of Non-Software Professionals 44
H. Ellis, A. Moreno, N. Mead, and S. Seidman

Soft(ware) Skills in Context: Corporate Usability Training Aiming at Cross-Disciplinary Collaboration..............52
B. Rummel and M. Latzina

Software Engineering and Industry 2 (Paper Session B)
Session Chair: Michael Ryan

On a Partnership between Software Industry and Academia..60
A. Kornecki, S. Khajenoori, D. Gluch, and N. Kameli

Aligning Workforce Development and Software Process Improvement Strategy for
Accelerated Adoption of Software Engineering Capability..70
J. Mason

Educating Software Engineering Managers...78
L. Peters

Software Engineering Curriculum 1 (Paper Session C)
Session Chair: Don Bagert

What Should Graduating Software Engineers Be Able To Do? 88
A. Cowling

Engineering an Introductory Software Engineering Curriculum 99
T. Hilburn, A. Sobel, G. Hislop, and R. Duley

A Coordinated Plan for Teaching Software Engineering in the
Rey Juan Carlos University 107
J. Pérez-Martínez and A. Sierra-Alonso

Software Engineering Curriculum 2 (Paper Session D)
Session Chair: Jocelyn Armarego

A Practical Approach of Teaching Software Engineering 120
M. Gnatz, L. Kof, F. Prilmeier, and T. Seifert

Software Engineering Education: Following a Moving Target 129
D. Rosca, W. Tepfenhart, and J. McDonald

Is Software Engineering Training Enough for Software Engineers? 140
I. Crnkovic, R. Land, and A. Sjögren

Software Engineering Curriculum 3 (Paper Session E)
Session Chair: Susan Mengel

Teaching Ethics in the Software Engineering Curriculum...150
    E. Towell

Reviewing the Curriculum of Software Engineering Undergraduate Courses to Incorporate
Communication and Interpersonal Skills Teaching 158
    V. Teles and C. de Oliveira

Reflections on a UK Masters Level Software Engineering Programme for the
Home and International Market...166
    H. Edwards and J. Thompson

Software Engineering Methods 1 (Paper Session F)
Session Chair: Pete Knoke

Teaching a Software Development Methodology: The Case of Extreme Programming 176
    O. Hazzan and Y. Dubinsky

Improving Project Planning/Tracking for Student Software Engineering Projects through SOPPTS....................185
    D. Zage, J. Zhang, and W. Zage

Together We Stand: Group Projects for Integrating Software Engineering in the Curriculum 193
    D. Dalcher and M. Woodman

Software Engineering Methods 2 (Paper Session G)
Session Chair: Pierre Bourque

Modelling: A Neglected Feature in the Software Engineering Curriculum...206
    A. Cowling

An Experimental Card Game for Teaching Software Engineering...216
    A. Baker, E. Navarro, and A. van der Hoek

What Cognitive Activities are Performed in Student Projects? 224
    E. Germain and P. Robillard

Software Engineering Methods 3 (Paper Session H)
Session Chair: Gregory Hislop

Reflecting Skills and Personality Internally as Means for Team Performance Improvement 234
    W. Zuser and T. Grechenig

Some Experiences with Evolution and Process-Focused Projects..242
    N. Wilde, L. White, L. Kerr, D. Ewing, and E. Krueger

The Cross-Course Software Engineering Project at the NTNU: Four Years of Experience..................................251
    G. Sindre, T. Stålhane, G. Brataas, and R. Conradi

Software Engineering Process (Paper Session I)
Session Chair: Joe Clifton

Can We Influence Students' Attitudes about Inspections? Can We Measure a Change in Attitude?....................260
D. Bailey, T. Conn, B. Hanks, and L. Werner

Assessing Attitude Towards, Knowledge of, and Ability to Apply, Software Development Process...................268
D. Klappholz, L. Bernstein, and D. Port

Introducing Testing Practices into *Objects and Design* Course...279
E. Barbosa, R. LeBlanc, M. Guzdial, and J. Maldonado

Software Engineering – Other Topics (Paper Session J)
Session Chair: Ana Moreno

Inspections and Historical Data in Teaching Software Engineering Project Course 288
T. Ahtee

A Study Program for Professional Software Engineering 298
E. Horn and M. Kupries

Learning Software Engineering with Group Work...309
M. Alfonso and F. Mora

Panels

Developing an Undergraduate Software Engineering Degree
Chair: J. Naveda
Panellists: J. Armarego, D. Bagert, S. Eisenbach, T. Hilburn, and S. Seidman

Panel Statement 318

Software Engineering Retraining — Different Perspectives
Chair: M. Murphy
Panellists: J. Diaz-Herrera, P. Thompson, and D. Ramsey

Panel Statement 322

Certification for Software Professionals: The IEEE Computer Society's CSDP Program
Chair: S. Seidman
Panellists: D. Bagert, D. Frailey, J. Mason, F. Naveda, A. Parrish, and A. Sobel

Panel Statement 323

Workshops

Preparing for the 2004 IEEE Computer Society International Design Competition (CSIDC)
S. Land and A. Clements

Workshop Statement 326

Software Engineering Course Materials
G. Hislop, T. Hilburn, M. Lutz, S. Mengel, and M. Sebern

Workshop Statement 327

Tailoring a Successful Project-Based Course — In Which Students Learn to Work in Teams on the Development of Useful Software Products for Real Clients — To the Needs and Resource Constraints of Individual Colleges and Universities
B. Boehm, D. Port, and D. Klappholz

Workshop Statement 329

Tools for Outcomes Assessment of Education and Training in the Software Development Process
D. Klappholz, L. Bernstein, D. Port, and P. Dominic

Workshop Statement 331

IEEE-CS/ACM Computing Curriculum Software Engineering Volume Project
S. Mengel, A. Sobel, R. LeBlanc, M. Ben-Menachem, T. Lethbridge, J. Diaz-Herrera, T. Hilburn, and B. Thompson

Workshop Statement 333

SWEBOK: Adjustments for Education
R. Dupuis and P. Bourque

Workshop Statement 335

Tutorials

Managing the Performance of Software Engineering Professionals
L. Peters

Tutorial Statement 338

Training Experts in the Fundamentals: An Experience in Providing Software Engineers with the Basis of Software Process Improvement
N. Ovalle and H. Egdorf

Tutorial Statement 339

Author Index **341**

Foreword

Welcome to the 16th International Conference on Software Engineering Education and Training (CSEE&T 2003). The conference provides a forum for discussion of software engineering education and training by members of the academic, industry, and government communities. It continues a tradition of offering direction, promoting innovation and collaboration, and stimulating new instructional approaches. Attendance at past conferences has been drawn from many countries, and this year for the first time it is being held outside the USA, in the beautiful and historic city of Madrid, Spain. We hope that you will be able to sample some of the charms of this area in addition to enjoying the conference program.

CSEE&T 2003 includes a wide range of activities that promote new ideas and new synergies and provide for an exciting program.

Its principal theme is 'Software Engineering in Industry and Education for the 21st Century'. Just as the 19th Century is sometimes described as the age of steam, and the 20th Century as the age of electricity, the 21st Century is likely to have software as a defining technology. The educational challenges involved in helping understand and develop this technology and apply it in a professional manner are clearly going to be of great importance in the years ahead.

The conference addresses these challenges in a number of ways.

Keynotes: Our four keynote speakers look at present and coming challenges in software engineering education and training. They draw on a wealth of experience, both academic and industrial, and are based in four different European countries. With the conference in Europe for the first time this year we felt it appropriate to try to capture a broad European viewpoint, and draw on as many European countries as possible. Our speakers are:

- Dr. Chris Horn, Chairman, Iona Technologies, Dublin, Ireland.
- Prof. Natalia Juristo, Universidad Poletechnica de Madrid, Spain
- Prof. Jeff Kramer, Department of Computing, Imperial College, London, UK
- Prof. Dr. Dieter Rombach, Fraunhofer Institut Experimentelles Software Engineering, Germany

Abstracts of their talks and brief biographical sketches can be found later in these proceedings.

Papers: We received a total of 54 papers. All were subject to multiple blind reviews, and a total of 30 selected for inclusion in the conference. These can be grouped under five main headings:

- Software Engineering in Industry/ Industry-University collaboration
- Software Engineering Curricula
- Software Engineering Methods
- Management/Process
- Other topics

In addition, there are four invited papers in commemoration of the late Norm Gibbs.

Panels: Three panels have been organized. "Certification for Software Professionals: The IEEE Computer Society's CSDP Program" gives an opportunity to discuss this important certification program with some of those involved in its development. "Developing an Undergraduate Software Engineering Degree" provides an opportunity for discussion with panelists who have been involved in doing just that, and "Software Engineering Retraining: Different Perspectives" deals with industry/university collaboration in software engineering education and training.

Workshops: Six workshops, including an invited workshop on SWEBOK, are included. "IEEE-CS/ACM Computing Curriculum Software Engineering Volume Project" gives an authoritative account of the work being done jointly by these organizations. "Software Engineering Course Materials" deals with materials being prepared as part of a SWENET project. "Tools for Outcomes Assessment of Education and Training in Software Development Process" looks at an important aspect of the pedagogic problems involved, "Tailoring a Successful Project-Based Course..." draws on six years experience of teaching by developing software for real clients, and "Preparing for the 2004 IEEE Computer Society International Design Competition" should be of real assistance to those whose students wish to enter this competition. The invited SWEBOK workshop deals with the ongoing work to codify the body of knowledge associated with software engineering.

Tutorials: There are two tutorials, "Managing the Performance of Software Engineering Professionals" and "Training Experts in the Fundamentals: An Experience in Providing Software Engineers with the Basis for Software Process Improvement." Both tutorials draw on extensive experience of software engineering in practice, and should be of particular interest to those involved with software development in industry.

Remembering Norm Gibbs: The program includes a special session in tribute to the late Norm Gibbs. The session includes four invited talks on Norm's accomplishments and legacy, plus a special presentation. Norm Gibbs was a distinguished pioneer in the fields of Software Engineering and Software Engineering Education, and among many other things founder of this annual conference.

We hope we can be forgiven for our Eurocentric choice of keynote speakers. The other activities above draw on participants from all over the World, and we believe that the conference should be of interest to a broad international audience. In designing the program we have also kept the needs of both industry and academia in mind, and we hope that both communities will find it relevant and of benefit.

We would like to thank all those who submitted papers, or suggestions for panels, workshops or tutorials; the members of the Program Committee for their advice and work; the members of the Conference Steering Committee (chairman Don Bagert) for their help and guidance; the IEEE Computer Society, especially our proceedings production manager Bob Werner, for help in preparing these proceedings; our Financial Chair (Dawn C Ramsey) and Publicity Chairs (Fernando Naveda and Claes Wohlin); and finally the local arrangements committee (Oscar Dieste, Xavier Ferré and Sira Vegas) whose sterling work has been at the core of everything that has happened. Many thanks also to the organizations that have supported CSEE&T 2003: the IEEE Computer Society, The University of Alaska Fairbanks, The Universidad Politécnica de Madrid, Dublin City University and AEP Systems Ltd.

Michael Ryan, Program Chair
Ana Moreno, Conference Co-Chair
Pete Knoke, Conference Co-Chair

Conference Organizers

General Chairs

Pete Knoke
University of Alaska Fairbanks
USA

Ana M. Moreno
Universidad Politécnica de Madrid
SPAIN

Program Chair
Michael Ryan
Dublin City University
IRELAND

Financial Chair
Dawn Ramsey
Southern Polytechnic University
USA

Publicity Chairs

J. Fernando Naveda
Rochester Institute of Technology
USA

Claes Wohlin
Blekinge Institute of Technology
SWEDEN

Steering Committee
Chair: Don Bagert
Rose-Hulman Institute of Technology
USA

Pierre Bourque, École de Technologie Supérieure, CANADA
David Budgen, Keele University, USA
Robert Dupuis, Université du Québec á Montréal, CANADA
Dennis Frailey, Raytheon, USA.
Tom Horton, University of Virginia, USA
Peter Knoke, University of Alaska Faribanks, USA
Mike McCracken, Georgia Tech, USA
Nancy Mead, Software Engineering Institute, USA
Susan Mengel, Texas Tech University, USA
Ana M. Moreno, Universidad Politécnica de Madrid, SPAIN
Dawn Ramsey, Southern Polytechnic University, USA
Michael Ryan, Dublin City University, IRELAND
Hossein Saiedian, University of Kansas, USA
Ann Sobel, Miami University, USA
Tim Lethbridge of the University of Ottawa, CANADA

General Chair of CSEE&T 2004 in Norfolk, Virginia, USA
Tom Horton
University of Virginia
USA

Program Committee

Dr. Jan van Amstel, Philips Research Laboratories, NETHERLANDS
Jocelyn Armarengo, Murdoch University, AUSTRALIA
Don Bagert, Rose-Hulman Institute of Technology, USA
J. Barrie Thompson, University of Sunderland, UK
M. Brian Blake, Georgetown University, USA
Robert Cochran, National Centre for Software Engineering, IRELAND
Mats Daniels, Uppsala University, SWEDEN
Fadi Deek, New Jersey Institute of Technology, USA
Prof. Dr. H. Dieter Rombach, Universität Kaiserslautern, GERMANY
Robert Dupuis, Universite de Quebec a Montreal, CANADA
Heidi Ellis, Rensselaer at Hartford, USA
Dennis J. Frailey, Raytheon Company, USA
Tom Hilburn, Embry-Riddle University, USA
Frank Houdek, Daimlerchrysler, GERMANY
Natalia Juristo, Universidad Politécnica de Madrid, SPAIN
Pete Knoke, University of Alaska, USA
Timothy C. Lethbridge, University of Ottawa, CANADA
Jochen Ludewig, Universitat Stuttgart, GERMANY
Ewa Lukasik, Technical University of Poznan, POLAND
Jeff Magee, Imperial College, UK
James Mason, SIAC, USA
Jim McDonald, Monmouth University, USA
Nancy Mead, SEI, Carnegie-Mellon University, USA
Ramanathan Narayanan, Tata Consultancy Services, INDIA
Heikki Saastamoinen, University of Jyvaskyla, FINLAND
Sotirios Skevoulis, Pace University, USA
Ann Sobel, Miami University, USA
Giancarlo Succi, Politécnico de Milano, ITALY
Laurie Williams, North Carolina State University, USA

Additional Reviewers

C.L. Campbell, New Jersey Institute of Technology, USA
Kyungsub Steve Choi, New Jersey Institute of Technology, USA
Marcus Ciolkowski, University of Kaiserslautern, GERMANY
Dr. Joanna DeFranco-Tommarello, New Jersey Institute of Technology, USA
Xavier Ferre, Universidad Politécnica de Madrid, SPAIN
T. Hampp, IBM T.J. Watson Research Center, USA
Ralf Kalmar, Fraunhofer IESE, Kaiserslautern, GERMANY
J. Fernando Naveda, Rochester Institute of Technology, USA
Stefan Opferkuch, Universitat Stuttgart, GERMANY
Rainer Schmidberger, Universitat Stuttgart, GERMANY

Remembering Norm Gibbs

Norm Gibbs

Norm Gibbs – A Leader in Software Engineering Education

Norm Gibbs obtained a Bachelor of Science degree in Mathematics from Ursinus College in 1964 and earned his MS and PhD in Computer Science from Purdue University in 1966 and 1969 respectively. Norm was the 14th student to be awarded a PhD from Purdue's Department of Computer Science.

While at Ursinus Norm set a goal to become a professor and upon graduation he accepted a teaching assistantship from the Division of Mathematical Sciences at Purdue University in West Lafayette, Indiana. During his first term he met his wife Barbara (also a TA) in an Abstract Algebra class. Barbara was a secondary school mathematics teacher until their two children were born. She now teaches part time for Ball State's Department of Mathematical Sciences. Their daughter Karen is an Associate of the Society of Actuaries and is employed by Nationwide Insurance in Columbus, Ohio and until recently Jennifer was a systems analyst at BTI (an integrated communications provider) in North Carolina's research triangle.

Norm's academic career consisted of professorships at Bowdoin College in Maine, Arizona State University, and the College of William and Mary in Virginia.

He spent over a decade as the first Director of Carnegie Mellon University's Software Engineering Institute's (CMU SEI) Education Program. During Norm's tenure, the Education Program led the effort to develop a model software engineering curriculum, which is still in use in a number of Masters of Software Engineering (MSE) degree programs throughout the world. He was also named professor of computer science and was the founding director of Carnegie Mellon's professional Master's of Software Engineering degree program. He later became Director of SEI's Products and Services Division. While he was at the SEI, he received an ACM award for outstanding contribution to computer science education in 1994

He then served as Director of Information Technology and Services at Guilford College in Greensboro, North Carolina. As the College's chief information officer, he took the lead in the redesign and implementation of an entirely new academic and administrative computing environment for the College that leveraged best practices in information technology.

Subsequently, he was at the University of Connecticut where he served as Executive Director of the Connecticut Information Technology Institute (CITI) located at the University of Connecticut's Stamford Campus and as professor of Operations and Information Management where he taught courses in e-Commerce Technology.

Norm joined Ball State's Computer Science Department as Chair on July 1, 2000, and remained there until he passed away on April 25, 2002.

He published numerous articles, edited many publications and has co-authored two books in the Information Technology field. He was a member of the Editorial Board for the Annals of Software Engineering, served on advisory committees and boards, held elected offices in ACM and was a computer science education consultant for colleges and universities throughout the United States.

Norm Gibbs and His Contribution to Software Engineering Education Through the SEI Curriculum Modules

David Budgen
Department of Computer Science
Keele University
Staffordshire ST5 5BG
U.K.
d.budgen@cs.keele.ac.uk
and
James E Tomayko
School of Computer Science
Carnegie Mellon University
Pittsburgh PA 15213
USA
jet@cs.cmu.edu

Abstract

The Software Engineering Institute (SEI) at Carnegie Mellon University started its first contract with a carte blanche opportunity and generous funding to improve the state of software engineering education. Norm Gibbs, the first Director of Education at the SEI guided efforts is thus area. One of his innovations, discussed here, were the "curriculum modules" encapsulating software engineering knowledge.

1. Introduction

Norm Gibbs was the founding Director of the Software Engineering Institute's (SEI) Education Group (later Program), and was appointed to this post in 1985 from Bowdoin College, where he was the founding chair. In this paper we look back at the early work of the Group, and in particular at its influence upon wider Software Engineering thinking through the pioneering role of the *Curriculum Modules* which formed part of its remit. Our paper is written largely from a personal and participating perspective and we have drawn upon our notes and records (as well as our memories) to try to recreate the sense of excitement that pervaded the early years of the SEI.

In this brief introduction we review the form and nature of the Education Group at that time, as well as its main activities. We then discuss the curriculum modules in a little more detail, followed by some personal experiences with the development of the early modules. Finally we reflect upon the wider influence of these modules.

1.1 The Education Group, circa 1986

At the start of 1986, when we were both first involved with the activities of the group, Norm was still building up his team and the core members at that point were:

Norm Gibbs as Director

Gary Ford (Senior Computer Scientist)

Jim Tomayko (on sabbatical leave from Wichita State University, KS, December 1985 to May 1987)

David Budgen (on sabbatical leave from the University of Stirling, Scotland, February-July 1986)

Albert Johnson (Technical Project Administration)

Alison Brunvand (Secretarial support)

and this continued to be the operative group over the period covered by this paper (circa 1986).

At this point, the SEI was still operating from its temporary location in Shadyside Place, and it is worth reviewing the then 'state of the art' computing resources that we employed at that time.

❑ Computing was performed using microVax computers running BSD Unix and dumb terminals.

❑ The postscript-based laserprinter had just become available and formed a key production tool.

❑ Text processing was performed using the *Scribe* system developed by Brian Reid (a CMU graduate), which is basically a mark-up formatting system that generates postscript for the laserprinters.

❑ For electronic internal communication, we employed the Carnegie Mellon *Bulletin Board* system (basically a set of structured mail lists) and e-mail.

❑ Networked e-mail was still in its relative infancy, but was improving rapidly[*].

The SEI itself was a rapidly expanding organisation that was still finding its feet and establishing its role (having only been founded in 1984). In that sense, the Education Group had a distinct advantage in that its mission was relatively specific (and there was a

---

[*] One of us at least has mixed memories about this. E-mail from Scotland might take a few minutes or a day or more to arrive, but it did mean that for the first time it was possible for the home department to contact someone who was away on sabbatical with all of those awkward questions about "what did you do about ... before you left?".

---

relatively large budget allowance for it too, no less than 10% of the total SEI budget having been allocated for the education programme).

1.2 Early activities of the Education Group

Despite being small, or even perhaps because of that, the group was certainly active. Much of the planning was undertaken during daily 'brown bag lunches', often centred around a copyboard! Some of the activities that resulted from the ideas generated in these sessions, and also derived from Norm's wider responsibilities, included the following.

1. The *Software Engineering Education Directory*, providing a summary of existing software engineering programmes.
2. The structure for the curriculum modules and the plans for the initial batch (we will say more about these in the next section).
3. The first Software Engineering Education conference since the pioneering one of 1975 [3 and 7].
4. A plan for a book series, with the contract for this being eventually agreed with Addison Wesley.

All in addition to Norm's other activities within the management structures of the SEI.

In many ways, Norm's chief role in much of this was to act as a *facilitator*. His own background was Mathematics, and this, together with his experience as an educator, enabled him to ask the questions and lead the discussions without necessarily getting involved in the technicalities. These latter aspects were then left to the remaining three academics to argue about (discuss constructively)!

2. The Curriculum Modules

In its original submission to the DoD, seeking to host the future SEI, Carnegie Mellon University included an Education Division in its plan, tasked with the aim of assisting with the wider development of graduate Software Engineering programmes. In many ways, the Curriculum Modules were then a key element in the strategy that Norm adopted for meeting this aim.

In 1986, there was still relatively little in the way of academic textbooks available for anyone wanting to teach units on software engineering topics. So, much of the practical knowledge about software engineering tended to be mainly possessed by researchers and practitioners, and although various courses were organised by industry for their own staff, these rarely produced published material that could be employed in academia. The aim of the curriculum modules was therefore to make that knowledge more accessible, as well as to assist the teacher in putting together their course units. Modules were intended to provide the outline for actual units, together with references to useful source material, examples etc. Each module therefore formed a *'roadmap'* for a particular topic.

Norm's vision for the curriculum modules was beyond simple teaching aids. When the group hosted the first curriculum conference in 1986, he made sure that Tomayko's collaboration with Jim Collofello on software engineering topics would be reviewed [2]. The curriculum modules would flesh out this topic list, similar to the nascent Software Engineering Body of Knowledge (SWEBOK) today [6]. These mainly consisted of an outline of the subject matter of the topic and an extensive bibliography. His idea was that, if a professor were required to teach a new subject, he or she would find a colleague's syllabus with an outline and bibliography of it. Norm proposed that we do these tasks for the potential instructor. He also saw that, after completing a module, an author had already completed a lot of the work towards producing a book, and several books have actually resulted from the series. For our own parts, David Budgen wrote a very successful book on software design based on the first curriculum module [1]; with a second edition imminent[†], while Jim Tomayko wrote a book on configuration management. It was never published, but was the text for a two-credit course on the subject at the Wichita State University

The Education Group was therefore faced with a number of tasks in developing these modules.

❏　　　　Creating a suitable framework for a curriculum module, to ensure that all aspects relevant to the needs of the end users were included.

❏　　　　Identifying the areas where curriculum modules were needed and where they could also sensibly be developed, guided as indicated above, by the pioneering work of Tomayko and Collofello.

❏　　　　Finding suitable external experts to develop curriculum modules over the summer vacation.

❏　　　　Identifying appropriate ways to review, revise and distribute the modules.

It would be fair to say that here, Norm's personal contacts with others in the field were often highly valuable, particularly in finding the first group of module developers.

Our own roles here were rather mixed, since we also developed the first prototype modules within the group, an activity that was particularly useful for assessing our ideas about structure. Since we report on these particular experiences in the next section, we will not enlarge upon them at this point.

Ideas about module structure evolved gradually, but the main headings that we employed in the early modules were as follows.

❏　　　　A *capsule description*, summarising the subject matter in a couple of sentences.

❏　　　　The *philosophy* section, where the underlying ideas for the module topic were explained.

❏　　　　The module *objectives* in terms of what a student should learn by studying a course unit based upon the module material.

❏　　　　The *prerequisite knowledge* necessary to study the topic.

❏　　　　Details of the *module interface* which was basically how the topic of the module interacted with the subject matter of other modules.

❏　　　　The actual *module content*, primarily in the form of an ***annotated outline***.

❏　　　　A section on *teaching considerations*, considering how the material might be presented, and (where applicable) adding worked examples and exercises.

[†] One lesson from this is that revising a book is rather like undertaking a software maintenance project. Every change can have potential side-effects, external references may need to be updated, there is a strong temptation to add too many bells and whistles; and it needs a good configuration management scheme!

❑   An annotated *bibliography* of books and papers that would underpin the material of the module.

Detailed structuring of these did vary as our ideas evolved, but the above summarises the main elements that could be found in a typical curriculum module.

In [2], the core consisted of topics under the headings of   *Technology* (Overview; Communication Techniques; Interface Engineering; Software Generation; Implementation; Tools, Correctness; Evolution and Quality) and *Management* (Project Management; Organisational Structures; Cost Estimation and Scheduling). It is interesting to compare this with Table 1, which summarises the details of the Curriculum Modules that were produced at the SEI[‡]. (It is difficult to be specific about the exact dates when modules were developed. The dates given are those of the final issued versions. As can be seen, while some modules never progressed beyond an initial version, several, including CM-2 discussed later, were quite extensively revised.)

Table 1. Summary of the SEI Curriculum Modules

Module No. & Version	Completed in	(Abbreviated) Topic	Authored by	Author Affiliation
CM-2-2	January 1989	Software Design	David Budgen	U. of Stirling, Scotland
CM-3.1.5	June 1988	Software Technical Review Process	James Collofello	Arizona State U.
CM-4-1.4	December 1990	Configuration Management	James Tomayko	SEI
CM-5-1.2	July 1987	Information Protection	Fred Cohen	Lehigh U.
CM-6-1.1	July 1987	Software Safety	Nancy Leveson	U. of California, Irvine
CM-7-1.1	July 1987	Software Quality Assurance	Bradley Brown	Boeing Military
CM-8-1.0	October 1987	Formal Specification	Alfs Berztiss	U. of Pittsburgh
CM-9-2.0	June 1992	Unit Analysis & Testing	Larry Morell & Lionel Deimel	Hampton U. & SEI
CM-10-1.0	October 1987	Software Evolution: Life Cycle & Process	Walt Scacchi	U. of Southern California
CM-11-2.1	January 1990	Software Specifications	Dieter Rombach	U. of Maryland
CM-12-1.1	December 1988	Software Metrics	Everald Mills	Seattle U.

[‡] Almost all of the Curriculum Modules can be downloaded from the SEI web site. They are indexed as a group after the 1986 publications.

8

CM-13-1.1	December 1988	Software Verification & Validation	James Collofello	Arizona State U.
CM-14-2.1	July 1989	Intellectual Property Protection	Pamela Samuelson & Kevin Deasy	U. of Pittsburgh
CM-16-1.1	December 1989	Software Development using VDM	Jan Pedersen	Computer Resources International A/S
CM-17-1.1		User Interface Development	G Perlman	M.I.T.
CM-19-1.2	January 1990	Software Requirements	John Brackett	Boston U.
CM-20-1.0	December 1988	Formal Verification of Programs	Alfs Berztiss & Mark Ardis	U. of Pittsburgh & SEI
CM-21-1.0	July 1989	Project Management	James Tomayko & Harvey Hallman	Wichita State & SEI
CM-22-1.0	December 1989	Design Methods for Real-Time Systems	Hassan Gomaa	George Mason U.
CM-23	November 1991	Technical Writing	Linda Levine, Linda Pesante and Susan Dunkle	SEI
CM-24	April 1990	Concurrent Programming	David Bustard	U. of Ulster
CM-25	April 1990	Support for Concurrent Programming	Michael Feldman	George Washington U.
CM-26	August 1990	Understanding Program Dependencies	Norman Wilde	U. of West Florida
CM-27-1.0	February 1993	Formal Specification & Verification of Concurrent Programs	Daniel Berry	Technion & SEI
CM-28		Measuring O-O Products	C Archer	Winthrop U.

The topics represented in Table 1 was driven by a number of factors. One of these was consideration of a topic's perceived importance in the curriculum. A more pragmatic issue was that of the availability of authors, who were chiefly drawn from academia. What is also noticeable is that the vast bulk of this material was assembled over quite a short time, most modules being produced between mid-1987 and the beginning of 1990. In that sense, the Curriculum Modules represented a very concentrated effort to make something available as quickly as possible.

3. Curriculum Module development and our personal experiences

Part of our individual involvement with the Education Group was to help with developing two of the first modules (CM-4: *Software Configuration Management* and CM-2: *Software Design*). In this section we briefly discuss our own experiences of what module development could entail.

3.1 Writing the Configuration Management module (*Jim Tomayko*)

As we mentioned above, David   Budgen wrote the first curriculum module, on software design, but Tomayko's module on configuration management was completed first. This was probably due to it being of a narrower scope than Budgen's, but more concretely, it was Budgen having reduced time to complete his, due to his return to his then position at Stirling.

A curriculum module was intended to be adaptable to full semesters, quarters, and tri-masters. Each module contained a capsule description, like a college catalogue course description, a philosophy statement (why this piece of knowledge?), a list of behavioural objectives, as well as the subject outline and annotated bibliography. Support materials, such as slides and exercises, may, as in the case of the configuration management module, accompany the document.

Many modules had some background research done by the author. One attraction that the Graduate Curriculum Project, as it was then known, had, were workshops consisting of experts in the field and several SEI personnel. We held a configuration management workshop in which their companies paid most expenses, that resulted in a technical report [4]. This module also had the advantage of being tested at several companies.

Both the module and the support materials are still being requested today. Therefore, it is one of the lasting legacies of Norm's work on graduate curricula.

3.2 Writing the Software Design module (*David Budgen*)

Having had a developing interest in the challenges of software design for a number of years before arriving at the SEI, my time at the SEI provided the opportunity to put this on a more systematic basis. This interest stemmed in part from my work on the UK Ministry of Defence's MASCOT (Modular Approach to Software Construction Operation and Test) approach to the design of real-time systems [5], but had widened over the following years into a greater interest in how design knowledge could be systematised and transferred.

One of the (several) major problems in developing this module was to find a way of giving it a structure. The literature on software design then (as now) was apt to be rather partisan, with each 'guru' advocating their own approach, notations, and rationale. The task of standing back and finding a framework for looking at this objectively, in order to teach *about* design, proved to be a source of real difficulty. The basic curriculum module structure identified major headings for the module, but (rightly) didn't really help much with the task of structuring the subject matter within this. Addressing this problem was a matter of producing drafts, getting reviews, and holding a small workshop with external participants. Norm, in fairness, recognised the difficulties all of these presented (not least for a non-US academic) and provided both encouragement and support. In the latter case, this was partly through the help of Dr Richard Sincovec, who was brought in during the later months to help to address the need to provide mappings of the curriculum module material to the structures used in US programmes.

Other aspects of module development, such as document preparation and gathering information were well supported by the SEI's developing structures and facilities. One of the problems of software design as a topic is that much of the material, on design methods at least, lies in books rather than journal papers and the resources of the SEI were particularly useful here.

The module itself was eventually revised and updated in 1988 for a number of reasons.

One was simply that the context we had originally envisaged, with this module providing a baseline and framework that would be expanded in later, more specialist modules, had not evolved in this way. A second was that our ideas about module structure had also evolved, and so some of the work in the summer of 1988 was primarily to restructure the module to fit the revised format. Lastly, there had been some further time to reflect upon how the subject matter could be structured, and the organisation of the material in the revised version was quite extensively modified to reflect this. Indeed, the revised structure then provided much of the basic format for [1].

Throughout all of this process, Norm's encouragement and support was an important element. Always willing to help bring in others to help and advise, he was nonetheless also aware that the author of a module needed to have the final say in its structure and content.

4. A Retrospective – what did the curriculum modules achieve?

Tracing the influence of so complex and wide-ranging a programme as that of the curriculum modules is bound to be rather difficult, and we have not attempted to undertake this on any systematic basis. Rather, we look at a number of related developments in Software Engineering and Software Engineering Education and ask how the modules are likely to have contributed to these.

a) **The emergence of a Software Engineering Education Community.** While this was primarily driven by the development of the Software Engineering Education Conferences (themselves originating with Norm and his group), in early days at least, the SEI-sponsored workshops at which new modules were presented to the user community were an important element in bringing software engineering educators together. These workshops were run in different parts of the USA, and enabled the module developers to present their work to the academic community, with related discussions that were a valuable element of these workshops. Overall, the workshops, and hence the curriculum modules, did certainly play a valuable role in creating a sense of a community of Software Engineering Educators.

b) **The codifying of Software Engineering Knowledge.** The most recent manifestation of this practice is of course the SWEBOK. However, the curriculum modules can reasonably be seen as representing a much earlier attempt to bring together and codify such knowledge and as such, they made an important contribution to our subject. Indeed, it is rather a pity that this work was not continued in some way over subsequent years, as much of this knowledge was then not gathered together again by the community until the SWEBOK programme got under way.

c) **Motivating other developments.** We have already mentioned that one book was certainly spawned out of our own work [1]and the modules provided an opportunity for others to assemble their ideas for possible publication. More recent work within the community to develop an undergraduate software engineering curriculum, and particularly in the context of the SEEK (Software Engineering Education Knowledge) efforts[§], can certainly be viewed as having its roots in the pioneering work of the curriculum modules.

To expand a little on the last point, it is interesting to match the span of the curriculum modules (Table 1), intended to support graduate software engineering programmes in the late 1980's, with the topics being identified by the SEEK as core for an undergraduate software engineering programme in the 2000's.

Table 2. Comparison of SEEK topics and the CMs

SEEK Topic	SEEK weighting (contact hours)	Curriculum Modules related to the topic
Fundamentals (mathematical, computing, engineering, modelling)	250	CM-8 (Formal Specification) CM-12 (Software Metrics) CM-28 (Measuring O-O Products)
Professional Practice (group dynamics/psychology, communications skills, professionalism)	35	CM-5 (Information Protection) CM-6 (Software Safety) CM-14 (Intellectual Property Protection) CM-23 (Technical Writing)
Software Requirements (fundamentals, eliciting requirements, modelling & analysis, documentation, validation, management)	43	CM-11 (Software Specifications) CM-19 (Software Requirements)
Software Design (concepts, strategies, architectural, user interface, detailed, notations & support tools, evaluation)	78	CM-2 (Introduction to Software Design) CM-17 (User Interface Development) CM-22 (Design methods for real-time systems)
Software Construction (language issues, technologies, tools, formal construction methods)	46	CM-16 (Software Development using VDM) CM-24 (Concurrent Programming) CM-25 (Support for Concurrent Programming)
Verification & Validation (terminology &	46	CM-3 (Technical Review Process) CM-9 (Unit Analysis & Testing)

[§] The SEEK project's URL is http://sites.computer.org/ccse/. For the comparison in Table 2, we have used the First Draft, dated August 2002.

foundations, reviews, testing, user interface testing and evaluation, problem analysis & reporting)		CM-13 (Software Verification & Validation) CM-20 (Formal Verification of Programs) CM-26 (Understanding Program Dependencies) CM-27 (Formal Specification & Verification of Concurrent Programs)
Software evolution (processes & activities)	9	CM-10 (Software Evoluton: Life Cycle & Processes)
Software Process (concepts, implementation)	16	
Software Quality (concepts & culture, standards, processes, process and product assurance)	17	CM-7 (Software Quality Assurance)
Software Management (concepts, project planning, personnel & organisation, control, configuration management)	20	CM-4 (Configuration Management) CM-21 (Software Project Management)

While Table 2 is the outcome of a fairly informal analysis (not unreasonably – the SEEK itself is still subject to revision and the material of some Curriculum Modules will almost certainly relate to more than one of the SEEK headings), it does demonstrate that the Curriculum Modules did address a good span of topics from Software Engineering Education. The one omission (Software Process) is almost certainly covered to some degree in the Curriculum Modules. Perhaps the most noticeable degree of imbalance is in the area of Verification & Validation, and also in the proportion of Curriculum Modules that are related in some way to concurrency, both of which probably reflect the balance of academic interest and strengths when the Curriculum Modules were being developed. Overall though, if we take the set of Curriculum Modules as a whole, they are clearly still quite well matched to current thinking about software engineering curricula as based upon 'expert judgement' (the SEEK).

Inevitably this is a very short and rather personal view of the curriculum modules, their initial evolution and their contribution to the development of the subject. However, it should suffice to make the point that the SEI's curriculum modules did provide a very important and pioneering element of software engineering education in the mid to late 1980's. On that basis alone, Norm's personal contribution to the development of software engineering knowledge, particularly but not wholly for purposes of education, was a major one, and it is one that we are pleased to be able to acknowledge and honour in this paper.

Acknowledgements

We are grateful to Nancy Mead for her very constructive suggestions and comments on an earlier draft of this paper, and of course, to Norm Gibbs for giving both of us the opportunity to participate in the pioneering work of the Education Group.

References

[1] Budgen D., *Software Design*. Addison Wesley 0-201-54403-2, 1993.

[2] Collofello J., ed by J. Tomayko, "Proposed Curriculum for a Master of Software Engineering (MSE)," in Gibbs & Fairley, *The Educational Needs*, pp. 420-431.

[3] Gibbs N.E. & Fairley R.E., *Software Engineering Education: The Educational Needs of the Software Community*. Springer-Verlag. 0-387-96469-X, 1987.

[4] Harvey K. , "Summary of the SEI Workshop on Software Configuration Management," *CMU Technical Report* CMU/SEI-86-TR-005, 1986.

[5] Simpson H.R. and Jackson K. "Process Synchronisation in MASCOT," *Computer J.*, **22**(4), 1979, pp. 332-345.

[6] SWEBOK, *Guide to the Software Engineering Body of Knowledge SWEBOK*, Eds. Bourque P. and Dupuis R., IEEE Computer Society Press, 2001.

[7] Wasserman A.I. & Freeman P, *Software Engineering Educati˙on: Needs and Objectives.*, Springer-Verlag. 0-387-90216-3,1976.

The Softer Side of Custom Software Development: Working with the Other Players

William G. Poole
Seattle University, Seattle, Washington, USA
bpoole@seattleu.edu

Abstract

Many university programs in Software Engineering educate students about various technical topics, programming, methodology, software, applications as well as other topics that are considered 'hard' subjects. However, in the practical industrial world of developing custom software applications, there are various other matters confronting the software engineer that involve the other stakeholders in the development setting. These other stakeholders might be from the 'softer' subjects: sales, marketing, graphical arts, management, etc. This article presents an overview of the other stakeholders and suggests, to the software engineer, how to interact with them effectively.

Introduction

University programs in Software Engineering [1] do a good job, more or less, of educating students about analysis, design, methodology, languages, programming, quality assurance, data structures, algorithms, mathematical foundations, system software, architecture and security, metrics, database systems, artificial intelligence, computer graphics, real-time systems, etc. The list can go on almost without end. However, in the practical industrial world of developing custom software applications, there are various other matters confronting the software engineer that involve the other stakeholders in the development setting.

The *custom application* or *professional services* environment differs from the world of developing *software products* in several ways. That topic will not be discussed here but a key difference is that, in the professional services world, there seem to be more players or people with a stake in the outcome and that some are within and some outside the professional services company. In software development, no matter how hard the marketing department and product managers try to understand the market of potential users, in the final analysis those internal organizations have to define the objectives. On the other hand, in the development of custom applications, there are people both within and without the company determining the project goals. The software engineer is only one among many who participate in the definition of the resulting application.

This article addresses those other *stakeholders* and their relationships with software engineers. All examples come from actual experiences of the author in his 20 years of working in professional service departments and companies.

1093-0175/03 $17.00 © 2003 IEEE

Stakeholders representing the professional services or developer firm

There are many people and roles involved in the definition, design, and development of a custom application. I will refer to everyone as *stakeholders* because each one holds a share, interest or stake in the project, although the stakes will differ from role to role. Most stakeholders have the tendency to focus on and overemphasize the importance of their particular role. This applies to junior software engineers as well as the client's vice president of marketing.

Every stakeholder is important and his or her perspectives, goals, questions and motivations contribute to the definition as well as to the success or failure of the project. Everyone involved has a sense of pride in her or his work, feels a challenge to succeed and wants the project to be successful if for no other reason than he or she may receive a promotion or salary increase based on the project's success. Let's evaluate the perspectives of several of those stakeholders, first on the professional services side of the fence.

Let's start initially from the technical viewpoint. *Software engineers* [2] are interested in the latest tools, programming styles, methodology, environment and languages. They care very much about the coding details, "neat" software and new "stuff". Just hand them a task specification and they will be content. They want to add something to their resumes. The rest of the stakeholders have quite different perspectives and the software engineers need to understand how to cooperate with all of them.

The *software engineering manager* certainly has a different viewpoint. He is concerned about having the properly prepared personnel available so the design and programming will be done with sufficient quality. He also cares about making the schedule, completing the total feature set, and not overlooking anything important. He evaluates whether or not the engineers will enjoy the project and grow from the experience. The manager wants the project to be viewed as a success so he will look good to higher management and he wants the engineers to succeed so they will appreciate their manager.

Quality assurance engineers and managers often have to worry about the specifications being finished in time so they can write a test plan and test cases. Also there can be concern as to whether their test cases are extensive enough to satisfy the quality needs. Scheduling their work is very difficult because the dates keep changing as the engineers and others finish their tasks ahead or behind schedule. They may be working on multiple projects simultaneously and since QA is the last step prior to deployment, this department ends up being responsible for making up time lost earlier in the project.

The final technical groups that will be considered here are the *information technology* and *information systems* departments. Some of their main concerns are system maintainability and compatibility with other systems, including the numerous databases they must maintain and with which they must connect. Software engineers may feel capable of doing some of these tasks better and faster but must learn to work with these groups.

A role that is usually non-technical but central to the success or failure of a project is *project management* [3]. This individual sees a project as a set of requirements, a plan for meeting those requirements with associated risks and contingencies, a schedule for carrying out the plan, resources assigned to tasks in the schedule, and a budget. She is required to trust what many other people tell her even though she may not understand all of the details. The project manager must persuade many individuals to make deadlines and quality goals while distributing a large amount of praise. She has overall responsibility for the project's success or failure but in most cases has very little direct power over the people she guides, most of whom are direct reports of other managers.

The user interface designer may fall into one of two categories. The first is the *graphic designer*. The graphic designer may have a marketing and advertising background and experience creating print or interactive materials used to communicate a message in a unique and appealing manner. She may be assigned to the project because she is a "graphics person" and is expected to put a face on an application that is designed by the software engineer and other stakeholders. The graphic designer has simultaneous but possibly competing goals of attractiveness and effectiveness - how to make something visually appealing while enhancing its usefulness. Her question may well be "will it win an award?" Her approach will differ considerably from the software engineer's.

The second and increasingly common UI design role is the *interaction designer*. The interaction designer's goal is to orient the functionality of an application towards a targeted type of end user. He will use a methodical process to profile this user, determine the user's goals, and map a series of tasks the user will undertake via the application to achieve these goals. This process is known as user-centered design and makes use of information architecture and usability principles. Like the graphic designer, he may also be motivated by peer recognition or the opportunity to build his portfolio.

The *usability specialist* [4] will focus on how intuitive or natural is the application's use, determining if navigation, content and process are well organized and whether or not the user will easily understand it. He wants to impart a structure that does not require the user to think too much about how it works - just as a driver is not required to understand how an internal combustion engine works in order to operate an automobile. He assumes the role of the end user and attempts to answer fundamental questions such as: "what is this?", "what can I do with it?" and "what is in it for me?"

Next are the business interests of the professional services firm. *Account management* is interested in keeping the client satisfied and wondering if this project will help meet ever-increasing revenue and satisfaction goals. In one sense, the account manager represents the client within the professional services firm. It is not unusual for the account manager and the software engineer to be in a contentious relationship because of conflicting goals.

The *sales* department is trying to get the client and the professional services company to sign the contract and, if unsuccessful, wondering if the project should be started without appropriate signatures. Her question might be "will it help me make my quota this quarter?" I do not mean to belittle the role of sales or account management for they play an absolutely key role in the overall process. Without their efforts, there would be no company revenue to pay the software engineering salaries.

The *marketing department* wants to know if the company will be presented in the best light and if this project fits the company's business plan and strategy. Their question might be "how does it tie in to our other products and projects?" or "can we easily re-brand this project for other clients?"

The *legal department* will want to protect the company's liability and financial situation. Concerns include non-disclosure agreements, work statements and contractual agreements. Finally, the *executive sponsor* will want to know if the company will make a profit and have a happy client.

This article does not list every possible role in a professional services company with an interest in a project but does give a representative sample of the roles with a significant stake. At one time or another, the author has played most of these roles. Clearly, software engineering shares interest in the success of the project with many other roles but is only a component of the total picture.

Stakeholders for the client

Next, let's survey the viewpoints of some of the stakeholders representing the client or customer side. First and foremost, there should be a *project champion* [5] or *advocate* who is the primary representative and sponsor of the project. The project often ties very closely to her position at the client firm. She may have several questions regarding this project: "will I lose my job if it fails?" or "will I get a promotion and pay raise if it succeeds?" She may be quite concerned about how she ever got into this mess in the first place. The advocate's job is often made difficult because she has to justify spending a considerable sum of money on building the system. If the individual in this role or her manager changes, the risk of project failure increases significantly.

The client's internal *information technology* or *information systems* departments will be concerned about hooking into existing databases, compatibility with existing systems and the general maintainability of the new system. An overriding concern will be with computer and information security.

There will almost always be a group of client *software engineering* staff. Some of them will be wondering why they aren't developing this application instead of being left with the maintenance tasks. They think they are smarter than the consultants and are wondering who these outsiders are. On the other hand, if they are very busy with other work or lacking in the proper skills, they may be very glad that they don't have to do this project. Their cooperation will be important, no matter what their opinions are.

If the project will be to develop an internal system or intranet, the affected *department users* will have much to say about the project. They mostly will be concerned about the ease of use and the speed of the system; also training will be important to them. Some of the users will object to changing to another system from one with which they are comfortable.

Any application that will be seen by the public, such as a public web site, will be under the watchful eye of the client *marketing director*. He will want the application to be presented in the best light. The application must fit their overall marketing plan and strategy, it must tie into their products and services offered to the public, and it must be easily modified as far as the marketing messages are concerned.

Representatives of the *finance* and *legal* departments will want to understand thoroughly the payment terms and provisions that determine what happens when there are disagreements about completion of the project. They may also be concerned with who owns the code or intellectual property once the project is completed. After all, they feel as though their company invented this application.

As with the professional services firm, this is just a sample of stakeholders for the client, many of whom are unseen by the software engineer.

When things go wrong: misunderstandings breed difficulties

Projects do exist for which there are few problems. You are fortunate when you are part of a team working on such a project. However, it is more likely that there will be some misunderstandings on a project ranging from simple to very difficult situations. Let's examine some of the causes and some potential solutions for difficulties.

One portrayal of the software development process has three items as sides of a triangle.

- Features and Quality: this involves the scope, definition or features of the application

- Time: the second side of the triangle represents the work breakdown structure, schedule and individual assignments for performing tasks
- Money: the third side represents the estimated cost which depends on labor rates and estimated hours

These three items are not evenly balanced. Usually, features influence the time and time controls the money. First, let's consider a few items that may go wrong with the most basic attribute – the scope.

Yes, Virginia, *changes in scope* actually do happen.

- People change their minds about what they want or about how they want something to look. The longer a project lasts and the more personnel changes involved, the more likely this will happen.
- Occasionally, needed features are not mentioned until an inconveniently late time ("of course, we need to allow the shipping department to directly connect to the FedEx system").
- Newly available technology may prescribe that some features must change or may offer some new capabilities that should be added.
- New stakeholders may decide that something must be in the system. This is more likely to happen if the newcomer has some authority in her position.

Some procedure for handling change orders should be implemented to handle these legitimate changes. Of course, the schedule and cost may need to be adjusted, a matter that may cause alarm on the client's part.

An *incomplete description* can lead to misunderstandings as well.

- For example, the font style, font size, color, and placement may be very important to the client marketing department but, unless carefully specified, you can be certain that they will not be understood by everyone.
- Connectivity to external databases often causes considerable problems. Fields must be described in great detail as well as frequency of look-up, polling or data migrations.
- How are exceptions to be handled? One can spend a lot of time writing requirements and still forget many exceptions.

Another type of problem that arises with the project scope can be nothing more than a *difference of opinion*.

- When all we have to base decisions on is a conversation and a few hand-written notes from two months ago, we should expect to have differences of opinion about what was said and decided.   Expectations are often set, but unless we probe the client they are rarely "announced." Expectations often find there way into a project in the form of "assumptions" which is always a losing proposition in terms of time and money.   It simply takes more work to correct for missed assumptions.
- Also, saying that a page or screen should be "intuitive" can mean significantly different things to different people.

Disagreements regarding the project scope can be lessened by *writing everything down* [6], reviewing it, revising it in more detail, signing off by both parties and building some type of screen shots, use cases or prototype. All of these help decrease the likelihood of misunderstanding. Notice, we didn't say eliminate the misunderstanding. You can usually count on there being some because we are imperfect communicators. However, we should strive to reduce the confusion. There is no known substitute for frequent and clear communications within the team and with the client stakeholders.

Of course, schedule problems also occur. It is difficult to avoid an *incomplete schedule*. For example, if the scheduler (usually the project manager) forgets to add a task for correcting errors after the tasks are reviewed, it is unlikely that the deadline will be met without some angst.

On some projects, as the end of the time limit approaches, it becomes clear that *not everything can be completed on time*. Then the question to be asked is "how much can be done in time?" The development and client teams must have some uncomfortable talks to decide what will be left out. This is the time that *versioning* ("what can we postpone until the next version?") can be discussed. Perhaps some of the features can be left out of the first version and put into later versions.

The *price* for developing a system is the cause of disagreements less often than one might expect. One situation occurs before the project begins: the client is not willing to pay as much as the developer estimates. Negotiations are necessary to cut the "gold plating", unnecessary features and the profit margin. You may hear the sales people or account manager say "we'll make it up on later projects if we can just land this one". Quality can also be negotiated but that is dangerous. For example, cutting out some of the fail-safe features can cut cost but may lead to expensive errors later. Another difficult situation occurs when versioning is being discussed and negotiation is needed about an adjusted price.

How to make communication and collaboration work effectively

Effective communication and collaboration do not come naturally to many people and software engineers in particular. There are things that we can do to be more effective. Rebecca E. Burnett [7] addresses several of these.

- Understand what the shared goals are of any project. Ideally, this is clarified before the requirements are established.
- Join in discussions with a cooperative and receptive attitude. After all, we are all in this together with the goal of completing an excellent piece of work with the developer and client both feeling satisfied.
- Be involved in the communication by being prepared, capable of conveying general objectives of the project as well as details regarding specific tasks. Meetings are costly and preparedness can make meetings worth their while.
- Be attentive when others speak and ask questions to get the information that you need. Do not let misunderstandings persist. Understand that others may have different ways of communicating their ideas.
- On the other hand, be willing to share your ideas with others on your team. Give specific information and keep collaborators up to date about your part of the project. Communication is a two-way street. Don't be afraid to admit your concerns and problems.
- Use appropriate technology. There are various software tools that may aid your collaboration such as a group calendar, shared folders and documents, e-mail and chat systems.

- Ponder the ideas and opinions that you have heard or read. You must take some time to filter the information that you collected so that you can discern what is important from what is not. Find a quiet place where you can concentrate.

Some of these may seem obvious to the reader but we don't always behave this way. A conscientious decision to act a different way is required.

Incorporating into software engineering curriculum

What does this have to do with software engineering? Well, these are realistic examples of the environments that software engineers may find themselves in day to day. We may prefer to stay in the world of bits, languages, design and classes but this article paints a more realistic, "larger" picture of what software engineers may encounter in their daily work. The sooner they understand this and learn to cooperate with all of the other stakeholders, the more successful and pleasant their work will be.

The author has tried to link this material to software engineering curriculum in several ways. Here are a few ideas.

- Invite guests representing several of the shareholder roles discussed in this article. They could give lectures and lead discussions in existing courses on Technical Communication, Project Management, Requirements Analysis, User Interface Design or Legal Aspects of Software. Almost any course could incorporate the perspective of one of the shareholders.
- Develop seminars and short courses for faculty development and practicing software engineers and their managers. Real-life examples are easy to find in industry. After presenting a problem, perhaps using role-playing, the students could be asked to work out a satisfactory solution.

Conclusion

In this article, I have tried to identify some of the key stakeholders for the professional services company and for the client and have tried to describe their concerns, goals and expectations. Many of them are very different from software engineers and view the project quite differently. It is important for all team members to understand the various roles and responsibilities. Furthermore, all team members should appreciate the limit of their expertise and the value of others.

Next, I listed some of the problems and their possible causes that are fairly common in project work. They are taken from my experience of working in professional services groups for twenty years.

Finally, I presented some ways that may help alleviate the severity of these problems. These are typically "soft" ways for approaching the problems – not the "learn another language" that most software engineers may be accustomed to. Understanding the perspective of others is a key ingredient of success.

Acknowledgements

This article is dedicated to the memory of Norman E. Gibbs. The author worked very closely with Professor Gibbs for nine years while both of them were beginning their careers as faculty members at the College of William and Mary. They worked together on developing the first Computer Science curriculum at William and Mary, they co-chaired a national ACM SIGCSE conference, they carried out research and published several papers together, and they were personal friends. Norm was interested in the students as individuals. He wanted to help prepare them for the jobs they would soon be taking – not just with the technical topics of the classroom but also with ideas regarding how to work with people. This article is written in that spirit.

The author wishes to thank Randy Rehn and Bobby Stevens of The Cobalt Group of Seattle, Washington, USA, for carefully reading and suggesting improvements to this article.

References

[1] For example, good places to start looking at software engineering curriculum and standards are http://www.sei.cmu.edu/ and http://standards.ieee.org/reading/ieee/std/se/.

[2] Numerous books on software engineering and the role of the software engineer contain useful discussions including Carlo Ghezzi, Mehdi Jazayeri and Dino Mandrioli, *Fundamentals of Software Engineering, Second Edition* (Upper Saddle River, NJ: Prentice Hall, 2003).

[3] The role of the project manager is detailed in several project management books such as Walker Royce, *Software Project Manager: A Unified Framework* (Boston, MA: Addison-Wesley, 1998). Also see *Project Management Journal: The Professional Journal* and *PM Network: The Professional Magazine* of the Project Management Institute and http://pmi.org/.

[4] The Usability Professionals' Association, http://www.upassoc.org/ is a place to start looking for information about usability roles.

[5] Scott E. Donaldson and Stanley G. Siegel, *Successful Software Development, Second Edition* (Upper Saddle River, NJ: Prentice Hall PTR, 2001) has numerous references to client roles and their interaction with software engineering team members.

[6] See Walker Royce, *Software Project Manager: A Unified Framework* (Boston, MA: Addison-Wesley, 1998), chapter 6, "Artifacts of the Process" for an approach to documenting an application.

[7] Rebecca E. Burnett, *Technical Communication, Fifth Edition* (Boston, MA: Thomson Heinle, 2001), pp. 138-144.

Norm's Legacy: A Perspective from the Next Generation

Donald J. Bagert
Rose-Hulman Institute of Technology
Don.Bagert@rose-hulman.edu

Abstract

The leaps and bounds that software engineering education has made over the last several years has been greatly influenced by the pioneering work of Norman Gibbs, especially during his tenure as director of the Education Program of the Software Engineering Institute - cited by in 1999 by FASE as one of the Top Ten Contributions in software engineering education, training and professional issues of the 20th century - during the Program's first five years of existence. Virtually everyone working in the software engineering education field today has been touched either directly or indirectly by the legacy Norm Gibbs left us. This talk will examine the influence that Norm and the Education Program have had on the current generation of the software engineering education community, including the author's personal experiences.

1. Introduction

In my opinion, no organization in the history of software engineering education and training (SEE&T) has had a greater and lasting impact on it than the Education Program of the Software Engineering Institute (SEI) of Carnegie Mellon University. This is despite the fact that the program only lasted for ten years and ended almost a decade ago. It has left a tremendous legacy as well as a void that the SEE&T community is still trying to fill.

For the first five years of its existence (1985-89), the Education Program was led by Norman E. Gibbs. Norm had a distinguished career in academia both before and after his time at the SEI [13]. At the time of his death in April 2002, he was the Chair of Computer Science at Ball State University in Muncie, Indiana, USA.

This paper discusses the impact that Norm Gibbs and the Education Program has had in shaping software engineering education and its current generation of leaders today. Section 2 contains a detailed discussion of the SEI Education Program, and Norm's role in shaping it. Section 3 will discuss the impact of Norm and the Education Program. In Section 4, I will provide some personal reflections on the influence that Norm and others at the SEI had on me. Section 5 will contain some final thoughts.

2. The SEI Education Program

2.1. Technical Reports and Other Documents

In its brief history, the Education Program produced a tremendous number of artifacts, many of which are still being used today. For instance, there were a series of Curriculum Modules (CMs) on various software engineering topics. Each CM contained a short description of the subject and overview of possible teaching methodologies, along with an extensive and annotated bibliography.

Besides the curriculum modules, there were a variety of other educational materials that could be used in the classroom. There was also a series of courses in which a set of lecture tapes for the entire class was available and could to help an instructor teach a particular subject for the first time.

A number of technical reports created and released by the Education Program set the tone for the direction and future of software engineering education. *Software Engineering Education: An Interim Report from the Software Engineering Institute* by Gary Ford, Norm Gibbs and Jim Tomayko [5] was an early example of this, discussing Education Program activities as a whole, including the outline for an undergraduate software engineering project course as well as a curriculum module for a professional-oriented Master of Software Engineering (MSE) degree. Jim's model for the project course, which was further described in [14], was used extensively for many years after that, and was commonly referred to as the "Tomayko model". Norm led the effort to develop the Master of Software Engineering degree model, and was also the founding director of Carnegie Mellon's own MSE program. Gary, along with Mark Ardis, provided a detailed description of the MSE curriculum and courses in a 1989 report that is still considered today to be the predominant model for graduate software engineering education [1].

In later years, the Education Program produced two reports devoted to undergraduate software engineering education and curricula. The 1990 report [7] by Gary was the first document widely-available in the U.S. that proposed an undergraduate software engineering curriculum model. (There was a report jointly published in the United Kingdom [4] by the British Computer Society and the Institution of Electrical Engineers, but had virtually no circulation in the United States – although Gary did reference it in his own report.) In 1994, a progress report on undergraduate software engineering education was released [9].

The Education Program also kept track of existing software engineering degree programs. A list of current graduate programs was included in [8], there were also later updates, the last of which was dated March 1996 and reprinted in [12].

Although it was published after the Education Program had ceased to exist, in January 1996 Gary and Norm wrote *A Mature Profession of Software Engineering*, which once again examined software engineering education along with other professional issues (such as licensing and certification) related to the development of software engineering as a discipline [10]. At the time, most of the components required for software engineering to be recognized and evolve as a profession, as outlined in that report, existed only in the United Kingdom.

2.2. Conferences and Workshops

Before the Education Program existed, there had only been one significant meeting that been devoted to software engineering education [15]. However, the success of the 1986 by-invitation workshop organized by Norm and Dick Fairley [11] led to the creation of the SEI-sponsored Conference on Software Engineering Education and Training (CSEE&T), as it is now called. CSEE&T has been held on a regular basis since the first conference in 1987; it was sponsored by the SEI until 1997, often had several hundred attendees during that period.

The Education Program also sponsored a number of Faculty Development Workshops. These workshops presented Curriculum Modules and other educational materials and in general provided a means by which faculty new to the teaching of software engineering could learn effective ways of doing so.

3. Impact

Even though there was a tremendous amount of material generated by the Education Program, and there were many events that they sponsored and hosted, I think that the greatest impact that it had was the inspiration they provided the software engineering education community. In fact, it could be argued that before the Education Program there was no actual SEE&T "community", or if there was, it had little focus. The work of Norm Gibbs and many others made the Education Program that focal point through which ideas and innovation could be generated throughout the field.

Most of the current "generation" of software engineering educators became part of the SEE&T community during the period when the Education Program existed. Several were SEI Visiting Scientists who worked in the Program, while other attended workshops or conferences they sponsored, or used the materials they generated.

One particular example of the influence that Norm and the Education Program has had on the current leaders of the SEE&T community comes from Hossein Saiedian, who is the Chair of the Education Committee of the IEEE-CS Technical Council on Software Engineering: "One of the earliest articles I read about software engineering education and one that really made an impact on my outlook on the field was one by Norm Gibbs (and Gary Ford) [6] in which I found the following few words, 'industry needs software engineers, but universities are supplying computer scientists. Thus it is time to promote widespread development of software engineering degree programs.' to be on the target. I found so much truth in those few words that I essentially decided to devote a major part of my academic efforts on developing and promoting such programs."

In December 1999, the editors Forum for Advancing Software engineering Education (FASE) electronic newsletter convened a panel to determine the top ten contributions to software engineering education, training and professional issues of the 20th century [3]. The results (listed in chronological order) contained not only the SEI Education Program, but two other contributions produced by it: CSEE&T and the SEI Graduate Curriculum Model/Carnegie Mellon MSE Program. In fact, FASE itself can be said to be descended from the Education Program, since it came about after some discussions held at one of the early CSEE&T conferences.

To attempt to fill some of the void left by the demise of the Education Program in 1994, Nancy Mead (who had succeeded Norm for the last five years of the Program's existence) formed the Working Group on Software Engineering Education and Training (WGSEET). The Working Group is a "think tank" of sorts, following the lead of the Education Program in attempting to devise innovative solutions to help advance the software engineering education and training field, and inspire its community. WGSEET has had some successes (notably an updated undergraduate curriculum model [2] which is currently the *de facto* standard), but is a volunteer organization which meets only twice per year, and so is not able to come close to matching the quantity of output generated by the Education Program. One way to partially meet this challenge is by seeking and obtaining grants; for instance, several WGSEET members has formed a consortium of schools which has obtained an NSF grant to update the SEI Curriculum Modules.

4. Personal Reflections

My dissertation was not in software engineering, but instead related to programming language environments, and I didn't really appreciate the potential of software engineering at the time. Soon after I arrived at Texas Tech two years after receiving my Ph.D. (in 1988), I was assigned to teach the graduate-level software engineering course. After teaching the course, I didn't think more of software engineering as a profession or as an academic discipline.

I first heard of the SEI through being on a panel with Gary Ford at the 1988 SIGCSE Computer Science Education Symposium. Shortly after that, I learned about the SEI Faculty Development Workshops, and convinced my department chair to send me to one. My first workshop was in 1989, and then in 1990 went to another workshop and the 4th Conference on Software Engineering Education (as CSEE&T was then called). It was at these workshops that I first met Norm Gibbs. I knew that he was the Director of the Software Engineering Program, and there I was, an Assistant Professor who was struggling in a new area of computing. Despite this, he always treated me as a peer, and I very much appreciated that. (In general, I have had uniformly good relationships with SEI staff involved with the Education Program, both during and after the program's existence. I believe that their great capacity for cooperation contributed to the enormous influence they have had on the SEE&T community.)

Over the years, I used many of the technical reports and education modules that the Education Program provided, much of it having been produced during Norm's tenure as director. The ones that had the most impact for me were those involving undergraduate and graduate curriculum models, which were first of their kind widely-published in the U.S. I know that others did much of the development of those models, but I could also see Norm's influence and vision at work. One of those times was in 1994, when Norm was given the ACM SIGCSE Award for Outstanding Contribution to Computer Science Education. The keynote speech he gave at the acceptance ceremony was titled "Computer Science: Past, Present and Future". In it, Norm gave his current thoughts on a software engineering undergraduate curriculum; at the time there were no BSSE programs in the United States. I remember thinking that this curriculum went farther than any that I had seen up to that time in distancing itself from both CS and traditional engineering curricula, and enjoyed the brief conversation we had afterwards about it.

Several years later, I was stunned when Norm asked me to be one of his references. I felt that I must have achieving some degree of success if Norm Gibbs thought that my recommendation would be useful! Norm ended up as the CS chair at Ball State. This past year, Norm did not know that I was considering a move to Rose-Hulman, but in fact, few people did. However, I was excited about the possibility of moving to Indiana and working with Norm and other well-known people in software engineering education that were working at various schools in that state. However, before I could make my announcement, word reached me that he has passed away.

5. Final Thoughts

The SEI Education Program was a special group that was fortunate to have great leadership and great personnel during its entire ten-year existence. It is something that was sorely needed at the time and is missed even today. However, its has inspired and influenced many in the software engineering education and training community and is therefore at least indirectly responsible for many of the current successes in the field involving new degree programs, curriculum models and accreditation. At the beginning of all this was Norman E. Gibbs.

I didn't know Norm well enough to call him a friend, and never worked with him closely. Despite this, his influence on me in my development as a software engineering educator has been considerable. Thanks, Norm.

6. References

[1] M. A. Ardis and G. A. Ford, 1989 SEI Report on Graduate Software Engineering Education, CMU/SEI-89-TR-2, Carnegie Mellon University, Pittsburgh PA, 1989.

[2] D. J. Bagert, T. B. Hilburn, G. Hislop, M. Lutz, M. McCracken and S. Mengel, Guidelines for Software Engineering Education Version 1.0, CMU/SEI-99-TR-032, Carnegie Mellon University, Pittsburgh PA, 1999.

[3] D. J. Bagert, D. Carter, T. B. Hilburn, N. R. Mead, M. Ryan, A. I. Wasserman and L. Werth, "Top Ten Contributions of the Century", Forum for Advancing Software engineering Education (FASE), 9, 12, December 1999. (electronic newsletter) <http://www.cs.ttu.edu/fase/v09n12.txt>

[4] British Computer Society and The Institution of Electrical Engineers, A Report on Undergraduate Curricula for Software Engineering, Institution of Electrical Engineers, 1989.

[5] G. A. Ford, N. E. Gibbs, and J. E. Tomayko, Software Engineering Education: An Interim Report from the Software Engineering Institute, CMU/SEI-TR-87-109, Carnegie Mellon University, Pittsburgh, Pennsylvania, USA, 1987.

[6] G. Ford and N. Gibbs, "A Master of Software Engineering" IEEE Computer, 22, 9, September 1989, 59-71.

[7] G. A. Ford, 1990 SEI Report on Undergraduate Software Engineering Education, CMU/SEI-90-TR-3, Carnegie Mellon University, Pittsburgh, Pennsylvania, USA, 1990.

[8] G. A. Ford, 1991 SEI Report on Graduate Software Engineering Education, CMU/SEI-91-TR-2, Carnegie Mellon University, Pittsburgh, Pennsylvania, USA, 1991.

[9] G. A. Ford, A Progress Report on Undergraduate Software Engineering Education, CMU/SEI-94-TR-11, Carnegie Mellon University, Pittsburgh, Pennsylvania, USA, 1994.

[10] G. A. Ford, N. E. Gibbs, A Mature Profession of Software Engineering, CMU/SEI-96-TR-004, Carnegie Mellon University, Pittsburgh, Pennsylvania, USA, 1996.

[11] N. E. Gibbs and R. E. Fairley eds., Software Engineering Education: The Educational Needs of the Software Community, Springer-Verlag, New York, New York, USA, 1987.

[12] P. J. Knoke, "Software Engineering Graduate Study Opportunities", Forum for Advancing Software engineering Education (FASE), 7, 4, November 1997. (electronic newsletter) <http://www.cs.ttu.edu/fase/v07n04.txt>

[13] N. R. Mead, "Norm Gibbs - A Leader in Software Engineering Education", Forum for Advancing Software engineering Education (FASE), 12, 5, May 2002. (electronic newsletter) <http://www.cs.ttu.edu/fase/v12n05.txt>

[14] J.E. Tomayko, Teaching a Project-Intensive Introduction to Software Engineering, Technical Report SEI-SR-87-1, Software Engineering Institute, Carnegie Mellon University, Pittsburgh, PA, 1987.

[15] A. I. Wasserman and P. Freeman, eds., Software Engineering Education: Needs and Objectives, Springer-Verlag, New York, USA, 1976.

Norm Gibbs – Department Chair, Facilitator, Motivator and Visionary

Norm Gibbs assumed the position of Chair of the Department of Computer Science at Ball State University in Muncie, IN in the fall of 2000. We saw the fire and spark in his eyes and he saw in us a place where he could make a difference. He wanted his work at BSU to be his last home run before he retired to that golf course in the south. His enthusiastic support greatly aided my decision to take on the directorship of the Software Engineering Research Center, SERC, an NSF Industry/University Cooperative Research Center, now headquartered at Ball State. Fortunately, a video clip was produced for the SERC containing Norm's views about the Center. On Thursday, April 25, 2002 Dr. Norman E. Gibbs passed away unexpectedly, but we have his vision, which was beyond the Norm.

Video follows.

Dr. Wayne M. Zage is Director of the Software Engineering Research Centre and Professor in the Computer Science Department, Ball State University, Muncie, IN 47306

Keynotes

Dieter Rombach
Fraunhofer IESE & Universität
Kaiserslautern, Germany

Jeff Kramer
Imperial College, UK

Christopher J. Horn
IONA Technologies, Ireland

Natalia Juristo
Universidad Politecnica de Madrid, Spain

Teaching how to engineer software

Engineering competence requires both a sound scientific foundation and engineering skills for solving concrete problems. Software engineering is based on scientific foundations from several areas including mathematics, computer science, and the economic and social sciences. Active experience exists in the form of empirical observations, laws and theories. Most software engineering curricula address foundations from computer science only, ignore the existing body of knowledge, and provide few means for actively practicing the actual engineering. It is not acceptable to release graduates into software engineering practice without basic ideas about economic value models for software and software engineering, team work, motivation and empirical methods. Neither is it acceptable to release graduates without comprehensive knowledge regarding the already existing body of software engineering knowledge to build upon. This talk provides an outline for comprehensive software engineering education; presents an overview of teachable software engineering knowledge in the form of empirical observations, laws and theories; discusses the use of empirical studies and experiments as an efficient form of learning engineering skills; and proposes different forms of integration with basic computer science curricula. Finally, a concrete software engineering curriculum at the University of Kaiserslautern and first experiences are presented.

Dr. H. Dieter Rombach is a Full Professor in the Fachbereich Informatik (i.e., Department of Computer Science) at the Universität Kaiserslautern, Germany. He holds a chair in software engineering, and is executive director of the Fraunhofer Institute for Experimental Software Engineering (IESE) which aims at shortening the time needed for transferring research technologies into industrial practice. His research interests are in software methodologies, modeling and measurement of the software process and resulting products, software reuse, and distributed systems. Results are documented in more than 120 publications in international journals and conference proceedings.

Prior to his current position, Dr. Rombach held faculty positions with the Computer Science Department and UMIACS (University of Maryland Institute for Advanced Computer Studies) at the University of Maryland, College Park, Maryland [1984-1991] and was a member of the SEL (Software Engineering Laboratory, a joint venture between NASA, Goddard Space Flight Center, Computer Sciences Corporation, and the University of Maryland) [1986-1991].

He received his B.S. degree in mathematics from the University of Karlsruhe, Federal Republic of Germany, in 1975, his M.S. degrees in mathematics and computer science from the University of Karlsruhe in 1978, and his Ph.D. degree in computer science from the University of Kaiserslautern, Federal Republic of Germany, in 1984. In 1990 he received the prestigious Presidential Young Investigator Award (US$ 500,000.00) from the National Science Foundation, USA, in recognition of his research accomplishments in software engineering. In 2000 he was awarded the Service Medal of the State of Rhineland-Palatinate, Germany, for his accomplishments in software engineering research and his contributions to the economic development of the state through the establishment of a Fraunhofer institute.

Dr. Rombach heads several research projects funded by German Government, European Union and Industry. He currently is the lead principal of a federally funded project (ViSEK) aimed at building up a German repository of knowledge about innovative software engineering technologies. He consults for numerous companies on issues including quality improvement, software measurement, software reuse, process modeling and software technology in general, and he is an advisor to Federal and State Government on software issues. He frequently gives industrial executive seminars on software quality improvement, software measurement, software reuse, and process modeling. He was Co-Guest-Editor of two Special Issues in IEEE Software, on Software Quality Assurance in September 1987 and Measurement-Based Process Improvement in July 1994, respectively, and organized the International Workshop on Experimental Software Engineering Issues in Dagstuhl, Germany, September 1992. He served as General Chair of the 18th International Conference on Software Engineering in Berlin, 1996. He is an associate editor of the Kluwer Journal "Empirical Software Engineering" and serves on the editorial boards of numerous other journals and magazines. He is a member of GI and ACM, and a Fellow of IEEE.

Abstraction - is it teachable? *'the devil is in the detail'*

Abstraction is a key skill for software engineers. It is essential during requirements engineering to elicit the critical aspects of the environment and required system while neglecting the unimportant. At design time, we need to articulate the software architecture and component functionalities which satisfy functional and non-functional requirements while avoiding unnecessary implementation constraints. Even at the implementation stage we use data abstraction and classes so as to generalize solutions

However, my experience is that abstraction is extremely difficult to teach and learn. How should we go about teaching this skill? Indeed, is it teachable?

This talk discusses the difficulties and challenges in learning and using abstraction. In particular, we consider whether or not the standard engineering technique of model construction and analysis can help in this venture. The importance of having associated tool support is also considered.

Professor Jeff Kramer is Head of the Department of Computing at Imperial College. His research interests include requirements engineering, software architectures and analysis techniques, particularly as applied to concurrent and distributed software. He was a principal investigator in the various research projects which led to the development of the CONIC environment for configuration programming and the Darwin architectural description language. His current research work is on behaviour analysis, the use of models in requirements elaboration and architectural approaches to self-organising software systems.

Jeff Kramer is a Chartered Engineer, Fellow of the IEE and Fellow of the ACM. He was program co-chair of the 21st ICSE in Los Angeles in 1999, Chair of the Steering Committee for ICSE from 2000 to 2002, and associate editor and member of the editorial board of TOSEM from 1995 to 2001. He is co-author of a recent book on Concurrency, co-author of a previous book on Distributed Systems and Computer Networks, and the author of over 150 journal and conference publications

using Animation
— p cf. Alan Kay — SQUEAK

Software Engineering in the 21st Century - a view from the trenches

The software industry has reverted back to normality after the dotcom era, but certain aspects appear irrevocably changed. Sometimes veteran programmers and commercial managers have complained in the past that software engineering courses taught by the universities are overly theoretical, impractical or irrelevant. At the start of the 21st century, is this long standing prejudice still true, or have academia and commercial practice at last caught up with each other - or are there now new pragmatic changes in the industry at the start of the 21st century which academia has yet to realise?

Our company, IONA, employs software engineers in four major locations across the planet, with employees of some twenty-five nationalities. Our core competence is the development of software products, which are sold and used in volume by our customers worldwide, and deployed in many varied industries. Apart from the typical software engineering management issues such as requirements capture, product version management, software operating environment configurations, testing, and release management, there is of course the commercial pressure of developing products to compete aggressively and agilely among some of the world's best software companies on the world stage. But in new century, there may be profound trends emerging which will change the old software engineering activity of the 20th century forever.

Dr. Christopher J. Horn is a co-founder of IONA Technologies (established 1991). He was the initial developer of Orbix® and held the joint offices of IONA's President, Chief Executive Officer and Chairman of the Board from IONA's inception until May 2000. Dr Horn is currently the Chairman of the Board of IONA. Dr Horn was an electronics graduate in 1978, and received his PhD in Computer Science in 1983. From 1984 until 1994, he was a lecturer in the Computer Science Department at Trinity College, Dublin, where he was involved in many pan-European IT research projects involving distributed computing. He also worked in Brussels, Belgium for the European Commission, and was an integral part of the ten-year "Esprit" program designed to improve the continent's technology industry.

Dr. Horn is a member of a number of company boards and advisory groups, including Sepro, CR2, Delta Partners, the AIB technology fund and HotOrigin. He is chairman of the Ireland China Association and of the Irish Management Institute, a Director of Science Foundation Ireland, and a member of the Board of Trinity College Dublin. He chaired the "Expert Group on Future Skills", part of Ireland's Educational Technology Investment Fund from 1998 to 1999. In 2001 he received an honorary Doctor of Science from Trinity College Dublin and became an honorary Fellow of the Institution of Engineers of Ireland. Dr Horn also received the Gold Medal for Industry from the Industry and Commerce Committee of the Royal Dublin Society in the same year. Dr Horn is involved with a number of charities, and serves as Chairman of the Irish Brain Research Foundation, of the UNICEF Ireland Committee, and of the Community Foundation for Ireland.

Undergraduate software engineering education options: independent programmes, specialisations or subjects

At the international level, there are now a range of alternatives for teaching software engineering (SE) in undergraduate programmes: pure SE programmes, computer science programmes offering a specialisation in SE with and without qualifications and computer science programmes including some SE subjects.

In this presentation, these alternatives are analysed, addressing aspects such as

- the official restrictions and conditions to which programme establishment is subject in different countries, which can help explain why there are different educational alternatives in these countries.

- the distribution of SE-related content in each of the programme types and the quantitative and qualitative differences there between them.

- the different alternatives for teaching SE compared to the teaching of other scientific and engineering disciplines.

This comparative analysis highlights the differences between the European and US perspective and gives an understanding of the socio-political and cultural reasons why different undergraduate SE teaching options are now in place in different countries.

Dr. Natalia Juristo is a professor of software engineering in the Computer Science School at the Universidad Politecnica de Madrid, and since 1992 has been Director of the MSc in Software Engineering there. Dr. Juristo has a B.S. and a Ph.D. in Computing. She was a fellow of the European Centre for Nuclear Research (CERN) in Switzerland in 1988, and a visiting staff member of the European Space Agency (ESA) in Italy in 1989 and 1990. During 1992 she was a resident affiliate of the Software Engineering Institute at Carnegie Mellon University. She was program chair for SEKE97 and general chair for SEKE01 and SNPD02. She has been guest editor of special issues in several journals, including the Journal of Software and Systems, Data and Knowledge Engineering and the International Journal of Software Engineering and Knowledge Engineering Dr. Juristo has been member of several editorial boards, including IEEE Software and the Journal of Empirial Software Engineering. She is senior member of IEEE.

Software Engineering and Industry 1 (Paper Session A)

Teaching Software Engineering Fundamentals
to Practicing Engineers

Paul Strooper[†], David Carrington[†], Sharron Newby[*], Terry Stevenson[*]

[†] *School of Information Technology and Electrical Engineering*
The University of Queensland, St Lucia, QLD 4072, Australia
{davec, pstroop}@itee.uq.edu.au

[*] *Boeing Australia Limited*
363 Adelaide St, Brisbane, QLD 4001, Australia
{Terry.Stevenson, Sharron.Newby}@Boeing.com

Abstract

This paper describes an ongoing collaboration between Boeing Australia Limited and the University of Queensland to develop and deliver an introductory course on software engineering for Boeing Australia. The aim of the course is to provide a common understanding for all Boeing Australia's engineering staff of the nature of software engineering and the practices used throughout Boeing Australia. It is meant as an introductory course that can be presented to people with varying backgrounds, such as recent software engineering graduates, systems engineers, quality assurance personnel, etc. The paper describes the structure and content of the course, and the evaluation techniques used to collect feedback from the participants and the corresponding results. The course has been well-received by the participants, but the feedback from the course has indicated a need for more advanced courses in specific areas.

1. Introduction

When Boeing Australia Limited (BAL) moved its corporate headquarters to Brisbane in 1998, Boeing management made it clear to the local universities that they were keen to establish collaborative partnerships. At the beginning of 2000, BAL asked for assistance to create an in-house course that provided an overview of software engineering. At this time, BAL was revising its Software Process Manual (SPM) and introducing an intranet facility known as EngNET, which provides uniform access to information for engineering staff. BAL wanted all staff to have a common base of knowledge about software engineering and its corporate best practice. Because the course was intended to be broad in scope, it was given the title "Software Engineering Fundamentals".

BAL is a wholly-owned subsidiary of the Boeing Company, and specialises in the design, installation and support of defence systems, and the development and application of complex systems support and communications solutions for commercial markets. The Boeing Company has been involved in Australian aircraft and defence businesses for more than sixty years. BAL conducts operations at thirteen locations throughout Australia and employs more than 3,000 people. Like most enterprises, BAL recognises the strategic importance of software to its business, and it is keen to identify ways to enhance the skills of its staff.

The course was assembled by BAL software engineering staff and the second author from a variety of sources, including an extensive library of in-depth courses available from the Boeing Company. Early drafts of the SWEBOK guide [1] were used to check that no important software engineering topics had been omitted. An early decision was to involve both academic and BAL presenters so the participants receive both theoretical and practical viewpoints of software engineering. Another was to make the course as practical as possible so participants have opportunities to experiment with their new knowledge. A particular challenge is that the course is intended for a wide audience; as a result, most practical work is organised as workshops to be done in groups.

The remainder of the paper is organised as follows: Section 2 discusses related work on collaborations between industry and universities to improve software engineering education and training. The structure of the course itself is presented in Section 3, while Section 4 discusses the feedback mechanisms that have been used to gather information from the course participants, the types of feedback received and how this feedback has been used to improve the course.

2. Related work

During the past fifteen years, there has been a growing realisation world-wide that universities and industry can both benefit from closer relationships. In the United States, the Working Group - Software Engineering Education and Training[1] has an active Industry/University (I/U) subgroup investigating collaborations between industry and academic institutions, in which non-software professionals and practitioners without formal software engineering education are re-educated to become software engineers. Between 1995 and 1999, the Software Engineering Institute published an annual "Directory of Industry and University Collaborations with a Focus on Software Engineering Education and Training"[2]. Members of the working group and its subgroups have a strong history of promoting industry-university interactions.

Ellis et al. [2] describe some of the work performed by the I/U subgroup and the common characteristics that they have found in successful I/U education collaborations. Although the focus of this subgroup (re-educating people without formal software engineering education to become software engineers) is somewhat different from the focus of our collaboration (providing an introduction to the field of software engineering and specific BAL practices for all engineering staff), it is interesting to note that our collaboration satisfies most of these common characteristics. In particular, the course was initiated by BAL (industrial initiative), the industrial partner is a sizeable company with significant financial resources, the course is practically oriented, and there are a limited number of students in each course. The only characteristic discussed in [2] that we do not satisfy is restricting the audience to software practitioners, but this is caused by the difference in focus of the I/U subgroup and our collaboration with BAL.

Similarly, Beckman et al. [3] discuss experience with three successful industry/university collaborations in the area of software engineering education. They also list the key benefits that can be gained by both industry and academics from such collaborations. Again, we have seen many of these benefits in our collaboration: for the industry partners, cost-effective, customized education and training, influence on academic programs, and access to university research, and for the academics placement of students (in project courses), insight into corporate issues at the applied level, research and continuing education opportunities, and special funding from a corporate partner. From their experience, they propose a model for collaboration based on: forming an industry-advisory board, defining common goals and sharing expectations, planning activities, measuring outcomes, and accommodating feedback.

---

[1] http://www.sei.cmu.edu/collaborating/ed/workgroup-ed.html
[2] http://www.sei.cmu.edu/publications/documents/99.reports/99sr001/99sr001chap01.html

McCabe et al. [4] describe the approach taken by McDonnell Douglas Aerospace to software engineering training and education, which is based on a mix of in-house developed courses and collaborative out-sourcing. Again, the focus of their courses is different from ours, in that it is to train and educate practising software engineers to do their job better. In 1992, their software engineering training consisted of four in-house courses ranging from 1.5 to 40 hours in duration. Over the next three years, this effort grew to 14 courses ranging from 1.5 to 40 hours, 8 of which were developed and presented in-house, and the other 6 were out-sourced through the Software Engineering Forum for Training (SEFT), a consortium of three companies interested in a common set of software engineering courses (the university partner in these courses is California State University at Long Beach). Based on their experience, they recommended that in-house training be used for organisation-specific, high-volume, process-oriented training, consortium training for generic, low-volume, process-oriented training, and other out-sourced training for generic training that is technically oriented.

3. Course overview

As we explain in Section 4, the structure of the course has changed since it was first introduced in September 2000. In this section, we describe the latest version of the course and in Section 4 we discuss some of the changes that we have made.

3.1 Aims and expected outcomes

The aims of the Software Engineering Fundamentals course are introduced in the first session of the course, and they are to:
  a) Provide a working understanding of Software Engineering principles.
  b) Introduce all software engineers to accepted software engineering practice within BAL.
  c) Demonstrate the role of the BAL Software Process Manual and EngNET in supporting software engineering at BAL.
We stress that this course is only introductory and that it is not meant to produce experts in any of the areas that are covered in the course. Although the second aim is phrased in terms of software engineers, the course is actually intended for a much wider audience, including systems engineers, quality assurance personnel, and even some of BAL's customers. As such, we expect that different people will value different aspects of the course. For example, for recent software engineering graduates employed by BAL, the most valuable part of the course is most likely to be the Boeing-specific aspects of the course, such as the BAL Software Process Manual and EngNET. For a systems engineer, it is more likely to be a general understanding of the software engineering discipline and how this is put in to practice at BAL. For others, it might be some of the specific techniques that we teach in the course.

3.2 Presenters

To ensure that both the theoretical and practical viewpoints of software engineering are covered, the course is presented by a combination of BAL staff and University academics. The BAL presenters are able to share experiences from recent and current projects, and several sessions are specifically designed for this purpose. Although the details vary from one version of the course to the next depending on exactly which staff are available, approximately half the sessions are presented by academics and the other half by BAL staff.

3.3 Sessions

Table 1 shows the current course structure. The course runs over four full days, with a mixture of theoretical and practical sessions. The formal breaks in the course are fairly lengthy, to provide ample opportunity for informal exchange of ideas and sharing of experiences. For that same reason, lunch is provided by BAL for each of the four days. Because the schedule is fairly packed and covers a lot of material, additional short breaks are also included as needed (by either the presenters or the audience). Each session is described briefly.

Table 1: Course structure

Time	Day 1	Day 2	Day 3	Day 4
8:30	Introduction & Overview	Review Exercise	Detailed Design	V&V, Quality Assurance
9:00				
9:30	Systems vs. Software	Design Principles	Build Software	Tools demo – EngNET/LLS
10:00				
10:30	Morning Tea		Morning Tea	Morning Tea
11:00	Requirements Principles	Morning Tea	Testing Principles	Software Project Management
11:30				
12:00		Design Workshop		Measurement
12:30	Lunch		Lunch	Lunch
13:00		Lunch		
13:30	Requirements Workshop	Software Domain Exper.	Test Workshop	Software Process Improvement
14:00				
14:30				
15:00	Afternoon Tea	Afternoon Tea	Afternoon Tea	Afternoon Tea
15:30	Software Reviews	CM Principles	Maintenance	Course Summary & Review
16:00				
16:30	Peer reviews	CM Exercise	Maint. Exper.	
17:00	Finish	Finish	Finish	Finish
	Homework: review preparation			

Introduction and Overview: explains the aims and expected outcomes of the course, provides both the presenters and attendees with an opportunity to introduce themselves, forms groups for the workshops in the course, and outlines the course structure. Because there is typically a mixed audience in the course, the working groups are formed to ensure a mix of experience level in each of the groups (this is done by asking all attendees to self-assess their experience with software). The second part of this session provides a brief introduction to the software engineering discipline, and an overview of various software lifecycle models, including BAL's preferred lifecycle model. Finally, the Software Process Manual and EngNET are briefly introduced, although typically several of the attendees are already familiar with both of these.

Systems vs. Software: discusses the relationship between systems and software engineering at BAL, and some of the challenges faced by BAL in both (mainly dealing with complexity). It also provides a brief overview of the Boeing Company and specifically the types of work carried out by BAL.

Requirements Principles and Requirements Workshop: are intended to provide an understanding of requirements and why they are important. They introduce various techniques for eliciting, recording, and analysing requirements. The theoretical session before lunch is followed by a workshop after lunch that provides an opportunity to gain practical experience with some of these techniques. During this workshop, a case study involving an Emergency Response System (ERS) is introduced. This case study is used in several of the workshops. During the Requirements workshop, the groups are asked to develop a set of use cases for the ERS. At the end of the workshop, each group presents their results to the other groups so that the attendees get a feel for different approaches to the same problem. This technique is used for most of the workshops.

Software Reviews and Review Exercise: provide a working understanding of objectives, methods, guidelines, and forms for software reviews as defined by BAL (essentially a form of Fagan inspection). The principles are introduced on the first day. The participants are then asked to do individual preparation as their homework (the only homework in the course) for the review meeting which is held at the beginning of the second day. The document that is reviewed is part of a hypothetical requirements document for the ERS.

Design Principles and Design Workshop: introduce the notion of software architecture and provide practical experience with some techniques for deriving an architecture during the workshop. In the workshop, the groups are asked to develop a sequence diagram for one of the scenarios developed in the requirements workshop and a corresponding initial class diagram for the ERS.

Software Domain Experience: is the first of the sessions where BAL personnel present practical experience from real projects related to the material presented in the course. No new material is typically presented in these sessions, rather they are included to illustrate how theory is being put into practice. In this session, a software manager presents the architecture (and the process used to create this architecture) of a significant current software project (which means that, in some cases, people working on that project are part of the audience).

CM Principles and CM Exercise: identify the purpose and application of Software Configuration Management. The exercise consists of two versions of a small shapes puzzle; after solving the puzzles, the groups are asked to provide detailed build instructions and version descriptions for both versions of the puzzle.

Detailed Design: introduces the notion of detailed design and presents several aspects that need to be considered when developing or evaluating a detailed design.

Build Software: presents pertinent aspects of the implementation phase, such as software development environments, and other tools and techniques that assist with writing and debugging code.

Testing Principles and Test Workshop: provide an introduction to what software testing is and where it is applied. They explain how to plan, develop and execute a software test program. The workshop focuses on applying black-box and white-box test case selection strategies to a small piece of software.

Maintenance: provides an understanding of software maintenance and its specific problems.

Maintenance Experience: is the second session in which BAL personnel discuss practical experience, in this case experience maintaining a large legacy software system.

V&V and Quality Assurance: introduces the terms Verification and Validation (V&V) and then identifies some techniques used in V&V (several of which have already been covered earlier in the course). It also provides a brief introduction into the area of Quality Assurance and how this relates to software projects at BAL.

EngNET/LLS Demo: demonstrates several on-line tools that are available to support software engineers at BAL in their day-to-day activities. In particular, it introduces the Engineering Network (EngNET) that provides on-line access to process and project documentation. It also introduces a recently developed Lessons Learned System (LLS) that allows software engineers to record and reuse lessons learned on projects at BAL.

Software Project Management: introduces the management cycle of a project, and how to apply general management principles to the management of software projects.

Measurement: provides an overview of the principles of software measurement and explains the ideas and benefits of a goal-driven measurement process. It also shows how measurement has been used in practice on a number of Boeing projects.

Software Process Improvement: identifies the need for process improvement and the BAL infrastructure and assets that are in place to support it. The session contains a small exercise to allow groups to develop some ideas for process improvements in their area of work.

Course Summary & Review: briefly reviews the aims of the course and then asks the participants to report on what they learnt from the course. The session is structured as informal presentations by the groups in which they briefly describe the important aspects from each session of the course.

4. Evaluation

Evaluation provides feedback from course participants that can be used to improve course content and presentation techniques. Many methods of evaluation exist. For this course, we have primarily used written questionnaires. We use a specific questionnaire for each day of the course so we can gather information about individual sessions, as well as an end-of-course questionnaire to gather overall impressions. We also intend to carry out long-term evaluation.

4.1 Short-term evaluation

Since it was first run in September 2000, the course has been run 9 times, with between 8 and 30 attendees each time. In addition to tracking the attendance at each course, the engineering training department at BAL has evaluated the course using questionnaires on individual sessions at the end of each day of the course, and a summary evaluation at the end of the course.

Both evaluations are carried out using questionnaires that contain a mix of rated and short answer questions. The sessions and presenters are rated using a scale of Excellent-Good-Average-Poor, and similarly each day as a whole is rated using this scale. The evaluations from the last course for the presenters and the workshops are shown in Figures 1 and 2. To convert the ratings to a numerical value, the following scales are used: 10 for Excellent, 7 for Good, 4 for Average, and 1 for Poor. In addition, the questionnaires ask the participants to nominate particular aspects of the sessions that they liked/disliked and that they found particularly useful.

As the data in Figures 1 and 2 shows, although there is some variability between presenters and the different sessions, the course is generally very well received. This has been the case from when the course was first offered, but there was a greater variability in the responses for the initial versions of the course. The ratings and responses of the attendees indicated that many of the attendees struggled with the amount and detail of material presented in some of the more technical sessions. This was particularly true for the Design Principles and Design Workshop sessions, and to a lesser extent for the Requirements and Testing sessions. As a result, the two most significant changes to the course have been to reduce the amount of detailed, technical material in these sessions, and to make the workshops more accessible to people with little or no background in software engineering. The testing workshop is now also preceded by a brief group tutorial to illustrate what is expected during the workshop on a small example.

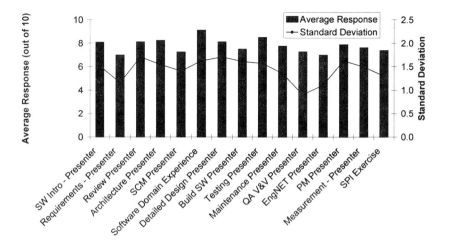

Figure 1: Presenter evaluation

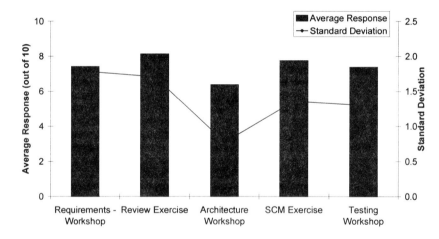

Figure 2: Workshop and exercise evaluation

The end-of-course summary evaluation asks participants to rate their knowledge of the subject matter before and after the course, the relevance of the course, as well as the course materials and the venue. Again, the feedback on all of these is very positive, although the self-ratings of knowledge vary widely both within and across different courses, reflecting the mixed background of the course participants

4.2 Long-term evaluation

Informal feedback on the course has been obtained from course participants and their project leaders through monthly process group meetings. Again, this information has been positive in general, with an indication for the need for more advanced follow-on courses in specific areas, often on a project-specific basis. We have also created a questionnaire for long-term evaluation, to examine if participants are able to apply the skills or knowledge they have gained through the course in their work. It includes more general questions related to the perceived training needs of the attendees. We plan to use this questionnaire in the near future and send it to people who have attended the course six or more months ago.

5. Conclusions

The BAL software engineering fundamentals course is an introductory course designed for the wide range of participants' backgrounds. The course has been developed and is presented as an on-going collaboration between BAL and the University of Queensland. The work presented in this paper differs from most other published industry/university collaborations on software engineering education, in that this course is an orientation course that is intended to provide staff from a variety of areas with an appreciation for the software engineering discipline. This appreciation is increasingly important as software becomes a larger part of BAL's business. Through a mixture of theoretical and practical sessions, we expose the participants to software engineering ideas and techniques. Despite the mix of people that attend the course, feedback indicates that we are meeting our participants' expectations, and that they value the knowledge and skills that result from their involvement. Based on the feedback, the two main changes have been reducing the amount of detailed, technical material in some of the sessions and making the workshops more accessible to people with little or no background in software engineering.

The authors plan further development of this course based on the on-going feedback and we are also considering which areas of software engineering require more advanced follow-on courses for BAL staff. These advanced courses are likely to be directed at upgrading the skills and knowledge of BAL's software engineering specialists.

6. Acknowledgements

The authors would like to thank Fiona Dobson, Ramayya Darbhamulla and other BAL staff who have helped prepare and present parts of the course. We would also like to thank Roger Duke for his constructive comments on an earlier version of this paper.

7. References

[1] Alain Abran et al. (eds.), Guide to the Software Engineering Body of Knowledge: Trial Version, IEEE Computer Society Press, 2001.
[2] H.J.C. Ellis, N.R. Mead, A. Moreno, C.D. Tanner and D. Ramsey, Characteristics of Successful Collaborations to Produce Educated Software Engineering Professionals, Computer Science Education, 12(1-2):119-140, 2002.
[3] K. Beckman, N. Coulter, S. Khajenoori, and N.R. Mead, Collaborations: Closing the Industry-Academia Gap, IEEE Software, 14(6):49-57, 1996.
[4] N. McCabe, G. O'Mary, and K. Powel, Stretching the McDonnell Douglas Software Training Budget: Striking a Balance Between In-House and Outsourcing, Proceedings of the Ninth Conference on Software Engineering Education, pg. 199-213, 1996.

Industry/University Software Engineering Collaborations for the Successful Reeducation of Non-Software Professionals

Heidi J. C. Ellis
Rensselaer at Hartford
heidic@rh.edu

Nancy R. Mead
Software Engineering Institute
nrm@sei.cmu.edu

Ana M. Moreno
Universidad Politécnica de Madrid
ammoreno@fi.upm.es

Stephen B. Seidman
New Jersey Institute of Technology
Stephen.Seidman@njit.edu

Abstract

Production of software is growing at a phenomenal rate worldwide. In addition, the increasingly global business climate has accelerated the need for business software. There are too few software engineers to produce and maintain software to meet this demand. One possible solution to correcting this shortfall is reeducating existing non-software employees to become software engineers. For the past two years, the Industry/University (I/U) subgroup of the Working Group on Software Engineering Education and Training (WGSEET) has been investigating active collaborations between companies and universities in which employees without formal software education are reeducated to become software engineers. This paper reports on our findings by discussing our approach to the investigation, outlining the factors involved in successful collaboration construction and execution, and describing alumni views of the knowledge and skills transferred by the collaboration.

1. Introduction

In its annual report (*Worldwide Software Market Forecast Summary 2001-2005* [15]), International Data Corp. has projected a growth rate of 11.8% for companies in the market of developing and deploying software applications in the year 2002, indicating rapid growth in the development and use of software. However, the number of software professionals available to develop and maintain this software is limited and is not growing at a rate equal to the growth rate of software. This lack of software professionals is also occurring in countries such as Canada, India, and most countries in Europe.

Educational institutions are expanding efforts to increase the number of software engineering graduates [13], but the rate of production is not keeping up with demand. The reeducation of existing non-software personnel to fill software engineering positions is one logical approach to meet this shortfall. Indeed, some companies have entered into cooperative partnerships with academic institutions to retrain employees with domain knowledge in order to retain this valuable resource [6]. In addition, various efforts have identified the need for incorporating a strong industry perspective into software engineering education programs [7, 8, 12, 14]. Thus, the construction of a collaborative relationship between industry and academic partners to reeducate a portion of the existing non-software workforce is one approach to providing a larger software engineering workforce.

This paper presents the findings of recent research performed by the Industry/University subgroup of the Working Group on Software Engineering Education and Training into collaborative reeducation efforts between industry and academic institutions for converting non-software professionals into software engineers.

1.1 The Working Group on Software Engineering Education and Training

The Working Group on Software Engineering Education and Training (WGSEET) (http://www.sei.cmu.edu/collaborating/ed/workgroup-ed.html) was formed in 1995 with the mission of improving the state of software engineering education and training. An ad hoc group of approximately 80 international professionals from academia, industry, and government, the focus of the group is on the education and professional development of software practitioners through degree programs, continuing education, on-the-job training, etc. The Industry/University (I/U) subgroup is a subset of WGSEET members whose focus is to explore and foster collaborations between academic institutions and industry [11]. Currently, the I/U group is investigating collaborations in which non-software professionals and practitioners without formal software education are reeducated to become software engineers.

Section 2 describes our approach and research framework, while Section 3 discusses the characteristics of successful collaborations. Section 4 describes the alumni opinions of the usefulness of the knowledge they gained in the collaborative programs, and Section 5 provides some general conclusions.

2. Investigation process

The motivation for investigating I/U reeducation collaborations occurred as a result of a talk given to the WGSEET by Dennis Frailey [6] in March 2000 in which he described a collaborative software engineering reeducation program between Texas Instruments/Raytheon and several Dallas area universities. Using Beckman's definition [1] of a collaboration as "a formal, joint effort by a university (or universities) and a business or government organization(s), where each party provides specified products and services to achieve common goals," we decided to focus on cooperative programs between academic institutions and industry partners to retrain non-software professionals to become software engineers. We decided to center our investigation on education programs that had a wider effect than several-day or week-long just-in-time training. In March 2000 we began our investigation by identifying nine industry-university collaborative programs. By February 2001, we had centered our investigation on five ongoing collaborations whose programs range in duration from eight months to two years. The outcomes of these collaborative programs ranged from students that obtained credit towards undergraduate courses to students who received Master's degrees. In the following sections we describe our approach to investigating I/U reeducation collaborations.

2.1 Our approach

The organization of the major steps taken in our investigation are shown in Figure 1.

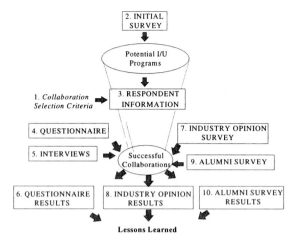

Figure 1. Process used to study I/U reeducation collaborations

Our investigation process has ten steps:

Step 1 Determine Collaboration Selection Criteria: We began our efforts in March 2000 by identifying a set of criteria that we used to select candidate collaborations. Criteria included programs with a focus on education/training for non-software professionals, programs that were currently in existence, and ongoing interaction between industrial and academic partners.

Step 2 Conduct Initial Survey: Based on our selection criteria, we developed a short survey that we used to identify candidate collaborations. Between April and June 2000, we distributed this survey to a variety of software engineering fora.

Step 3 Filter Respondent Information: In December 2000 we applied the selection criteria to the results of the initial survey to determine collaborations and identified a pool of nine successful collaborations, six located in the United States and three located in Europe. Details of these results are described in [5].

Step 4 Administer Questionnaire: An in-depth questionnaire was constructed in November 2000, focusing on the organizational and participational factors that may have contributed to the success of the collaboration.

Step 5 Conduct Interviews: During January and February 2001, the questionnaire was administered to the candidate collaborations identified in Step 3.

Step 6 Evaluate Questionnaire Results: During the month of February 2001, the results of the questionnaire were tabulated to determine characteristics of successful industry/university collaborations. Ellis et al. [2] provide the initial results of the questionnaire, and an overview of features of successful collaborations is included in Section 3.

Step 7 Create Industry Opinion Survey: Results from the questionnaires and interviews indicated a possible academic bias in our information. Therefore, in order to elicit industry views, we constructed a short industry opinion survey during February 2001.

Step 8 Incorporate Industry Opinion Results: The industry opinion survey was administered to the industry partners participating in the collaborations in April 2001, and during May

2001 the results were tabulated. An overview of industry opinions on successful collaboration development is included in Section 3, and details are provided by Ellis et al. [3].

Step 9 Conduct Alumni Survey: During October 2001, the I/U subgroup constructed a survey to elicit information on the breadth of knowledge gained from the collaboration and its usefulness. Survey details are provided in Section 4.

Step 10 Interpret Alumni Survey Results: In February 2002, the I/U subgroup evaluated the results of the alumni survey. While we lacked sufficient responses to obtain statistically significant results, we were able to make some useful observations on the transfer of skills, which we discuss in Section 4.

3. Successful collaboration construction and execution

Based on our observations of the ongoing collaborations over the course of two years, we have identified characteristics of successful collaborative efforts to reeducate software engineers. A more complete discussion of our observations can be found in [4].

3.1 Common characteristics

Based on our observations, it appears that successful collaborations share factors related to industry participation. Common characteristics of the collaborations we studied include:

Industrial Initiative: A majority of the collaborations were initiated by the industry partner(s) as a result of recognizing the need to expand their workforce.

Strong Industrial Partners: The industry partners in the collaborations are either sizeable companies or collections of companies that have significant financial resources, and almost all are either government agencies or private companies that handle government contracts.

Practically Oriented Programs: All of the collaborative programs studied were practically oriented, focusing on the application of knowledge and skills.

Software Practitioners as Students: All of the students who participated in the collaborative programs had been employed in some aspect of the software field for two to over ten years.

Limited Number of Students: The successful collaborations that we examined all had between 10 and 25 students per offering.

3.2 Dissimilar characteristics

We also identified several differences between the programs including:

Content Definition for the Program: Content definition alternatives included determination by the industry partners, by the university partner, or by a mixed group.

Admission Procedure: In some collaborations the industry partner selected students or dictated student selection, while in others students were required to fulfill the academic institution's program entrance requirements.

Financial Models: In some collaborations the industry partner paid on a per student basis, while in others the industry partner provided the academic partner with a specific amount of funding, irrespective of the number of students.

Other minor differences between the programs included location, timing of class offerings, and content.

3.3 Benefits

In the process of evaluating the collaborations, we identified four benefits that resulted from the collaborative reeducation efforts:

Knowledge Enrichment of University Teachers: Practical knowledge migrated into the curriculum as faculty gained increased exposure to real-world software development practices.

Self-Supporting Programs: All of the collaborations that we studied were entirely self-supporting and in some instances financially profitable.

Knowledge Enrichment of Industry Employees: The expanded knowledge and skill set of employees is the primary benefit identified by industry partners.

More Competitive Software Industries: Reeducation collaborations result in a benefit to the software industry as a whole through the production of better quality software.

Other indirect benefits obtained from the collaborative programs are that employees are less likely to leave the company when they are participating in a collaborative reeducation program.

3.4 Industry viewpoint

In general, the industry partners appeared to be very satisfied with the collaborations and their outcome [3]. All of the industry partners indicated that they were satisfied or very satisfied with the program development and participant selection. All industry partners thought that the program management and oversight, student enrollment procedure, and format, content, and pace of the program were acceptable. The majority of the industry respondents rated both the instructors' knowledge and the facilities as outstanding, while the instructors' teaching skills were rated sufficient by most respondents. All of the respondents indicated that they felt that the number of participants in the program was the correct size. All of the industry partners indicated that they felt that the program was successful and that they gained knowledgeable, competent employees.

The main area for improvement identified by industry partners was the incorporation of domain knowledge in program content.

4. Evaluating knowledge/skill transfer

In October 2001, the I/U subgroup decided to try to assess the efficacy and efficiency of knowledge and skill transfer that occurs in the collaborative reeducation programs (Figure 1 steps 9-10). We constructed a survey to educe the opinions of alumni of the collaborative programs in which they participated. The first part of the survey asked students the emphasis placed on each of the subjects, the usefulness of the knowledge acquired in each subject for alumni's current job tasks, and the sufficiency of knowledge gained for each subject using the ten major SWEBOK topics [9]. The second focus area of the surveys dealt with the impact of the programs on the professional and educational status of the alumni. In this section, we describe our effort and the results.

4.2. Results analysis

Alumni of four different collaborations were surveyed to analyze knowledge transfer in their collaborations. A total of 31 surveys for the four collaborations were collected. Two collaborations were located in Spain (Madrid) and two in the United States (Georgia, Pennsylvania). Although the final number of surveys is insufficient for a formal statistical analysis, the survey results allow us to make some general observations about the efficacy of the programs.

In order to understand how the alumni's current jobs were impacted by their education, we surveyed alumni to determine the software engineering activities performed in their current positions. Table 1 shows the activities performed by the alumni. Note that the percentage column does not add up to 100, as some alumni performed more than one activity type.

Table 1: Current alumni job types

Job Type	Requirements	Design	Code	Test	CM	Maintenance	Documentation	QA	Project Management
% alumni	36%	25%	14%	29%	11%	25%	21%	11%	50%

4.2.1. Results of content measurement: A set of emphasis, usefulness and sufficiency of knowledge gradients were used to ascertain alumni opinions on the skills gained from their educational experience. Figure 2 shows the results for all 31 alumni for the part of our survey based on these gradients. Overall, practitioners who participated in the collaborative programs have a positive impression of the effectiveness and usefulness of the skills that they gained. These results differ somewhat from Lethbridge's study on the applicability of software engineering knowledge [10], which indicates a larger gap between transferred knowledge and its usefulness in industry. One reason for this difference could be the fact that the majority of the collaborative efforts we investigated involved postgraduate (Master's level) education, which is typically more focused than undergraduate education.

Figure 2 indicates that alumni consider the knowledge acquired about the topics of software management and software requirements most useful, whereas the knowledge related to software construction, software testing, and software maintenance is somewhat less useful. Since Table 1 Indicates that a higher percentage of alumni perform project and requirements management tasks, this is not an unexpected result. The results for the topics of testing and maintenance indicate that alumni do not consider the knowledge acquired on these topics to be very useful.

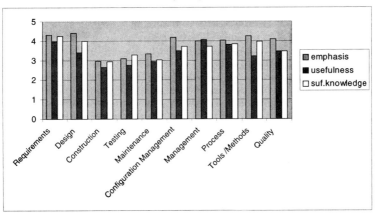

Figure 2. Weighted values of emphasis, usefulness, and sufficiency of knowledge

The ideal result would be for all three measures (emphasis, usefulness, and sufficiency) to be equal for each subject. An analysis of the chart in Figure 2 shows that the average pair-wise correlation for the three characteristics is .79 between usefulness and sufficiency of knowledge, .78 between emphasis and usefulness, and .89 between emphasis and sufficiency of knowledge.

The relationship between usefulness and sufficiency of knowledge indicates the effectiveness of the programs. Figure 2 shows that except for software management, the knowledge sufficiency for each subject is at least as great as the usefulness, indicating that the programs are viewed as very effective. For software management, the emphasis rating is slightly lower than the usefulness rating, which may indicate a need for programs to reexamine content related to software management, as well as to review the process by which this topic is taught.

Overall, the .79 correlation between usefulness and sufficiency of knowledge shows that alumni are satisfied with the knowledge gained from the collaboration. A large difference between the sufficiency of knowledge rating and a greater usefulness rating, as seen in the software tools/methods and software design areas, indicates that programs are providing more knowledge or skills than required by the alumni. Since only 25% of alumni perform design tasks (see Table 1), alumni may benefit from education and skills at a higher level of abstraction.

The relationship between content emphasis and the sufficiency of knowledge determines the efficiency of the education. The .89 correlation between these two characteristics indicates a relatively efficient transfer of skills. The largest differences are found for software quality and software configuration management; alumni believe that these topics receive more emphasis than their usefulness warrants. The results for software testing show that the sufficiency of knowledge rating is higher than the level of emphasis.

The relationship between content emphasis and knowledge usefulness can provide an indication of the overall success of the collaboration. The relatively high correlation of .78 indicates that the reeducation programs are producing individuals that, from the alumni point of view, are highly qualified to step into software engineering positions.

4.2.2. Results of subjective assessment: The second part of the survey asked alumni to assess the program's effect on the educational and professional status of the alumni by indicating the extent they agreed (strongly agree, agree, disagree, or strongly disagree) with statements:

My software engineering education has adequately prepared me for my current job.
My education provided me with knowledge and skills that contribute to my job performance.
My education has improved my software development skills.
My education has improved my communication skills.
My education has improved my technical skills.
My education has improved my organizational skills.
My education was highly relevant to state-of-the-art practices in my field.
My education provided me with a useful reputation as a software engineer.
My education contributed to the development of my professional career.
I would recommend participation in my educational program to others.

The results indicate that the alumni generally agree that the programs improved their skills, with 70% of alumni stating that the programs improved their technical skills and almost 90% of alumni indicating that they would recommend the program to colleagues.

Although a majority of the alumni stated that management supported the use of the newly acquired knowledge and skills, 25% of alumni indicated that they received no such assistance. Another unexpected result of the subjective assessment was that alumni have a relatively low perception of the reputation that they received as a result of their educational experience. One possible reason for this result is that most of the alumni surveyed were within two years or less of their graduation and the impact of the reputation may not be felt until later in their careers.

5. Conclusion

In the course of its two-year investigation into industry/university collaborations to reeducate non-software personnel to become software engineers, the I/U subgroup of the WGSEET has compiled several useful observations about such collaborations. The primary observation is that these collaborations provide significant benefits for all three major stakeholders: the industry partner, the academic partner, and the students. Industry feedback indicates that companies benefit from a larger, more highly trained workforce with a higher level of knowledge and skills while retaining large stores of domain knowledge held by the existing employees. Universities benefit from increased visibility of their programs, as well as from the dissemination of a real-world vision of software engineering throughout the faculty. Students benefit by becoming more highly skilled workers, with higher job satisfaction and more career mobility.

One area of concern that we identified in our investigation was the apparent relatively short life of industry/university collaborations for reeducating software engineers. Given the amount of effort required to construct such a program and the continuing shortfall of qualified software engineers, we believe that maintaining these programs is of value to both the partners involved, as well as to the larger discipline of software engineering.

Acknowledgements

The authors would like to acknowledge and thank Dawn Ramsey and Cynthia Tanner for their efforts in support of this work.

References

[1] Beckman, K., "Directory of Industry and University Collaborations with a Focus on Software Engineering Education and Training," Version 7, Technical Report, CMU/SEI-99-SR-0001, 1999.

[2] Ellis, H. J. C., N. R. Mead, A. Moreno, and P. MacNeil, "Can Industry and Academia Collaborate to Meet the Need for Software Engineers?" *Cutter IT Journal*, June 2001.

[3] Ellis, H. J. C., N. R. Mead, A. Moreno, C. D. Tanner, and D. Ramsey, "Characteristics of Successful Collaborations to Produce Educated Software Engineering Professionals," *Computer Science Education Journal*, , Spring 2002.

[4] Ellis H.J.C., Ana Moreno, Nancy R. Mead, Stephen B. Seidman "Reeducation to Expand the Software Engineering Workforce: Successful Industry/University Collaborations," SEI Technical Report, *CMU/SEI-2002-SR-001*, Aug. 2002.

[5] Ellis, H. J. C., "Summary of the Initial Results of the University/Industry Survey Performed by the Industry/University Subgroup of the Working Group on Software Engineering Education and Training," FASE Vol. 11, No. 1, Jan. 2001.

[6] Frailey, D., and F. Moore, "Maintaining a Capable Software Engineering Pool," Proceedings, *1998 Software Technology Conference*, Apr. 1998.

[7] Frezza, S. T., and S. L. Hazen, "Integrating an Industrial Practicum into a Graduate Embedded Software Engineering Program," *Frontiers in Education Conference*, Nov. 1999.

[8] Hazen, S. L., and S. T. Frezza, "An Integrated Embedded Software Engineering Program and Practicum," *Frontiers in Education Conference*, Nov. 1997.

[9] Hilburn, T., et al., "A Software Engineering Body of Knowledge," Version 1.0, CMU/SEI-99-TR-004.

[10] Lethbridge, T., "What Knowledge is Important to a Software Engineer?" *IEEE Computer*, May, 2001.

[11] Mead, N. R., et al., "Industry/University Collaborations: Different Perspectives Heighten Mutual Opportunities," *Journal of Systems and Software* (49) 2-3 (1999).

[12] Mingas, C., et al., "How We Teach Software Engineering," *Journal of Object-Oriented Programming*, Feb. 1999.

[13] Modesitt, K., D. Bagert, and L. Werth, "International Academic Software Engineering: Results of the First Annual Survey," Proceedings, *IASTED International Conference on Applied Informatics*, Feb. 2001.

[14] Wholin, C., and B. Regnell, "Achieving Industrial Relevance in Software Engineering Education," Proceedings, *12th Conference on Software Engineering Education and Training*, Mar. 1999.

[15] IDC Worldwide Software Market Forecast Summary, 2001-2005, (IDC #25569), Oct. 2001.

Soft(ware) Skills in Context: Corporate Usability Training Aiming at Cross-Disciplinary Collaboration

Markus Latzina, Bernard Rummel
SAP AG
markus.latzina@sap.com, bernard.rummel@sap.com

Abstract

Employing user-centered instructional design methodology, we developed a usability training workshop for developers which has remarkable impact on participants' attitudes towards the cross-disciplinary collaboration in the software development team. Based mainly on learning experiences during a simulation game, participants gain insights regarding typical pitfalls and opportunities of collaboration with user experience specialists and other non-technical professionals. Rather than teaching abstract, high-level usability principles, we use the "reflected practice" approach [1] as a guiding workshop theme, in order to achieve lasting effects for the succeeding professional practice of software development teams.

We include evaluative data based on participants' feedback and in-class statements.

Keywords: *Usability Training, Simulation Game, Collaboration, Instructional Design, Human-Computer Interaction*

1. Introduction: what & how to teach developers?

Computer science curriculum studies are still slow to embrace user-centered development methods [2]. Consequently, much of the usability training and education for developers is left to corporate training organizations. In their specific context, corporate instructional designers need to address a set of typical problems in order to create effective usability training for developers.

Because usability is not the professional focus of a developer, the allotted time and resources for training are limited. As usability and interaction design experts, we face the problem that condensing our expertise to a 2-day course often results in commonplace statements. Additionally, developers are not, and will not be, usability specialists, no matter how hard we train them.

The variety of products common in a large software company, and rapidly evolving technical platforms, make it hard for instructional designers to develop focused training content. Therefore, meta knowledge on how to access and use standards is often more useful than knowledge of specific product standards.

Furthermore, user-centered development being a multidisciplinary activity, trainees need to acquire cross-disciplinary cooperation skills. Consequently, social and motivational aspects are much more important to convey in training than encyclopedic knowledge.

In this paper we present an approach to these problems which exemplifies the cross-disciplinary collaboration between Usability and Instructional Design experts.

2. User-centered instructional design

The authors' professional background lies in the fields of HCI and Instructional Design. While the User-Centered Development approach to software engineering and the Instructional Design methodology [3] bear striking similarities for the purpose of

52 1093-0175/03 $17.00 © 2003 IEEE

our course design project they complemented each other extremely well (in terms of subject matter expertise and methodological conduct).

2.1. Needs analysis

2.1.1. Organizational setting: SAP favors a user-centered development approach as introduced in the Enjoy initiative, which resulted in the SAP R/3 "Enjoy" release 4.6. In recent years, SAP has built up a strong in-house network of usability and interaction design professionals (User Interface Designers) a developer can expect to have in his/her team.

SAP's corporate culture treasures customer orientation, continuous learning, and teamwork. The training situation must respect and foster this attitude.

Due to SAP's world-wide operations, a multi-cultural audience is to be expected. In fact, we had up to 18 nations represented in a course.

2.1.2. Job & task analysis: Since a developer at SAP can expect support from usability experts, he/she does not need to make UI design decisions on his or her own, but rather to cooperate with UI experts and other professionals, such as product and quality management specialists. This cooperation requires enough basic knowledge of user centered development methodology to participate in the process, and a basic motivation to do so. Since user-centered development activities are better accepted if they visibly speed up the development process, the training situation should demonstrate this benefit.

There is a vast amount of usability resources available at SAP (e.g. the publicly available SAP Design Guild [4], and various intranet resources). A developer needs to know how to use and navigate within these resources to quickly find standards, guidelines, tools, and methodology support.

2.1.3. Target group analysis: We built on a database of interviews with beginning developers, and a collection of contextual work models of typical development practices in the company. We also created two primary personas [5] as archetypical participants in our training. From this analysis, we found additional requirements with implications for the course design in terms of guiding ideas.

Beginning developers are eager to demonstrate their skills in the teams they are joining. Consequently, they need to acquire skills which can be readily applied. Knowledge of the user-centered development process enables participants to demonstrate project management skills, thereby fostering their careers.

2.1.4. Training constraints: For years SAP had been offering an introductory usability course for newly-hired developers. The course used to be a short introduction into usability principles and techniques, which was exactly what developers and management expected and still would expect after our redesign.

Beginning SAP developers go through several months of training - Usability is one course among many others.

3. Course design

3.1. Definition of learning goals

Based upon the needs analysis, we focused our training and education efforts on effective cooperation with the professional User Interface Designers a developer can expect to have in his/her team. According to our analysis, a developer needs to:

(1)   Accept and understand the division of labor with User Interface Designers, entailing the cross-disciplinary collaboration among professionals. This requires a certain change of attitude towards a better acceptance of / cooperation with non-technical professional roles.

(2)   Be able to participate in a User Centered Development Process, including specific User Interface (UI) design activities.

(3)   Know where to find, and how to use, usability resources at SAP, such as contacts, guidelines, infrastructure, learning materials and text/web resources

3.2. Designing learning tasks

In order to achieve the learning goals we needed to design appropriate learning tasks [6]. For this purpose we had to break down the learning goals into specific learning objectives. Besides goals in the cognitive domain we needed to address skills in problem-solving, motivation, and individual and social action. Learning methods would need to accommodate these various areas.

For example, to accomplish learning objectives in the motivational domain, the learning task needs to be intrinsically motivating. In the social action domain, the learning situation needs to involve a collaborative situation combined with social reinforcements.

Therefore, as the core learning method within the 2 day training course we devised a theme-oriented process simulation game of about one day duration. Differently from other simulation game implementations [7, 8, 9], we did not choose a purely computerized solution but just rely on the use of networked computing for the participants to accomplish the learning tasks.

This decision was guided by the overall goal to come up with an adult-oriented training method which would be suited for professionals. More specifically, we wanted participants to experience typical situations which arise during a development project, and to have them develop solutions to typical problems on their own (rather than telling them which solutions to apply) [10].

In order to accept and participate in UI design activities, participants need to be motivated, and the effectiveness of the respective techniques needs to be demonstrated. We chose short introductory lecturettes, and immediate hands-on experience with slightly simplified interaction design and usability methods to achieve this objective.

Participants expect to be instructed in basic usability principles and solving design problems, but encyclopedic completeness was not required. Self-guided problem solving in the context of the simulation game, assisted by trainers, is appropriate to achieve this.

As an introduction to SAP Usability Resources, and how to find and use them, we chose to conduct a simulated low-fi usability test of usability-related intranet sites and other resources. This approach enabled us to combine the demonstration of a usability technique with research and navigation training. We also regularly make use of this opportunity to collect feedback for our own intranet site.

4. Course outline

The final course design is a two day workshop for 18-36 participants. During the course of learning events, the group is split in several subgroups, which need to coordinate their activities. In the following we describe the overall course outline.

4.1 Preparation of the learning setting

We begin with a self-assessment of learning styles and ask participants to enter their scores in an (anonymized) group chart. Participants learn about the large diversity in the training group, and are told that the course is set up to accommodate each of the various styles with different learning tasks at various points in time.

4.2 UI design evaluation

We introduce Personas [4] as a tool for evaluating the interaction design quality of web sites. This block is a lot of fun; it activates participants and motivates them for the experience-based learning in the next block.

4.3 Simulation game: pizza service solution

The simulation game is the core learning experience of the course. Participants design a pizza service solution, which includes three different but related user scenarios and technical platforms: a web scenario for the consumer, a mobile/ handheld solution for the delivery driver, and a client/ server platform for a pizza manager/ dispatcher. Three ("development") groups design and develop paper prototypes for these scenarios under time pressure. A fourth group ("Task Force") does research on user scenarios, style guides for the various platforms, and terminology issues. This group is also supposed to coordinate the development groups. In the final phase of the game, the Task Force tries to support the design process, based upon their own results. Finally, each team's achievements are evaluated by user tests, style guide reviews, and terminology reviews, comprising both assessments by peers and by the trainers.

In a dedicated reflection phase, participants state which lessons they learned from the game. They spontaneously discover and state key factors for implementing a user-centered development process. We just collect these statements without interfering.

4.4 SAP usability resources

Participants form groups of three and conduct a simulated low-fi usability test of usability-related intranet and web resources. We introduce the method and provide task descriptions. Results are collected on a voluntary basis.

4.5 Transfer of knowledge preparation

In order to transfer participants' learning achievements to their jobs and daily work practice, participants are motivated to form intentions, and to build commitment. Participants form small "buddy" groups, in which they negotiate and sign a learning contract. The contract states usability-related goals the participants have defined for themselves, how they intend to pursue them, and how they plan to deal with obstacles.

5. Evaluation

5.1 Goals of evaluation

Our training activities at SAP are explicitly embedded in a larger knowledge management strategy, aiming at the dissemination of usability knowledge to the User Interface Designers and developers community, by means of training and education (including self-study materials), intranet and web presence, and toolkits. Consequently, we continuously evaluate our activities with regard to benefits, redesign needs, and remaining training needs. Results are reported to management, the UI community, and course participants to provide them with an overall picture of the course group's learning achievements.

5.2 Data gathering

For the overall course, we used the computer-based standard SAP University course evaluation questionnaire each course participant is required to fill out.

For the simulation game, we collected anonymous, voluntary statements from participants, what they liked or disliked about themselves, their team, and the simulation game. During the reflection phase of the simulation game, we additionally collected informal minutes of the participants' "lessons learned" statements.

5.3 Data analysis

Data were analyzed qualitatively, partly with enumerating, by clustering statements in terms of evaluative feedback. We focused on identifying factors fostering or inhibiting learning achievements, and indicating opportunities for course redesign and training needs.

5.4 Results

Participants' feedback ranges from enthusiasm (~80%: "great simulation, great techniques, great fun") to disappointment (~20%: missing "usability theory/ principles"). The key differentiator in whether participants like or dislike the course is whether or not they understand the connection between project management problems in the simulation game, and usability problems. Those who understand the connection like the course; the others often don't.

However, even participants who dislike the simulation game as such make interesting statements in the simulation game reflection phase. Based upon our evaluations of a number of courses we conducted, we find that participants repeatedly state insights in accordance with our learning goals. Here are some samples:

- *Time and proper project management are required to roll in user/ task information, usability standards*
- *The user perspective has advantages when compared to a purely technical perspective*
- *Data-based design is a necessity*
- *Developers feel bothered by Task Force - Task Force is disappointed by lack of interest in their results*
- *Development teams become aware of their autistic behavior*
- *Task force members become aware of communication needs*
- *Everyone sees the cost of communication, and that you need to look beyond your team to see the benefits*

Participants also develop their own solution ideas (which they will better remember later at work than any trainer's statement):

- *The Task Force needs a coordinating role in the development process*
- *Development teams need coordinators talking to adjacent teams*
- *Network communication structure; a Task Force member switches between groups*
- *Creation of an internal Design Reviewer role*

In terms of redesign and remaining training needs, participants often request more specific training in UI design for specific platforms, such as web or handheld devices.

We take this as an indicator that we achieved strong motivation for further participation in usability training.

6. Summary

Based on the understanding that, in a corporate setting, developers need to cooperate with UI professionals rather than design on their own, we developed a usability training workshop for beginning developers focusing on motivational and social action issues rather than theoretical usability knowledge. Using user-centered instructional design methodology, we developed a training workshop which has remarkable impact on participants' attitudes towards collaboration with non-technical professions. Participants reproducibly make spontaneous statements, indicating key insights for successfully implementing a user-centered development methodology and effective cooperation between technical and non-technical professional roles.

7. References

[1] Schön, D.A., Educating the reflective practitioner. Jossey Bass, San Francisco, CA, 1987.

[2] Kaasinen, E., and A. Clarke, Design for Adaptable Usability Training Materials. (USINACTS: Deliverable Nr. 15), 1998. Available at http://atwww.hhi.de/USINACTS/d15final.html.

[3] Leshin, C., J. Pollock, and C. Reigeluth, Instructional Design Strategies & Tactics, Educational Technology Publications, Englewood Cliffs, NJ, 1992.

[4] SAP Design Guild. Available at http://www.sapdesignguild.org.

[5] Cooper, A., The Inmates are Running the Asylum, SAMS Indianapolis, IN, 1999.

[6] Schott, F., and M. Latzina, PLANA, a Method of Generic Task Analysis for Improving Mental Modeling and the Transfer of Learning, Journal of Structural Learning, 12, 1995, 175-95.

[7] Oh, E., and A. van der Hoek, Adapting Game Technology to Support Individual and Organizational Learning, In: Proceedings of the 13th International Conference on Software Engineering and Knowledge Engineering, Buenos Aires, Argentina, June 2001. Available at http://www1.ics.uci.edu/~emilyo/papers/SEKE2001.pdf

[8] Pfahl, D., M. Klemm, and G. Ruhe, Using System Dynamics Simulation Models for Software Project Management Education and Training, IESE-Report No. 035.00/E, 2000. Available at http://sern.ucalgary.ca/-~ruhe/Research_Publications/techn_reports/iese-035_00.pdf.

[9] Adelsberger, H.H., M.H. Bick, U.F. Kraus, and J.M. Pawlowski, A Simulation Game Approach for Efficient Education in Enterprise Resource Planning Systems, In: Proc. of ESM 99 - Modeling & Simulation: a Tool for the next Millennium, Warsaw, 1.-4. June 1999. Available at http://wip.wi-inf.uni-essen.de/research/-publications/esm99.pdf.

[10] Kolb, D.A., Experiential learning. Prentice Hall, Englewood Cliffs, NJ, 1984.

Software Engineering and Industry 2 (Paper Session B)

On a Partnership between Software Industry and Academia

Andrew J. Kornecki, Soheil Khajenoori, David Gluch
{andrew.kornecki,soheil.khajenoori,david.gluch}@erau.edu
Department of Computing
Embry Riddle Aeronautical University, Daytona Beach, FL
and
Nader Kameli
nader.kameli@guidant.com
CRM Guidant, St.Paul, MN

Abstract

This paper discusses a role for industry in software engineering education, specifically presenting a university-industry partnership between the Cardiac Rhythm Management (CRM) organization at the Guidant Corporation and Embry-Riddle Aeronautical University (ERAU). The focus of the partnership is technology transition. The partnership involves fostering students' professional development, providing students experience solving real-world problems, and exploring modern directions of software engineering. The critical component of the partnership is a student-oriented research laboratory. After discussing the background and history of the project, we focus on the partnership's accomplishments. These include facilitating the transition of graduates from student to employee by developing in them extended software engineering skills and in-depth understanding of the application domain.

1. Introduction

Safety is a system property that assures the system's operation will not endanger human life or adversely impact the environment. Any system controlling energy is an example of safety-critical system. Safety critical software-intensive systems are found in diverse human endeavors, from controlling a nuclear power station to pacing a human heart. Examples of such applications are found in military, aerospace, aviation, transportation, and medical industries. Most of these applications are embedded real-time systems requiring exceptional performance and high reliability. Their development requires rigorous development processes and an intimate knowledge of the application domain.

In most cases industry is interested in application-oriented activities that bring more immediate solutions, help in the implementation of new products, or improve the bottom line of everyday operations. Industry is competing for college graduates with the skills to meet the challenges of developing safety-critical software-intensive systems. It is difficult to find individuals with the requisite expertise and experience in the discipline of software engineering: its lifecycle, artifacts, and processes. Companies focusing on software-intensive safety-critical products understand the importance of having a steady influx of qualified personnel and reliable external source of technology assessment.

One way to assist in these personnel and technology assessment issues is to have a permanent academic partner familiar with the company domain and culture. The selection of such partner may depend on many factors. One of them is the physical proximity. It is much easier to co-operate with the partner located across the street for a steady stream of graduating students. However, most often the selection of partner depends on the academic program

1093-0175/03 $17.00 © 2003 IEEE

focus and qualifications that cannot be found locally. Such factors as the university's technology focus, environment and culture need also to be considered.

One of the ways to bridge the gap between industry and academia and improve the current situation is through close cooperation between academia and industry. This paper describes a program for such cooperation.

2. Past Collaboration Efforts

There are a variety of ways that industry and academia can cooperate. Many academic institutions have installed departmental or other academic unit-wide Industrial Advisory Boards. These groups, consisting of managers and engineers from industries closely associated with the academic organization, are one of the vehicles that provide feedback about an academic program's direction. Other typical forms of cooperation are occasional short-term projects, meeting the current needs of industry. Such projects allow faculty and students to become familiar with the domain and often contribute to the industrial partner's goals. Other vehicles of cooperation are student co-op and faculty internship programs. They facilitate understanding of industry needs and allow the university to make appropriate program corrections. All these approaches can be effective. However, they do not provide a complete solution.

In the mid-90's Embry Riddle Aeronautical University's computing department launched the Software Center. The Software Center was designed to provide a process-centered, measurement driven environment for educating future software engineers. We organized it with shared resources of the university and industry partners. It consisted of faculty, students, and industry collaborators engaged in projects organized to utilize software engineering's best practices. It was a resource center using faculty and students. It was dedicated to addressing selected software engineering problems, providing technology assessments and solutions to participating industrial partners. The Software Center provided feedback for the software engineering curriculum enhancement while providing support and solutions for the industry partners.

The initial concept was to attract a few committed industrial partners to sponsor the Center's operational budget. In three years of operations, the support was associated with a specific project. Even though specific projects brought value to our department by enabling faculty and students to work on realistic industry problems, the sporadic nature of the relationships was difficult to manage in an academic setting. Timing of projects and their deliverables became major complications in managing resources within an academic environment. In most cases when the department had available resources, our industry partners did not have an appropriate project or available funds. When our industry partners had a prospective project, the faculty had already been assigned to other academic responsibilities.

3. Overview of the Strategic Cooperation

The specific partnership presented here is a long-term program composed of the following elements:
o Fellowships and other financial sponsorships for students and faculty.
o Ongoing internships for students to spend a summer or selected term at the industrial partner's research and development facilities.

- o Faculty and technical personnel exchange programs (the faculty may spend a summer or selected term at the industrial partner's facility and technical personnel from industrial partner may spend time at the university).
- o A laboratory in support of the industrial partner's software engineering areas of interest; involving the following two steps:
  - o to create an infrastructure at the university in support of specific industry principal application domain (with equipment, documentation, and matching configuration), and
  - o to conduct related software engineering research in the areas of mutual interest.
- o Transfer of solutions and technologies to the industrial partner.

The Mission statement for the project is: "To provide a challenging and rewarding environment for the development of students and faculty, one that enables important contributions to the professional community and the discipline."

The mission is realized in three areas: student development, faculty development, and contribution to the profession. The program consists of specific activities in each of these areas. In the area of student development, we include recruitment focused on the industry partner program, student-centered research, producing quality graduates educated in the practical aspects of the discipline of software engineering with a special emphasis on safety-critical systems, and student publications and presentations. Faculty development is realized by creating and expanding the body of knowledge in the practical application of science and technology to the field of safety-critical systems, providing an incubation environment to jump start junior software engineering faculty's research in the field of safety critical systems, improving teaching strategies and curricula, and improving faculty capabilities in technology exchange between academia and industry. The contribution to the profession includes publications of research findings s.

4. Implementation Details

The collaboration approach presented here is a joint venture between the Cardiac Rhythm Management (CRM) of the Guidant Corporation with its main office located in St.Paul, Minnesota, and Embry Riddle Aeronautical University (ERAU) located in Daytona Beach, FL. Guidant is a leader in development of cardiac devices. ERAU is a leading academic institution in aviation and aerospace education ranked between top engineering schools without doctoral programs according to the recent US News and World Report ranking. The computing programs at ERAU, currently affiliated with the Department of Computing in the College of Engineering, are producing students with bachelor degrees in Computer Science, Computer Engineering and Software Engineering, as well as master degrees in Software Engineering. The department is actively involved in software engineering education contributing to the identification of the software engineering body of knowledge and the related software engineering curricula [1].

The contact started in 1997 when two alumni from our graduate programs got positions with the Guidant/CRM and made significant impression on their management. It appears that the skills and knowledge of the graduates were at the time directly in sync with the company requirements. The appropriate elements of our student education included knowledge of the software technical project management (lifecycle and process management, metrics and measurement, estimation techniques, effort and defect tracking - in addition to the software

63

engineering practices such as requirements engineering, software architecture and design, and a focus on safety critical real-time embedded systems [2]).

Guidant approached the computing department and, after several rounds of negotiations, including on-site visits by the faculty and industry representatives, an agreement was signed. Guidant committed a continuous level of funding to support building the infrastructure and the operations of a dedicated laboratory housed at ERAU. The university provided personnel (the student researchers and faculty mentors) primarily involved in building domain knowledge. Due to the selected topics and the direction of research, the students who worked in the laboratory gained significant experience in the company operation, knowing the products and industrial partner processes. In the long term the work has resulted in building software engineering expertise, with the special focus on safety critical systems in both students and faculty. It is important to note, that as per agreed mission statement, the university does not provide solutions to the industrial partner. The program is focused on providing benefits to the university, particularly to the computing programs and professional community that is interested in engineering software for safety critical systems. Figure 1 illustrates the structure of the Guidant Program at ERAU.

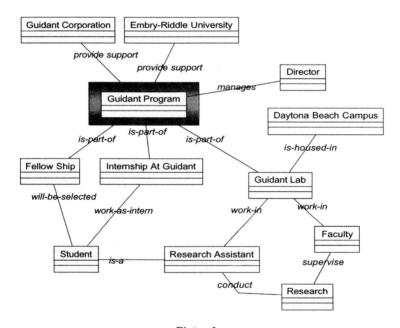

Figure 1

The specific topics addressed during the last three years of the Guidant Program operation were architecture for safety critical systems and model based verification.

The laboratory operations are realized on two orthogonal planes. They are:

o   Problem Oriented - result driven investigation of contemporary software technology issues (with focus on advancing state of the art and practice) o   Student Oriented - providing learning experiences for graduate students while investigating contemporary software technology issues (with focus on knowledge exchange and technology transition)

Historically, most of entry-level software engineers are assigned to the tail end activities of software engineering life cycle, such as testing or maintenance. This is primarily to learn the product and gain experience with a company's operations. It is not an easy task to mold a fresh college graduate into the industrial environment. However, entry-level software engineers have a better chance of participating in other life cycle activities when:

o   They are familiar with the technical aspects of software engineering project management in addition to other skills such design and coding, and
o   They are familiar with the domain, the product concept, and the used hardware/software platforms

The ERAU students meet the first condition. In their graduate software engineering program student focus on practical aspects of software development, using Personal and Team Software Processes proposed by Watts Humphrey [3,4] (http://www.sei.cmu.edu/tsp/). The second condition was made possible by creation of a dedicated laboratory working on real projects. The industrial partner provides software engineering challenges or problems that they have once faced and solved, in a particular way, through their product development process. However, it is critical to note that, even though the research projects focus is provided by the industrial partner, the research team will attempt to solve the problem in a generic form as oppose to being specific to the partners case. This is due to the important mission of the program to provide benefit to the community of safety critical system developers as oppose to any direct benefit to the partner.

The research philosophy is student-centered and explorative. To enhance the learning opportunity, it is the students who carry out the research in the lab. The faculty members serve as mentors by providing guidance, insight, and a conceptual framework for conducting the research, and assessing and providing feedback. Such learning must be marked by strong self-direction, willingness to take risks, and integration of the learning that life teaches outside of academic environment – "a journey of exploration that corrects its course as it proceeds" [5]. In addition, the faculty mentors have advisory roles in overseeing the projects from the perspective of achieving overall goals of the program and managerial liaison with the industry partner. The faculty mentors have control over hiring students. They also define the research direction of the program and provide continuity, building upon the knowledge gained in the previous years. A designated industry representative is the technical liaison with the laboratory serving as an advisor and a required "sanity check".

Embry Riddle submits a three-year proposal indicating overall research direction, required level of funding, and expected outcomes. The industry acceptance of the proposal in principal is indication of a commitment to the continuous level of funding, given that the program progress and achievements are consistent with the objectives of the industrial partner. This process eliminates the need and effort for every year proposal development and provides basis for three year planning. But, continuation of funding is contingent on the assessment and satisfaction of the industrial partner of the progress and the program achievements. At the beginning of each academic year, the ERAU develops and submits a yearly plan of operation. The plan details the research projects, methods, personnel, techniques and deliverables. Once the industrial partner approves the plan, it is executed throughout the year. To track the project progress and interact with the research teams, the industry liaison, often with accompanying technical or managerial representatives, visits the lab at least twice during the academic year, typically at the beginning and the end of the planning cycle. Furthermore, to keep the interaction alive during each year, the academic team participates in the technical seminars organized at the industry site. In addition, to further enhance the relationship, practical knowledge and skills of students and faculty, some of the students spend summer internships at the industry site. And thus far, one faculty has completed and another has just started an additional sabbatical assignment sponsored by the Guidant.

The tasks assigned in the laboratory are executed using software engineering conventions. Each task is planned and a detailed record is kept during task execution. For example, one of the early areas of research was related to the acquisition, retaining, and replicating knowledge in a software engineering domain. The particular application was in the area of software understanding. The Software companies often face the following issue: given the requirement documents and the source code what is the best way to have new software engineer understand the software. By *understanding* we mean to have enough expertise to answer questions about the software operation as well as to be able to propose modifications and improvements.

The logistics of collaboration have included regular visits at the university and the industry sites, planning discussions, regular e-mail exchanges, weekly minutes, teleconferences, presentations on technical meetings, one-to-one contacts between student researchers and industry representatives, etc. These means worked well over the last four years despite the physical distance between Minnesota and Florida.

5. Accomplishments

The first year of the program was geared toward gaining overall knowledge and familiarity with different aspects of software intensive applications in the safety critical systems domain. Guidant equipment, product, processes, problems, and insights where made available to the research team. These served as representative instances of the domain, focusing on the critical elements. For example, one of our early projects involved understanding the implicit and explicit relationship between the requirements for an early generation pacemaker product and its associated test suites. The research team analyzed (reverse engineered) portions of the test suite, and attempted to understand the requirements. This was accomplished in part by contrasting the requirements against the test suites and identifying potential new test cases. We also explored issues of reliability assessment and certification [6].

Subsequent years have allowed us to embark into more substantial activities. We ported one of the testing subsystems to different compiler platform and analyzed possible architectural solutions for testing software. We developed a prototype implementation of software architecture for testing real-time embedded safety critical systems enhancing capabilities of the existing testing software. In the course of work the team did extensive research on identifying software requirements for testing software system to effectively test safety critical devices or products. The first phase of the research resulted in creating software requirements, identifying software architecture for the test system and design documents. Subsequently, to validate the resulted architecture and to ensure that it satisfies the desired properties and attributes the team selected to develop prototype test system and implement and evaluate the architecture in the prototype. Implementation platforms were evaluated and selected. A prototype of the testing software architecture was implemented, using an incremental development process to construct and test each build and then integrate with the previous build. The specific outcomes of the work were clear identification of requirements of testing software and good understanding of the selected architecture. The students gained familiarity and skills with tools and process for software construction and advanced their knowledge about testing software: requirements, architecture, design and implementation.

5.1. Knowledge Patterns

The temporary nature of student employment graduating in two-year cycle required detailed planning and assurance that there are always "old" workers in the lab who could help newcomers with the knowledge of the lab operation and domain. This resulted in the need to explore the techniques and mechanism for knowledge capturing artifacts.

In the process of software understanding we have identified three basic elements. The first element is related to the question *WHAT?* Analysis of the software requirements documentation, coupled with the familiarity of the system domain, allows one to address this question. The second element is related to the question *HOW?* Here, the most useful is the analysis of a source code and the knowledge of the applicable hardware platform. The most difficult is the third element. It is related to question *WHY?* To answer this question one needs to get rather thorough familiarity with both: the application domain and the software.

In the situation with fluctuating a workforce and new student employees, it is imperative to have good documentation. Granted, all mature organizations have an appropriate amount of documentation for young engineers to study. The idea has been, however, to capture various aspects of the work in a standard and easy to understand format. To support the process of understanding we have used the concept of patterns. Patterns originated in the architectural domain [7]. A pattern is an abstraction from a concrete form that may reoccur in a specific context. Patterns constitute a template for problem-solving documentation, which, for a given context and the problem, describe a proven solution. Patterns are particularly applicable for re-use and knowledge retention, since the context and problems reoccur and the workforce changes. The patterns describe practical solutions while may also identify good practice and processes. Having such Knowledge Pattern Library we may provide a base for better understanding the domain, tasks, products, organization, and the company operations. Patterns may help capture domain expertise documenting design/solution decisions and rationale. They convey expert insight to novices reusing wisdom and experience of master practitioners. Additionally, they also constitute shared vocabulary for the discussion. Of course, the patterns must not to be treated as all solving silver bullet.

After analysis of the pattern applicability, we decided to create a template meeting our project needs. Using the presented format we recorded few selected elements of the project in both the organizational and technical domain. Significant work was spent on capturing the software system understanding. The software system we have analyzed was a testing system. The testing process is structured into chunks defined as "features". To test one of the features it is required a significant knowledge of domain, the product, test station hardware and software. A preparation of the first Knowledge Pattern Template (KPT) for a testing feature was a lengthy task. It has been shown, however, that the subsequent students, learning from the information captured and documented in KPT, were capable to develop not only understanding of the specific feature but also create new templates for completely different features. This process was significantly shorter, compared to our first experiment of understanding the features.

5.2. Software Architecture

In the last two years, one of the main research trust of the lab has been on software architecture. Over the course of last year the team engaged in Knowledge-Based Assessment of Safety Concerns in the Software Architecture. An objective of this activity has been to evaluate the emerging discipline of software architecture for its application in development of safety critical systems. Software architecture is the stepping-stone between the requirements and the design stages. There is an evident contrast between these phases of software development. The *requirements* are concerned with the determination of the information, processing, and the characteristics of that information and processing needed by the user of the system. The *architecture* is concerned with the selection of architectural elements, their interactions, and the constraints on those elements and their interactions necessary to provide a framework in which to satisfy the requirements and serve as a basis for design. The *design* is concerned with the modularization and detailed interfaces of the design elements, their algorithms and procedures, and the data types needed to support the architecture and to satisfy the requirements.

As mentioned previously, the first architecture research project focused on identifying appropriate software architecture for testing safety critical software systems. The tasks conducted by the team included:

o   identification and assessment of architectures for software intensive safety critical systems,

o   identification of the features and metrics for software architectures (as related to safety needs and requirements for safety critical systems),

o   development of an appropriate architecture that meets the requirements of a testing environment for safety critical systems,

o   architectural trade-off analysis for safety critical systems, and

o   development of a prototype to demonstrate the proposed architecture for testing safety critical systems.

The most recent software architecture research project has concentrated on investigating a mechanism to increase product safety and minimizing the risk of failure. The research has been focusing on identifying techniques and mechanism for more effective deign and assessment of safety critical systems. The long-term goal of this research project is to design and develop a knowledge-centered framework for effective detection and prevention of defect in software architecture, design and implementation of safety critical systems. The architecture research team objectives have been developing tools and techniques for reducing cost of quality while maintaining or improving product field quality. Their goal is to achieve the objectives by focusing on early defect detection and resolution through better assessment techniques and tools and defect prevention through providing insight and tools for architecting and designing software for safety critical systems [8].

5.3 Model-Based Verification

The objective of the Model Based Verification (MBV) effort is to investigate software model checking practices and technologies and to explore their role as part of verification and validation processes. This work is based upon the approaches presented in [9]. The focus of the work is on identifying defects early in the development cycle. In a model-centered approach, models are the basis for automated code generation. Verification and validation techniques are used on the models and the code to assure the quality of the software. The investigation focus has been on acquiring insight into the potential for model checking, both as an autonomous verification practice and as a coordinated activity with testing, to provide greater efficiency and effectiveness in testing processes and increased assurance in the quality of software. It explores the technical factors and practice issues, considering the effectiveness of the techniques, the process implications, and the expertise required to implement the approach.

In the program, we have applied the MBV methodology and a specific tool, the Symbolic Model Verifier SMV, on a portion of the requirements for a pacemaker. This effort also

68

defined a process, used metrics to compile costs, and captured engineering observations and rationale associated with model checking techniques [10]. In this work we evaluated the processes and skills required to use this MBV. We also explored different notations and their applicability in building SMV models as well as issues relating to translating state machine representations into SMV models [11]. These efforts are aimed at facilitating the transition of the processes and technologies into routine software engineering practice.

6. Conclusions

The collaboration has had a positive effect on both partners. The university has a venue for research and financial support for that research. These provide exceptional learning experiences as well as scholarships and stipends for our graduate students. The program also provides incentives for faculty to engage in applied research, publish research results, and contribute to the solution of industry problems. The results of the lab activities are also used in the classroom, where the students present their work and course content is enhanced with insights and examples from the research. These activities have had significant impact on graduate classes in the Master of Software Engineering program including Software Architecture, Software Quality, and Software Safety. The support for this claim can be found in the course evaluations. For example, the data on software architecture course evaluation demonstrate evidence of instructor's increased performance in the term following the research ("excellent" evaluations increased from 12% to 55%)

One of the assumptions for the program was that the laboratory activities must not provide deliverables directly applicable to day-to-day operations of the industrial partner. In addition, the technical reports produced in the laboratory are available and accessible to other organizations directly from the Lab website (http://erau.computing.edu/guidantlab).

While the sponsor provides the technical challenge, the research conducted in the lab and the published results address solutions to the generic problems in safety critical software systems. For other activities like specific projects supporting the sponsor's business operation (e.g. training, reports, travel) we receive separate funding. The direct involvement of students and faculty through summer internships and mutual visits and hiring some of the Lab graduates, are part of the technology transfer component of the program. The industrial partner has ready access to graduates, specifically to evaluate them as potential employees. Over the last three years eight out of 16 students who worked in the Lab have joined Guidant/CRM, and the others have taken employment with companies such as Lockheed Martin, Boeing, and Carrier.

7. References:

[1] D.Bagert, T.Hilburn, G.Hislop, M.Lutz, M.McCracken, S.Mengel, Guidelines for Software Engineering Education, Version 1.0 (CMU/SEI-99-TR-032, ESC-TR-99-002). Pittsburgh, PA, SEI, Carnegie Mellon University, 1999, http://www.sei.cmu.edu/pub/documents/99.reports/pdf/99tr032.pdf
[2] S.Khajenoori, "Process-Oriented Software Education," IEEE Software, No. 6, November 1994.
[3] W. Humphrey, Introduction to the Personal Software Process, Addison Wesley, 1997
[4] W. Humphrey, Introduction to the Team Software Process, Addison Wesley, 2000
[5] P.B.Vaill, Learning As A Way Of Being: Strategies for Survival in a World of Permanent White Water, Jossey-Bass, A Wiley Company, 1996
[6] A.Kornecki, S.Khajenoori, W.Thabet, H.Li, J.Chapman, "Reliability Assessment through Certification Activities", Fast Abstracts and Industry Practices Proceeding of the International Symposium on Software Reliability, ISSRE'99, Boca Raton, FL, November 1999, pp 41-42
[7] C.Alexander, A Pattern Language: Towns, Buildings, Construction; Oxford University Press, 1977
[8] Khajenoori, L.Prem, K.Stevens, B.Kang, N.Kameli, "Knowledge Centered Assessment Patterns: An Effective Tool For Assessing Safety Concerns in Software Architecture," accepted for printing, Journal of Systems and Software, 2003

[9]   D.Gluch, C.Weinstock, Model-Based Verification: A Technology for Dependable System Upgrade (CMU/SEI-98-TR-009, ADA354756). Pittsburgh, PA, SEI, Carnegie Mellon University, 1998, http://www.sei.cmu.edu/pub/documents/98.reports/pdf/98tr009.pdf

[10] K.Myers, K.Dionne J.Cruz, V.Vijay, S.Dunlap, D.Gluch, "The Practical use of Model Checking in Software Development," Proceedings of the IEEE Southeastcon 2002, April 5 –7, 2002, pp. 21-27.

[11] H.Li, A.Kornecki, D.Gluch, "SM2SMV - A Tool for Facilitating Dependable Software Requirements Analysis Using Model Checking", Fast Abstract in Proceeding of International Conference on Dependable Systems and Network, New York, NY, June 2000, pp B.36-37

Aligning Workforce Development & Software Process Improvement Strategy for Accelerated Adoption of Software Engineering Capability

James Mason

Securities Industry Automation Corporation (SIAC)

jmason@siac.com

Abstract

This paper explores the process of aligning a Workforce Development Program with Software Process Improvement strategies in order to accelerate the adoption of Software Engineering practices in a major software organization – the Securities Industry Automation Corporation (SIAC). Some of the ideas and conclusions presented here are drawn from "Using SWEBOK for Education Programs in Industry and Academia" [6].

1. ORGANIZATION OF THIS DOCUMENT

Sections 2 through 5 examine some of the many management challenges technology organizations face in trying to keep workforce capability in step with the evolution of best practices. Topics include challenges related to Software Process Improvement (SPI) efforts – and issues related to workforce development in lower maturity organizations. Sections 6 through 9 examine an approach implemented at SIAC to accelerate the adoption of best Software Engineering practices in support of the SPI effort – and to assure the ongoing capability of the workforce.

2. THE DILEMMA FACING SOFTWARE ORGANIZATIONS

Partially because of the nature of technology, and partially because of the youth of the discipline, accepted practices in software development are supplanted several times over a typical practitioner's career. Unless there is an overt effort to assure that the capability of the workforce remains consistent with these practices, software development organizations – and the systems they develop and support – may fall behind.

Even though this is widely understood, with the exception of "tools training," few I/T organizations upgrade the "process & methods" capability of their workforce with any regularity. This effectively institutionalizes methods that are becoming increasingly out of sync with "newer" best practices.

Laboring under this trend, software organizations are finding that the talented people who had successfully met one crisis after another for many years are increasingly straining in the face of progressively complex issues.

3. THE SOFTWARE PROCESS IMPROVEMENT SOLUTION

Of the wide range of responses that industry has made to this challenge, applying the Software Engineering Institute's Capability Maturity Model for Software (SW-CMM) has been one of the most successful [5]. Organizations successfully using the SW-CMM have sometimes dramatically increased their ability to meet their challenges. Despite the efficacy of the CMM, many Software Process Improvement (SPI) efforts fail. An underlying reason for the less than wholehearted response to SPI efforts is that lower maturity organizations do not know what return to expect for its investment in process improvement activity. The Sy Simms slogan "An educated consumer is our best customer" is well appreciated by SPI professionals – who feel their jobs would be easier if their organizations better understood the benefits derived from applying engineering practices to software. The implication here is that, in addition to its general value in maintaining workforce capability, education is a central component of process improvement – at both the task and management level.

4. EDUCATION IN LOW MATURITY-LEVEL ORGANIZATIONS

In lower maturity-level organizations, everyone is typically so busy with the heroics needed to meet product development commitments that everything else takes a back seat. This often makes formal workforce development activities a "nice to have". Even in organizations where budget is allocated for development activities, it is the exceptional case where there is a plan that [4] comprehensively addresses workforce capability versus the process improvement capability development strategy. The SEI developed the People Capability Maturity Model (P-CMM) in recognition of the importance of workforce development practices in moving an organization up the SW-CMM ladder. Its creation was also recognition of how rare it was for a lower maturity level organization to focus concerted management attention on workforce development practices. Yet, developing software engineering capability in an individual or an organization is both central to success [1] and a non-trivial task.

5. SIAC EDUCATION PROGRAM

SIAC builds and operates floor-trading systems for the New York Stock Exchange. These are highly complex, high volume, transaction-processing systems that demand the highest levels of dependability & reliability. SIAC values education and training. Its policies in this area feature a number of notable characteristics:

- ❐ A tuition assistance program that provides up-front loans to employees
- ❐ Substantial investment in leadership development training
- ❐ Substantial investment in "technical" training (languages, operating systems, DBMS's and tools) – both at the corporate and division levels.

Despite these progressive policies, the trade-off between finding the time for employees to attend training and meeting product development commitments is sometimes challenging – and a management infrastructure with robust linkages between product development processes, education & training and assessed workforce capability remains elusive.

6. SPI WORKFORCE DEVELOPMENT STRATEGY

A decision was made to align the development of the organization (and therefore the training program) with the Software Development Lifecycle. Alignment with the lifecycle was one of the basic tenets of the SPI strategy. Taking the view wherein workforce development occurs in increments that are aligned with the Lifecycle provides support for the simultaneous development of product development processes and people. It also allows a strategic focus to be applied to targeted workforce development efforts. The matrix in Figure 1 indicates the relationship between training offerings, the lifecycle, and high-level SPI goals.

Figure 1: Development Programs versus the lifecycle, and high-level SPI goals

Course Name	Project Planning	Requirements	Analysis & Design	Coding and Implementation	Testing	Roll Out	Post Implementation	Change Management	Management	Predictability of Effort and Schedule	Quality and Efficiency	Customer Communication and Satisfaction
SMU Software Engineering Program	X	X	X	X	X				X	X	X	
Software Inspections classes		X	X	X	X						X	
OOA&D w\UML class		X	X	X								
Commercial Project Management classes	X					X	X	X	X	X		X
Project Leadership Seminar	X								X			X
Requirements Engineering Program		X	X	X								
Software Testing classes		X		X							X	
Estimating	X									X		
Post Implementation Review							X	X	X		X	X

7. SMU MASTERS PROGRAM

Another key decision that was made was to develop engineering capability in the workforce via a Masters Degree Program. After an extensive assessment of available programs, SIAC met with Southern Methodist University (SMU) representatives to discuss how their employee development needs might be met using SMU courses. SIAC elected to work with SMU for several reasons.

- ❏ SMU introduced a software engineering masters degree in 1993, and, therefore, had one of the oldest and most respected programs in the country

- ❏ SMU faculty utilize many adjunct faculty, consisting of working practitioners – who where therefore able to bring real world experience to the classroom.

- ❏ SMU has a distance learning capability, which SIAC elected to use in conjunction with classroom instruction.

- ❏ Two senior members of the SPI team were graduates and could attest to the quality of the program

8. ALIGNING SIAC REQUIREMENTS WITH SMU COURSES USING THE SWEBOK

SMU and SIAC worked jointly to develop an approach for SIAC personnel to acquire identified knowledge in the most effective manner. The Software Engineering Body of Knowledge (SWEBOK) proved to be useful in devising an approach for aligning the SMU Masters Degree program with the lifecycle and SIAC's development needs.

The SWEBOK structure provided a common ground by which courses in the SMU program could be associated with the development needs identified by SIAC. SWEBOK made it easy to relate job functions to specific components of software engineering knowledge for SIAC practitioners – and it allowed SMU professors to indicate similar linkages to the course in the SMU Masters Curricula.

Because the Knowledge Area (KA) structure of the SWEBOK aligns with the major workflows in the software development lifecycle, SIAC practitioners were able to identify themselves as individuals who perform their professional tasks within the domain of one or more KA. Identification with the KA's was immediate, and did not require an extensive competency modeling exercise – which is little understood and often viewed as low-value-added overhead by software practitioners.

A chart similar to that of Figure 2, except taken to considerably more detail, made it possible to do a comprehensive assessment of the SMU program versus the SWEBOK KA's. A chart similar to that of Figure 3, made it possible for SIAC personnel to identify individual and unit development requirements versus the Lifecycle, SWEBOK and SMU program.

SMU MASTERS PROGRAM	SOFTWARE ENGINEERING FUNDAMENTALS	SOFTWARE REQUIREMENTS ENGINEERING	SOFTWARE DESIGN ENGINEERING	...	SOFTWARE MANAGEMENT
Course 1	X	X			
Course 2			x		
Course 3			x		
Course 4		x			
Course 5				x	
Course ...					x

Figure 2: SMU Course content versus SWEBOK Knowledge Areas

SIAC DEPARTMENT	SOFTWARE ENGINEERING FUNDAMENTALS	SOFTWARE REQUIREMENTS ENGINEERING	SOFTWARE DESIGN ENGINEERING	...	SOFTWARE MANAGEMENT
Employee a	X	X			
Employee b	X				X
Employee c	X		X		
Employee d	X				
Employee e				X	
Employee f		X			

Figure 3: Employee development plans versus SWEBOK Knowledge Areas

9. A STRATEGY FOR ACCELERATED ADOPTION

A comprehensive educational program -- such as an MS in Software Engineering -- can be a daunting proposition to many employees. Furthermore, our analysis showed that many employees did not need such a comprehensive program -- at least not initially. Taking a cue from the CMM and its layered model, SIAC and SMU developed a series of certificate programs, building up knowledge in layers, with intermediate plateaus. The final level of accomplishment is, indeed, a complete masters degree. But by making the knowledge available in a series of smaller steps, the prospect of participation is less intimidating – both at the individual and business unit level.

Under the program, individuals receive a certificate after completing a core curriculum and another after the completion of any of five specialties. Employees have the option of taking multiple specialty programs and later completing the MS – or stopping after completion of one or more individual certificates (figure 4 displays the overall structure of the program). A business unit might encourage employees to take the core and a specialty applicable to the business function and the employee may then choose whether to progress further on the basis of individual career development needs.

Smaller increments are particularly important in industrial applications where productivity spent away from product development activities is precious. Use of the SWEBOK KA's and subcategories provides a focus for those increments that aligns with the major development workflows. This, in turn, provides a scope to management expectation regarding return on investment that is comprehensible – and therefore supportable. Individuals completing a program of study in requirements engineering, for example, would be expected to help produce better requirements. Individuals completing a program of study in test engineering would be expected to help contribute to more effective testing.

From the university's perspective, the certificates provide units of courseware that appeal to many companies needing a structured education program that aligns with generally accepted views of software engineering while not requiring completion of a full masters degree. The tables 1 and 2 provide a summary level view of the objectives, and courses comprising the certificate programs.

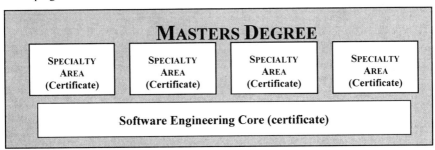

Figure 4: Structure of the overall program

Certificate Program Components	
Component	**Objective**
Core Curriculum	The common, "foundation knowledge" from the software engineering discipline that would providing grounding in, and support for, continued development in any of the other knowledge areas. This core will be common to each certification program.
Software Requirements Engineering	A certification program that produces individuals capable of applying engineering discipline and a wide range of tools & techniques to the practice of Software Requirements Engineering (development, analysis and maintenance of software requirements)
Software Design Engineering	A certification program that produces individuals capable of applying engineering discipline and a wide range of tools & techniques to the practice of Designing Software
Software Construction Engineering	A certification program that produces individuals capable of applying engineering discipline and a wide range of tools & techniques to the practice of Constructing (building) Software
Software Test Engineering	A certification program that produces individuals capable of applying engineering discipline and a wide range of tools & techniques to the practice of Testing Software
Software Engineering Management	A certification program that produces individuals capable of applying disciplined tools and methods to planning and management of software engineering

Table #1: Certificate Program Components

Course Name	CORE	REQUIREMENTS	DESIGN	CONSTRUCTION	TESTING	MANAGEMENT
Software Requirements and Design Engineering	x					
Software Testing and Quality Assurance	x					
Software Project Planning and Management	x					
Software System Engineering		x				
Object Oriented Analysis and Design		x	x			
User Interface Design			x	x		
Software Generation and Maintenance				x		
Software Reliability and Safety					x	
Software Metrics and Quality Engineering					x	x
Software Acquisition Practices, Legal and Economic Issues						x

Table #2: SMU Courses Mapped to Certificate Programs

10. CONCLUSIONS

The response to this approach has been enthusiastic. Approximately 90 individuals participated in a 2-day overview of Software Engineering course as a precursor to signing up for graduate courses. The table #3 below illustrate the levels of participation in the graduate classes. Table #4 indicates the number of individuals requesting to pursue specific certificates. A combination of live classroom (executive style) and distance education techniques is being used to provide flexibility in the way the courses are offered – to accommodate differing student needs.

Summary of Enrollment by Class		
Course #	Class Name	#
CSE 7315	Software Project Planning and Management	43
CSE 7313	Software Requirements and Design Engineering	43
CSE 7314	Software Testing & Quality Assurance	18
CSE 8313	Object Oriented Analysis and Design	12
CSE 8317	Software Reliability and Safety	5
CSE 7345	Advanced Java Programming	1
CSE 7312	Software System Engineering	1

Table # 3: Summary of Enrollment by Class

Count of Requests for Certificates by Program	
Certificate Name	#
Certificate in Software Engineering Fundamentals	66
Certificate in Software Requirements Engineering	50
Certificate in Software Engineering Management	45
Certificate in Software Design Engineering	44
Certificate in Software Test Engineering	25
Certificate in Software Construction Engineering	24

Table # 4: Count of Certificate Requests by Program

References

[1] Curtis, Bill, William Hefley and Sally A. Miller, *People Capability Maturity Model (P-CMM)*, 2001, Carnegie Mellon University

[2] IEEE, *Guide to the Software Engineering Body of Knowledge*, 2001, www.swebok.org

[3] Motorola, *Motorola on Training And Continuous Learning*, www.fed.org./u.../labor/a_m/Motorola.html

[4] Robinson, Dana G. and James C., *Training for Impact, How to Link Training to Business Needs and Measure Results*, 1989 Jossey-Bass In., pages 7 – 8.

[5] SEI, Software Engineering Measurement and Analysis Team, *Process Maturity Profile of the Software Community 2001 Mid-Year Update*

[6] IEEE, CSEE&T Dennis Frailey and James Mason, Using SWEBOK for Education Programs in Industry and Academia, 2002

Educating Software Engineering Managers

Lawrence Peters

Software Consultants International Limited

lpeters@sci-ltd.net

Abstract

The term, "Software Engineering," has been in use for more than 30 years. In that time, the software community has undergone many changes including the introduction of new programming languages, new analysis and design methods and more advanced, easier to use development environments. Even with all these improvements, software continues to be a source of problems and increased risk for most corporations. If the "software problem" were truly of a technical nature, the problems (e.g. late delivery, cost overruns, low quality) would have been largely solved. More recently, the source of these problems has been attributed to the people who direct software development and maintenance efforts – the Software Engineering Manager. This paper examines the nature of Software Engineers, the skills needed to effectively manage them, presents a method for solving most intractable problems associated with managing Software Engineers and discusses the educational issues associated with training effective Software Engineering Managers.

1. Introduction

Software Engineering was originally proposed as a concept by some very bright, well educated, technical people. As they looked into the future of computing in general and to Software Engineering in particular, they foresaw a large number of challenges. Unfortunately, they viewed these challenges almost exclusively from a technical, not a managerial or business standpoint. As a result, the software industry has produced more than three dozen methods and techniques [1,2], hundreds of software tools, dozens of new programming languages and programming aids, numerous textbooks and training classes with, ". . . disappointingly small effects" [3]. We now recognize that the single most important factor in the success or failure of a software project is its management [4], not its technology. This paper examines the nature of Software Engineers, Software Engineering Managers and the most serious management issues. An example of a solution to the most intractable of these problems is provided. Challenges to educators are pointed out throughout the paper closing with a discussion of possible ways of training Software Engineering Managers, the problems this presents to universities and industrial educators and how they can be addressed.

2. Historical perspective

The founding fathers of Software Engineering could not have foreseen the size and complexity of the systems of the future and the large numbers of people required to build and maintain them. Hence, they may have had difficulty in foreseeing the need for effective management skills to pull all the pieces together in a rational manner. But that is where we are today. The fact that the software industry, ". . . has failed to produce a cadre of competent software engineering managers" [5] and little has been done about it in the decade since that quote was published indicates the low priority the profession places on the training of Software Engineering Managers and research into management science as it applies to them.

3. The nature of Software Engineers

One of the first issues which the new Software Engineering Manager must come to grips with in their leadership role is the fact that the people to be directed do not lend themselves to working as a team nor being directed by someone who is not (in the Software Engineer's opinion) their technical superior. This is partly a result of the unique psychological and behavioral characteristics exhibited by this group. These were documented and studied a long time ago [6] without much fanfare in the Software Engineering Community. These characteristics are:

- High Growth Need Strength (GNS) – This refers to the fact that Software Engineers are attracted toward difficult, challenging problems. This is one of the reasons why it is so difficult to get Software Engineers to do simple tasks (e.g. create even modest program documentation, fix bugs for an extended period, and so forth).
- Low Social Need Strength (SNS) – This characteristic manifests itself in the form of working independently. High GNS pushes the Software Engineer to work on difficult problems but low SNS makes working on them independently quite attractive. For example, it is common to participate in a meeting to discuss some serious technical problem and have a Software Engineer at the meeting volunteer to fix it by saying, "I can take a look and probably have it fixed this week." The use of "I" rather than "We" indicates low SNS.

A fair question to ask is, "How many Software Engineering Managers are aware of the nature of Software Engineers as described above?" An informal survey of professional managers in seminars [7] on advanced software engineering topics in Australia, the United States, Canada, the United Kingdom, Spain, Italy, Germany and France indicated practically none (less than 5%) had ever heard of these factors. An equally important question to ask is, "What difference does it make whether or not a Software Engineering Manager is aware of the nature of Software Engineers?" The answer is that knowing that this group has a strong tendency to work independently and only want to tackle hard problems means that the manager should put increased emphasis on team building within the group, maintaining open communications with all Software Engineers reporting to them and rotate assignments to ensure no one works long periods on unchallenging tasks. From an educational standpoint, the Software Engineering Manager needs training in interpersonal skills, communication skills and some basic psychology in order to have the possibility of being a success in this role.

As if the above characteristics were not enough of a challenge, at least one expert in the field [8] believes that many Software Engineers exhibit symptoms of attention deficit disorder. The keys here are the rapid rate at which information can be consumed, the rapid pace of change, concepts mastered and the continual desire to change or improve the software.

4. The nature of Software Engineering Managers

In some ways, management is a very simple role within the company. According to some authors, management's role is to plan, schedule, control, staff and motivate [9]. Other responsibilities have evolved over the years, but these basic five cover most of what managers do. One may wonder how Software Engineering Managers could be so different from Software Engineers when Software Engineering Managers used to be Software Engineers? The fact is that there is considerable evidence indicating important differences exist between managers and their non-manager [10]. These differences are best illustrated by examining the value system of each group (Table 1). Note the differences in what each holds as their highest value and what this implies about communication between these groups.

Any manager who wonders why someone left the firm after getting a raise is clearly unaware of this work. What the raise says to someone who is in an assignment they do not like is that the company is not only happy with their performance but it is likely they will continue in that role. Hence, they feel almost obligated to leave. What Table 1 also indicates is that what the Software Engineer values most is being appreciated for work done. This is not synonymous with a merit increase but is free to the company. The simple act by the Software Engineering Manager of telling the Software Engineer that they are appreciated (i.e. telling them, "Thank you") will suffice. Since money is the highest priority for the Software Engineering Manager, we have what may constitute a "Retention Paradox." That is, the Software Engineering Manager uses the most costly and least effective means of rewarding the Software Engineer when the least expensive and most effective means is often overlooked.

Table 1. Value systems of Managers and Subordinates (where 1 = highest value, 10 = lowest)

Value Description	Manager	Engineer
Salary	1	5
Job Security	2	4
Promotion/Growth Opportunities	3	7
Working Conditions	4	9
Interesting/Challenging Work	5	6
Personal Loyalty to Workers	6	8
Tactful Discipline	7	10
Appreciation for Work Done	8	1
Help with Personal Problems	9	3
Being in on Things	10	2

5. The role of the Software Engineering Manager

There are many facets of managing Software Engineers that are overlooked by people making the move into management. One of the most uncomfortable is having to evaluate the performance of each Software Engineer on a regular basis. This is so uncomfortable, that some Software Engineering Managers simply avoid the issue by not reviewing their people at all. More than one multi-billion dollar gross revenue company has had this situation go on for a year or more. Of course, these firms had high turnover in the departments where Software Engineering Managers had been remiss in conducting performance reviews. This high turnover rate is consistent with the points made in the previous section.

The discomfort associated with performance reviews stems from two sources:
- Evaluating someone else is always difficult and uncomfortable. This is especially true if the review is a negative one or may lead to dismissal.

- The review format and content is usually not very relevant [11]. It is usually constructed in such a way as to be used by every manager in every department, whether or not there are any Software Engineers in it. This "one size fits all" approach is generally unsuitable for use with Software Engineers.

Another serious issue is that the role of the Software Engineering Manager is no longer a tactical one but is now a strategic one. In their tactical role as a Software Engineer, they were tasked with achieving a well defined set of programming goals within a local domain. The impact of software within the corporation is such that it impacts nearly every aspect of the company. This has resulted in software being an important part of strategic planning within the corporation. That is, Software Engineering Managers are now charged with planning, leading and directing relative to corporate strategies and goals as well as at the project or program level. Most Software Engineering Managers are very uncomfortable with developing strategy (let alone achieving it). That discomfort combined with the lack of training in strategy formulation and execution causes them to revert back to being Software Engineers leaving the organization without a full time leader.

6. Sources of problems for the Software Engineering Manager

Software Engineering Managers incur several issues which their technical skills, training and experience leave them ill equipped for. These fall in three broad categories:
- Conceptual – The notion that management is, ". . . an art" [12], not a technical discipline [18] is difficult to accept. Instead of technological expertise, management requires a high degree of creativity and innovation.
- Perceptual – The impact software has on the entire corporation has resulted in the Software Engineering Manager being tasked to support (and occasionally develop) corporate strategy and "balance" decision making on more than just money.
- Human Resource Performance Management – The notion that people will always do their best if we just pay them well is a common misconception. The greatest leverage with respect to benefit to cost ratio can be obtained by taking actions that are free and motivate Software Engineers to perform at higher levels.

The sections which follow will address the above and present an example solution which addresses the second and third items the same time.

7. Training Software Engineering Managers

Software Engineering Managers start out as Software Engineers. Therefore, it is safe to assume that they have acquired some level of technical knowledge. In their management role, they should only need to know enough, technically, to ask appropriate questions and how to dig deeper into some technical issue they may be unfamiliar with or have concerns about. From an educational standpoint, this more technical aspect of Software Engineering Management is, generally, well covered during university training, professional education programs and through reading journals and texts in technical topics. However, the role of management demands new, less technically specific skills which the new manager has not developed. Since they will determine the success or failure of the manager, the most important and least addressed by the Software Engineering community of these are:
- Human Resource Management
- Strategic Project Management

Both of these are elaborated upon in the sections which follow.

7.3 Training in Human Resource Management

Of all the cost saving, productivity improving measures that a Software Engineering Manager can employ, improving the performance of their team is at once the most cost effective and the least expensive [9,14,15]. As we have seen, this is because Software Engineers are not driven to higher levels of performance by money. Instead, they are driven by having challenging problems to solve and contributing by doing important tasks. Other branches of engineering have begun to recognize this [11]. A key issue is whether it is possible to integrate this aspect seamlessly into the practice of Software Engineering management. This will be demonstrated later in this paper.

7.4 Strategic Project Management training

There are dozens of universities offering Software Engineering degree programs at the graduate and undergraduate levels worldwide. While many of these programs do a very credible job of providing solid technical training, the earlier discussions can only cause one to conclude that training in Software Engineering Management is lacking to some extent. The issue here is that textbooks and classes on Software Engineering Management tend to focus on the standard issues such as planning, scheduling, controlling and quality. Textbook topics include PERT and Gantt charts, COCOMO [16], CMM [17] and other day-to-day operational skills. One popular book in this area [18] is typical of the texts used in Software Engineering Management curricula. It discusses the process of managing software efforts and related topics very well but ignores discussion of the strategic role of the Software Engineering Manager within the corporation. Even the PMI Body of Knowledge ignores strategy [19]. The pervasive nature of software within the corporation has expanded of the role of the Software Engineering Manager from managing efforts with local impact to ones which are vital to corporate survival. As a result, the type of training being provided to Software Engineer Managers at the university level is analogous to training someone how to use the tools necessary to build a house without ever having taken that person to a construction site where houses are being built. The result is they know how to use the tools but do not, necessarily, know why they are important because they do not know what their role is within the effort.

8.0 Incorporating strategy into Software Engineering Management training – an example

Training Software Engineering Managers in the creation, use and implementation of strategy at the group, project and/or corporate level(s) offers the prospect of multiple benefits because it links corporate (or group) strategies, improves the effectiveness of performance evaluations and increases the motivation and performance of Software Engineers. At least one method currently exists that lends itself to use in this multifaceted way – the Balanced Scorecard [20]. It has been adapted for use in the Software Engineering arena and called SEM (Strategy-based Evaluation Method). It is presented herein as an example of what can be achieved when methods outside of the Software Engineering community are adapted for use within it.

8.1 Introducing SEM (Strategy Based Evaluation Method)

The Balanced Scorecard Method (BSC) is a multi-dimensional view of strategy and operation. The key advantage it offers over earlier methods in this area is its all inclusive, multi-dimensional view and the fact that it provides measurable objectives for what is relevant to each dimension. While the concept of measurable objectives is not new [2], the multi-dimensional viewpoint is.

Extensions to the BSC have been added by this author in order to make it more suitable for typical Software Engineering Project Management situations [14,15,21]. These added factors are, "Owner" and "Supplier." Descriptions of the complete set of factors are presented in Table 2. The results of applying the method to a hypothetical software company are presented in Table 3. Note that for each "Strategic Theme" there is not only an objective but measurement mechanism, desired outcome and, essentially, a baseline value. All of these make performance reviews more objective and effective at motivating and improving performance.

Table 2: Summary SEM Concepts

Element of the Method	Description
Strategic Theme	The overriding goal prompting the effort
Business Perspectives (4)	Financial – the costs and savings that accrue
	Customer – the impact on the customer
	Internal – the impact on internal operations
	Learning/Growth – what training would be required
Objectives/Actions	Measurement – the metric used to assess progress
	Target – threshold at which we have achieved the goal
	Initiative – the process by which we will achieve the objective
	Ownership – person or group responsible for achieving this objective
	Supplier – outside vendor or contractor involved

Table 3: Example of the Application of SEM

Strategic Theme: Faster Bug Correction / perspective	Objective	Measurement	Target	Initiative	Owner	Supplier
Financial	- Lower support costs	- Support resource costs total	< 25% of software costs	- Bug Cost Tracking Task	- Finance TBD by Finance Department	- Student / Temporary hire
Customer	-Rapid response -Less complaints	- Flow time - Customer responses	< 48 hours - TBD	- CRM – Quality and Retention	- CRM Director and team	- Product development – n beta sites
Internal	- Reduce bug correction resources	- Flow time by severity	< 48 hours	- Develop error correction process	- Product Software Engineering	- Not applicable
Learning	- Software team education	- % of team trained over time	- 50% 1st year - 100%, 2nd yr	- Software Engineer and Manager Train	- Dual role – Product SWE & Education Department	- Possible vendor, research sources

8.2 Benefits of SEM to the education of Software Engineering Managers

The typical review of Software Engineers by Software Engineering Managers usually involves subjective observations Examples include improvements in proficiency with a particular programming language and acquired knowledge of new systems. This does not address what drives Software Engineers to higher performance levels (i.e. challenging work).

The use of SEM is not restricted to supporting corporate strategic initiatives but can be applied at the division or project level. Note how the baseline measurement, measurement method and target or goal value lend themselves to more relevant evaluation. This gives the Software Engineering Manager and Software Engineer a concise, objective means of setting goals as colleagues. This also plays into the concept of participative decision making in that the Software Engineer perceives her/himself to be part of the process, not a servant of it. At evaluation time, these are reviewed and have either been achieved or not achieved. The benefits to the Software Engineer are that the manager's expectations of the individual are clearly stated, the current state of affairs is noted, the measurement mechanism to be used is stated and the target results and stated, the impact on what is relevant to the corporation stated and the importance of their work obvious. This is more motivating to the Software Engineer than more subjective approaches. The overall benefits of SEM are listed in Table 4. Regardless of what method or approach used, the key point to keep in mind is that, "The central question in how to improve the software art centers, as it always has, on people" [13].

Table 4: Traditional Performance Evaluation Methods versus SEM

Characteristic	Traditional	SEM
Scope of Evaluation	Local, Task	Corporate, Group, Individual
Explicit Linkage to Strategy	No	Yes
Positive feedback (Self-worth, importance	Low	High
Explicit linkage to Manager's Goals	Infrequently	Always
Reinforces value of role in group	Infrequently	Always
Objectivity of Evaluation	Infrequently	Always
Goal development participation, measurable outcomes	Low	High

9. The challenge to educators

One fact about training Software Engineering Managers that should be obvious by now is that the instructors need to have had the experience of successfully (i.e. on time, on budget, meeting requirements) managing software projects. Some well known authors in this area have never managed a software project, while others have not managed in 10 or 20 years. This type of education is experiential, both for the instructor's previous experience and the student's experience as part of the course. This rules out use of texts by many famous authors who both the anecdotal and practical knowledge needed.

It is vital that instructors involved in Software Engineering Management training have the commitment, the current/relevant experience and the communication skills needed to bring about the kind of change needed in the practice of Software Engineering Management. Where do we find such individuals? Obviously, not all university professors have the industry experience nor can they acquire it quickly. This does not preclude them from successfully instructing Software Engineering Managers. There are several ways to address this problem:

- Use Adjunct Professors who currently manage software projects
- Team teach with currently practicing Software Engineering Managers
- Contract with a training firm to teach the course and/or license their materials

Finally, finding candidate projects to plan, analyze and execute as part of the course could be difficult. However, at least one Master of Science in Software Engineering program [22] takes on software projects for charities and small businesses to their mutual benefit.

10. Conclusions

Software Engineering has matured to the point that certain persistent problems can no longer be attributed to technical issues. They are now seen as being management issues. An easy to learn and use method which lends itself to motivating Software Engineers now exists by which many of these issues can be addressed together in an objective manner. The issue now becomes whether or not the Software Engineering Management and educational community can advance to the next level of maturity.

11. References

[1] L.J. Peters, *Software Design: Methods and Techniques*, Prentice-Hall, Englewood Cliffs, NJ, 1981.

[2] L.J. Peters, *Advanced Structured Analysis and Design*; Prentice-Hall, Englewood Cliffs, NJ, 1988.

[3] B. Curtis, H. Krasner and N. Iscoe, "A Field Study of the Software Design Process for large Systems," Communications of the ACM, Vol. 31, No. 11, pp. 1268-1287.

[4] M. Schlumberger, "Software Engineering Management," Position paper in the Proceedings of the 13th International Conference on Software Engineering, pp. 152-153, 1991.

[5] M.I. Kellner, Panel Session Chairman, "Non-technological issues in software engineering," IEEE, Proceedings of the 13th International Conference on Software Engineering, pp. 144-146, 1991.

[6] D.J. Couger and R.A. Zawacki, *Motivating and Managing Computer Personnel*, Wiley-Interscience, New York, NY, 1980.

[7] L.J. Peters, Unpublished notes collected 1988 to 1998, Software Consultants International Ltd., Kent WA.

[8] Interview with Dr. J.J. Ratey (co-author with E.M. Hallowell of, *Driven to Distraction: Recognizing and Coping with Attention Deficit Disorder from Childhood through Adulthood*, Simon and Schuster, New York, N.Y., 1995) on KUOW radio, Seattle, WA, April 26, 2001.

[9] R. Kreitner, *Management*, Houghton-Mifflin Company, Boston, MA: 1998.

[10] K.R. Linberg, *Job Satisfaction Among Software Developers*, Ph.D. Dissertation, Walden University, St. Paul, MN, May, 1999.

[11] R.E. Crandall, "Keys to Better Performance Management," IEEE, IEEE Management Review, Vol. 30, No. 3, pp. 58-63, Third Quarter 200.

[12] P.F. Drucker, *The Essential Drucker*, Josey-Bass Publishing Co., San Francisco, California, 2001.

[13] F.P. Brooks, "No Silver Bullet," Computer, pp. 10-19, Vol. 20, No. 4, April 1987.

[14] L.J. Peters, *Software Engineers and Their Managers: Motivation, Retention and Evaluation*, Ph.D. Dissertation, California Coast University, Santa Ana, CA, February, 2002.

[15] L.J. Peters, "Managing Software Professionals," submitted to ICSE-2003, September 2002.

[16] B.W. Boehm, *Software Economics*, Prentice-Hall, Englewood Cliffs, NJ: 1981.

[17] M. Paulk, B. Curtis, M.B. Chrissis, and C. Weber, "Capability Maturity Model for Software, Version 1.1," Technical Report CMU/SEI-93-TR-024, ESC-TR-93-177, Software Engineering Institute, Carnegie Mellon University, Pittsburgh, Pennsylvania, February, 1993.

[18] W.S. Humphrey, *Managing the Software Process*, Addison Wesley, Reading, Mass., 1990

[19] Project Management Institute, *A Guide to the Project Management Body of Knowledge (PMBOK® Guide)*, Newtown Square, Pennsylvania, 2000.

[20] R.S. Kaplan and D.P. Norton, "Linking the Balanced Scorecard to Strategy," California Management Review, Vol. 39, No. 1, Fall 1996.

[21] L.J. Peters, "Managing the Performance of Software Professionals Seminar," Software Consultants International Ltd., Kent, WA, 2001.

[22] L.J. Peters, "Software Project Management Curriculum," Developed as part of the Master of Science in Software Engineering Program at Seattle University, Seattle, WA, 1989 – present.

Software Engineering Curriculum 1
(Paper Session C)

What Should Graduating Software Engineers Be Able To Do?

A. J. Cowling
Department of Computer Science,
University of Sheffield,
Regent Court, Portobello Street,
Sheffield, S1 4DP, United Kingdom
Email: A.Cowling @ dcs.shef.ac.uk

Abstract

This paper is concerned with trying to characterise the skills that students should develop during the course of a degree programme in software engineering. It is based on a generic framework that has been developed within the UK to describe the abilities that engineering students should possess on graduation, and the paper discusses how this framework could be applied to software engineering graduates at the levels of both bachelor's and master's degrees. The discussion covers the kinds of systems that graduates should be capable of developing, the process model within which this development can be described as taking place, and the levels of ability that could be expected for each of the activities within this process model.

Keywords

Software engineering education, software engineering curriculum, engineering practice, engineering abilities, software development skills.

1. Introduction

The fundamental purpose of any engineering degree programme is to equip students to function as engineers, and this involves them both in acquiring knowledge and learning how to use it. Most of the recent discussion of the curriculum for software engineering (SE from now on) has focused on the aspect of knowledge, starting with the specific knowledge that is required by a practising engineer, as documented in the SE Body of Knowledge project [1] (SWEBOK from now on). In a degree programme this must then be underpinned by more basic knowledge, and the part of the Computing Curricula 2001 project [2] (CC2001 from now on) concerned with developing an SE volume is attempting to document this whole package of SE Education Knowledge [3] (SEEK from now on). To complement these efforts, it therefore seems timely to give some attention to the role of the skills that software engineering students should be expected to develop while studying on these degree programmes, and this is the purpose of this paper.

The starting point for the paper is a problem that had been encountered in the UK with the current accreditation criteria for British engineering degrees, and the background to this problem is described in section 2. Section 3 describes the project that was undertaken to try to produce a generic solution to this problem, and section 4 outlines the principles used in trying to instantiate this for programmes in SE. Sections 5, 6 and 7 then discuss various aspects of this instantiation, and particularly the differences between bachelor's and master's level programmes. Finally, section 8 summarises the conclusions of the paper.

1093-0175/03 $17.00 © 2003 IEEE

2. Background

In the UK, the engineering profession is regulated by a set of bodies that form a hierarchical structure with two levels. At the top level is the Engineering Council, which sets the generic standards for what it terms registration (ie certification), in the form of a document known as SARTOR [4] (an acronym for "Standards and Routes to Registration"). The lower level of the hierarchy consists of the various professional institutions for different branches of engineering, such as the British Computer Society and the Institution of Electrical Engineers. These administer the processes of registration and accreditation, on the basis of guidelines (such as [5]) that interpret the requirements of SARTOR for their particular discipline.

The processes are under constant development, and the most recent major development (the 1997 version of SARTOR) was mainly to bring UK standards closer to those in other European countries. This involved emphasising the distinction between "Chartered Engineers" (those responsible for innovating technology) and "Incorporated Engineers" (those responsible for managing existing technology), and in particular it raised the educational requirements for chartered engineers from a bachelor's degree to master's level qualifications.

Along with this, it expected the master's programmes to be aimed at the most able students, in the sense of progressing through material at a rate that would stretch them, and so possibly be beyond the less able. It could not specify this directly in terms of the "speed of the course", though, for there is no defined unit in which to measure it: "knowledge units per hour" would not be practical, since the size of a knowledge unit is usually described in terms of curriculum hours. The alternative approach, of trying to define directly the amount of material to be covered, would effectively have led to a national curriculum for engineering, and this was neither feasible at the generic level nor politically acceptable. Thus, the approach that was taken was to define this requirement in terms of the ability of the students, as measured by their qualifications on entry, although this was also recognised to be politically unsatisfactory.

To try to improve on it, an academic body, the Engineering Professors Council, set up a project to try to develop a standard that could be used to define the levels of achievement of graduates from engineering degree programmes. The initial results of this were published in December 2000, in the form of what they called their Graduate Output Standard [6], which is a generic document, in the sense of applying to all branches of engineering. An attempt has been made to create an instantiation of it for bachelor's degree programmes in SE [7], and this paper seeks to extend this to master's level programmes as well, but before discussing how this could be done it is necessary to describe the framework set by the generic standard.

3. The Generic Standard

The generic standard focuses entirely on the abilities and skills that the graduates will have developed to actually do engineering, and it is framed in terms of a generic model of the process by which engineers develop systems, which has six main stages. For each stage it then identifies the key activities, and hence the abilities of graduates to carry out these activities. This therefore gives a structure of 25 "Ability to" statements, divided into six groups, plus another 6 statements covering the application of general transferable skills. The complete set is listed in table 1.

The actual levels of ability implied by these statements are effectively determined by the complexity of the systems being developed, and so the generic standard requires instantiations to be created for different branches of engineering, so as to define one or more benchmark systems. Then, each "Ability to" statement in such an instantiation will be interpreted in the context of these benchmark systems.

Table 1. The generic "Ability To" statements

1.	**Ability to exercise Key Skills in the completion of engineering-related tasks at a level implied by the benchmarks associated with the following statements.**
a)	Communication
b)	Information Technology
c)	Application of Number
d)	Working with Others
e)	Problem Solving
f)	Improving Own Learning and Performance
2.	**Ability to transform existing systems into conceptual models**
a)	Elicit and clarify client's true needs *VS User goals*
b)	Identify, classify and describe engineering systems
c)	Define real target systems in terms of objective functions, performance specifications and other constraints (ie, define the problem)
d)	Take account of risk assessment, and social and environmental impacts, in the setting of constraints (including legal, and health and safety issues)
e)	Select, review and experiment with existing engineering systems in order to obtain a database of knowledge and understanding that will contribute to the creation of specific real target systems
f)	Resolve difficulties created by imperfect and incomplete information
g)	Derive conceptual models of real target systems, identifying the key parameters
3.	**Ability to transform conceptual models into determinable models**
a)	Construct determinable models over a range of complexity to suit a range of conceptual models
b)	Use mathematics and computing skills to create determinable models by deriving appropriate constitutive equations and specifying appropriate boundary conditions
c)	Use industry standard software tools and platforms to set up determinable models
d)	Recognise the value of Determinable Models of different complexity and the limitations of their application
4.	**Ability to use determinable models to obtain system specifications in terms of parametric values**
a)	Use mathematics and computing skills to manipulate and solve determinable models; and use data sheets in an appropriate way to supplement solutions
b)	Use industry standard software platforms and tools to solve determinable models
c)	Carry out a parametric sensitivity analysis
d)	Critically assess results and, if inadequate or invalid, improve knowledge database by further reference to existing systems, and/or improve performance of determinable models
5.	**Ability to select optimum specifications and create physical models**
a)	Use objective functions and constraints to identify optimum specifications
b)	Plan physical modelling studies, based on determinable modelling, in order to produce critical information
c)	Test and collate results, feeding these back into determinable models
6.	**Ability to apply the results from physical models to create real target systems**
a)	Write sufficiently detailed specifications of real target systems, including risk assessments and impact statements
b)	Select production methods and write method statements

c)	Implement production and deliver products fit for purpose, in a timely and efficient manner
d)	Operate within relevant legislative frameworks
7.	**Ability to critically review real target systems and personal performance**
a)	Test and evaluate real systems in service against specification and client needs
b)	Recognise and make critical judgements about related environmental, social, ethical and professional issues
c)	Identify professional, technical and personal development needs and undertake appropriate training and independent research

The other key feature of the standard is that it defines a threshold, meaning that every graduate should be expected to have achieved every one of these abilities to at least the specified level. Hence, the individual "ability to" statements in an instantiation must define minimum levels of capability, rather than average levels, and so the benchmark systems must similarly specify minimum rather than average levels of complexity.

4. The Standard and Software Engineering

The previous work on instantiating this standard for SE was aimed just at the level of the UK's honours bachelor's degree, which is also recognised (eg by the Washington Accord [8]) as equivalent to the bachelor's degree in North America. As yet, though, such degrees are very rare in the rest of Europe, although they are beginning to be introduced in a process of harmonisation of standards resulting from the Bologna Declaration [9]. Currently, though, in these countries most degrees in professional disciplines are at the master's level, and this is particularly true for engineering [10]. Hence, the main aim of this paper is to extend the previous work to cover master's degrees as well. As with the bachelor's level instantiation, this has involved three main issues. The first is the definition of a benchmark system or systems. The second is to map the process model used for the generic standard into typical SE process models, since there are significant differences between the two. The third is then to define the actual levels of ability that should be specified for each of the generic "Ability to" statements.

Underlying all of these issues is the impact that such a standard might have on the way in which students' work is assessed. The project to create the generic standard was intended to lead eventually to a specification of output standards that could replace the current specification of input qualifications in the UK's accreditation criteria. This would imply that programmes seeking accreditation should be able to show that their graduates were developing these abilities to the specified levels, and so the assessment mechanisms in the programmes would need to be able to support this. Many of these abilities are quite general, and so their assessment is not a simple process [11], but a major component of it will be the assessment of practical projects that the students undertake, and particularly capstone projects. This results in a variety of links between an instantiation of the standard and the requirements for such projects.

5. Benchmark Systems

In particular, any requirements for benchmark systems will effectively become requirements for the kinds of systems that should be developed during such projects, and practical constraints on such projects, such as curriculum time, will also constrain what can reasonably be specified as benchmark systems. In the trial instantiations that were produced as part of the original work on the generic standard, this had been reflected in the choice of specific example systems, such as an audio amplifier with a particular range of performance characteristics as a benchmark system for electronic engineering. In proposing requirements for an instantiation for SE at the bachelor's level, however, key concepts from project estimation methods (such as function points [12] and object points [13]) were used to describe the complexity of benchmark systems more directly. Thus, target ranges were developed for four aspects of system complexity: the number of entities or business classes in the data model; the number of relationships or associations per entity or business class; the number of menu functions in the external view of the processing model; and the number of sub-systems in the internal view of this model.

In extending these requirements to master's level, a key issue was how the constraints of curriculum time for capstone projects might vary. This requires further study, but it appears that typically a master's project has more time allocated than a bachelor's project, by a factor that lies roughly in the range 1.2 to 1.5. Using typical parameters from effort estimation models (eg [14]), this would mean that a master's project might be expected to be roughly between 1.1 and 1.3 times more complex than a bachelor's project, which should be reflected in the requirements for benchmark systems. The other important constraint is Miller's limit of seven plus or minus two [15], which implies that each aspect may need to involve a minimum of ten components in order to ensure that systematic development methods have to be employed, which is obviously an important feature in demonstrating practical ability to do SE.

For the data model, experience of running various kinds of projects in the undergraduate curriculum at Sheffield [16] had shown that for this purpose the most important components for the effective complexity were not the business classes (or entities), but the associations (or relationships). Since five business classes gives ten possible pairs that could be involved in associations, the requirement that had been derived from this was that a benchmark system at bachelor's level should have between five and seven business classes. Then, the need to avoid some particularly simple topologies for the model had given rise to a second requirement, that at least two of the business classes should each be involved in more than two associations.

At master's level this could be scaled up to give a range such as six to nine business classes, but because of the threshold property of the requirements it is only the lower limit that is vital. Here, the possible variations in the number of associations is actually more significant than the difference between five and six business classes, and so there is little point in having different ranges for the two levels, and it is proposed that this requirement should be the same at both.

For the processing model, the requirement that had been proposed at the bachelor's level was that the external view should contain between twenty and thirty basic functions, but the arguments used to derive this were based closely on the provision of separate functions to create, edit and delete data for each of the main business classes and associations. In considering how to adapt this range for the master's level, a number of the projects that had been undertaken by students in the author's department were reviewed. This demonstrated clearly that this notion of expecting separate functions was not valid, since in many cases the data sets had fairly complex structures, so that functions could not sensibly be broken down into separate external operations on different business classes. Hence, it was concluded that it was inappropriate to require benchmark systems to have any particular level of complexity for the external view of the processing model, and the only requirement should be based on the internal view of it.

Here the underlying structure is invariably hierarchical, but in practice the complexity can be measured for this purpose by the number of components (ie sub-systems) in the top layer of the hierarchy, which will be determined by the basic architecture of the system. In many cases this will use three layers, for the user interface, the business logic and the persistent storage, and so the basic requirement proposed at bachelor's level was that a benchmark system should involve three sub-systems, but without any requirement that these be organised as layers. To reflect the different ways in which software engineers actually develop sub-systems, though, the other requirement that was imposed was that at least one of them should be developed by configuring existing components, using the interfaces that they provided, and at least one should be developed from first principles.

Qualitatively, these two requirements for the processing model are obviously still valid at master's level, and quantitatively the parameters described above would not justify any changes to the numbers. Consequently, the specification of a benchmark system is identical at both levels, and is as summarised in table 2. This does not mean that typical master's projects will not be more complex than the bachelor's ones, but the additional complexity will arise in other ways, such as a more specialised context for the development of the system, and hence more difficulty in analysing the requirements or designing a system to meet them.

Table 2. The proposed specification for a benchmark software system.

At both bachelor's and master's level, a benchmark software system is any system whose complexity lies within the following bounds.	
i)	Its data model consists of between five and seven entities or business classes, of which at least two are each involved in more than two relationships or associations.
ii)	Its processing model consists of three sub-systems, of which at least one is to be developed by configuring existing components using the interfaces that they provide, and at least one is to be developed from first principles.

One other issue is that of whether the specification given in table 2 should be augmented with actual examples of typical systems, as have been given in the other trial instantiations. This, though, is really for others to judge rather than the author, and so must be left as an aspect of this work that still requires further development.

6. Development Process Models

The most difficult part of instantiating the generic standard for SE was trying to reconcile the process model underlying the generic standard with the ones commonly used in SE, since they also assume different sets of product models. As table 1 implies, the generic standard assumes just three kinds of product model, which it calls conceptual, determinable and physical models respectively, and the definitions of these are given in table 3. The way in which they are meant to be used at different stages in the generic process can be inferred from table 1, and in the following description references to stages of this process identify the sections of this table.

Requirements analysis is stage 2, and is described as delivering a conceptual model, or possibly a set of alternatives, so that it also includes some aspects of concept design. These designs are formalised in stage 3, to deliver a range of determinable models, which are then evaluated and optimised in stages 4 and 5, with stage 4 relying mainly on mathematical analysis and stage 5 on the use of physical models for validation. Stage 6 translates the selected optimal design into a suitable form for the production process, and stage 7 covers the activities of project evaluation and further development, of both the project and the person.

Hence, the distinction between conceptual and determinable models is fundamental to this process, but it has little relevance to the current state of SE, where the main kinds of models used in both requirements analysis and design are diagrammatic ones, typically expressed in UML [17], and so they would all be classed here as conceptual models. As described in a separate paper [18], within SE the distinction that the generic standard makes between these two kinds of models would usually be regarded as the one between qualitative and quantitative models. Also, reflecting the need to model problem domains as well as solutions, SE puts much more emphasis on the different perspectives from which modelling is carried out [19], and in particular it typically uses the term conceptual model for one (usually qualitative) that is developed during requirements analysis from the conceptual perspective [20]. Furthermore, as work on methods integration (such as the precise UML project [21]) progresses, so qualitative models developed from the specification perspective may well become sufficiently precise and formalisable (if not actually formal) that they should be classed instead as determinable rather than conceptual models. This therefore leads to the mapping for product models that is given in table 4, and this applies to both bachelor's and master's levels.

Table 3. Definitions of the product models used in the generic standard.

Conceptual model	A graphical, diagrammatic, symbolic or otherwise mentally apprehensible representation of an engineering system illustrating the relationship between key parameters in a form that may be transformed into a determinable model. (For example, the model used in a process diagram, a circuit diagram, a pipe network, a structural frame, a magnetic field pattern.)
Determinable model	A mathematical, computer/numerical, or logical representation of a conceptual model which enables the key system parameters to be firmly decided or definitely ascertained. (For example, a finite element computer model, a set of algebraic equations.)
Physical model	A physical representation of all or part of a real target system capable of being tested practically to determine or verify key system parameters. A prototype of the real target system. (For example, a wind tunnel test, a materials test, a field trial.)

With this mapping of the product models, there are then three main differences that need to be accommodated in mapping SE process models into the generic one. These are: the different breakdown of the design activity, the different treatment of construction, and the extent to which feedback loops are incorporated.

Table 4. The proposed mapping for the kinds of product models.

Generic Product Models	SE Product Models
Conceptual model, as the term is used in the activities of the requirements analysis stage.	Qualitative model, constructed from the conceptual perspective.
Conceptual model, as defined.	Qualitative model.
Determinable model, as the term is used in the activities corresponding to the architectural design stage.	Qualitative model plus derivable formal models or specifications.
Determinable model, as the term is used in the activities corresponding to analysis of performance or quality.	Quantitative model.
Physical model.	Prototype.

In SE the design activity is usually just broken down into two stages, architectural design and detailed design, whereas the generic model assumes three stages. Given the mapping that is proposed for the product models, two of these stages (3 and 4 in table 1) can be regarded as corresponding roughly to the two stages that are recognised in SE, which just leaves stage 5 in table 1 unaccounted for. This, though, is primarily a reflection on the relative immaturity of SE, where it is still commonplace (particularly in student projects) to regard any reasonably feasible solution as sufficient, rather than expecting any form of optimal solution. As the discipline matures, so one can expect that the activity of optimising designs (as in stage 5 of the generic process) will become increasingly significant, and this should start to be reflected first in degree programmes at master's level, and then work its way down to bachelor's level.

For the treatment of construction, the generic model implicitly assumes that the engineer only has to design and manage this, rather than actually undertake it, since this is the normal practice in other branches of engineering. By contrast, SE still treats it as an activity that is conducted by engineers rather than technicians, and one approach (particularly associated with agile methodologies such as XP [22] is that this reflects the inherent flexibility of software, and can be expected to continue. The opposing approach is that, particularly as code generation tools develop, so the main focus of SE should move from construction to design, as in other branches of engineering. Until this has happened, though, graduates from SE programmes at either level will still need to achieve a reasonable level of competence at actually undertaking construction (ie activity 6(c) of table 1), rather than simply managing it (ie activity 6(b)). Again, though, one can expect to see changes in this occurring first at master's level, and then working down to bachelor's level.

The third feature of the generic process model is the very limited occurrence of explicit feedback loops by comparison with typical SE processes: indeed, it is effectively a straight waterfall model with big-bang delivery. In part this reflects what other branches of engineering would regard as inherent limitations on their kinds of artefacts, which mean that they could not be developed on any kind of evolutionary or incremental basis, although arguably their view is only valid because they fail to look at the lifecycles over a long enough time scale. Within SE, though, these sort of development processes are commonplace, and so the activities of managing them are important. In particular, there is an expectation that a student of SE at either bachelor's or master's level should, in the course of their capstone project, take some role in planning its process, rather than simply following one prescribed by a project supervisor. The proposed instantiation of the standard for SE at bachelor's level could not reflect this, since the relevant activities just do not appear in the generic model. The only way in which this could be solved for either level would be to create an additional "ability to" statement, along the lines of "plan and manage a development process that will match the client's true needs", and add this somewhere to the set in table 1 – probably in section 2, or maybe 7.

7. Levels of Ability

In the trial instantiations that were produced as part of the project to develop the generic standard, the phrase "ability to" was left unqualified, except for one that suggested that lower levels of attainment (such as "experience of" or "knowledge of") might be substituted in some of the statements. In part this reflected the threshold characteristic of the standard, which means that every graduate should be expected to achieve the specified level in every one of the abilities listed in table 1, and this effectively implies a binary decision. In working towards an instantiation for SE, it was felt that this approach was unlikely to be adequate at both bachelor's and master's levels, where the difference between the two was likely to be reflected in a need to specify just what level of ability was being required in performing the various activities. Thus, in the proposals at bachelor's level an attempt was made to define the level of ability more precisely, using the general wording "a software engineering graduate must be capable of carrying out the basic activity correctly, but not necessarily getting every detail right, or understanding every fine nuance of either the activity or the system to which it is being applied".

By contrast, for master's graduates one would expect a higher level of ability, but it is not obvious how much higher this should be, and whether it should apply to all of the "ability to" statements or just some of them. One would expect the generic guidelines for accreditation in the Engineering Council's SARTOR document to shed some light on this, and the UK's Quality Assurance Agency (QAA) has also produced a National Qualifications Framework [23]. This tries to describe the different levels of post-school qualifications in the UK, from sub-degree ones through to doctorates, although it does so in terms that are generic across all disciplines.

Most of what SARTOR has to say about the distinction between the two levels is expressed in terms of knowledge that is to be gained. For instance, master's graduates should have "a broader and more general educational base", an "increased depth and range of specialist knowledge", and this should demonstrate a "greater extent of industrial relevance". It does also make some statements about abilities, but the majority of these (such as "use IT effectively", or "manage projects, people, resources and time") are common to both levels. The most notable difference is that master's level includes an additional statement, "be creative and innovative", and also one or two other statements specify more complex forms of ability at master's level.

In addition, SARTOR requires master's graduates to have undertaken both an interdisciplinary group and an individual research project (either of which could play a capstone role, but does not have to), whereas a bachelor's graduate simply has to undertake an individual capstone project. In terms of the key skills that are listed in section 1 of table 1, this means that master's graduates can be expected to have achieved a much higher level than bachelor's graduates in ability 1(d) ("working with others"), but otherwise the differences in the abilities that should be demonstrated at the two levels lie mainly in the contexts in which the projects are carried out. In particular, at master's level SARTOR expects that the abilities relating to requirements analysis (in section 2 of table 1) should be demonstrated in application domains that require both a wider range of knowledge than at bachelor's level, and possibly also more specialised knowledge, and this need for additional knowledge also feeds through into the design activities.

Table 5. The general abilities required by the UK National Qualifications Framework.

Honours Bachelor's Level	Master's Level
apply the methods and techniques that they have learned to review, consolidate, extend and apply their knowledge and understanding, and to initiate and carry out projects;	deal with complex issues both systematically and creatively, make sound judgements in the absence of complete data, and communicate their conclusions clearly to specialist and non-specialist audiences;
critically evaluate arguments, assumptions, abstract concepts and data (that may be incomplete), to make judgements, and to frame appropriate questions to achieve a solution - or identify a range of solutions - to a problem;	demonstrate self-direction and originality in tackling and solving problems, and act autonomously in planning and implementing tasks at a professional or equivalent level;
communicate information, ideas, problems, and solutions to both specialist and non-specialist audiences;	continue to advance their knowledge and understanding, and to develop new skills to a high level;

Much the same is true of the National Qualifications Framework, which describes (in very general terms) both the kinds of knowledge that graduates should possess at each level, and the abilities that they should be able to demonstrate to apply this knowledge. The latter are set out in table 5, but their organisation renders point-by-point comparisons difficult. Where they can be made, though, they reinforce the approach of the accreditation criteria, in that the main difference is in the complexity of the problems to be solved, and the levels of knowledge, originality and creativity required to solve them.

This requirement to apply a greater depth and range of specialist knowledge at master's level is reflected to some extent in the first draft of the SEEK, which proposes a list of what it calls "Systems and Applications Specialities", and it suggests that students may either specialise in one or more of these areas, or by deeper study of some of the core knowledge areas. Putting the ideas from these documents together thus suggests that, at master's level, the "either ... or" should disappear, so that these students should be required to study both one or more of these application areas, and also specialisms within the core. This could then be incorporated into the "ability to" statements, in two ways. Firstly, it could be specified that at master's level the benchmark system should be one that is drawn from the specialist application area, and so should incorporate requirements that reflect the specialised features of this area. Secondly, in place of the general wording suggested at the beginning of this section, one would expect master's graduates to be able to get more details right in carrying out the activities, and in particular to understand more of the nuances of the activities or the systems to which they are being applied.

The application of this higher level of knowledge could then be demonstrated by specifically demanding a higher level of performance from master's graduates in the ability to evaluate the significance of details, particularly in those activities that they have studied to greater depth. Beyond this, though, the specification of the particular activities where this knowledge would be demonstrated could not be done generically, and so instead it would have to be specified for each individual degree programme by its designers, so as to reflect the particular focus of that programme.

8. Conclusions

The overall conclusion of this paper is that the generic graduate output standard can be instantiated for SE, at both bachelor's and master's levels, and this provides a good definition of what graduates in SE should be able to do, as an important complement to descriptions of what they should know. In particular, it provides a sound basis for characterising the kinds of systems that they should be expected to develop competently, although whether this needs to be supplemented by descriptions of typical example systems is still an open question.

The work described here has, though, highlighted two weaknesses of the generic standard. One is that its set of product models needs to be made richer, to reflect the extent to which SE, as a socio-technical branch of engineering, needs to model problem domains as well as solutions. The other is that it needs to recognise the more extensive set of feedback loops that exist within typical SE development processes, and in particular it needs to incorporate explicitly an ability to manage these processes.

The work has also highlighted three weaknesses of the current state of SE, reflecting its relative immaturity as a branch of engineering. One is the extent to which it still relies on relatively informal product models, rather than rigorous ones. The second is the very limited attention given to trying to achieve optimal designs, rather than ones that are merely feasible. The third is the extent to which it still treats construction as an engineering activity, rather than simply a technical one.

As SE matures, one can expect that developments in all of these areas will appear in master's level programmes first, and then work their way down to bachelor's level ones. This illustrates the final conclusion, which is that while master's level graduates can be expected to demonstrate greater levels of the abilities described here than bachelor's graduates, the differences between these two levels need to be described mainly in terms of the additional knowledge that is being

98

applied. This can not be done at the level of SE as a discipline, but rather it will need to be documented separately for each individual degree programme.

References

1 IEEE Computer Society, *Guide to the Software Engineering Body of Knowledge: Trial Version (0.95),* IEEE Computer Society (May 2001), and also at <http://www.swebok.org/stoneman/version095.html>.
2 IEEE-CS and ACM Joint Task Force on Computing Curricula, Approved Final Draft Version of Computing Curricula 2001 (15th December 2001), <http://computer.org/education/cc2001/final/index.htm>.
3 A E K Sobel (ed), *Computing Curricula - Software Engineering Volume: First Draft of the Software Engineering Education Knowledge (SEEK),* 28th August 2002, <http://sites.computer.org/ccse/artifacts/FirstDraft.pdf>.
4 Engineering Council, *Standards and Routes to Registration (SARTOR),* 3rd edition, London (1997).
5 British Computer Society, *Guidelines on Course Exemption & Accreditation,* Swindon, UK (September 2001), and at < http://www1.bcs.org.uk/>.
6 Engineering Professors Council, *The EPC Graduate Output Standard: Interim Report of the EPC Output Standard Project,* Occasional Paper No. 10, Coventry, England (December 2000), and at <http://www.engprofc.ac.uk/op/op10.html>.
7 A J Cowling, Towards a Graduate Output Standard for Software Engineering, to appear in J B Thompson & H Edwards, *Post-Summit Proceedings of the International Summit on Software Engineering Professionalism,* (co-located with the International Conference on Software Engineering (ICSE) 2002), Orlando, Florida, to be published by Sunderland University Press (2002).
8 Washington Accord, *Recognition of Equivalency of Accredited Engineering Education Programs Leading to the Engineering Degree,* (1989), <http://www.washingtonaccord.org/>.
9 Confederation of EU Rectors Conferences and the Association of European Universities (CRE), *The Bologna Declaration on the European space for higher education: an explanation,* (2000), <http://europa.eu.int/comm/education/socrates/erasmus/bologna.pdf>.
10 R Kirby (ed), *European Engineering Yearbook 1996,* Cambridge Market Intelligence Ltd with FEANI, London, (1996).
11 Engineering Professors Council Assessment Working Group, The EPC Engineering Graduate Output Standard: Assessment of complex outcomes, Institution of Mechanical Engineers, London, England (January 2002), and at <http://www.engprofc.ac.uk/pap/EPC%20AWG%20TF%20Report%20TF%2012Feb02.pdf>.
12 C R Symons, *Software Sizing and Estimating: Mark II Function Point Analysis,* Wiley, New York (1991).
13 B W Boehm, B Clarke, E Horowitz *et al,* Cost Models for Future Life Cycle Processes: COCOMO 2.0, *Annals of Software Engineering* 1 (November 1995), pp 57-94.
14 B W Boehm, *Software Engineering Economics,* Prentice Hall, Englewood Cliffs NJ (1981).
15 G A Miller, The magical number seven, plus or minus two: some limits on our capacity for processing information, *Psychological Review* 63, 81 – 97 (1956).
16 A J Cowling, The first decade of an undergraduate degree programme in software engineering, *Annals of Software Engineering* 6, 61 – 90 (1998).
17 G Booch, J Rumbaugh & I Jacobson, *The Unified Modelling Language User Guide,* Addison Wesley, Reading MA (1999)
18 A. J. Cowling, Modelling: A Neglected Feature in the Software Engineering Curriculum, these proceedings.
19 S Cook & J Daniels, *Designing Object Systems: Object-Oriented Modeling with Syntropy,* Prentice Hall, Englewood Cliffs NJ (1994)
20 M Fowler with K Scott, *UML Distilled: Applying the Standard Object Modeling Language,* Addison Wesley, Reading MA (1997).
21 A Evans, *The precise UML group: main details,* <http://www.cs.york.ac.uk/puml/maindetails.html> (2002).
22 K Beck, *Extreme Programming Explained: Embrace Change,* Addison Wesley, Reading MA (2000).
23 QAA, *The framework for higher education qualifications in England, Wales and Northern Ireland,* Quality Assurance Agency, Gloucester, England (2001).

Engineering an Introductory Software Engineering Curriculum

Rick Duley
Edith Cowan University
r.duley@cowan.edu.au

Gregory W. Hislop
Drexel University
hislopg@drexel.edu

Thomas B. Hilburn
Embry-Riddle Aeronautical University
hilburn@erau.edu

Ann E. K. Sobel
Miami University
sobelae@muohio.edu

Abstract

This paper presents ideas and issues related to the design and implementation of a curriculum for the introductory part of a B.S. degree in Software Engineering (BSSE). It provides a framework for designing curriculum units and other learning activities that will help prepare students for more advanced study in software engineering. The curriculum is called "introductory" because it represents the beginning knowledge and practices that software engineering students must acquire in the first year or two to adequately prepare them for more advanced study.

1. Introduction

In a 1987 study of the profession of SE [5], Gary Ford and Norman Gibbs cited "initial professional education" as one of the areas of weakness in advancing SE as a profession. Since then, there have been a number of undergraduate and graduate programs in software engineering established throughout the world. Unfortunately, these new programs are few in number and many commentators say they do not come close to meeting industry needs.

The ACM and the IEEE Computer Society have sponsored a number of activities and projects intended to advance the state of software engineering as a profession. These have included the development of the following:

- the Guide to the Software Engineering Body of Knowledge (SWEBOK) [4]
- the Software Engineering Code of Ethics and Professional Practice [1]
- Computing Curriculum, Software Engineering (CCSE) [http://sites.computer.org/ccse/], a volume of Computing Curriculum 2001 that will provide guidance for undergraduate software engineering education
- the Certified Software Development Professional program (CSDP) [http://computer.org/certification/].

Another group that has been active in the helping to improve software engineering education is the Working Group in Software Engineering Education and Training (WGSEET). WGSEET is sponsored by the Software Engineering Institute (SEI) and consists of about eighty individuals interested in and engaged in software engineering education and training. The mission of the WGSEET is to improve the state of software engineering education and training with a focus on the education and professional development of software practitioners.

In recent years, the working group has undertaken a series of projects related to SE curriculum and academic-industry collaboration. The curriculum sub-group has selected projects with an eye to complementing the ACM and IEEE efforts listed above. In 1999, the curriculum sub-group developed a document that provided guidance on the development of software engineering programs [2]. More recently, the curriculum subgroup (membership listed in the Acknowledgements section) has been working on the development of guidance to support the introductory part of an undergraduate SE program. This paper presents the results of that work.

Early versions of the WGSEET work have been provided to the CCSE Steering Committee to support their work effort. Because of space limitations much of that material has not been included in this paper. We expect to review the resulting CCSE document so that the final version of the WGSEET work may accurately reference the resulting CCSE curriculum guidelines.

The remaining sections of this paper include a discussion of the objectives and prerequisites of an introductory curriculum that is followed by recommended development strategies and a definition model for the introductory SE curriculum.

2. Objectives

As a means of achieving this transition, the WGSEET first identified the student learning objectives of an introductory SE curriculum; namely, what knowledge should an undergraduate student possess after completing the first year or two of an SE curriculum These are listed in Table 1.

Verbs used relate to the expected level and depth of student capability. This approach is similar to the one taken in Bloom's taxonomy [3]. For example, objectives 1, 2, 6 and 7 refer to knowledge of software engineering topics that is at Bloom's "knowledge" and "comprehension" levels, while objectives 3, 4, and 5 would be at Bloom's "application" level.

Objectives 4 and 5 both concern development of software and use the term "modest-sized". Here the intent is to prepare students capable of engaging in "software-engineering in the small". That is, they would experience and become competent in various aspects of software engineering (requirements, design, coding, review and testing, etc.) as applied to the development of programs with size and complexity appropriate for the first year or so of the a software engineering program (up to a few hundred lines of code). Objective 6 highlights the importance of communication and teamwork in the very beginning of the curriculum. The curriculum subgroup's expectation is that the coverage of these same topics will continue in greater depth later in the undergraduate SE curriculum.

Table 1 : Introductory Curriculum Objectives

Upon completion of the introduct ry curriculum, students should be able to:
1. Describe the problems in software system development and evolution.
2. Discuss the basic concepts and practices of software engineering in the areas of requirements, design, construction, quality, testing, evolution and management.
3. Model, develop and document a modest-sized high-quality program in an high-level language
4. Apply core Computer Science concepts that include basic data structures, and to design and implement a modest-sized program.
5. Model a software artifact's properties and argue its correctness using sound but informal reasoning.
6. Appreciate basic cooperative team skills and communicate contributions and other issues with other members in a clear and timely manner.
7. Describe the importance of ethical behavior and professional practice by a Software Engineer.

In the working group discussions that provided the basis for this paper, there was a clear tension between wanting to cover all the "important" topics, and trying to be realistic about what could be covered early in the curriculum. In considering the material below, it is important to remember that our expectation is that coverage of this material will extend beyond the first year, but should easily be manageable within the first two years.

3. Prerequisites

After much discussion the subgroup agreed that:

- Students entering the introductory SE curriculum must be competent in pre-calculus mathematics;
- There are no prerequisites for programming skills or knowledge.

The problem with specifying prerequisites for a curriculum designed to support a wide variety of programs is that there are significant differences in what can or should be expected of them. In order to serve the widest group we decided to not place any requirement on prior programming experience.

4. Curriculum Strategies

In this section we present ideas and issues that we believe should be employed in the development and delivery of an introductory curriculum.

Catch Student Imagination - Students should engage in software engineering experiences they find both interesting and challenging.

Introduce Principles Early - Students should learn a combination of software engineering principles and their application starting early in the curriculum. Comparing and contrasting software engineering with science, technology, and other engineering fields can help students better understand the discipline, see the rationale for their studies, and start to comprehend the nature of their future professional life.

Start with a Defined Process - Beginning students should learn about and use a defined process for phased development of small programs.

Emphasize Problem Solving - An introductory curriculum should emphasize the teaching of problem solving and critical thinking.

104

Emphasize Modeling - Abstraction and modeling (a black box approach) should be used to teach software engineering principles.

Table 2: Introductory Curriculum Modules

Module	Description
Software Engineering Knowledge Overview	Introduces the discipline of software engineering to students new to computing.
Software Unit Development	Introduces students to basic concepts of a software development process.
Software Design Principles and Methods	Covers basic design principles and methods including abstraction, modularity, information hiding, encapsulation, mathematical modeling, specification, and verification.
Programming Tools and Techniques	Covers basic tools and techniques of programming including high-level language fundamentals .
Discrete Mathematics	Introduces discrete mathematics as a tool for software engineering.
Communication and Teamwork	Motivates and provides a foundation for the development of presentation, inter-personal and team skills
Society and the Software Engineering Profession	Introduces students to concepts and issues related to professional ethics, professional activities, and life-long learning.

Introduce Modeling with Mathematics - Students should begin to understand how to use mathematics as a software-modeling tool for small programs.

Balance Principles and Practice - Lectures and class discussions should be used to teach concepts and

principles, while laboratories and tutorials should be
used to teach software tools, processes, and practices.

5. A Model for Implementation

In Table 2 we propose a set of seven modules that
implement the objectives and strategies discussed in
the previous sections. The intent here is not to define
courses or even parts of courses. Rather, these
modules are meant to demonstrate one possible logical
grouping of topics. It is recognized that how various
institutions map these topics into courses will vary
considerably.

6. Conclusions

Any Introductory Software Engineering Curriculum
must lay a firm foundation on which the rest of a
program may build. WGSEET has worked to develop
a sound framework for designing curriculum units that
will facilitate the preparation of students for more
advanced study in software engineering. While none
of the ideas presented here are revolutionary or
necessarily innovative, we believe that their collation
into a single, coherent document based on the
collective experience of a diverse, international group
has created a useful guide for all those involved in
introductory curriculum development.

The WGSEET is continuing the effort to contribute
to this definition. Future efforts by the group will
continue to be selected in an effort to complement and
support the projects of the professional societies. The
WGSEET will welcome and carefully consider any
feedback or advice as they seek to further develop and
refine their work.

Acknowledgements

Most of the ideas and recommendations in this
paper were developed in meetings of the WGSEET in
October of 2001 and February 2002. Those working
group members most directly involved included the

following: Jocelyn Armarego (Murdoch University), Joe Clifton (University of Wisconsin – Platteville), Jorge Diaz-Herrera (Rochester Institute of Technology), Rick Duley (Edith Cowan University), Rob Hasker(University of Wisconsin – Platteville), Peter B. Henderson (Butler University), Tom Hilburn (Embry-Riddle Aeronautical University), Greg Hislop (Drexel University), Peter Knoke (University of Alaska), Mike Lutz (Rochester Institute of Technology), Paul E. MacNeil (Mercer University), Jim McDonald (Monmouth University), Michael Ryan (Dublin City University), Mark Sebern (Milwaukee School of Engineering), Ann Sobel (Miami University), Massood Towhidnejad (Embry-Riddle Aeronautical University).

References

1. ACM/IEEE-CS Joint Task Force on Software Engineering Ethics and Professional Practices, *Software Engineering Code of Ethics and Professional Practice*, Version 5.2, http://www.acm.org/serving/se/code.htm, September 1998.

2. Bagert, D., et. al., *Guidelines for Software Engineering Education*, Version 1.0, CMU/SEI-99-TR-032, Software Engineering Institute, Carnegie Mellon University, 1999.

3. Bloom, B.S. (Ed.) *Taxonomy of educational objectives: The classification of educational goals: Handbook I, cognitive domain*. New York; Toronto: Longmans, Green, 1956.

4. Bourque P. and R. Dupuis, eds. *Guide to the Software Engineering Body of Knowledge*, IEEE CS Press, Los Alamitos, Calif., 2001.

5. Ford, G. and Gibbs, N., *A Mature Profession of Software Engineering*, CMU/SEI-96-TR-004, Software Engineering Institute, Carnegie Mellon University, http://www.sei.cmu.edu/publications/documents/96.reports/9 6.tr.004.html , Pittsburgh, PA, 1996.

A Coordinated Plan for Teaching Software Engineering in the Rey Juan Carlos University

Jorge Enrique Pérez-Martínez, Almudena Sierra-Alonso
Rey Juan Carlos University
C/Tulipán s/n, 28933
Móstoles (Madrid)- Spain
{j.perez, a.sierra}@escet.urjc.es

Abstract

Nowadays both industry and academic environments are showing a lot of interest in the Software Engineering discipline. Therefore, it is a challenge for universities to provide students with appropriate training in this area, preparing them for their future professional practice. There are many difficulties to provide that training. The outstanding ones are: the Software Engineering area is too broad and class hours are scarce; the discipline requires a high level of abstraction; it is difficult to reproduce real world situations in the classroom to provide a practical learning environment; the number of students per professor is very high (at least in Spain); companies develop software with a maturity level rarely over level 2 of the CMM for Software (again, at least in Spain) as opposed to what is taught at the University. Besides, there are different levels and study plans, making more difficult to structure the contents to teach in each term and degree. In this paper we present a plan for teaching Software Engineering trying to overcome some of the difficulties above.

1. Introduction

In Spain there are three Computer Science degrees: Technical Engineer in Software Management (TESM) (this degree specializes in Information Systems), Technical Engineer in Systems Computing (TESC) and Computer Engineer (CE). The two first degrees are given after a first level (somewhat similar in contents to the bachelor degree) with a three year duration. Students with one of these degrees can continue studies in CE (similar in contents to Master studies) with a duration of two years (see Figure 1). The Ministry of Education establishes by law [4] the minimum number of credits of a set of disciplines considered essential and mandatory to obtain these degrees. One credit is equivalent to 10 class hours. There are theory credits and practical (laboratory) credits. Disciplines are organized in different courses and academic years. Afterwards, each university, taking into account the mandatory disciplines, defines its study plan orienting and specializing such studies. Specialization is accomplished by increasing the number of credits of certain mandatory subjects and/or including elective courses. Consequently, in Spain there is a common set of courses for all students in the same degree, with a high diversity of study plans (one per university).

In Table 1 we show the credits established by the Ministry of Education for the Software Engineering (SE) discipline in the three degrees.

The Rey Juan Carlos University offers the three degrees described above. In Table 2 we show the credits established by this university to obtain the three degrees in Computer Science. Mandatory and elective credits are specified in this table. The credit load for SE, divided into theory and practical credits, varies significantly from one degree to another (see Table 3). For example, this table shows that the number of credits assigned to SE for the TESM degree is almost three times the number assigned for the TESC degree. On the other hand, students arriving to the CE degree may have different levels of training, since they can come from TESM studies or from TESC studies. To this, we can add the fact that in the first year of the CE studies we can have students coming, not only from our university, but from any other university in Spain, which implies a high diversity in levels of training because of differences among study plans.

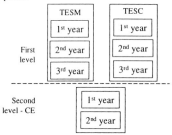

Figure 1. Organization in academic years of degrees TESM, TESC and CE.

Degree	Mandatory credits
Technical Engineer in Software Management	12
Technical Engineer in Systems Computing	0
Computer Engineer	18

Table 1. Mandatory credits for SE in Computer Science degrees in Spain.

Finally, we have to point out that the SE discipline is taught in several courses in the three degrees and it is necessary to coordinate the contents included in each of them in order to assure that the SE training obtained by the students is complete and non-redundant. In Figure 2 we show those SE courses. The courses defined as mandatory by the Ministry of Education or by the study plan in the University are marked as (M). The elective courses are marked as (E). Following the name of the course, we show the number of credits: theory credits + practical credits. We also show whether the course is taught in the first or second semester of the year. Observe that some courses extend over the two semesters.

	Credits to obtain a degree		
	TESM	TESC	CE
Mandatory	180	180	93
Electives	45	45	54
Total	225	225	147

Table 2. Credits in Computer Science degrees in the Rey Juan Carlos University.

Degree	SE mandatory credits
Technical Engineer in Software Management	6 theory + 6 practical
Technical Engineer in Systems Computing	3 theory + 1.5 practical
Computer Engineer	10.5 theory + 7.5 practical

Table 3. Credits established for SE in the Rey Juan Carlos University study plan.

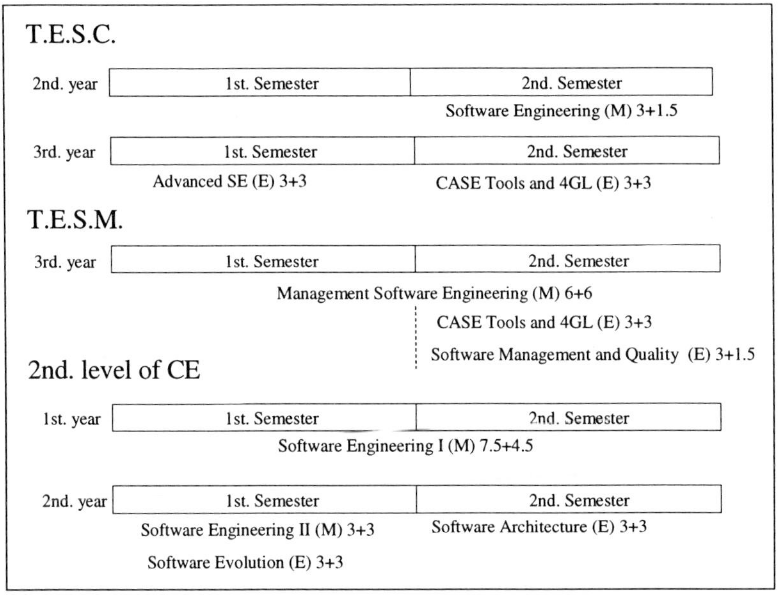

Figure 2. Distribution of SE courses by degrees, years and semesters.

Some elective courses present in the study plan have not been offered yet. That is the case with the courses *Software Management and Quality* and *Software Evolution*.

Summarizing the information presented, Computer Science studies are structured in two levels, and students may end their studies after the first one or continue studying CE. In this framework, our paper tries to solve the difficulties arising from the training differences among students of SE when they access the CE degree studies. At the same time, it tries to coordinate the set of courses in the SE area to provide a consistent view of this discipline along the different periods in which it is taught. More specifically, our goals are:

1. To give students who finish the first level (in TESM or TESC) a wide knowledge of areas related to SE as described in SWEBOK [5] and in the Computing Curricula 2001 [2] (pp. 147-153). The IEEE SE curriculum [3] has not been considered because

it is only a draft at the moment. In the second level we will deepen in this knowledge and will extend it with specialized techniques of SE and with the last advances in the discipline.

2. To establish mechanisms to provide students that access the second level from any first level degree with a similar body of knowledge in SE.

Besides, this work takes into account other problems like the extent of the Software Engineering area, the scarce number of class hours, the high level of abstraction required by this discipline, the difficulty to reproduce real world situations in the classroom, the high number of students per professor (in Spain) and the reality of companies developing software rarely over level 2 of the Capability Maturity Model for Software (again, in Spain).

The rest of the paper is structured as follows. In sections 2 and 3 we present a plan oriented to achieve the previous goals. In section 4 we show some relationships among the courses of SE. Section 5 describes some results obtained since the start of this plan. In section 6 we present the main conclusions of this work, and finally, in section 7 we outline some future work for the improvement of the proposed plan.

2. Planning for the TESC and TESM degrees

Figure 2 shows that there is an unbalance in credits between the degrees TESC and TESM in relation with the study of SE. The mandatory course has 12 credits assigned in TESM and only 4.5 credits in TESC. The only way to palliate this difference is to recommend students in the TESC studies who plan to continue with the second level to take the elective course *Advanced Software Engineering*. This way, in the TESC degree students take 10.5 credits of SE as opposed to 12 taken in the TESM degree.

Given that students in the TESC studies are free to choose or not the course *Advanced Software Engineering,* the teaching of SE must be structured in such a way that the basic knowledge of SE is assigned to the second year, and more specialized knowledge is assigned to the third year. With this idea in mind, the course *Management Software Engineering* of the TESM degree (focused on SE techniques for information systems) can be structured in two parts: the first one corresponding in contents with a deeper treatment of the course *Software Engineering* of the TESC studies and the second one with the contents included in the course *Advanced Software Engineering* of the TESC degree (see Figure 3).

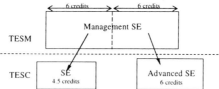

Figure 3. Relationships among the SE courses in the TESM and TESC studies.

In the way just described, we satisfy the two goals in our introduction, that is, to teach the basic concepts of the discipline and to provide students in both degrees with a similar body of knowledge in SE. The SE courses in both degrees have been developed following this plan. The contents covered in these courses are shown in Table 4. This table also includes the description of the type of practical works to develop and the tools used for them.

Tech. Engineer in Software Management	Technical Engineer in Systems Computing
MANAGEMENT SOFTWARE ENGINEERING	**SOFTWARE ENGINEERING**
Goals: to provide the student with the basic principles of Software Engineering as a framework for the construction of reliable and maintainable software. It studies current methods, techniques and tools provided for Software Engineering, and provides students with a global view of the different activities and variables to consider in the software development process.	**Goals**: to introduce the student in the knowledge of the basic principles of Software Engineering. It studies the basic tasks of software development from an object oriented point of view.
Contents	**Contents**
SOFTWARE ENGINEERING	SOFTWARE ENGINEERING
Introduction to software engineering	Introduction to software engineering
Software development models	Software development models
Software development methodologies	Software development methodologies
O.O. SOFTWARE DEVELOPMENT	O.O. SOFTWARE DEVELOPMENT
Object oriented basic concepts	Object Oriented Basic Concepts
Requirement engineering	Requirement engineering
Object oriented analysis	Object oriented analysis
Object oriented design	Object oriented design
Implementation	Implementation
Object oriented software testing	Object oriented software testing
STRUCTURED SOFTWARE DEVELOPMENT	SOFTWARE MAINTENANCE
Structured analysis	Introduction to software maintenance
Structured design	**Laboratory work**
Structured software testing	To do the O.O. analysis and design of a small application (1 or 2 use cases) from its specification, using the Unified Software Development Process.
SOFTWARE DEVELOPMENT MANAGEMENT	**Tools**: Rational Rose.
Introduction to management tasks	**ADVANCED SOFTW. ENGINEERING**
Software project management	**Goals**: to learn the basic aspects of software development management and to apply methods and techniques of the structured development paradigm.
Configuration management	**Contents**
SOFTWARE MAINTENANCE	SOFTWARE DEVELOPMENT MANAGEMENT
Introduction to software maintenance	Introduction to management tasks
Laboratory work	Software project management
To do the O.O. analysis and design of a small application (4 or 5 use cases) from its specification, using the Unified Software Development Process.	Configuration management
To do the time and resource planning for a software development problem.	STRUCTURED SOFTWARE DEVELOPMENT
Tools: Rational Rose and Microsoft Project.	Structured analysis
	Structured design
	Structured software testing
	Laboratory work
	To do the time and resource planning for a software development problem.
	Tools: Microsoft Project.

Table 4. Contents of the SE courses for the TESM and TESC degrees.

The elaboration of the contents is based on the topics described in the SWEBOK. In Figure 4 we enclose with dotted lines the topics of the SWEBOK treated in the TESM studies. The figure shows that students must have a global view of development activities, and must learn some management aspects and the basic concepts of software maintenance. Evidently, not all topics are studied with the same wideness and depth described in the SWEBOK. The topics studied with more depth are the object oriented requirements, analysis, design and testing. Students will do some practical work about these topics.

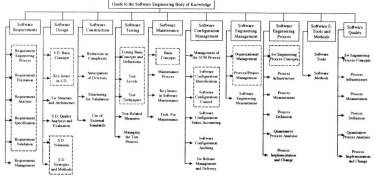

Figure 4. Contents of the SWEBOK included in the TESM studies.

In Figure 5 we show the topics treated in the TESC degree. With a uniform dotted line we enclose the topics of the mandatory course. With a non-uniform dotted line and rounded corners we enclose the topics covered in the elective course (*Advanced Software Engineering*). This figure shows that adding the two courses, we cover the same topics, but with a different depth in some of them due to the difference in the number of credits. Students that take only the mandatory credits know at least the basic development activities using the OO paradigm.

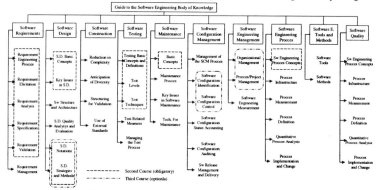

Figure 5. Contents of the SWEBOK included in the TESC studies.

Technical Engineer in Software Management and Technical Engineer in Systems Computing
CASE TOOLS AND 4GL
Goals: To learn the importance of the CASE tools in the lifecycle of a software product, both in the development and maintenance stages.
Contents   INTRODUCTION   COMPONENTS OF THE CASE SYSTEM: TOOLS   SOFTWARE DEVELOPMENT SUPPORT   TOPICS RELATED TO THE CASE TECHNOLOGY
Laboratory work   To develop the use case model, analysis and design of a given application.
Tools: Rational Rose

Table 5. Contents of the course *CASE Tools and 4GL* taught in the TESM and TESC degrees.

Finally, there is an elective course, *Software Management and Quality*, that has not been opened yet. This course will make more emphasis on quality aspects because software management has already been introduced in mandatory courses.

3. Planning for the CE degree

To plan the courses of SE corresponding to the CE degree we assume that students already have a wide knowledge of all the activities in the discipline, and that they have done some practical work in development (in particular with the Unified Software Development Process).

The contents proposed for the course *Software Engineering I* of the first year, study with some depth some activities related to the discipline (with less emphasis in implementation activities for which students are supposed to have the required ability). The table of contents for this course is shown in the left column of Table 6.

For the course *Software Engineering II* of the second year, we propose the table of contents shown in the right column of Table 6.

As in the previous case, the elaboration of these contents is based on the topics described in the SWEBOK for the CE degree. In Figure 6 we enclose with a dotted line the topics of the mandatory course of the first year. With non-uniform dotted line and rounded corners we mark the topics covered in the mandatory course of the second year. As can be seen, some of the topics marked in this figure were already covered in the first level degrees. The difference is that in the second level, these topics are treated with more depth and more complex techniques are studied.

Furthermore, in the course of the second year newer subjects are treated not yet included in any of the knowledge areas of the SWEBOK. Such is the case with components or reengineering, topics included in appendix D of the SWEBOK.

In the course *Software Architecture* the student learns the last advances in this discipline that, despite its youngness, is starting to consolidate some principles and to stand out like one of the key pieces in software construction and maintenance. The contents of this course (see Table 7) correspond partially to the topic *Software Structure and Architecture* of the knowledge area *Software Design* and partially to contents treated in appendix D of the SWEBOK.

Computer Engineer	
SOFTWARE ENGINEERING I. **Goals**: to study in depth the main tasks done in the software engineering discipline: requirements, architecture, low level design, verification and validation, project management, software quality and reengineering. The student must be able to work in any of the stages of the software development and maintenance, from the management and development points of view. **Contents** INTRODUCTION: SOFTWARE PROCESS SOFTw. DEVELOPMENT MANAGEMENT REQUIREMENT ENGINEERING SOFTWARE ARCHITECTURES DESIGN PATTERNS VERIFICATION AND VALIDATION SOFTWARE QUALITY REENGINEERING **Laboratory work** To do the planning and management of the project (configuration management, planning adjustments). To elaborate a requirement specification according to the standard IEEE 830. To develop an application from the specification, using patterns, defining the architecture, … To do the unitary and functional testing. **Tools**: RequisitePro, Rational Rose and Rational testing tools.	**SOFTWARE ENGINEERING II**. **Goals**: • To understand what a software process is and the problems to design it, and to familiarize with the metaprocess level of the Unified Software Development Process. • Familiarize students with specialized techniques of SE in environments like critical systems or formal specification. • To learn the last advances in SE like WEB engineering, component engineering or extreme programming. **Contents** SOFTWARE DEVELOPMENT METAPROCESSES DISTRIBUTED OBJECTS ENG. COMPONENT BASED SE CRITICAL SYSTEMS WEB ENGINEERING FORMAL METHODS "EXTREME PROGRAMMING" **Laboratory work** It varies every year, but it is always related to theoretical contents. **Tools**: Rational, free distribution middleware, .NET.

Table 6. Contents for the mandatory SE courses in the CE degree.

4. Relationships among the courses

The plan proposed has been implanted in the second and third year of the TESM and TESC studies. During the academic year 2002-2003, it will be implanted in the course *Software Engineering I* (first year of the second level of CE) and during the next academic year in the courses *Software Engineering II*, *Software Architecture* and *Software Evolution* (second year of the second level of CE) completing the implantation of the whole plan. Up to now, the new plan implanted in the first level has existed side by side with the previous one in the second level of CE. Because of that, the relationships among the courses shown in Figure 2 are the following:

- The course *CASE Tools and 4GL* shows the use of the tool Rational Suite Enterprise Edition 2001A. This tool is used in the practical work of the courses *Management Software Engineering*, *Software Engineering I*, *Software Engineering II* and *Software*

Architecture.

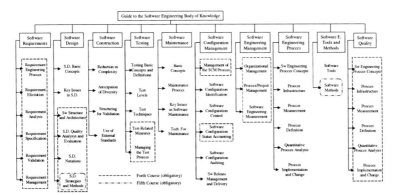

Figure 6. Topics of the SWEBOK included in the second level of the CE degree.

Computer Engineer
SOFTWARE ARCHITECTURE.
Goals:
• To recognize the architectonical styles existing in software systems.
• To estimate reasonable architectures for an application and choose among them.
• To be able to reason about the properties of different style architectures.
• To understand how to use the domain knowledge to specialize an architecture for a particular family of applications.
Contents
INTRODUCTION
ARCHITECTONIC STYLES
STUDY CASES
TOWARDS A SOFTWARE ARCHITECTURE
DOMAIN SPECIFIC ARCHITECTURES
SOFTWARE CONNECTORS
ARCHITECTURE DESCRIPTION LANGUAGES
SOFTWARE ARCHITECTURE DINAMISM
THE ROLE OF UML IN SOFTWARE ARCHITECTURES
FROM THE ARCHITECTURE TO THE IMPLEMENTATION
QUALITY ATTRIBUTES OF AN ARCHITECTURE
SOFTWARE ARCHITECTURES FOR USER INTERFACES
Laboratory work
Architecture analysis and design
Tools: free distribution (ArchStudio 3.0, ACME, ...)

Table 7. Contents for the course Software Architecture of the CE degree.

• The practical work done by students of the course *Software Engineering II* (consisting on the elaboration of a software requirements document) is used as the specification for the practical work to do by students of the course *Management Software Engineering* of the TESM degree.

- The practical work done during the first semester in the course *Management Software Engineering* is used as the specification for one of the practical works of the course *CASE Tools and 4GL*.
- The practical work done in the course *Software Engineering II* constitutes the specification for the practical work to develop in the course *Software Architecture*.

Our goal is to increase the number of relationships in the direction shown in section 7, related to future work.

5. Some results

Following, we describe some of the most interesting results observed after the two-year period since the plan was implanted.

5.1. How to simulate some real world situations

One of the classical difficulties teaching Software Engineering is to transmit students the problems and situations that take place in real projects. It is very difficult to reproduce such situations in the classroom. On the other hand, one of the stages of development essential for the success of the project is the acquisition and analysis of requirements. In this context, we have done an experiment consisting on providing the students of the course *Management Software Engineering* with a requirement specification document prepared by students of the course *Software Engineering II* instead of by the course professors. Of course, the document has inconsistencies, contradictions, lack of precision and almost all those deficiencies that a real project document would have. Students must be able to solve those problems with the professor on the role of user. Afterwards they have to do an analysis of the application. The experience has been very positive because:

- It allowed students to face a specification document with deficiencies, which will be customary in their professional experience.
- It encouraged a higher interaction professor-student, by having the professor in the role of final user.
- Students used a specification that conforms to a standard (IEEE 830-1998) that, even if it is not used in their future professional experience, provides a model with a lot of similarities.

5.2. Selected tools

The tools used for the realization of practical work are Rational™ products. Specifically, students used Rational RequisitePro for the requirement capture and Rational Rose for the use case modeling, analysis and design of the application. Despite the fact that for modeling there are some free distribution tools like ArgoUML, we consider more likely that in the professional environment students find tools like Rational. The main disadvantage is the high price of these tools. Even with the 80% discount for Universities, to equip a laboratory for 20 users with Rose and RequisitePro costs about 33245 euros.

The experience with this tool has been positive. Students have been able to experiment the facilities of a very powerful CASE tool and to see the effort it saves. However, we have also seen that they use very few facilities of the tool, just the ones required to do the practical work. We must find ways to encourage students curiosity in this respect.

5.3. SE in the second year

Everybody knows that learning SE is a difficult task, not only because of required previous knowledge, but because of the abstraction level necessary. In the TESC degree, this discipline is taught in the second year, having only 4.5 mandatory credits assigned (see Figure 2). In the second year, simultaneously to SE, students take the course *Data and Information Structure* and they have not taken yet any courses on databases. This implies that students have not developed yet an adequate ability for abstraction, essential for the analysis and design stages. On the other hand, they do not have any notions about data repositories (important for modeling and implementation). To this, we have to add that this course is the only mandatory one of SE in the degree, and because of that, it is the only opportunity that the professor has to provide the student with a minimum set of knowledge about SE.

To solve these problems, and given that the study plan cannot be modified, this course focuses on analysis and design, without considering management aspects proper of more advanced courses. These topics are treated in an applied way, taking into account the existing restriction of practical credits. Besides, the object oriented paradigm has been selected because its knowledge is considered essential nowadays for a Computer Science degree.

6. Conclusions

A plan for teaching SE in two levels has been developed:
- The first one covers the most important aspects of software development and some management ones.
- The second one extends the previous concepts and presents the student more advanced topics of SE, such as software architecture, reengineering or components. It also extends the knowledge in management and covers some topics not seen in the first level, like software quality.

In this manner, we achieve a continuous line of learning in two levels, in such a way that students finishing the first level have the basic knowledge of the SE discipline and may start developing software by applying some engineering principles. On the other hand, students finishing the second level have a more solid knowledge of the basic principles and extend their knowledge on the development stages, strengthening the concepts already acquired in the first level. Furthermore, these students come out prepared for an essential task in any engineering: the planning and management of projects. Students finishing the second level have also acquired some perspective on the newest advances in the area, which may attract their interest towards a wider training.

7. Future work

As we already said, the first goal in the short term is the implantation of the whole plan described, that will take place in the academic year 2003-2004. In parallel with this, we have to design the contents of the SE courses that will be taught in the CE degree that will start in the academic year 2002-2003. We also have to work on the next renewal of the study plan for the TESM and TESC degrees. All this will happen in the framework of a near review of the European university structure according to the Bologna Declaration and the Bricall report [1].

In the meanwhile, we have to concentrate on those aspects open to improvement. On the one hand, we may attack one of the major problems that the teaching of SE has, that is, the time restriction (in credits) of the courses. This restriction prevents the development of software projects with an appropriate size, that would show the true power of this engineering. We think that a possible solution (already implanted in other universities) is the realization of a medium size project along several academic years. We know the efforts of planning and coordination that this idea entails, but we think that this practice will notably improve the quality of SE teaching. On the other hand, we think that we may improve the interrelations among the courses that configure this discipline. In section 5 we indicate the relationships currently existing among these courses. However, these relationships will disappear with the start of the new stages of the proposed plan, but new relationships will appear. An example is the course *Software Evolution* that may takes its practical input from the practical work done in the course *Software Engineering I*.

With respect to the tools to use for the practical work, we will continue making an effort to get the necessary equipment in the laboratories. We have already asked for the licenses for Rational Robot, Test Manager and PurifyPlus to be able to undertake the testing activities. Depending on the budget of the Rey Juan Carlos University and the policies of Rational Rose for university centers, we will try to equip a laboratory with all the tools necessary to support the software development and maintenance activities.

Finally, but not less importantly, we are starting to study the future integration of the disciplines SE and Databases (DB). Nowadays it is almost impossible to find a software product that does not have a database associated, or in more general terms, a data repository. The integration of both disciplines is a fact in industrial environments and we think it must be in the academic environment. Setting the inter-relations among the courses of SE and DB should drive us to achieve this goal.

8. References

[1] Bricall, J.M. (2000). *University Report 2000*. Retrieved on April 3, 2002 from http://www.campus-oei.org/oeivirt/bricall.htm

[2] Computing Curricula (December 2001). *Computer Curricula - Computer Science Volume*. (Final Report). The Joint Task Force on Computing Curricula, IEEE Computer Society and Association for Computing Machinery.

[3] Computing Curricula (August 2002). *Computer Curricula – Software Engineering Volume*. (First Report). The Joint Task Force on Computing Curricula, IEEE Computer Society and Association for Computing Machinery.

[4] University Council (1993). *New studies for the computer engineer, the technical engineer in software management and the technical engineer in systems computing* [Professional Monographs]. Universidad-Empresa Foundation and University Council.

[5] SWEBOK (May 2001). *Guide to the Software Engineering Body of Knowledge*, trial version (Version 1.00). Software Engineering Coordinating Committee.

Software Engineering Curriculum 2
(Paper Session D)

A Practical Approach of Teaching Software Engineering

Michael Gnatz, Leonid Kof, Franz Prilmeier, Tilman Seifert

Institut für Informatik
Technische Universität München
85748 Garching

{*gnatzm, kof, prilmeie, seifert*} *@in.tum.de*

Abstract

In today's software industry a software engineer is not only expected to successfully cope with technical challenges, but also to deal with non-technical issues arising from difficult project situations. These issues typically include understanding the customer's domain and requirements, working in a team, organizing the division of work, and coping with time pressure and hard deadlines. Thus, in our opinion teaching Software Engineering (SE) not only requires studying theory using text books, but also providing students with the experience of typical non-technical issues in a software project. This article reports experiences with the concept of a course focusing on providing practical know-how.

1: Introduction

This article describes a practical approach of teaching SE know-how at the Technical University of Munich in a course called "Software Engineering Project" (SEP) conducted by the authors during summer term 2002.

1.1: Motivation

The major objective of the SEP is to provide students with the experience of an industry-like software development project. A typical software project is challenging in many ways: A new domain must be understood, "maybe" requirements are inconsistent and need to be clarified with the customer; the technology used might be new to team members, so they must learn and gain experience using that particular technology. Deadlines might be set a bit too optimistically, and developers need to solve unexpected technical problems. Besides all this, social aspects are to be considered as well: How do team members communicate with each other, how do they like each other's working style, habits, and so on.

There are many SE text books that describe all these difficulties and challenges; some of them like [3] focus more on design aspects, while others like [8] emphasize project management issues. But the only way that really prepares anyone for doing successful project work is learning by doing. From a university's perspective it is a challenging task to find a teaching concept for providing students with practical know-how regarding project work.

1093-0175/03 $17.00 © 2003 IEEE

1.2: Project Goals

One major goal is to teach students what it means to work in a team and how to go through the whole project life cycle with all phases from requirements engineering to delivery. The second goal is the development of a correctly working and useful piece of software which serves at least as a prototype. This software should be well documented and maintainable. During the course of 2002 the tool prototype APE, which is explained in section 3, was developed.

About half of the students had already heard the lectures on SE and knew about typical problems and methods useful in solving them. They knew in theory what to do. Our project showed once more how important it is not only to theorize about developing software, but to actually do it. Only when time becomes short and deadlines come closer, everyone (including students and supervisors) realize the importance and difficulties of social communication and stable interface definitions on the technical side.

1.3: Overview

In section 2 we will discuss the setup of the SEP focusing on the question of doing a real project. Section 3 outlines the domain and purpose of the tool APE to be developed and some technical background as well as the initial project plan. Section 4 describes what actually occurred, while section 5 summarizes lessons learned – not only by the students but by us as well. A short conclusion is given in section 6.

2: Project setup – Doing a Real Project

2.1: Students

The announcement of the course looked similar to a job advertisement. Besides offering real project experience, which is almost unique among university courses, the announcement emphasized the higher work load and time demand in comparison to other courses.

For successful team work during the course it is important that the differences between students with respect to motivation and knowledge are not too great. Therefore, as in real industry life we conducted interviews with all applying students. The major criterion for choosing a student was his/her motivation and commitment for doing project work. In these interviews 12 students from advanced semesters were chosen. This number of participants has proved sufficient for experiencing team work and the difficulties of communication.

There were even more factors that one can usually find in industrial projects: the team was brought together only for this project, and most of the members did not know each other before. Large parts of the used technology were new to most of the team members. The students were expected to spend a large amount of time on this project, but they had other courses on their schedules as well.

2.2: Customer

To provide a real setting for the project a "real" customer was involved in the course. A nearby company took over the role of the customer and provided an initial and slightly fuzzy requirement specification document for the software to be developed. Of course, this requirements document was not a formal specification at all, but provided a lot of space for interpretation and clearly needed clarification. A further difficulty was the bulk of requirements given by the initial requirements document. Having too many requirements and only little time is not an untypical project situation. Students had to negotiate the functionality that can actually be done in a three months project with the customer.

During the project the customer was intended to be the primary address for the students' questions regarding requirements. After one presentation of the results in the middle of the project the customer was involved in acceptance testing. After the final presentation the customer had to decide whether to accept or to decline the delivered software. The delivery deadline was a hard deadline, i.e. the end of the term.

2.3: Teachers' Roles

There were five supervisors (four staff members and one senior student). While four of the supervisors focused their work guiding their respective student team through the development process, the remaining supervisor was designated for quality assurance, thus being responsible for reviewing all the documents produced along the way. The intention behind this division of responsibilities was to assure his independence from the students and their work and his objectivity in reviewing these documents. Of course all other supervisors read and reviewed the documents as well.

Coaching included solving technical problems as well as moderating discussions about the use cases to be realized, the architecture of the application or planning of the next steps. Last but not least coaches had to maintain the motivation of the teams. The project leader (one of the supervisors) additionally took care of further organizational issues and kept in contact with the customer.

2.4: Limitations as Compared to a Real Project

This course tried to be as close as possible to reality. But still, some differences remained. The main goal of teaching sometimes conflicts with the aim of a real-life setting. There were three months time – just enough to go through a full life cycle of a small software project. But there was no chance to touch maintenance issues.

The project started with 12 students, and each had to be occupied from day one. Typically, team sizes vary over time with some developers deciding on the architecture and a larger team joining in when it comes to implementation. In every real software project there is at least one experienced architect. In our project we wanted all students to do the entire job, including software architecture. We had inexperienced students and therefore could not expect them to design a perfect software architecture.

This approach makes sense for teaching, but it becomes a real problem if you want to get a solid architecture. But the teaching goal was to let the students experience the challenges of designing a good architecture. We believe that we did achieve this goal.

The incentives for developers, however, are quite different. In this project, no real money changed hands. Instead, students received credit points for attending. The product was meant only as a prototype and not for productive use, which seemed to change the attitude quite remarkably. The customer was not a "real" customer who was anxious to use the tool but a company willing to support this kind of university project.

3: Background for the Project "APE"

The Living Software Development Process Today's software development projects are confronted with a frequently changing environment: rapidly altering business domains and processes, fast technology evolution, great variety of evolving methods and development processes. Therefore, a highly flexible and adaptable software development process is required that allows a project to react to changes quickly and to adopt existing development methods to comply with the project's actual needs. We call such a process a living software development process – a process which allows tailoring according to a given project situation as well as evolutionary process improvement. The concept is based on process patterns. Further reading on the concept of process patterns can be found in [2], [5], [6].

APE The tool APE ("Applied Patterns Environment") was to be developed in the project. Project managers can use APE for configuring a project plan based on their company's process pattern library. APE supports the tailoring a generic process model containing alternative methods for the specific project. During project execution the team members are guided through the project by means of process patterns. APE can suggest applicable process patterns based on the state of the documents under development. For example, the pattern "find test cases" might be considered useful when the use case document reaches the status "accepted".

Although APE remains a prototype it shows that the concept of process patterns is sufficiently powerful to provide a basic platform for a living software development process, which guarantees the required balance between flexibility and control in a process model. For more information on APE see [7].

Technical Background Practical SE requires know-how of a broad range of technologies upon which the project is based, and tools which are used in the development process. This project was no exception, quite a few tools and technologies were new to the students.

CVS (concurrent versions system) was used for version control. LaTeX was standard for writing all the documentation. TogetherJ [12] was used as UML editor for modeling and code generation; a number of Java libraries were used: JUnit [10] for regression testing and a setup for daily build and smoke tests, XML libraries (we used JAXP [11]), and Log4J [1] which provides a flexible and powerful logging mechanism. The Bugzilla bugtracking System [9] was installed and used extensively.

Finally the Eclipse IDE [4] was development tool and target platform at the same time: APE was designed as a plug-in for Eclipse, which meant extending and using the Eclipse APIs, like the SWT library (standard widget toolkit) for the GUI. Eclipse was the greatest technical challenge because it is a very young technology. Not many documentation resources existed describing how to extend Eclipse or use the services provided by its APIs.

Altogether there was an impressively broad range of tools and technologies with which not all students were familiar. Surprisingly most students said this was not the primary challenge for them – being either an indication for their high motivation and preparedness for learning new technologies, or indicating that other problems arising in the software development process are much more challenging.

Team Organization We devided our 12 developers into three teams of four students each and assigned them according to the layers of a classical three-layered architecture. Negotiation among the teams was necessary in several areas. During requirements clarification each team was responsible for writing a different part of a requirements specification document. In the end this document, of course, had to be consistent and complete. The teams were responsible for designing and negotiating interfaces between the layers. Since little experience regarding interfaces was available, a change board comprised of representatives of each team had to discuss necessary changes of the architecture document.

Coordination among teams was achieved through weekly project meetings attended by all participants. During the meeting each team reported accomplished work and further steps were discussed. The meeting results were captured by protocols, which were written by revolving students authors. Besides this weekly meeting, the teams contacted their supervisors on a regular basis where team-specific problems were discussed.

4: The Actual Project Run

The available time of three months was divided into five phases[1], as listed in table 1. At the time of project kick-off, the team agreed to this plan. It was considered to be ambitious but feasible. Minor deviations in the plan were expected, but there was no serious doubt about the success of the project. In the project run it turned out that some tasks were much more time-consuming than initially thought. Table 1 gives an overview of the temporal deviations.

Project Phase	Planned Duration	Actual Duration
Analysis phase resulting in a requirements specification document	3 weeks	5 weeks
Design phase leading to a architecture document, containing the detailed descriptions of interfaces between the layered architecture	2 weeks	4 weeks
Development of the first increment including integration, testing and delivery	4 weeks	6 weeks
Development of the second increment	4 weeks	—
Integration as well as acceptance testing	2.5 weeks	0.5 weeks

Table 1. The Initial Plan and the Actual Project Run

In retrospect the initial plan was overly optimistic (which might also be considered typical for software projects). The delays of the analysis and architecture phases led to the necessary plan adjustment of formally dropping the second development increment. We had to inform our customer that some of the use cases promised only a few weeks ago in the requirements specification might not be realistic for the remaining project time.

Not even this adjustment allowed the continuation of the project with the planned functionality and with proper documentation. In contrast to the official plan, the team (including the project leader) decided to achieve the initially planned functionality. In the

---

[1]Some of the mentioned phases did overlap to fit into the project duration of three months

end, about three days remained for the integration of the separately developed layers. For acceptance testing by the customer we had one day left.

During the implementation phase we experienced necessary changes to the interface specification document almost daily, although the document had been formally reviewed by the whole team.

Quality of the Developed Software In the end, the resulting software is not too bad. In spite of some issues regarding user guidance, the customer was satisfied with the result. Among the features realized there is full access to the imported XML data produced by a neighbour system, and the tool integrates nicely into the Eclipse IDE. On the other hand, APE falls short of supporting concurrent access by different users, but this deficiency was realized early and accepted by the customer through his signing of the requirements specification.

Finally, we were able to deliver a productive version of APE with limited functionality and a prototype version realizing almost the entire functionality as planned albeit with minor deficiencies. The code contains 10.500 lines of code (LOC, blank lines and comments excluded) in 120 Java classes.

5: Lessons learned

Communication Students were asked to fill in an anonymous questionnaire about the course with questions about the achievement of teaching goals and the experiences they gained. They all agree that the most difficult issue in software development is not a technical one, but a social one.

What is the right way to communicate in a larger group? There are about 700 emails in APE's mailing list archive (25 of them sent after 10pm). In this course, we did not answer the question of the perfect way, but students learned about the importance and difficulty of communication.

They also learned how to communicate with the customer. It was not possible to deliver all the functionality the customer ordered – and the students had to explain why some of the ideas could not be part of the first roll-out. There were good reasons, but they had to be presented in an appropriate way.

Technical Issues Students learned a lot about practical software development: They had to manage several tools as well as some new technology, and were required to handle an amount of code with continuously increasing size. Only towards the end, where the project became too complex for a single programmer, they realized the importance of modularization and stable interfaces by experiencing an overly increasing need of communication.

Process Knowledge Students also learned about the software development process in two ways: The domain of their project was about software processes, and they experienced one full development cycle.

> "...Conducting a project from the beginning until the end was very interesting, as one saw the major differences between large projects and just a few days of programming on your own. Also seeing the supervisor's tasks (even if

you are just the one being supervised) was interesting. ... " (from a student's questionnaire)

Management Problems Not only the students learned in this course – it was also a very interesting project from the supervisors' perspective and a good way to experience practical problems of project management. The project plan had to be adjusted several times. There was serious misjudgment about how time consuming certain activities can be. What are the reasons for that?

First, the way from the initial customer specification to our requirements specification was much longer than anticipated. Knowing the domain, we initially thought it might be a small task. Second, before the start of the project we did not invest much time in a thorough evaluation of our base technology Eclipse. The GUI widgets of Eclipse turned out to be a rather difficult technology, especially when you have to use "trial and error" because of insufficient documentation.

Another mistake was that the list of features to be realized was not adapted according to the actual state of the project. Although the development phase for the second increment was dropped, due to our unfounded optimism, we tried to catch up with the original plan. At the end of the project we did not manage to stop coding at the proper time, in order to be able to test and properly document the software: The major part of code was written and tested in the last 2.5 weeks before delivery.

Documentation The elaboration of the requirements specification as well as the architecture document took much time, and was of poor quality in the end. Why was that?

"...Subject of future improvement might be the communication of tasks. Sometimes it was not clear at all what the expectations were – causing some delay of the project ... " (from a student's questionnaire)

The early process phases were only roughly planned and prepared. We used a document template for the requirements specification, which turned out to be difficult to use, because explanations for its application were missing. For the architecture document, we only provided oral instructions, but no template, exemplary document, guidelines, or checklist. It is no surprise that the architecture was not a stable document but kept being changed continously throughout the following phases. Also some useful architectural issues are missing completely in our document, for instance the description of the exception handling concept. This lead to problems during implementation and some deficiencies in the resulting software.

All in all the documentation does not seem to facilitate the further development of the tool APE – some reverse engineering might be necessary. On the other hand, the code itself is thoroughly documented using JavaDOC comments. We even have a comment ratio of 37 percent compared to the total number of lines of code.

Clearly, in providing useful templates together with checklists, we see great potential for improving the project performance.

Team Organization Another problem arose from inflexibility regarding the size of our development team. Untypically for a real project, we did analysis and architecture with the full team size of 12 developers.

From the teacher's perspective the approach has been valuable. All participants were involved in all life-cycle phases. In the end students may have learned the advantages of stable interface definitions. In the beginning of implementation, the GUI team gave the impression of not being able to cope with the whole functionality because of difficulties with the Eclipse GUI widgets. At the same time, the application layer team did not seem to have much to do. This had some influence on the motivation of the whole team. At the end of the project, when Eclipse finally turned out to be manageable, we simply did not have enough time for both implementing application layer features and testing them properly. We considered rebuilding the teams as a reaction to shifted work load. This might have been advantageous, but in our opinion changing teams could also have resulted in a major time loss for the integration of new team members.

5.1: Why did it work anyway?

Sometimes work was accomplished in a practical manner, clearly resulting in some trade-offs, as for example an imperfect architecture. But finally the software functioned – even after a dramatically shorter implementation and testing phase. Analysis and architecture activities did not lead to high quality documents, but at the begin of implementation developers seemed to have understood the application domain quite well. So the thorough preparation of the implementation phase led to much quicker coding.

During implementation some practices proved very helpful. We established a nightly build and test run and sent emails to all project members in case of failure. Developers committed new code to the CVS repository very carefully, making team work smooth.

We established a formal procedure for change management regarding changes to the interface specifications. A change management team had to be informed about necessary architectural changes, approve or reject them and distribute approved changes by email to all parties involved. Furthermore the use of a bug tracking system as a means of communication proved quite helpful. 234 bugs or reminders have been noted in APE's bugtracking system.

Integration and testing were quite short but nevertheless did work. During the implementation a large part of the requirements were tested using automated unit tests. Judging the quality and completeness of the test cases written, one must say, quality is rather poor, but even the focus on test cases seems to have led to careful development so that integration in the end did not produce major problems.

The most important factor that saved the project's success certainly was good communication. Although we did not have a perfect plan all the time, we always knew the actual state and problems of the project. A good working atmosphere, high motivation of all participants, sometimes resulting in late night work, helped us in solving (almost) all problems during the project. An important factor for the success was probably that all participants had fun.

5.2: Lessons that Still Need to be Learned

Several things could be done better. Some open questions remain.

How can we get closer to reality? The SEP still has kind of a sandbox character. To make the project more realistic we should not give the same type of tasks to all the

128

students. Furthermore, in a real project team size would vary over time. On the other hand three months time is too short for changing teams or tasks frequently.

How can we better reach our teaching goals? It is hard to teach how important it is to write good documentation (and how to do it). The value of good documentation only surfaces during the maintenance phase, which was not included in the project time.

Asked about their estimation for the ease of maintenance or developing additional features in the future, students told us at the end of the project that they did not see any problems in understanding their code after a year's time. This is fundamentally in contrast with the supervisors' opinion. From the teaching point of view we were not able to provide the "maintenance experience".

6: Conclusion

Is this the right way to teach SE? We believe it is, even though we still see shortcomings in setting up a real industrial project environment. Every year we are supported by companies that invest time and money just for playing the role of the customer. We interpret this fact as a sign that our approach helps provide students with the knowledge and experience that industry expects from computer science graduates.

By no means would we argue against studying standard SE text books. Courses like the one presented here demonstrate that we need both: Studying SE methods and creating an atmosphere as close as possible to real software project life.

Acknowledgements We are grateful to Rainer Frömming for acting as the customer and Robert Abright for his thoughtful comments on a draft version of this paper.

References

[1] Apache Software Foundation. *Log4j*, 2002. http://jakarta.apache.org/log4j/.
[2] Klaus Bergner, Andreas Rausch, Marc Sihling, and Alexander Vilbig. A Componentware Development Methodology based on Process Patterns. *Proceedings of the 5th Annual Conference on the Pattern Languages of Programs*, 1998.
[3] Bernd Brügge and Allen Dutoit. *Object-Oriented Software Engineering: Conquering Complex and Changing Systems*. Prentice-Hall, Inc., 2001.
[4] The Eclipse Project. *Eclipse*, 2002. http://www.eclipse.com.
[5] Michael Gnatz, Frank Marschall, Gerhard Popp, Andreas Rausch, and Wolfgang Schwerin. Towards a Living Software Development Process Based on Process Patterns. *Lecture Notes in Computer Science*, 2077, 2001.
[6] Michael Gnatz, Frank Marschall, Gerhard Popp, Andreas Rausch, and Wolfgang Schwerin. Modular Process Patterns Supporting an Evolutionary Software Development Process. *Lecture Notes in Computer Science*, 2188, 2001.
[7] Michael Gnatz, Frank Marschall, Gerhard Popp, Andreas Rausch, and Wolfgang Schwerin. Towards a Tool Support for a Living Software Development Process. *Proceedings of the 35th Hawaii International Conference on System Sciences*, 2002.
[8] Steve C. McConnell. *Software Project Survival Guide*. Microsoft press, 1997.
[9] Mozilla.org. *The Bugzilla Bugtracking System*, 2002. http://bugzilla.mozilla.org/.
[10] Object Mentor, Inc. *JUnit*, 2002. http://www.junit.org/.
[11] Sun Microsystems, Inc. *Java API for XML Processing (JAXP)*, 2002. http://java.sun.com/xml/jaxp/index.html.
[12] TogetherSoft. *TogetherJ - The Model, Build, Deploy Platform*, 2002. http://www.togethersoft.com/.

Software Engineering Education: Following a Moving Target

Daniela Rosca   William Tepfenhart   James McDonald
Software Engineering Department
Monmouth University
West Long Branch, NJ 07764
{drosca, btepfenh, jamesmc@monmouth.edu}

Abstract

This paper presents the main lessons learned over 16 years in offering a graduate degree in software engineering at Monmouth University. It covers the challenges in delivering a program that meets the needs of industry and students in a highly dynamic field. The evolution of the curriculum induced by the continuous advances in the field and industry practice is presented. This evolution is an example of a transition from a "computer science curriculum with an engineering flavor", towards a software engineering curriculum. The special meaning of continuous course content development in software engineering is argued through issues pertaining to dated textbooks, ever-changing programming languages, operating systems, and software tools. The paper also presents our experience in dealing with the diversity of the student body, and its influence on the curriculum and course content. We conclude with the presentation of future directions for this program.

1. Introduction

Although software engineering was recognized as a field in 1968 at the NATO sponsored conference on the subject [Nau68], it took universities and colleges a significant amount of time to respond to that fact. It wasn't until 1986 that Monmouth University (MU) started one of the first graduate programs in the nation dedicated to software engineering, which was offered by its Computer Science Department. In 1995 Monmouth created the first Software Engineering Department in Unites States. Now it is one of a growing number of universities offering a bachelor's degree in software engineering.

One motivation for creating a separate software engineering program and department, was the awareness of the skills that industry would like students to have upon graduation, which are not stressed by most computer science curricula. These skills include teamwork, communications, time management, engineering problem solving, quantitative and qualitative process management, reuse, requirements management, system architecture, testing and project management.

As one of the few universities with such an extensive and comprehensive experience in offering software engineering programs, we have learned much about providing such a program. With more and more undergraduate software engineering programs appearing, we feel it would be beneficial to other institutions for us to share our problems and lessons learned. A summary of the problems encountered and the lessons learned are presented here:

- **Revolutionary Curriculum Changes**. One can expect to revisit the overall curriculum of the program every four to five years, in order to accommodate changes in industry practice and educational expectations.
- **Continuous Development Of Course Content.** It is critically needed due to the dynamics of the field. The continuous development of course content implies also a continuous development of course projects, and dealing with dated textbook, ever changing operating systems, programming languages and software tools.

•**Difficulties Attracting and Retaining Faculty.** The need for new faculty to have a record of sustained scholarly accomplishments and industrial experience imposes great restrictions on the number of available candidates.

•**Diversity of the Student Body.** Issues raised by a diversity of educational backgrounds, employment status, educational goals, and communication skills impose challenges that need to be dealt with by any software engineering program.

The remainder of the paper discusses in detail the topics presented above. Section 2 presents the evolution of curriculum over the history of our program. Section 3 discusses various issues involved in the continuous changes of the software engineering course content. Section 4 shows our experience in hiring and retaining the faculty, while Section 5 presents the influence of the diversity of the student body on the curriculum and course content. Section 6 identifies where we expect the program to head in the future.

2 . Revolutionary Curriculum Changes

Over its short history, software engineering (SE) as a field has been a moving target. We have observed the introduction of the Capability Maturity Model, the Unified Modeling Language, Personal and Team Software Process, and corporate adherence to ISO Standards emerge as major forces within software engineering organizations. Therefore, a curriculum that addresses the skills and practices required by professionals in this field, needs to continuously reinvent itself over time. In order to accommodate industry's needs and to keep pace with the advances of software engineering as a field, we have added or dropped courses, and added new tracks and programs. The decisions were made in the context of creating and maintaining a balance between the theory, technology and practical aspects of software engineering.

Next we present some examples of curricula that reflect the evolution of the Monmouth University's Graduate Software Engineering Curriculum. They show a gradual transition from a software engineering program created inside a Computer Science department, towards a program with engineering courses that span the entire software lifecycle. The evolution of the curricula illustrates the kinds of responses that result from academic and industrial forces.

2.1. The Initial Curriculum (1991)

The initial curriculum consisted of 30 credits, with 6 core courses and 4 electives (see Figure 1). The core courses covered in detail only the design and project management aspects of the software lifecycle, due to the limited availability of faculty with an appropriate background. The curriculum looked more like "a computer science curriculum with an engineering flavor"[Dar97]. It included an artificial intelligence course, 4 courses of mathematical foundations and formal methods in SE, and 4 courses in network technology (due to our geographic location in an area dominated by the telecommunications industry). The practical training of students was accomplished in a 3-credit practicum course, which consisted of a team project that would develop a software system from initial requirements to the final, tested and documented product. The early curriculum was biased more on theoretical aspects, with less exposure to specific SE technology and practice.

Core Courses (6 Courses = 18 Credits)
SE 501 Mathematical Foundation of Software Engineering I (3 credits)
SE 505 Software System Design (3 credits)
SE 506 Formal Methods in Programming (3 credits)
SE 516 Software Engineering (3 credits)
SE 518 Project Management (3 credits)

SE 525 System Project Implementation (3 credits)

Elective Courses (4 Courses = 12 Credits)
SE 502 Mathematical Foundation of Software Engineering II (3 Credits)
SE 503 Intro. to Computer-Communication Networking (3 Credits)
SE 509 Programming Languages (3 Credits)
SE 510 Computer Network Design (3 Credits)
SE 511 Protocol Engineering (3 Credits)
SE 519 Database Management (3 Credits)
SE 522 Software Engineering Environments (3 Credits)
SE 532 Software Process Quality (3 Credits)
SE 534 Formal Specifications of Software Systems (3 Credits)
SE 536 Fundamentals of Computer Security (3 Credits)
SE 538 Advanced Topics in Networking Topology (3 Credits)
SE 540 Introduction to Artificial Intelligence (3 Credits)

Figure 1. First Curriculum

2.2. 1995 Curriculum Changes

In 1995 the curriculum was substantially changed to include 36 credits, with 10 core and 2 elective courses (see Figure 2), in order to comply with the Software Engineering Institute model curriculum [Ard89]. That curriculum covered the entire software lifecycle in detail, by offering 3 new courses, specifically in requirements, implementation and reuse, and testing and quality. A former elective, software systems security, became a core course. Having such a heavy core, this curriculum offered little flexibility to students for learning aspects of SE that they would be most interested in. Another major change was reflected in the introduction of several new courses that would form 6 credit elective specialization tracks, in distributed software systems, software management, information systems, and real-time systems. These tracks were introduced as a response to the needs and feedback from our local industry, and government collaborators [Pow97]. The curriculum change was possible because of the newly hired faculty with both theoretical background and working experience in industry, supplemented with a substantial help from adjunct faculty with expertise in specialized areas of SE.

Core Courses (10 Courses = 30 Credits)
SE 501 Mathematical Foundation of Software Engineering I (3 credits)
SE 504 Principles of Software Engineering (3 credits)
SE 505 Software System Design (3 credits)
SE 506 Formal Methods in Software (3 credits)
SE 507 Software Systems Requirements (3 Credits)
SE 508 Software Implementation and Reuse (3 Credits)
SE 512 Software Testing and Quality (3 Credits)
SE 513 Software Systems Security (3 Credits)
SE 518 Software Project Management (3 credits)
SE 525 System Project Implementation (3 credits)

Advanced/Elective Specialization Tracks (2-course track = 6 Credits)

Distributed Software Systems	SE 526 Networked Software Systems I
	SE 527 Networked Software Systems II
Software Management	SE 531 Software Organization Management
	SE 532 Software Quality Management
Information Systems	SE 541 Information Systems Architecture
	SE 542 Information Systems Engineering
Real-Time Systems	SE 551 Real-Time Software Analysis & specification
	SE 552 Real-Time Software Design & Implementation

Figure 2. The 1995 Curriculum

2.3. 1996 Curriculum Changes

In 1996 minor changes were made in the curriculum. It remained a 36-credit program, but students now had 9 core and 3 elective courses, which offered a bit more flexibility than the previous program. The curriculum covered all the aspects of the software lifecycle, but the capstone course was either a 3-credit practicum, or 6 credits of thesis research. The introduction of a thesis option was made possible by attracting faculty with the desire to engage in research activities.

2.4. 1998 Curriculum Changes

The 1998 curriculum, which is the curriculum that we currently follow, represented another major change by providing for much more flexibility in a 36 credit program, with 5 core, 5 elective courses, and a 6 credit practicum or a 6 credit thesis (see Figure 3). All the knowledge areas of the Software Engineering Body of Knowledge (SWEBOK) project, as described in the Stone Man report [StM00] can be identified in this curriculum. The recognition of the importance of exposure to practical experience in a software engineering program has lead to the increase of the practicum project from 3 to 6 credits. Practical experience is also gained through project work in most of the courses offered in our program.

The 1998 curriculum has added a new course, The Process of Engineering Software, which largely follows Watts Humphrey's Personal Software Process (PSP) principles [Hum97]. The introduction of this course was justified by the need for graduates who are aware and have the necessary skills for predictably producing high quality systems, in a timely and cost effective manner, using reusable components as much as possible in their work. In spite of the hard work necessary for the manual input of the data for the various forms and templates involved in the PSP, students have given us very positive feedback about the usefulness of the principles learned in this course. For alleviating the clerical work related to the manual input of data, we created a semi-automated tool to support the PSP process [Ros01]. This tool was the result of a two-semester practicum project of one group of students.

The elective courses included in this curriculum were necessary for completing a chosen specialization track, such as organizational management, telecommunications, embedded systems, and information systems. These 15 credit tracks, were much more comprehensive, adding courses from other disciplines such as business, electrical engineering and computer science. However, students have been able to select electives across tracks if they didn't choose a specialization.

The Organisational Management track prepares students to become software development managers or specialists in software process improvement. Topics of study include process improvement, quality management, organisational development and management, risk management and project planning and management.

Preparatory Courses (15 Credits)

    CS 500 Program Development

    CS 503 Fundamental Algorithms I

    CS 505 Operating Systems

    SE 501 Mathematical Foundation of Software Engineering

    SE 504 Principles of Software Engineering

Core Courses (15 Credits)

    SE 500 The Process of Engineering Software

    SE 505 Software System Design

    SE 506 Formal Methods in Software

    SE 507 Software Systems Requirements

    SE 512 Software Testing and Quality

Capstone Course (6 credits) – Practicum/Thesis

Specialisation Tracks (15 Credits)

Organizational Management Track	Telecommunications Track
Required (9 Credits)	**Required Courses** (9 Credits)
SE 531 Software Organizational Management	EE 537 Wireless Communications
SE 532 Software Quality Management	SE 526 Network Software System I
SE 518 Software Project Management	SE 527 Network Software System II
Guided Electives (6 Credits)	**Guided Electives** (6 Credits)
BM 525 Management of Human Resources	CS 526 Performance Evaluation
BM 565 Management of Technology	CS 535 Telecommunications
SE 560 Software Risk Management	EE 505 Communications Technology
SE 565 Software Metrics	EE 581 Data Networks
	SE 513 Software System Security
	SE 598T Special Topics (Telecommunications)
Embedded Systems Track	**Information Management Track**
Required Courses (9 Credits)	**Required Courses** (9 Credits)
SE 526 Network Software System I	SE 541 Information Systems Architecture
SE 551 Real-Time Software Analysis and Spec.	SE 542 Information System Engineering
SE 552 Real-Time Software Design and Impl.	SE 518 Software Project Management
Guided Electives (6 Credits)	**Guided Electives** (6 Credits)
CS 525 Simulation	BM 520 Information System in Organisation
CS 526 Performance Evaluation	BM 565 Management of Technology
EE 509 Digital Signal Processing	BM 571 Introduction to US Health Care
SE 508 Software Implementation and Reuse	CS 517 Database Systems
SE 513 Software System Security	CS 530 Knowledge-Based Systems
SE 527 Network Software System II	SE 508 Software Implementation and Reuse
	SE 526 Network Software System I

Figure 3. The 1998 Curriculum

The Telecommunications track prepares students to become specialists in telecommunications. Topics of study include networks, software systems security, and evaluation of telecommunications systems.

The Embedded Systems track prepares students to become specialists in embedded systems development. Topics of study include specification and analysis of embedded real-time systems requirements, design and implementation of embedded real-time software systems, performance evaluation of embedded real-time software systems, and development of real-time components.

The Information Management track prepares students to become chief information officers or specialists in information systems integration and development. Topics of study include information technology management, specification and analysis of information systems, evaluation of information systems, and development of information systems software components.

Two of the former core courses, mathematical foundations of SE, and principles of SE, have been transformed into preparatory (bridge) courses (see Figure 3). Together with three other programming courses the "bridge" program is offered for students with an undergraduate major other than computer science, computer engineering, electrical engineering, or information systems. After taking the 15 credit preparatory courses and a one-semester project course, students can receive a certificate in software development.

2.5. 2002 Curriculum Changes

The 2002 curriculum added a new specialization track: the Management of Software Technology. It is offered in collaboration with the Monmouth University School of Business. The idea of this track grew out of the recognition that industry is outsourcing increasing amounts of software development. This track prepares students to be chief technology officers or specialists in the acquisition of software systems for businesses. Topics of study include assessing the impact that software can have on organizations, the development of requirements for system acquisition via purchase or outsourcing, the assessment of software technologies with regard to organizational needs, and implementing a controlled introduction of technology into an organization.

3. Continuous Development Of Course Content

Technologically, the computing field has undergone significant changes that have forced alterations in the material taught within Software Engineering courses. Since the inception of our SE Master's program, we have witnessed the wide-spread adoption of Object-Orientation (along with massive changes in techniques and methodologies), the phenomenal explosion of the World Wide Web, the emergence of Java, and the move of security requirements from corporate to consumer platforms, just to name a few of these changes. Therefore, the material covered within a curriculum that addresses the technological understanding required by professionals in this field, needs to be continuously updated over time.

This problem emerges in several different forms. In particular,
- Continuous Course Content Changes
- Dated Textbooks
- Operating System/Programming Language Bigotry
- Continuous Development Of Course Projects

Each of these areas is discussed in greater detail in the paragraphs that follow.

3.1. Course Content Changes

One can expect to have to revise course material every year. This is necessary to accommodate technological changes and to incorporate new industrial practices. For example, since the inception of our program we have changed the programming languages taught in class from Pascal to C, C++, and Java; we have added object-oriented analysis methods to the structured analysis methods in the requirements engineering course; in the design course we have made the transition from structured design to object-oriented design, component-based design, and architectural design. In the testing course we have added segments on testing applications that are constructed using commercial off-the-shelf (COTS) components and using automated testing and test management tools. For project management we have gradually introduced more content on the use of scheduling tools, such as MS project, risk simulators, like Risk+, and discussion of the use of buffer tasks in the planning of software development projects.

3.2. Dated Textbooks

As technology changes and software engineering evolves, the ability of texts to keep up with the changes is severely stressed. An instructor will find himself or herself utilizing three or four texts in order to properly cover a topic area. Books will seemingly contradict each other, only because they were published two years apart. Often, a book that is only three years old will contain many concepts that have been already superceded. Many excellent textbooks have not been updated to use current representations, such as UML, for example.

3.3. Operating System/Programming Language Bigotry.

Few topics seem to generate as much debate as the selection of which operating system or programming language should be the lingua franca for course work. It seems that everyone has an opinion or a realistic need to learn one environment over another. The selection of one environment over the other has significant impacts on the tools available for use by the instructor, the knowledge that the instructor has to bring into the classroom, and the equipment that must be maintained. In our case, over the years we have migrated from UNIX platforms, to Windows, and to dual-boot machines that run both Windows and Linux for a greater flexibility.

3.4. Continuous development of Course Projects

Faculty, students, and industry have universally recognized the need for hands-on experience. Without practical training, students and industry complain that the material will be too theoretical and that graduates would have trouble applying the theory to real world projects. This has led us to incorporate projects into the majority of courses taught in the program, while maintaining a balance between the theoretical and practical aspects of the courses. The projects are administered at the beginning of the semester, and have a couple of milestones spread along the semester. The instructors check the documents and/or software applications delivered at each milestone and provide feedback to the students. For some projects the problem to be solved is proposed by the instructor, for others, students can propose their own project theme. The members of the project teams are either established by the students, when they are not new to the program, or when no preferences are expressed, the instructor chooses the members. The teams have the authority to choose their leaders, and the roles each member will play in the team.

The introduction of projects into a Software Engineering course encompasses its own set of difficulties. While a simple program for shuffling cards may suffice to teach students about algorithms and data structures in a programming course, software engineering has to deal with much larger problems in order to demonstrate the value and need for an engineering process. The result is that projects have to be big, but not so big that they cannot be performed within the confines of the course. Because the project has to be big, it has to be structured such that the students can develop it as the course is presented.

As the course content, technology and available tools change, the course projects need to change too

4.Difficulties Attracting and Retaining Faculty

Software Engineers, even in the current difficult economic times, are a highly sought after commodity. It is extremely difficult for any software engineering program to both attract and retain their faculty. We noticed that the stability of the faculty makes a program more attractive to prospective students.

It is very difficult to attract appropriate faculty. In particular, faculty members usually have to be acquired from computer science backgrounds and/or from industrial practice. The problem with faculty from computer science backgrounds is that their backgrounds are in computer science rather than software engineering. The problem with acquiring faculty from industry is that often they do not have documented credentials and a documented trace of their scholarly work.

With the need to continuously update course content and curricula, to keep up or advance the state of the field, the load on a faculty member in software engineering tends to be significantly greater than in some other academic areas. Given that it is very difficult to hire faculty with the appropriate academic and industrial backgrounds, many of the hires are often non-tenure track. Thus, these faculty members can not be retained after their terms of contract. Faculty that have the appropriate backgrounds are in such high demand that they can have their choice of jobs. It is very difficult to retain faculty when they can be given higher visibility positions in Universities of their choosing.

The only real solution for the administration is to provide competitive salaries and support consulting activities. This enables faculty to make up any shortfalls in salary and keeps them active in industry. Faculty are also given one day a week to spend on research or consulting activities.

5.Diversity of the student body

In the 16-year history of the software engineering program at MU we have observed increasing diversity within the student population. The diversity spans several dimensions: educational background, employment status, educational goals and native language. The successful program must address all these dimensions of diversity.

5.1 Educational Backgrounds

Consistent with the origins of the program, many students in the graduate program achieved undergraduate degrees in computer science. These students have strong programming skills, but very seldom have the engineering discipline that emphasizes understanding the problem to be solved or the process to be followed. These students tend to immediately start coding once they receive a problem to be solved. Instructors have been asked on more than one occasion why it was necessary to design a program when they could write one faster.

We also have a large population of students that are coming into the graduate program from other engineering and non-engineering disciplines. These students usually are much more accepting of engineering processes, but have relatively weak programming skills and minimal knowledge about how computers function. To accommodate them we have had to incorporate a set of preparatory courses to provide the programming skills and computer knowledge necessary to succeed in the program.

We are expecting a new group of students to begin entering into the graduate program in two years. These students will have undergraduate degrees in software engineering and will already have a good understanding of engineering practices balanced with programming skills. At this point, we anticipate that our program will have to address increasingly more advanced software engineering topics that may be beyond the knowledge of the other two groups of students.

5.2 Employment Status

The employment status of students has significant impact on the program. It affects how long students are in the program, the effort that they put into assignments, their willingness to accept course material, and when classes are offered. It should be noted that (with a few exceptions) students entering into the program full-time usually find work at the end of their first year and become part-time students. The majority of our student population attends school part-time with full-time employment in the software industry. Most of our classes are offered in the early evening to accommodate them.

The fact that the average student is employed full-time and attends classes part-time means that they may be in the program for as long as 8 years. In fact, the population of students is much more stable than the curriculum. Some students have graduated on curriculums that have been replaced twice since they enrolled in the program.

Employment in the software industry has significant impact on the willingness of some students to accept the concepts taught in the classroom. These students have already acquired work habits that are not consistent with best practices. Students often state that they don't perform a particular engineering practice at work and that they don't see a need for it. Of course, many of these same students talk about how their projects at work tend to be chaotic. Other students report the difficulties they've encountered in trying to practice in their conservative organizations what they've learned in class. Either case tends to undermine the instructor in presenting new material in the classroom. Here is one of the situations where the industrial practice of the instructor plays an important role, in both selecting the material to be taught and in responding to student concerns regarding the usefulness in the real world of the topics learned.

Employed students also tend to focus on what they immediately need to succeed in today's workplace. There is often an insistence on learning a product (such as Oracle or Sybase) rather than the concepts (i.e., database principles). This emphasis on skill rather than knowledge runs counter to the goals of the program that are the development of software engineers who can lead their organizations into the future. We have included some of these products into our classrooms, but the main goals of the courses remain to teach the engineering principles of the field, which can be applied to a large number of products.

Students who are not employed in the industry have problems prioritizing the material being taught or placing it in the context of delivering a product. If they are required to know C++, they assume that all employers develop code in C++. They are often surprised when they get a job and discover that they will have to learn a new programming language. Students are occasionally concerned that courses cover many different methods and approaches to achieve a given goal rather than emphasize one method. They have to be taught to understand that the knowledge and skill they acquire in school will have to blend into whatever organization they join, and that they need to engage in a lifelong learning process that is inevitable in this dynamic field.

5.3 Educational Goals

It would be nice if all students entered the program with the desire and goal of becoming a software engineer and delivering a specific kind of product. However, the educational goals of the students range from wanting to know all about software and engineering to the other extreme where they only want to get the credentials that will allow them to earn a higher salary. Our student body appears to be driven by a small number of educational goals. These are:

- Get the business and process knowledge that will allow them to manage software projects and people.
- Get the skills and knowledge that will allow them to be more productive in their chosen career.
- Start a career in which they can have a significant income
- Get a job in the software field that does not involve a lot of coding.

The major impact of these goals concerns the subject areas that interest the student. We have had to tailor our curriculum to respond to these different goals. We find a significant fraction of the students are very interested in the process, project management, and organizational management courses. Others find that the courses on requirements and software testing gives them an entry point into a part of the software business that does not appear to require major coding efforts. Finally, the courses that emphasize specific types of software systems (real-time, information, and embedded systems) attract those students that are interested in gaining the particular knowledge and skills that will allow them to master their chosen field of work.

5.4 Communications Skills

There is significant diversity among our students in terms of their communication skills. However, communication skills are critical in software engineering. The average software engineering student will probably produce more documents and make more public presentations than the average English major. Communications have to be precise, unambiguous, complete, logically sound and well structured. Oral presentations have to convey complex information under time constraints. Students have to learn to gauge how much information is to be conveyed. This requires that they judge what their audience can be expected to know and what must be presented. Although typical undergraduate general education programs attempt to teach these skills most students who enter our graduate program require additional coaching and training in this area.

International students are often at a disadvantage due to the fact that English is their second language. This affects their writing ability where a weakness in vocabulary often prevents them from expressing themselves clearly and succinctly. It also undermines their confidence in public speaking due to concerns about their command of the language and fears that others will not understand them because of their accents.

International students are not the only ones with problems in communications. Many of the students, particularly those with computer science backgrounds, are not used to writing technical documents. While they may be good at writing code, they often have difficulties in expressing themselves succinctly in a written document.

The most direct approach to dealing with significant changes in the student population has been to adapt the curriculum and individual courses to meet the changing needs of our students. Employed students are encouraged to express their perspectives on the material so that their experiences can be shared with students that have yet entered the field. In some classes, programming assignments can be written in Java or C++ depending upon the students choice.

Another change has been the incorporation of more papers into course work so that our students get greater experience in writing. Papers are graded on technical content, structure, adherence to topic, and on the use of language. Corrections are suggested and students have a chance to resubmit corrected work.

6. Future Directions

Having looked at the past, it is now appropriate to look to the future for our program. In particular, we recognize a need for another set of changes. The introduction of an undergraduate software engineering program will have profound consequences on the graduate program, forcing severe changes in its curriculum. The redesigned curricula should allow the new graduates of the bachelors degree in software engineering to have the opportunity of extending their knowledge and skills to new frontiers.

With this respect, we plan on modifying our graduate program, such that the students with a bachelor's degree in SE will be required to take 7 elective SE courses and a 6-credit thesis. This would make our SE graduate program similar in structure to masters programs in electrical engineering, mechanical engineering, etc. throughout the United States.

Another issue, that is beyond the scope of this paper though, is the awareness of the influence that the licensing of software engineers shall have on the design of the undergraduate curriculum. However, the directions and discussions that are taking place with regard to licensing have to be followed so that appropriate changes can be implemented in the curriculum.

7. Conclusions

This paper has presented the main problems and lessons learned from one of the oldest programs in software engineering in the country. The evolution of the graduate curriculum over its 16 years of existence, as well as the first undergraduate curriculum, have been shown as an example for other colleges and universities considering the addition of a software engineering degree. We expect this evolution to continue in the future as the SE field is a continuously moving target, and as we will graduate the first class of bachelors in SE.

We have argued that the continuous update of the course content has a special meaning in software engineering, due to the dynamics of the field. With this respect, we have shown the impact of the advances in the field on the textbooks used, the need for continuous reevaluation of the chosen programming language, operating system, or software tools used in class.

Also, we have emphasized the importance of practice in a software engineering program, supported by several examples of current projects students are working on in their academic training.

The paper has shown the difficulties we have experienced in attracting and retaining the faculty over the years, due to the need of the new faculty to have both a record of scholarly accomplishments and industrial experience. The emphasis here is on the conjunction of these two requirements, which imposes great restrictions on the pool of available candidates.

Finally, we presented how various issues related to the diversity of the student body influence the curriculum and course content. As such, the educational backgrounds, employment status, educational goals, and communications skills of the student body are challenges any software engineering program has to solve.

As a measure of success of our continuous efforts to improve, we have seen the program enrollment increasing steadily, and doubling in the last three years. Apparently our strategy to continually update the program appears to be working, as mentioned by one of our alumni, Kevin McKee, VP Information Services - Health Network America, Eatontown, NJ: "The education I received while getting my Masters Degree in Software Engineering at Monmouth University has been invaluable. Not a day goes by when I do not use something that I learned in the program."

References

[Ard89] M. Ardis, G. Ford – "SEI Report on Graduate Software Engineering Education", *Proceedings of the Software Engineering Education Conference*, Springer-Verlag, 1989.

[Dar97] P. Dart, L. Johnston, C. Schmidt, L. Sonenberg – "Developing an Accredited SE Program", IEEE *Software*, Nov/Dec 1997, pp. 66-70.

[Hum97] W. Humphrey – "A Discipline of Software Engineering", *Addison Wesley*, 1997.

[McD00] J. McDonald – "Teaching Software Project Management in Industrial and Academic Environments", Proceedings of CSEE&T, 2000, pp. 151-160.

[Nau68] P. Naur, B. Randall (eds) - "Software Engineering: A report on a Conference Sponsored by the NATO Science Committee", NATO, 1968.

[Pow97] G.Powell, J. Diaz-Perrera, D. Turner – "Achieving Synergy in Collaborative Education", IEEE *Software*, Nov/Dec 1997, pp. 58-65.

[Ros00] D. Rosca – "An Active/Collaborative Approach in Teaching Requirements Engineering", *Proceedings of* FIE'00, pp. T2C9-12

[Ros01] D. Rosca, C. Li, K. Moore, M. Stephan, S. Weiner – "PSP-EAT – Enhancing a Personal Software Process Course", *Proceedings of* FIE'01, pp. T2D18

[StM00] Guide to the Software Engineering Body of Knowledge – Stone Man Version, SWEBOK, Feb. 2000, http://www.swebok.org/

Is Software Engineering Training Enough for Software Engineers?

Ivica Crnkovic, Rikard Land, Andreas Sjögren
Mälardalen University, Department of Computer Science and Engineering
PO Box 883, SE-721 23 Västerås, Sweden
{ivica.crnkovic, rikard.land, andreas.sjogren}@mdh.se
http://www.idt.mdh.se/{~icc,~rld,~ase}

Abstract

Most software engineering courses focus exclusively on the software development process, often referring to problems related to the complexity of software products and processes. In practice, however, many problems of a complex nature arise in which system engineering and other engineering disciplines are important in the development of systems. In such cases software engineers may have difficulty in coping with the entire problem, in the same way that engineers in other fields may have difficulty in understanding the software part. This suggests that the software engineering education of today is inadequate in certain respects. This paper presents a case study of a software engineering course and discusses the difficulty for computer science students to understand and to develop a system which also requires skills in engineering of a non-software nature.

1. Introduction

During recent years, as the use of software has increased and software has become more complex, there have been many discussions about education in software engineering, today and in the future [15,16]. The main challenge of such education is to prepare students for the "real world" [8,9,17], which is inconsistent, unpredictable, complex and always in a state of change. There are different approaches to meet this challenge; one example being the execution of projects based on real examples from industry [9]. Another approach is to "simulate" the real world by introducing a number of unpredictable obstacles into student exercises, the "dirty-tricks" method [10]. There are approaches which are focused on different areas of software engineering, such as requirements engineering, software design, validation and verification, others focused on the management of the complexity of products and processes. Surprisingly, the relation between software engineering and other engineering disciplines such as electrical engineering, mechanical engineering, different aspects of civil engineering is seldom discussed. In emerging as an independent discipline, software engineering has moved away from other classic engineering disciplines. The use of many classic engineering methods has been decreased or even removed from the software engineering curricula. While we can argue that this process is natural since there is no immediately apparent need for knowledge of classic engineering subjects for software development, we must also note that the frequency of project failure due to problems in software is significantly greater than that due to problems in other engineering disciplines. In too many cases the causes of failure originate in a misunderstanding of requirements, mismatches in system design and implementation, unrealistic expectations, and bad project planning [14]. The question is how much these problems are the results of a lack of formal engineering methods and procedures, and from the inability to manage the development of complex systems without using a systematic and analytical approach.

We believe that software engineering education should also include the training of future software developers in understanding and using (at least to some extent) the methods of classical engineering. We also believe that software engineers will increasingly encounter problems which are not of a pure software character, the software being only one part of a complex system. To understand the entire system, knowledge from pure software engineering will not be sufficient. Finally, we suggest that it is important to develop a culture of a systematic and analytical approach to the solution of problems, widely absent in the software community. For this reason we have updated our software engineering course for computer science students with additional elements: an analysis and modeling of a non-software system [1]. This gave us the possibility of analyzing the student's ability to cope with software and non-software related problems. This paper describes the experience from the course and suggests the importance of the inclusion of elements from other engineering disciplines in software engineering.

2. System Engineering vs. Software Engineering

In many products of today which embody the knowledge and skills of engineers from different fields, software is becoming the major and the most important part. Software increasingly controls the functionality and the overall behavior of the entire product. To develop these products successfully, extensive knowledge of software and of other engineering disciplines is required of the project team. However, understanding system requirements and their relation to software requirements remains one of the main difficulties in the development of computer-based systems [11]. It is not only because of the different nature of the requirements and characteristics of systems and software but also because of the different approaches to the development process [6]. A standard approach in a system development is a top-down approach; the system design beginning with the specification of the system architecture, the architecture defining the components and their interactions. Technologies and engineering methods from different engineering fields are then applied to the specification, design and development of components. While classical engineering disciplines follow this strict approach, software development process may be significantly differently. The top-down approach is often replaced by a bottom-up approach, sequential development processes are often experienced as non-appropriate models, and evolutionary models (incremental, rapid-prototype, spiral model, etc.) are used. Software developers have no strong culture of exact and formal specification. This incompatibility of approaches causes the mismatching of requirements, specifications and finally in the products. Our opinion is that this difficulty can be alleviated to a degree by making "system thinking" more explicit in software engineering courses, as we describe.

3. Case Study: Software Engineering Course

The software engineering course we analyze here [7] was attended by computer science students. They have attended basic courses in mathematics but very few courses that are parts of traditional engineering curricula, for example physics. The course concerned was presented during one semester and was divided into two parts: the first half of the course consisting of lectures and labs; the second half being devoted to project work. In the project phase, the students worked in independent groups with large grade of freedom, but the milestones and final results were specified by the teachers who also were involved in the project as customers and a steering group.

In the project, the two main elements given specially attention were a system analysis and architectural issues. The goal was to give the students an understanding of the need for a formal specification, based on the engineering methods associated with the system being developed.

3.1 The System Engineering Problem

The main idea of the project was to give students a problem not of a pure software character and which it would not be possible to solve by software development alone. The main assignment was to explain the capsize of the Vasa, a 17th century Swedish warship [2] and to develop a simulation model which would visualize the stability of the Vasa, or a user-configured ship [1].

Stability calculations are derived from basic forces of physics: gravity and buoyancy. Due to limited space, we do not explain the details, but Figure 1 visualizes the forces in action and the interaction between these. W denotes the wind force, G the gravity force, B the buoyancy force, and h the horizontal projection of the distance between the centers of gravity and buoyancy. The ship stops heeling in a position at which the forces and torques (leverage effects) are in a state of equilibrium. In case a) shown in the figure the resulting force will keep the ship in a stable position while in case b) the ship will capsize.

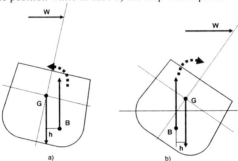

Figure 1.   Stable and unstable attitudes of a ship

3.2 The Project Assignments

During the project work period the students were required to analyze the problem to be solved, define and process requirements, and design and implement the system. The project work was focused on project planning, process measurement, teamwork, and an analysis of the work performed. In addition to "standard" assignments such as project management and negotiating with a "customer", two specific requirements were added:

- _Modifiability._ The system was required to be designed and implemented in such a way that it would be easy to modify. The students were expected to refine this requirement and describe how they intended to accomplish this, and analyze how well they succeeded.
- _Mathematical Model._ The mathematical model used for stability calculations was to be documented, and its correctness and accuracy analyzed.

The aim of these two additional requirements was to make the students familiar with long-term requirements and with quality issues.

4. The Students' Project Work

The project was to serve as an experiment. It was to indicate the ability of computer science students to cope with more complex problems related to a) software engineering and b) other engineering disciplines. The project was to show if the students are able to achieve similar results (i.e. a similar level of quality) in solving problems of a similar degree of difficulty but related to other domains than software engineering. It was also to investigate the student's ability to cope with unfamiliar problems as is very likely in their professional life. We shall concentrate on these additional requirements in the following.

4.1 Modifiability

The students discussed modifiability in two senses:

- In a general sense, by using e.g. a design pattern [12] and an architecture [3,5] that are believed to support modifiability, by using an object-oriented approach, or by establishing coding guidelines, structuring the code commenting it well etc.

– In a more specific sense, by assuming particular future changes which are more probable, and preparing their design for these modifications (similar to the way scenarios are used in the Software Architecture Analysis Method, SAAM [3,13]).

It was apparently difficult for the students to understand "modifiability" and the groups succeeded to different degrees. All of the groups had a modifiability requirement in their requirements document; however, when refining it, there were quite different approaches. Two groups explained modifiability with both a general description and a description of specific changes which could be used to test whether the system was modifiable.

In the design documentation, we expected to see documentation of the design decisions that were motivated by the modifiability requirements, according to the groups' own definitions in the requirements document. Three groups provided no explanation of how they had achieved modifiability, two groups showed how it was possible to implement the particular scenarios they had specified in the requirements document (although one group omitted their most interesting scenarios – making the system non-web-based and changing calculation model – and instead focused on "lower-level" scenarios, e.g. how to add a new deck), and one group explained that the system was modifiable both through their choice of architecture and through specific scenarios. Only one group discussed modifiability elsewhere than in a separate section, which might imply that they had a slightly deeper understanding of the issue.

The groups' achievements are summarized in Table 1.

Table 1: A summary of how the six groups treated modifiability

Group No:		1	2	3	4	5	6
Requirements Specification	General	x	-	-	x	-	x
	Specific scenarios	-	x	x	x	x	x
Design Specification	General	x	-	-	-	-	-
	Specific scenarios	x	-	-	x	x	-

We can conclude that the students achieved a certain understanding of modifiability. While they understood the requirements and to some extent their design was influenced by these requirements, they showed less ability in analyzing and explicitly documenting their decisions. The design was more "construction" oriented than property-oriented.

4.2 Mathematical Model

The most interesting, and complicated, part of the system was its ability to visualize the stability of a proposed ship. A part of the assignment was to develop the configuration of the ship: a ship can be built with different numbers of decks, different numbers of guns per deck, with or without ammunition and with different amounts of ballast. These configuration parameters and the form of the ship determine the center of mass of the ship. The center of buoyancy is defined by the shape, weight and heel angle of the ship.

Given a certain wind speed, the resulting heel angle of the ship can be determined. At some wind speed, the ship will capsize. The students thus had to develop and implement a mathematical model of the physics involved. To help the students, we gave a separate lecture describing the model and the basic physical principles such as methods for calculating the center of mass and the equilibrium state of an object.

4.2.1 The Models: The main difficulty was the determination of the center of buoyancy, which is at the center of the area of the displaced water. The shape of the cross section of that part of the ship under water when the ship is heeling may be quite complicated. However, it is possible to divide this area into a set of simple geometrical forms, and then its center can be calculated from the geometrical centers of these forms. The students thus had to model the ship's shape, take into account the heel angle, and by geometrical means divide the area into a set of simple shapes, find their the geometrical centers and from them calculate the geometrical center of the complete area.

The students specified basically three types of models:

- Four groups approximated the shape of the ship to a rectangle and calculated the center of buoyancy in either of two different ways, as shown in Figure 2A and 2B.
- One group approximated the shape to a rectangle with the corners "cut off". To find the center of the area they approximated the area using vertical bars, as shown in Figure 2C. Using this strategy, it would have been possible to choose a more realistic shape and – with more subdivisions of the polygon – any level of detail of the area of displaced water, but the group chose this very simple shape without further analysis.
- The last group also approximated the area as that specified by a set of points in the coordinate system, but used a simple but elegant method to approximate the shape of the ship: they superimposed a cross-section of the ship on a coordinate system and obtained a number of coordinates (arbitrarily chosen). The area was then divided into triangles, which made it easy to find the center of buoyancy. See Figure 2D.

Figure 2. The shapes and the calculation principles of the area of the ship's crosscut.

It is quite apparent that the calculations needed when using only three triangles (as in 2A) are not significantly less complex than those needed using several triangles (as in 2D), but that the latter approach will give a much more exact result. There were thus no implementation reasons for the students to choose a solution with a simple approximation of the shape of the ship – the calculations needed still required a sequence of calculations of coordinates. This observation leads us to believe that the students had decided that "just choosing a very simple shape of the ship will make the mathematics and the implementation easier" – which is a misconception. Furthermore, there are no signs that they even considered other alternatives. They had learned the basic physics from a lecture and then used the most direct method of approximating the shape of the ship in their determination of the center of buoyancy.

5.2.2 Documenting the Models: As the projects proceeded, the steering group and the customer were somewhat surprised that no group documented their model – nor were there any descriptions given of how they approximated the shape of the ship nor of how they divided the area under water into simpler shapes. Therefore, in the middle of the project, we requested documentation of their model, and the performance of some kind of analysis or verification of the accuracy of their model. The most common reaction to this was that they were now assigned an additional task in the middle of the project – which they felt to be unfair. From project documentation and group meetings during the project, there is no sign of any group having begun their project work by even considering that they should evaluate the mathematical model they found or developed – many of them did not understand they had already developed a model. Only one group began immediately the documentation requested; presenting satisfactory documentation the next week; the other groups did not document the model until the very last week of the project.

Three groups at first documented their model by describing the algorithm they had implemented, two groups using flowcharts and one group a pseudo-code. Although this was a good beginning, they did not perceive that they should also document the model as such.

5.2.3 Analyzing the Models: We did not expect any major analysis or verification of their models; we considered it sufficient to use one example of a ship fully equipped (one particular set of cannons etc.), using the original Vasa data. The crucial approximation incorporated in the models is that of the ship's shape, which affects the center of buoyancy and the center of mass. One means of verifying the model considered was to model the ship's shape more exactly (for this single case) and to find the center of buoyancy and the torque through some advanced method, analytical or numerical, available in some powerful mathematics program. One would then expect the students to analyze the consequences of a set of heel angles by comparing the torque of their model with that of "reality" – or at least as close to reality as possible. It would then be easy to present the accuracy of their model in a plot such as that schematically shown in Figure 3 in which they would indicate the differences in calculation of their model with a "real" model. Additional analysis would include a study of the difference between the critical angles with different wind speeds and different configurations of the ship.

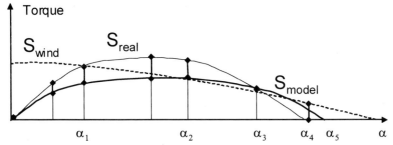

Figure 3.A schematic plot showing an analysis of the model.

The group that had approximated the ship's shape most closely (Figure 2D) used another approach: they verified their method, not their model. They approximated another shape, a hull with a semicircular cross section shaped as a semicircle, with 10 points, and compared the exact area (simple to calculate for a semicircle) with the approximated shape, as a number of triangles. However, they did not analyze the effect of the number of points on the accuracy – how much would 20 points have improved the accuracy? But this example shows a typical engineering approach; if you cannot calculate (or do not know how to calculate), use measurements from a particular case. Similarly, the group using the shape presented in Figure 2C did not analyze the effects of a larger number of coordinates on the accuracy.

Two of the groups had a smarter and more scientific and engineering approach. Using a recognized formula for calculating the torque, given the wind speed [4], they compared the results thus obtained with those they obtained by their own method, one group used two different wind speeds, the other one only (4 m/s, that when the Vasa capsized). This should be considered a respectable analysis, although we would have preferred the analysis of a larger number of heel angles or wind speeds.

One group performed a series of comparisons with different wind speeds, but compared their rectangular cross section hull not with a "real" ship but with a ship with a semi-circular cross section; they seemed to understand that this was not a verification, only a comparison between two crude approximations, but this was the best idea they had. This approach would show how close are the different approximations and assuming that the real shape is something between these two shapes, the correct result would probably lie between these approximations.

The other verifications did not reach this level. Two groups made a drawing of their rectangular ship and of the real ship (from a photo) on a graph paper, and counted the number of squares covered by the ship. Needless to say, this was a very inexact verification – perhaps more inexact than their model? One group performed no analysis or verification at all; they only discussed briefly the difficulty of modeling the ship sufficiently accurately.

Our impression is that this task proved difficult for the students to understand. Not all of them seemed to understand the purpose of verifying the model in this way at all. Others understood the purpose of such an analysis, but had no idea of how it was to be performed.

And we daresay that not until the end did some of the students realize that such an analysis could have been used at the beginning of the project to choose a suitable model.

The groups' models and their verifications are summarized in Table 2.

Table 2: A summary of how the six groups verified their mathematical models.

Group No:	1	2	3	4	5	6
Shape of ship	⊔	⊔	∪	⊔	⊔	∪
Checked paper	x	x	-	-	-	-
Center of Buoyancy[1]	x	-	-	-	x	-
Verification of method	-	-	-	x	-	x

[1]The center of buoyancy was compared with the formula found in [4].

6. Conclusion

The students knew quite well how to design and implement software to fulfill requirements; all groups produced design documents that were at least acceptable. The execution of the project was also satisfactory with very good teamwork. The issue of modifiability was seemingly harder; they understood that software should be easy to modify since one can always expect new requirements or changing environments, but it was hard for the students to know how to make the requirement of the software being modifiable more specific, and to show that they had succeeded. Finally, all groups certainly implemented a model of a ship; but its documentation and analysis was obviously a hard assignment.

Of course, students of computer science have limited experience in physics, so it is perhaps unfair to expect them to perform equally well in the physical modeling as the software modeling. However, although a physics student could be expected to implement a better model or a better numerical algorithm (and probably have problems with the software part), our point is rather that the students easily lost sight of the software as (part of) a system. They happily performed a software design and implemented it, and we had in general no serious remarks on their project work, but they seemed to view the software without reflecting on the result from a system perspective.

What are the lessons learned from the course result? We can discern at least two:

- *Previous education.* Two and a half years of studying computer science or computer engineering at university level had not given them "system thinking"; they focused on the software and the project work.
- *Teachers.* The assistants, at first, neither appreciated the importance of the model nor its documentation; they probably gave the impression that this was indeed a "new assignment" which turned up in the middle of the project. They had thus finished their education without sufficient awareness of system thinking! The main teacher, being also the customer, did not explicitly state the requirements of model and analysis and did not place them within the perspective of computer science students. This was an exemplary case of a misunderstanding between stakeholders due to different assumptions.

Execution of a project is today an established part of most Software Engineering courses [1,7,8,10,14-17]. Such projects usually cover different phases, from the requirements elicitation and specification to the implementation, validation and verification. We can designate these parts as "Software Engineering centric" tasks, as opposed to what we would prefer to call "System-Engineering centric" tasks. We claim that the focus on modifiability (and on other non-functional properties) requires more of a holistic and system perspective. The tasks that require particular knowledge from other engineering or basic disciplines such as physics and mathematical modeling (and analysis) can be denoted as "Domain Engineering centric" tasks. We argue that these parts are even more difficult for software engineers (see Figure 4).

When the students leave university, many of them will build software systems that are a part of larger systems – mechanical systems, electronics systems, web sites, etc. So, we arrive at a very serious question: are they prepared for this task? Will they be able to create "good systems", or will they be limited to creating "good software"? We believe that software engineers and students of computer science should have more insight into engineering disciplines other than pure software engineering.

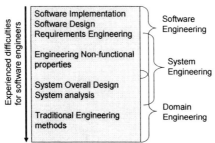

Figure 4. The difficulty of performing engineering tasks for software engineers

7. References

[1] *Mälardalen University, Software Engineering Course*, URL: http://www.idt.mdh.se/kurser/cd5360/, 2002

[2] *The Vasa Museum*, URL: http://www.vasamuseet.se/indexeng.html, 2002

[3] Bass L., Clements P. and Kazman R., *Software Architecture in Practice*, Addison-Wesley, 1998.

[4] Borgenstam K. and Sandström A., *Why Vasa capsized*, Vasa Museum, 1995.

[5] Bushmann F., Meunier R., Rohnert H., Sommerlad P., and Stal M., *Pattern-Oriented Software Architecture - A System of Patterns*, John Wiley & Sons, 1996.

[6] Crnkovic I., "Component-based Software Engineering: Building Systems from Software Components", In *Proceedings of 26th Computer Software and Application Conference (COMPSAC)*, IEEE, 2002.

[7] Crnkovic I., Larsson M., and Lüders F., "Implementation of a Software Engineering Course for Computer Science Students", In *Proceedings of 7th Asia-Pacific Software Engineering Conference (APSEC)*, 2000.

[8] Daniels M., Faulkner X., and Newman I., "Open ended group projects, motivating students and preparing them for the 'real world'", In *Proceedings of 15th Conference on Software Engineering Education and Training (CSEE&T)*, IEEE, 2002.

[9] Dawson R.J., Newsham R. W., and Fernley B. W., Bringing the 'real world' of software engineering to university undergraduate courses, *Software Engineering.IEE Proceedings*, volume 144, issue 5, 1997.

[10] Dawson R., "Twenty Dirty Tricks to Train Software Engineers", In *Proceedings of 22nd International Conference on Software Engineering (ICSE)*, ACM, 2000.

[11] Farbman White S., Melhart B. E., and Lawson H. W., Engineering Computer-based Systems: Meeting the Challenge, *IEEE Computer*, volume 34, issue 11, 2001.

[12] Gamma E., Helm R., Johnson R., and Vlissidies J., *Design Patterns - Elements of Reusable Object-Oriented Software*, Addison-Wesley, 1995.

[13] Kazman R., Bass L., Abowd G., and Webb M., "SAAM: A Method for Analyzing the Properties of Software Architectures", In *Proceedings of The 16th International Conference on Software Engineering*, 1994.

[14] Pfleeger S. L., *Software Engineering, Theory and Practice*, Prentice-Hall, Inc., 1998.

[15] Shaw M., We Can Teach Software Better, *Computing Research News*, volume 4, issue 4, 1992.

[16] Shaw M., "Software Engineering Education: A Roadmap", In *Proceedings of 22nd International Conference on Software Engineering (ICSE)*, ACM, 2000.

[17] Wohlin C. and Regnell B., "Achieving industrial relevance in software engineering education", In *Proceedings of 12th Conference on Software Engineering Education and Training*, IEEE, 1999.

Software Engineering Curriculum 3
(Paper Session E)

vgl ISO-Standards?

Teaching Ethics in the Software Engineering Curriculum

Elizabeth Towell
Carroll College, 100 N. East Avenue, Waukesha, WI 53186
etowell@cc.edu

Abstract

This paper describes a pilot study conducted to explore the teaching of ethics in Software Engineering programs. The author reviewed existing literature and then constructed a tentative survey, which was sent to 127 educators. Questions involved ethical topics encountered, methods of delivery, and the use of codes of ethics. Results provide only an informal snapshot of trends but responses are being used to create a revised survey, which will be sent to a larger population.

1. Introduction

Webster defines ethics as "1: a branch of philosophy, dealing with what is good and bad and with moral duty and obligation, 2: the principles of moral conduct governing an individual or a group." The study of ethics includes meta-ethics (general principles), moral theory (ethical systems consisting of criteria and procedures) and practical or applied ethics (the application of ethical systems to situations) [6]. The teaching of ethics in professional programs is generally focused on practical or applied ethics.

This manuscript explores the study of ethics in Software Engineering programs. We attempt to address the why, what and how questions of current ethics education. In addition to conducting a literature review, one hundred and twenty-seven previous CSEET conference attendees in academic positions were sent a questionnaire via email regarding teaching ethics. Thirty-six responses were received (28.3%). Undergraduate programs as well as graduate programs were represented, predominantly in Computer Science and Software Engineering fields. School sizes ranged widely but the greatest number of respondents were from larger schools with over 10,000 students. Most respondents were from North America but responses were also received from Asia, Australia, and Europe. The results cannot be construed to reflect any population other than recent CSEET attendees but they may provide an informal snapshot of trends.

The paper is organized in six sections following this introduction. In section two, we distinguish what is meant by ethics for the purposes of this paper and provide basic assumptions made by the author. In section three, specific ethics topics encountered in Software Engineering curricula are addressed. Section four explores methods of delivery for teaching ethical decision-making. Section five outlines the codes of ethics of various professional computing organizations. Section six explores the relationship of a code of ethics and professional conduct. The final section presents questions and conclusions that have been drawn from the study.

1093-0175/03 $17.00 © 2003 IEEE

2. Basic assumptions

The general goals of teaching ethics in any venue include deterrence, inspiration and guidance, and a shared understanding of ethical norms and expectations. This paper is premised on the specific assumption that facing ethical dilemmas is an integral part of a Software Engineer's career and that academia should prepare Software Engineers for this aspect of their career. Evidence that this is a widely held belief can be found in accreditation standards for Software Engineering programs. In the US, institutions seeking accreditation in engineering related programs by the Accreditation Board for Engineering and Technology (ABET) initially complete a self-study. Applicants are asked to answer this question, "Describe how this program assures the development of an understanding of the ethical, social, and economic considerations in professional practice" [1]. The model accreditation criteria for Software Engineering undergraduate programs established by the Education Task Force of the Joint Steering Committee of the IEEE Computer Society and ACM also specifies, "engineering responsibility and practice must be stressed, which includes conveying ethical, social, legal, economic and safety issues. These concerns must be reinforced in advanced work, as must the appropriate use of Software Engineering standards" [14].

A second assumption of this paper is that the teaching of Software Engineering ethics must necessarily focus on the process involved in the production of a software product. The concept of Software Engineering ethics should be distinguished from the myriad of abuses that occur via the use of a computer. As Gotterbarn [10] indicates, if any use of a computer to commit a crime can be construed as a case involving computer ethics, "then my use of a scalpel to rob someone is a problem of medical ethics." If we start with too big of a concept it becomes everybody's concern and nobody's business. Furthermore, there is a difference between what is ethical and what is illegal or should be made illegal. It may not be illegal to subtly undermine the efforts of programmers on your team but it is clearly unethical. We can break the law for ethical reasons and we can follow the law for reasons other than ethical ones. The following section continues to refine the context for what is meant by ethics topics in the Software Engineering curriculum.

3. Ethics topics covered in the Software Engineering curriculum

A review of books, case studies, and journal articles was used to generate a set of ethics topics that are routinely taught in Computer Science and Software Engineering programs. These topics are briefly defined in **Table 1**. The definitions cannot be considered comprehensive and there is obvious overlap among the topics. The grouping together of topics may also be arguable.

The results from the survey of recent CSEET attendees are shown in **Figure 1**. The survey asked respondents to rate each ethical area as *critical, important* or *unimportant* with respect to coverage in their program. The percent of respondents that believed that coverage of a specific topic was *critical* is shown. (It is interesting to note that in only two cases out of the nine, did a majority of the respondents think that coverage of the topic was critical: 1) quality and testing and 2) liability and risks in health and safety critical environments.) The three topics with the largest number of *unimportant* ratings were: encryption and privacy, fairness and discrimination, and whistle-blowing.

Table 1. Ethics topics in the Software Engineering curriculum

Confidentiality involves the control of information about an individual or an organization provided to an entrusted party.
Conflict of interest involves avoiding compromised decision-making due to offers of financial or other considerations.
Encryption and privacy involves communication of secret information and the bounds of governmental access for the public good.
Fairness and discrimination involves conditions of employment and equality of opportunity.
Intellectual property involves ownership of software, data, and ideas as well as the related legal protections such as copyrights, patents, trademarks, and oaths of confidentiality.
Liability and risks in health and safety critical environments involves legal obligations to protection of the quality of life and the environment.
Quality and testing involves the appropriate comparison of expected and observed behavior of software systems.
Unauthorized access and computer security involves the authorized use of computers and communications.
Whistle-blowing involves rights and responsibilities in terms of making revelations which call attention to threats to the public interest.

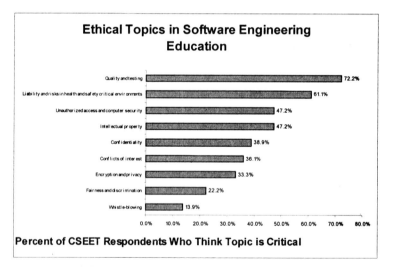

Figure 1. Ethical topics in Software Engineering education and the percent of CSEET respondents that believe the coverage is critical in a software development program

Other topics that were added by respondents included employment agreements, trade secrets, commercial integrity, professional responsibility, research ethics, measurement-related ethics and measurement dysfunction, power relationships, clear thinking about ethical responsibility, social impact and professional responsibility to society, internationalization, and data protection.

4. Methods for Teaching Ethics in a Professional Program

It is difficult to find definitive advice on how the teaching of ethics is best accomplished. What are the most critical topics (or are they all equally critical)? Curricular models do not address this. How are they best explored? There are limited standards in this area as well. Kevin Bowyer [7] offers this suggestion: ethics should be taught in three ways: discussion of real-world case studies, participation in active learning (exercises), and reading papers by distinguished authors.

The top five methods used from survey results are shown in **Figure 2** below. The most popular techniques were discussing personal experiences and discussing codes of ethics. Other methods employed that were mentioned included guest speakers, news articles, simulations, and risk forums. **Figure 3** gives a general indication of classroom time devoted to teaching ethics. Almost twenty-eight percent of respondents to this survey indicated that less than 1% of classroom time was devoted to teaching ethics. This would equate to less than half an hour total in a three-contact-hour class that meets for 15 weeks.

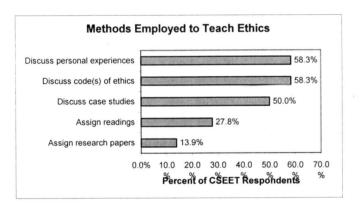

Figure 2. Methods used by CSEET attendees to teach ethics

The survey also queried how ethics instruction should be distributed throughout a program. One could argue that ethical behavior, like "proper documentation" or "logical analysis" is not a topic that can be or should be separated or isolated from the rest of the curriculum. **Figure 4** provides a snapshot of how ethics instruction is distributed throughout the curriculum in programs represented by CSEET attendees responding to the survey. Most respondents indicated that the teaching of ethics is focused in a few courses. (This might provide some explanation for the results in **Figure 3**.) Surprisingly, over 19% of the respondents indicated that the teaching of ethics in their curriculum is largely ignored.

154

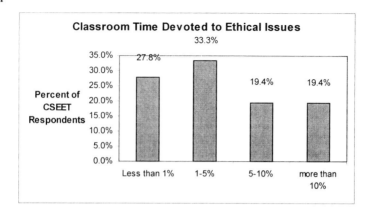

Figure 3. Classroom time devoted to ethical issues

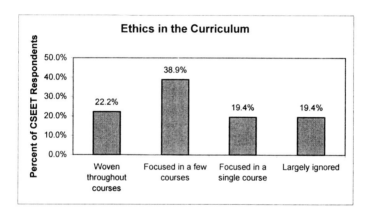

Figure 4. How ethics instruction is distributed throughout the curriculum

5. Codes of Ethics

A very popular technique for teaching ethics involves review of a published code of ethics. Nearly every professional computing organization has published a code of ethics. A brief description of seven prominent codes of ethics in the computing professions is provided in **Table 2**. A code of ethics is used to promote a variety of purposes and goals. Luegenbiehl [13] identifies 12 overlapping functions that can be served by a code of ethics: symbolize professionalism, protect group interests, specify membership etiquette, inspire good conduct, educate members, discipline members, foster external relations, enumerate principles, express ideals, put forth rules, offer guidelines, and codify rights.

CSEET attendees that responded to the survey indicated that they were most familiar with these codes: ACM, IEEE Computer Society, and the Software Engineering Code of Ethics and Professional Practice (adopted by ACM and the IEEE). Other codes named included National

Society of Professional Engineers, Engineering Council, Institution of Electrical Engineers, Southeast Asia Regional Computer Confederation and Computer Society of South Africa.

6. The Relationship of a Code of Ethics and Professional Conduct

Software Engineering is becoming a recognized profession both from societal pressures and within the ranks [11]. ACM and IEEE are working jointly to establish criteria and norms for the professional practice of Software Engineering. Three task forces have been formed to provide a foundation for this daunting goal. They are charged with 1) defining the Software Engineering Body of Knowledge (SWEBOK), 2) defining ethical and professional standards, and 3) defining educational curricula. These three pieces are highly related. The current version of SWEBOK [17] provides many examples of the emerging discipline of Software Engineering including the following:

- Universities throughout the world now offer undergraduate degrees in Software Engineering.
- The Accreditation Board for Engineering and Technology (ABET) and the Computing Science Accreditation Board (CSAB) have reached an agreement to cooperate in the accreditation of Software Engineering programs in the US.
- SEI's Capability Maturity Model for Software and ISO-9000 standards are now used to assess organizational capability for Software Engineering.
- The Software Engineering Code of Ethics and Professional Practice has been adopted by the ACM and the IEEE Computer Society. This code is intended to be one of three pieces that together will form criteria and norms for professional practice of Software Engineering.
- The Texas Board of Professional Engineers, the Association of Professional Engineers and Geoscientists of British Columbia (APEGBC) and the Professional Engineers of Ontario (PEO) have all established requirements for the licensing of Software Engineers.

The general nature of a professional organization is to confer privileges on its members (such as licensing) and to conduct disciplinary action for misconduct (such as disenfranchisement). Does this movement towards Software Engineering as a profession and the cooperation and consolidation of professional organizations signal a movement towards licensing of the profession? This seems to be the case, at least in the United States, where the title of engineer is protected and the practice of other forms of engineering is restricted. It is clear that one purpose of the development of SWEBOK is to establish a body of knowledge that license holders will need to possess. Equally clear is that one purpose of the Software Engineering Code of Ethics is to establish guidelines for disciplinary action involving license holders. The licensing of Software Engineers is a contentious issue. For example, in the survey taken for this study, 44% thought Software Engineering should be a licensed profession, 39% thought it should not be a licensed profession, and the remaining 17% were ambiguous for various reasons or undecided.

156

TABLE 2. Codes of ethics for various professional computing societies
(NOTE: this table has been abbreviated due to the proceedings page limitation)

Association for Computing Machinery (ACM) [2]
Canadian Information Processing Society (CIPS) [8]
New Zealand Computer Society (NZCS) [15]
Software Engineering Code of Ethics and Professional Practice 5.2 [16]
Australian Computer Society (ACS) [3]
British Computer Society (BCS) [4,5]
Institute of Electrical and Electronics Engineers (IEEE) [12]

7. Conclusions and Future Research

We teach ethics in a professional academic program for a variety of reasons including developing a shared understanding of ethical norms and expectations. Accrediting bodies in the Software Engineering field reinforce this notion in specific language calling for ethical consideration in the curriculum. Even if we are not seeking accreditation, we teach ethics because we realize that to do something well a student must not only develop good intellectual habits, he or she must also nurture good ethical habits as well.

There are a variety of topics and a variety of modes employed to cover ethical issues in Software Engineering programs. The data in this study suggests that quality and reliability issues are considered to be of greatest importance. These issues are often explored through discussion of personal experience, case studies, or review of codes of ethics. Three codes that are widely recognized are those of the ACM, the IEEE, and Software Engineering Code of Ethics adopted more recently by both ACM and IEEE. These codes seem aimed at the development of Software Engineering as a profession and the establishment of guidelines for disciplinary action involving license holders.

This paper was written for presentation and discussion at CSEET and is exploratory in nature. The population that was surveyed (CSEET attendees) involves an obvious bias and the number of responses was somewhat limited. For these reasons, more significant analysis of the data at this time is not warranted. Still, much has been learned that will be used as the manuscript is expanded. Future efforts will include:
1) Collection of more data from academicians to study
   a) the relationship between time spent teaching ethics and factors such as size of school and type of program;
   b) the relationship between time spent teaching ethics and factors such as support for the licensing of Software Engineers and accreditation status
2) Collection of data from practitioners to determine ethical areas considered most critical for inclusion
3) Development of a model for testing the effectiveness of different styles of teaching ethical conduct in Software Engineering program

References

[1] ABET, Applied Science Accreditation, 2002. "Volume I Self-Study Questionnaire 2002-3 Edition," Available http://www.abet.org/info_prgs_rac.html downloaded July 3, 2002.

[2] ACM, 2002. "ACM Code of Ethics and Professional Conduct," Available http://www.acm.org/constitution/code.html downloaded July 3, 2002.

[3] ACS, 2002. "Australian Computer Society Code of Ethics," Available http://www.acs.org.au/static/national/pospaper/acs131.htm downloaded July 3, 2002.

[4] BCS, 2002a. "BCS Code of Practice," Available http://www1.bcs.org.uk/homepages/533/ downloaded July 3, 2002.

[5] BCS, 2002b. "BCS Code of Conduct," Available http://www1.bcs.org.uk/homepages/518/ downloaded, July 3, 2002.

[6] Bott, F., Coleman, A., Eaton, J., Rowland, A. 2001. "Professional Issues in Software Engineering," 3rd edition, Taylor and Francis, p. 10.

[7] Bowyer, K. 2001. "Ethics and Computing, Living Responsibly in a Computerized World," IEEE Press.

[8] CIPS, 2002. "Code of Ethics & Standards of Conduct," Available http://www.cips.ca/about/ethics/ downloaded July 3, 2002.

[9] Gotterbarn, D., Miller, K., Rogerson, S. 1999. "Computer Society and ACM Approve Software Engineering Code of Ethics," Computer, October, pp. 84-88.

[10] Gotterbarn, D. 2002a. "Computer Ethics: Responsibility Regained [Online] Available http://www-cs.etsu-tn.edu/gotterbarn/artpp1.htm downloaded June 19, 2002

[11] Gotterbarn, D. 2002b. "An Evolution of Computing's Codes of Ethics and Professional Conduct," Available http://www-cs.etsu.edu/gotterbarn/artge1.htm downloaded June 19, 2002.

[12] IEEE, 2002. "IEEE Code of Ethics," Available http://www.shop.ieee.org/organizations/eab/apc/ceaa/operations/code_of_ethics.htm downloaded July 3, 2002.

[13] Luegenbiehl, H.C. "Computer Professionals: Moral Autonomy and a Code of Ethics," Journal of Systems and Software, Volume 17, 1992, pp. 61-68.

[14] Model Accreditation Criteria, 2002. "Model Accreditation Criteria For Software Engineering Undergraduate Programs," Available from the Education Task Force of the Joint Steering Committee of the IEEE Computer Society and ACM at http://www.computer.org/tab/seprof/Accreditation.html, downloaded July 3, 2002.

[15] NZCS, 2002. "The New Zealand Computer Society, Inc. Code of Ethics & Professional Conduct," Available http://www.nzcs.org.nz/membership/membership.htm downloaded July 3, 2002.

[16] Software Engineering Code, 2002. "Software Engineering Code of Ethics and Professional Practice, Version 5.2" Available http://www.computer.org/tab/seprof/code.htm downloaded July 3, 2002.

[17] SWEBOK, 2001. "Guide to the Software Engineering Body of Knowledge, Trial Version 1.00," Available http://www.swebok.org/ downloaded July 3, 2002.

Reviewing the Curriculum of Software Engineering Undergraduate Courses to Incorporate Communication and Interpersonal Skills Teaching

Vinícius Manhães Teles
Universidade Federal do Rio de Janeiro
Núcleo de Computação Eletrônica
vinicius@improveit.com.br

Carlo Emmanoel Tolla de Oliveira
Universidade Federal do Rio de Janeiro
Núcleo de Computação Eletrônica
carlo@ufrj.br

Abstract

The major problems of software development projects are not so much technical as sociological in nature. The industry seems to agree very much with this statement while the university seems to give it little importance. The article begins analyzing some related work and proposes changes in software engineering undergraduate courses to accommodate new ways of teaching and to incorporate professional skills teaching. It also describes a course on extreme programming where some techniques will be used and evaluated.

1. Introduction

The main emphasis of Computer Science courses is the development of technical skills by students undertaking the course (IEEE/ACM *cited in* Pham, 1997). This focus on technical skills poses problems for future professionals when they are supposed to build information systems where their activities are part of a team effort. According to DeMarco et al. [1] since they work in teams and projects and other tightly knit working groups, they are mostly in the human communication business. Their successes stem from good human interactions by all participants in the effort.

Researches conduced in Australia seem to confirm the statement above. In Australia, surveys of employers have shown that the qualities they consistently rate most highly in graduates relate to their communication skills, their ability to work together in teams and their technical writing skills, besides their basic technical knowledge. (Business Higher Education Round Table and Department of Employment, Education and Training *cited in* Keen, 1998)

The Business/Higher Education Round Table, Australia conducted a survey in 1992 in which both business and university were asked to rank the desired characteristics of university graduates. The results are shown in Table 1. [2].

Table 1. Desired characteristics of university graduates (where 1 is the most desired).

Desired Characteristics of Graduates	Rank Business	University
Communication skills	1	7
Capacity to learn new skills and procedures	2	5
Capacity for cooperation and teamwork	3	8
Capacity to make decision and solve problems	4	3
Ability to apply knowledge to workplace	5	4
Capacity to work with minimum supervision	6	6
Theoretical knowledge in a professional field	7	1

Capacity to use computer technology	8	2	6 X
Understanding of business ethics	9	12	3
General business knowledge	10	11	1
Special work skills	11	9	2
A broad background of general knowledge	12	10	2

This survey indicates that business and university differ in their ranking of the importance of characteristics in the graduates in two major areas:

1. Communication skills, a capacity to learn new skills and procedures, and a capacity for cooperation and teamwork. In each of these cases the university rankings are well below those of business, particularly in the area of communication skills.
2. Theoretical knowledge in a professional field and a capacity to use computer technology. In these cases university has rated these characteristics higher than has business. [2]

These results are consistent with the views of some authors, like DeMarco and Lister [1], Goguen and Linde [15] and Goguen [9]. They state that software development is strongly affected by social issues. So, it cannot be treated in a purely technological way.

Other researchers have been studying methods to improve the education of software engineering in order to address these social issues. In this paper, the authors review some recent developments in this area and propose a review in the computer science curriculum in order to accommodate these methods. In particular, they start proposing the introduction of an extreme programming course which will use some of the techniques presented in this article.

2. Related work

Researchers are working in two different propositions:

*   Changes in technical content teaching
*   Introduction of professional skills teaching

Each of these alternatives are described in the sections ahead.

2.1. Changes in technical content teaching

The Software Factory

Tvedt et at. [13] propose the "Software Factory", an eight-semester sequence of courses. These courses expose students to large-scale, team-oriented development in a software development organization. Each course represents a specific software engineering role or job within the development organization.

The eight semester sequence progresses the students through the following roles: (1) Software Factory process and tools trainee, (2) software system tests, (3 & 4) software developer and maintainer, (5) requirements analyst and test planner, (6) software designer and (7 & 8) software project manager.

Students from all courses in the Software Factory sequence meet simultaneously to fulfill their roles in the software organization. The enrollment in the program allows for multiple teams within the organization.

The Software Factory approach is rather interesting since students begin to work in a long term project early, exercise teamwork and face non-technical issues. Furthermore, it seems to bring students closer to what happens in the "real-world". On the other hand, the adoption of this approach has considerable impact on the way faculty staff is used to work and demands a significant infrastructure.

Large-scale software development

Sebern [16] also works with the idea of large-scale software development. He proposes a software development laboratory in which student teams' work for extended periods on large-scale, ongoing projects in the context of a standardized and evolving development process. It's composed of a three-course sequence.

Students in this course believe they have achieved the objectives related to teamwork, process improvement and software development practice. As in the case of Tvedt [13] this sequence reflects much of the experience in the "real-world". But it is also hard to be implemented by faculty staff.

The Activity Weekends

Ratcliffe et al. [11] describe the adoption of an integral activity weekend as part of the faculty's introductory software engineering course and a second weekend to reinforce industrial awareness in the student's second year.

These weekends have been developed to improve motivation and staff-student relations, emphasizing on life skills and adaptability. The idea is to introduce students to the concept of team skills. With specific attention to personal challenge and team dynamics, these weekends where carefully designed to both improve motivation and enhance the general employability of the students.

They follow a series of specially tailored outdoor activities that are designed to promote self and inter-personal skills through a series of shared group experiences. The activities are personally challenging and are heavily teamwork oriented. They cannot be carried out successfully without group co-operation and group encouragement.

Ratcliffe et al. [11] state that the response from the weekends is overwhelming. The students obviously enjoy themselves a great deal but more importantly they learn a great deal about themselves and working with others. It seems that the students learn far more about team working in one weekend than could have been taught to them through a whole series of class projects.

Although the approach is very interesting and effective, the costs are high. Considering the limitation of resources that affect many universities, it's necessary to find a way to implement these weekends with lower costs.

Open Ended Group Projects

Daniels et al. [10] describe the use of Open Ended Group Projects (OEGP). OEGP is a form of experimental learning (Kolb *cited in* Daniels et al., 2002) which can, in principle, be used to advantage to teach any subject with a practical application.

Daniels et al. [10], state that in addition to supporting knowledge acquisition, OEGP can be used to help the students gain and improve skills. The most obvious skill areas which are involved are interpersonal communication and group working. However, a suitably designed OEGP can ensure that students must consider the problems of communication with manager and client and can help improve both report writing and presentation skills. OEGP also assist in getting students to analyze problems and synthesize solutions while examining, and trying to mitigate the risks of things going wrong, all valuable skills for the software engineering project managers of the future.

The experience of group project work prepares the students for their subsequent careers where group working is the norm. Undertaking open ended projects also appears to have the benefit that they force the students to think about the problem rather than spending time searching for the 'correct' answer.

It is also noted that OEGP appear to have measurable beneficial effects on student performance in other academic subjects. Improved motivation and greater enthusiasm seem to carry over into general performance, confidence levels go up and problem solving skills improve so that students are more willing to attempt difficult tasks. OEGP can also be used to encourage students to apply theory which should lead to a better understanding of the theory and thus to improved performance in examinations.

Daniels et al. [10] describe several projects run in the classroom and they describe the students' reaction. Firstly, feedback from the students has been generally very positive. In all of the OEGP with which the authors have been involved there has been positive feedback from the students both during the module and afterwards. It is also noticeable that the levels of motivation of the students appeared to be higher with better completion rates, less plagiarism and very few drop outs or failures.

But OEGPs raise some criticism. Daniels et al. [10] explains that the main concerns that are expressed when the use of OEGP is suggested relate either to the use of group projects at all ("weak students get 'carried', good students get 'pulled down'") or to the fact that the outcome for an OEGP is inherently unknown i.e. that there is no 'right' answer. The necessity for group working is, however, becoming more widely accepted now (Ford *cited in* Daniels et al., 2002), thus it is the concerns about the open ended nature of the project and the need for fair assessment based on problems for which there is a correct answer, which are addressed here.

The obvious counter argument is that OEGP mirror real life software engineering projects which do not usually have known 'right' answers and there is a need to assist students to learn this before they start to work. Part of this learning process includes the intrinsically difficult process of finding out what the client thinks is required (Veryard *cited in* Daniels et al., 2002), negotiating with the client to agree what can be done and, later, explain what has actually been done and how it relates to the requirements. An alternative argument is that, ultimately, all criteria are established and judged by people and are, therefore, subjective. Objective criteria are only regarded as objective because there is agreement about the 'correct' way in which something should be done, or said. History suggests that most such agreements change over time and current 'right' way may well be revised later.

A different perspective on the fair assessment of OEGP can be provided by considering the way in which science and engineering are advanced. All research projects have unknown outcomes but the methods used to undertake and present research are common. Thus it is possible to provide a fair assessment process for OEGP by focusing on the process which the students use rather than the product they produce [10].

2.2. Introduction of professional skills teaching

Lamp et al. [3] state that changes to the traditional systems development life cycle towards use of package software, prototyping, distributed computing, JAD etc have all placed a further demand on interpersonal skills as opposed to technical skills. They described a major revision of the undergraduate teaching programme of the Department of Computer Science at the University of Tasmania, Australia.

This review introduced the teaching of professional skills. The objectives were:

- To introduce students to a range of professional skills considered essential for their effective operation as IT professionals;
- To develop skills and attitudes in students appropriate to IT professionals;
- To ensure that all times the acquisition of these professional skills are seen by the students as relevant to the technical and theoretical programmes which they are concurrently receiving, and as being essential for the well grounded graduate.

The second objective ensured that the professional skills training was a genuine skills-based programme, and not just an attempt to impart knowledge. Students are required to actively participate and to acquire appropriate levels of skills through experiential learning. The programme encompasses subjects that are taught along four years.

Table 2. Subjects' distribution.

First Year	Second Year	Third Year	Honours
What is the role of an IT professional? Ethics in computing Study skills Report writing Cross cultural communication Legal Issues Information gathering Interviewing Organizations: groups & teams Meetings & decision making Marketing, presentation skills Presentations by students	Groups and Teams Information Gathering Interviewing and ethics Interviewing Interviewing Exercises Metaphors Groups dynamics Meetings Team decision making Group problem solving Presenting a proposal Group presentations	Teamwork Team leadership Presentation skills Assertiveness Negotiation, conflict resolution Career visualization Skills/education for life Contract negotiation Detailed case study analysis	Advanced ethics, legal issues Critical analysis Research skills Presentation skills Thesis writing Organizational contexts

According to Lamp et al. [3] the inclusion of the professional skills programme complements the social and human aspects of information systems by giving real experience in organizational and team based activities, and focuses understanding of the impact of information technology at the interpersonal level.

3. Proposal

Based on the evidences given before, the authors of this paper are working on a research project in order to change the way software engineering is taught at Federal University of Rio de Janeiro. They are trying some of the techniques presented in this paper in order to change the way technical subjects are taught.

At the present moment, experiments are underway in a technical course on Extreme Programming. The authors are using concepts presented in this paper such as:

- The adoption of a large-scale project
- The involvement of an external client
- Open ended group project

Their approach is to change the curriculum gradually trying the techniques in different subjects.

The Extreme Programming Course

This is a semester long course for a class composed of 20 students. The content is based on the books of Beck [4], Beck and Fowler [14] and Jeffries et al. [7]. The introduction of extreme programming teaching to computer science undergraduate courses is not new. It has already been described in the works of Shukla and Williams [12] and Müller and Tichy [6].

Shukla and Williams [12] describe a course based on a 16-week semester class where the students completed four Java programming projects during the course of the semester. Three of the projects were completed as the students were learning and using more traditional software development practices. These practices were based on the Collaborative Software ProcessSM

(CSPSM) developed by Williams. They found that one semester is not long enough to teach two very different methodologies nor for the students to perform meaningful assignments using them. Furthermore, the students didn't work at all times co-located and with a customer on site. So, the experience didn't reflect the work of a real extreme programming project where co-location is strongly recommended and the customer should be present.

Müller and Tichy [6] developed an extreme programming course where, in the first three weeks students solved small programming exercises to familiarize themselves with the programming environment and to learn XP practices. The exercises introduced jUnit (the testing framework used throughout the course), pair programming, the test practices of XP (write test cases before coding, execute them automatically with jUnit), and refactoring. The remaining eight weeks were devoted to a project on visual traffic simulation. The course language was Java. All students had experience with Java from their early undergraduate courses. As in the case described by Williams, the students didn't work at all times co-located and with a customer on site which brought some problems.

The proposal of this paper tries to overcome the problems found in both cases. Firstly, it focuses only in one methodology, the extreme programming. Secondly, the students work only in one project through the course. And they develop software during the classes, so they are always co-located and they always have the customer on-site.

The project is the development of software to support the dissertation of a graduate student who acts as the customer all over the course. This approach is interesting, because the teacher doesn't act as the customer. He acts as the coach of the team. This project use Java as its development language.

The class is divided by five to form five teams of four students each. In each team, the students work in pairs. They practice pair-programming at all times following the recommendations of Williams et at. [5][8].

The students are evaluated in two ways, according to their individual achievements and their behavior working in the team. Every week the teacher proposes a reading assignment for the students. They have to read a text and answer some questions posed by the teacher in the following class. The texts are used so that students can learn more about each characteristic of the methodology. This evaluation represents half of the week grade.

The other half is based on teamwork. Students are observed while they work in pairs and the teacher grant marks according to the way they work with the pair and the other teammates. The teacher doesn't evaluate the final product, but only the process used by students to build the product. So, the students are not supposed to work on the project when they are not in class.

Each class takes four hours and there's one class per week. In the first hour the teacher asks the students about the text they've read along the week before the class. In the second hour the teacher gives a lecture on the subject of the class. And in the remaining two hours the students work on the project.

4. Results

In order to evaluate the results of this teaching method, the teacher has created a few forms which have been fulfilled by students. After each class the students received a form containing four questions about the method. The students were always supposed to answer the questions anonymously.

In the first class the teacher has proposed a group dynamic so that students could get to know each other. On the following class, they've been asked if they felt better posing questions and making comments after knowing their classmates. For 63% of them the group dynamic has been really useful and gave them more confidence to take part of the class' discussions.

They also agreed on the evaluation system. The teacher has proposed this system on the first class and the students were asked about it a few classes latter. For 94% of the students this evaluation system assesses fairly each student's learning. As the evaluation takes place every week, the teacher sends the evaluation results to the students every week, which gives them feedback about their achievements. Among the students, 83% believe this feedback is very useful and helps to motivated them so that they become more interested on the course. When asked whether this evaluation system should be applied to other technical disciplines 89% of the students answered affirmatively.

Pair programming was also very well accepted by students. All of them said they enjoyed the first exercises with pairs. In particular, they were also very enthusiastic about doing their exercises at the class. For 94% of the students doing their exercises at the class is far more effective than doing them at home. They said they learn more this way because they have the opportunity to discuss some ideas with their friends about the subject they've just learnt. This reinforces the learning process.

5. Conclusion

This paper began describing the concerns of business towards software engineering professionals in the areas of communication and interpersonal skills. Both empirical research and anecdotal evidence confirms that business remains strongly concerned over the teaching of this area. The authors presented some works that try to address those concerns. They do that changing the teaching of technical content or introducing the teaching of professional skills. Finally, they propose the adoption of some of these techniques in order to change the teaching of software engineering at the Federal University of Rio de Janeiro.

6. Future Work

This experiment is the first of a series of experiments the authors intend to put in action in their research which looks for new ways of teaching computer science courses in order to shorten the gap between industry expectation and university expectation. The results of this experiment will be available in the future in the form of a new paper.

7. References

[1] T. DeMarco, T. Lister, *Peopleware Productive Projects and Teams,* Dorset House Publishing Co., New York:, 1987.

[2] C. Keen, C. Lockwood, J. Lamp, "A Client-focused, Team-of-Teams Approach to Software Development Projects", *Proceedings of Software Engineering Education & Practice (SE: E&P'98)*, IEEE Computer Society Press Dunedin, 34-41

[3] J. Lamp, C. Keen, C. Urquhart, "Integrating Professional Skills into the Curriculum", *Proceedings of the First Australasian Conference on Computer Science Education*, Sydney, Australia, pp. 309-316, July 1996.

[4] K. Beck, *Extreme Programming Explained – Embrace Change*, Addison Wesley, 2000.

[5] L. Williams, R.Kessler, W. Cunningham, R. Jeffries, "Strengthening the Case for Pair Programming", *IEEE Software*, vol. 17, pp. 19-25, July 2000.

[6] M. Müller, W. Tichy, "Case Study: Extreme Programming in a University Environment", *Proceedings of the International Conference on Software Engineering 2001 (ICSE 2001).*

[7] R. Jeffries, A. Anderson, C. Hendrickson, "Extreme Programming Installed", Addison-Wesley, 2001.

[8] L. Williams, R. Kessler, "All I Really Need to Know about Pair Programming I learned in Kindergarten," *Communications of the ACM*, vol. 43, pp. 108-114, May 2000.

[9] J. Gouguen, "Requirements Engineering as the Reconciliation of Technical and Social Issues", in Requirements Engineering: Social and Technical Issues, edited with Marina Jirotka, Academic Press, 1994, pp. 165-199.

[10] M. Daniels, X. Faulkner, I. Newman, "Open Ended Groups Projects, Motivating Students and Preparing them for the 'Real World'", *Proceedings of the 15th Conference on Software Engineering Education and Training (CSEET'02)*.

[11] M. Ratcliffe, J. Woodbury, L. Thomas, "Improveint Motivation and Performance Through Personal Development in Large Introductory Software Engineering Courses", *Proceedings of the 15th Conference on Software Engineering Education and Training (CSEET'02)*.

[12] A. Shukla, L. Williams, "Adapting Extreme Programming for a Core Software Engineering Course", *Proceedings of the 15th Conference on Software Engineering Education and Training (CSEET'02)*.

[13] J. Tvedt, R. Tesoriero, K. Gary, "The Software Factory: Combining Undergraduate Computer Science and Software Engineering Education, *Proceedings of the International Conference on Software Engineering 2001 (ICSE 2001)*.

[14] K. Beck, M. Fowler, *Planning Extreme Programming*, Addison Wesley, 2001.

[15] J. A. Goguen, C. Linde, "Techniques for Requirements Elicitation", *Proceedings of Requirements Engineering (RE'98), IEEE Computer Society*, 1998, pp. 152-164.

[16] M. J. Sebern, "The Software Development Laboratory: Incorporating Industrial Practice in an Academic Environment", *Proceedings of the 15th Conference on Software Engineering Education and Training (CSEET'02)*.

[17] B. Pham. "The changing curriculum of computing and information technology in Australia". In *2nd Australasian SIGCSE Conference*, pages 149-154, The University of Melbourne, July, 1997.

Reflections on a UK Masters Level Software Engineering Programme Intended for the Home and International Market

Helen M. Edwards and J. Barrie Thompson
School of Computing and Technology
University of Sunderland, St Peter's Way,
Sunderland SR6 0DD, United Kingdom.
E-mail: {helen.edwards, barrie.thompson}@sunderland.ac.uk

Abstract

There are currently insufficient skilled Software Engineers to meet the needs of industry across the world. Intensive taught Masters level programmes represent one solution to this shortfall. One such programme is the MSc in Software Engineering offered by the University of Sunderland in the UK. This was developed to satisfy student needs both within and outside the European Union.. The constraints and challenges that needed to be addressed in the development of the programme are outlined. The programme and the various pathways through it are described. Student feedback on the programme is reported. The programme is evaluated and some of the lessons learned since its inception in 1999 are reviewed.

1. Introduction

In this paper we are describing an educational provision that will result in successful students being awarded a Masters degree in Software Engineering (SE). We will refer to it as a postgraduate programme and its constituent academic parts as modules because those are the terms that are used in the formal documents that define it. However, others may use terms such as: graduate, course, program, subject, unit etc. as the names for the equivalents within their particular frame of reference. Also, our past experiences in running international events associated with SE education (e.g. [3]) have clearly shown that without appropriate contextual information misunderstandings can occur. Therefore we will commence by outlining the types of Masters level programmes that can be found in the UK.

As we have explained previously [8], in the UK there is a broad range of general Masters qualifications: MSc., MA, MEng, and MPhil. There are also Masters qualifications associated with particular named disciplines, for example, Master in Business Administration (MBA). The majority of Masters qualifications are gained within taught programmes and the minority by independent research programmes. A taught Masters programme will normally involve one year of full time study (45/48 weeks) or the equivalent part time study. It will typically have approximately two thirds of its provision based on taught modules and the final third focused on an independent project which has a substantial research component. A Masters degree that is gained by wholly independent research is usually awarded as M.Phil or in traditional "older" universities as MSc or MA. These are awarded purely as Masters without any specific award title (such as Software Engineering). In such research Masters the student is allied to an individual academic supervisor (or supervisory team). There may be some supporting academic study to provide skills required for the research but these are determined on an individual basis. A research Masters will typically involve two years of full time study (90/96 weeks) or the equivalent part study. A third type of Masters award is the MEng. Students on this type of programme effectively join an undergraduate programme that has an additional "Masters" year.

The remainder of this paper is concerned with a Masters programme in SE which has been developed at the University of Sunderland to be both attractive to home students (including those from other countries within the European Union) and those who we class as international students (i.e. those from countries outside the European Union). In section two we consider the factors that had to be taken into account by the staff who were developing the programme. Section three provides a description of the Sunderland MSc in SE and the various pathways through it. Finally, section four provides an evaluation of the programme and outlines the lessons that have been learnt from the initial cohorts regarding its operation (since September 1999).

2. The Factors that Shaped the SE Programme at Sunderland

It is clear that, world-wide, the total number of SE undergraduate programmes has for years been insufficient to provide industry with enough SE graduates who will meet its requirements. For example, internet-collected data on US provision, which was reported in 2001, indicated only 16 programmes which are either bachelor degrees in SE, or in computer science with SE as a specific option/route [4]. Current provision in the UK , as we reported in late 2001 [8], appears good compared with the US. For the 2002/2003 University and College academic year we identified a total of 55 single subject undergraduate programmes (plus many more where SE could be combined with another subject for a "joint" degree). However, these will not produce graduates for another three or four years and even then it is unlikely that the numbers will meet industry's needs. One possible means of addressing the shortfall is to provide intensive Masters level programmes in SE for graduates who already possess an undergraduate degree in other computing or (appropriate) engineering subjects. This was the view taken by the staff at Sunderland in 1998 when they decided to develop their MSc in SE.

When developing a programme at the University of Sunderland there is a process of formal validation which involves taking expert opinion from both within and outside the University. A case must be presented that addresses the rationale (intellectual, academic, and market) for the programme Additional constraints that must be considered include meeting the UK government standards for educational programmes as defined by the Quality Assurance Agency for Higher Education (QAA) [5]. Also, if the programme is to be accredited by the British Computer Society (BCS), then the society's requirements for standards in content and assessment regime [1] must be satisfied.

2.1. Intellectual Rationale

The intellectual rationale that justified the programme at its inception was as follows [9]:
"This programme is distinctive from any currently offered within the School in that it is an advanced masters course in a mainstream computing discipline (i.e. Software Engineering). Existing masters computing provision within the school focuses on specialised areas, conversion courses and hybrid courses. Nationwide there are few advanced masters that explicitly focus on Software Engineering. Moreover although many computing degrees include Software Engineering elements within them there are few courses that are specifically B.Scs in Software Engineering, therefore, exposure to advanced elements of Software Engineering are rarely encountered by students undertaking their first degree. The M.Sc. in Software Engineering concentrates on the core concepts of the discipline. However, it is distinctive in that it is built upon expertise (both research and practitioner) that exists within the School. Thus students have the opportunity to use the best current industrial practice in a selection of areas within the field of Software Engineering and also to have exposure to current research thinking and results."

168

2.2. Academic Rationale

The academic rationale was based primarily on the profile of the School's SE research group. Ten members of academic staff who were active within this group had direct input into the creation of the programme. The research focus for the group has always been on applied SE. Particular strengths were in: Methods, CASE and metaCASE , Metrics, Quality and Standards, Testing, and Formal Methods. The importance of research was a key element in the developed programme and this obviously matches perfectly with what is highlighted by QAA in its Masters Level qualification descriptor [5].

2.3. Market rationale

The market need for the programme was demonstrated by consideration of the national and international shortage of highly skilled Software Engineers. This was a need that had frequently been discussed in both the industry's press and also in academic circles. Written support for the programme was also received from industrialists and national figures. The University was seeking to extend its market provision across the taught Masters sector and the School had a strategic objective to widen its own provision in this sphere. In doing so it was believed that the programme would meet local, regional, national and international needs and prepare appropriate students:

- to undertake effective research in SE, thus building upon the School's current strengths in this area, or
- to be highly effective professionals in the SE industry, working to accepted professional standards. Such standards are typified by those defined in the Software Engineering Code of Ethics and Professional Practice [6].

2.4 British Computer Society and Accreditation

For those in the field of computing (including SE) within the UK the relevant professional body is the British Computer Society (BCS). Full details of the society can be found at its web site [1]. A programme that has accreditation with the BCS is believed to give "added value" to students since this provides exemption from part of the BCS's qualifying examinations.

It was felt that having the programme accredited by the BCS would not only make it more attractive to those who wished to work in the UK but that it would also provide a further indication of the quality of the programme to students from overseas. Hence, in the development, steps were taken to ensure that the programme's content and assessment regime satisfied the BCS's standards.

3. The Sunderland M.Sc. in Software Engineering

The programme was developed with regard to the factors outlined above and in May 1999 it was formally validated and approved. Subsequently it ran with its first cohort in September 1999. The full-time programme lasts for 45 weeks within a calendar year whilst the part-time programme is normally scheduled for 30 weeks in each of three consecutive calendar years with students attending two evenings each week. For a full Masters award students must gain 180 M-level credits within the University's Credit Accumulation and Transfer Scheme (CATS) scheme. Intermediate awards of Postgraduate Certificate and Postgraduate Diploma are available for students who wish to leave the course during or at the end of the taught part having gained 60 or 120 credits respectively.

3.1. Programme Aim

The aim of the programme is to equip graduates in computing (or in another subject containing significant computing content) with advanced knowledge and skills in the field of SE. The objectives of the programme are to provide a postgraduate course of study that will allow students, on successful completion of the course, to [9]:

- Demonstrate knowledge and understanding of the fundamental principles of SE.
- Use the best of current industrial practice in a selection of areas within the field of SE .
- Devise creative and appropriate solutions to complex problems by the application and synthesis of the contents of the modules studied.
- Take a reflective, critical and scholarly approach to their work as software professionals.
- Independently study further areas, especially new and developing areas, in the field of SE.
- Demonstrate their ability to devise, plan, control and execute a substantial SE project.
- Demonstrate their ability to undertake effective research in SE.

3.2 The Programme Structure

The programme consists of three 15 week phases (each worth 60 M level CATS credits):

- a postgraduate certificate phase comprising four taught modules,
- a postgraduate diploma phase comprising four taught modules, and
- a project phase, requiring students to undertake individual, externally sponsored, projects supervised by a specific member of the Software Engineering faculty.

The general teaching, learning, and assessment strategy used within this programme reflects the School standard for postgraduate taught programmes. In particular, the students are expected to have the abilities that are required to undertake a significant quantity of unsupervised study. This may take the form of directed reading of research papers and advanced technical material or practical work on various software problems and environments. The objective of the student-staff contact time (typically 40 hours per module) is to set milestones and learning goals, and make new ideas and concepts accessible to the students. These ideas are then followed up in tutorials and in the students' own time. Tutorials are used within each module to provide support for lectures. The prime objectives of tutorial time is to allow in-depth study of particular topics which have been introduced and also for practical exercises (often machine-based). A tutorial group is expected to consist of no more than 18 students. In addition to significant individual study, group working (although not group assessment) is encouraged. This is in recognition of the fact that a graduate of the programme will normally be employed in environments where significant demands will be made upon his or her ability to co-operate and collaborate with others.

3.3. Taught Modules

Within the taught component of the original programme, students take six core and two optional modules, where each module has 150 learning hours associated with it. The core modules are:

- Research, Ethical, Professional and Legal Issues (REPLI),
- Project Proposal,
- Advanced Object Oriented Development (AOOD),
- Software Engineering Tools and Environments (SETE),
- Software Production Measurement and Control (SPMC),
- Database Systems Engineering (DBSE).

The optional modules are defined in pairs and pathways. These pathways provide a different emphasis on SE to reflect students' interests or career aspirations. These paths are:

- Technical Software Engineering with modules in Formal Methods in Software Engineering (FMSE) and Concurrent and Distributed Software Systems (CDSS).
- Sociotechnical Software Engineering with modules in Interactive Systems Development (ISD) and Method Engineering (ME).
- Computational Intelligence with modules in Knowledge Based Systems Engineering (KBSE) and Adaptive Systems (AS), and
- Management of Software Engineering with modules in IT Project Management (ITPM) and Quality Information Systems Strategies (QISS).

Each taught module typically has two pieces of assessed coursework and most also contain examinations. The assessments used vary according to the modules under study but include: technical reports, academic papers, discussion papers, practicals, presentations, portfolio, control assessment, traditional examinations, viva voce examinations and dissertation. The quality and standards of assessment are preserved through external and internal moderation of coursework and examinations. All assignments are accompanied with assessment criteria and these are made known, and explained, to students at the start of each module.

3.4. Project Module

The project phase lasts for 15 weeks (600 learning hours). Each student is expected to engineer a technically challenging software product that satisfies a sponsor's need. Projects may be sought from inside or outside the University. However, projects proposed internally must demonstrate that they satisfy a real requirement (such as the development of software for industry or a research group) and are not simply artificially generated by the programme team. Therefore, there must be a client associated with each project who will have a use for the practical deliverable ("the product"). The client's experience of the finished product will be an important ingredient of the student's final report. The student must gather the appropriate information to demonstrate the client's satisfaction. Credit is given for evidence that the student has elicited the client's requirements and satisfaction in a systematic and objective way.

4. An evaluation of the programme and lessons learnt.

The programme has had five cohorts of students: 9 students in September 1999, 22 in September 2000, 7 in Jan 2001, 15 in September 2001, and 20 in September 2002. The overall intake has been predominantly from overseas (particularly recruiting from India, Pakistan, and the Far East). The main issue we have had to address within the programme is the explanation of exactly what a British Masters course is. Unfortunately, this requires constant re-emphasis of the distinction between vocational training courses and a Masters qualification (which must have a focus on research). This is the case whenever we discuss the programme but it is especially important to get the message across to overseas applicants, since the gap between their expectations and the reality of the programme can demotivate them during the study period. What has been surprising is that so few UK nationals have been recruited to the programme. However, discussions with our undergraduate students suggest that they do not see the need for a postgraduate qualification in SE since the job market is buoyant and student debt accrued during their undergraduate courses makes immediate employment a more attractive option. This contrasts with overseas students' perceptions where one (or more) Masters qualifications are seen as necessary to "get ahead" in industry.

4.1. Intake standards

The minimum requirement for admission onto the programme was set as "[normally] a minimum of a lower second class honours degree in a computing subject (or in another subject which contains a significant computing element) and competency in a object oriented programming language (such as C++)". [9] Where applicants have a UK degree this is easy to assess, although often the programme leader needs to follow up on whether object orientation has been studied/practised. Where there is doubt about an applicant other information is taken into account (such as strength of academic reference, work experience). Where applicants are from overseas equivalency is looked for in their qualifications. The University has specific information on the broad comparability of many countries' qualifications (provided by the British Council). Overseas students frequently have degrees in technical subjects with some computing content supplemented by computing diplomas from training and consultancy agencies. The process of determining the fit of an overseas applicant to the entry requirements is, therefore, an inexact science.

However, an analysis of student results against entry status for the academic years 1999-2001 has demonstrated that (a) a standard entrant joining with our "normal entry qualifications" copes well with the course (b) that positive references can be deceptive (c) that there is no guarantee that any other type of computing qualification will bring students to the required standard for entry. Therefore the admissions process has been tightened to accept applicants with standard entrant qualifications and only in exceptional circumstances accept non-standard entrants, for instance where there is rigorous evidence of the applicants ability and /or experience (not simply "references").

4.2. Student expectation of the programme and the extent to which that expectation needs a Masters level programme

In May 2001 a short web-based questionnaire was posted to gather feedback from the, then current, students on their expectations and experiences of the programme . The results are summarised here. Eight out of the nineteen in the September 2000 cohort and three of the seven in the January 2001 cohort responded. The questions asked were:

- What did you think this Masters programme involved before you came here? Seven expected substantial teaching in practical skills (especially programming). Two thought it would make them "good software engineers" and one had an expectation of substantial theory backed up by practicals.
- What did you hope to get out of this Masters programme ? For five the ambition was to gain an MSc, four expected an enhanced skill set, one was looking for "depth of knowledge" and one expected to gain professional standing and another "a general idea of how you can organise the development a software project".
- How did you see this programme helping your career? For six simply having such an MSc was seen as an asset, four students expected the programme to provide depth of knowledge and thus to increase confidence and competency.
- What do you now think this Masters programme is about? There were a variety of answers but a common perception was that it was more about research and less about training in practical skills.
- What was your key interest in this programme ? This question was really answered from the perspective of "what they believe they got out of the programme so far" and the

range of answers was varied. However, again the predominant view was that those modules with a practical technical element, particularly java/OO, database and tools, were of most value. On an individual level there were favourable comments received once each for research, formal methods, concurrent and distributed systems, and project proposal.

- Which aspects of this programme have you found most satisfying? One student stated that the programme has "changed my way of thinking". By far the most satisfaction was expressed about lectures and tutorials (stated five times), staff accessibility and communication were identified four times and facilities were mentioned twice. Individual comments were made about formal methods, CASE and research.
- Which aspects of this programme have you found most disappointing? Most of the negative comments relate to problems in scheduling and organisation. Particular mention was made of the first phase for the September cohort: which had suffered staff changes and illnesses impacting on the cohesiveness of modules. Three students commented on material being irrelevant in their opinion (two identified formal methods and metrics in this) two commented on lack of depth (one citing AOOD as an example). One student was disappointed about the lack of choice for the pathway to be studied.
- If you had the choice, which programme title would have interested you most? Six of the students declared they would have chosen a "Software Engineering " title. Other titles identified included multimedia, web/internet design, intelligent systems, networking, advanced object orientation, distributed and concurrent systems, electronic commerce. Each of these was mentioned once each.

4.3. Summary and Analysis of the Student-expectation data.

The overall impression that can be gained from the feedback is that:
- The students see the benefit of the programme most strongly in terms of the qualification they will gain.
- There is no other programme that would have attracted them overall, and Software Engineering is still the appropriate title in terms of their ambitions.
- The students expected a much greater level of teaching of programming skills and much less in the way of research .
- The students have, on the whole, a positive attitude towards the content and delivery of the programme (in terms of lectures, tutorials, staff commitment and facilities).
- The positive and negative remarks about individual modules more or less balanced each other out (and each tended only to reflect one individual's view).
- The most negative experience for most students revolves around atypical organisational problems of resourcing the programme: staffing and timetabling.

From the programme team's viewpoint, the most significant points to come from the (limited) data were that although the ambition of the students is generally to get an M.Sc., in order to gain an advantage in the job market, their initial expectations of what a Masters programme involves is at variance with reality and their experience. Therefore, for a programme such as ours (working within the constraints of both matching QAA expectations of a Masters programme and the BCS requirements for professional accreditation) we need to "market" the programme, clearly emphasising:
(i) the need for applicants to have strong, existing, programme design and implementation skills and
(ii) the focus in the programme is on fundamental Software Engineering concepts, which are illustrated through practical activities

(iii) it is not a training programme and there is a significant focus on developing and applying research skills and independent learning.

4.4. Programme Modification

As a result of reviewing the students' progress on the programme, their interest areas and the schools research strengths, the original programme has now been modified. The modification has resulted in the removal of the Project Proposal module from the diploma phase. When projects were compared across a range of Masters level programmes within the School, most of which did not contain this module, there was no perceived benefit from it. The module "Concurrent and Distributed Software Systems" has become a core module, since there was a perception that it was "fitting" and essential module for current industrial needs. This module was taken from the technical pathway and as a result the pathway has been removed from the programme (thus losing the formal methods module). In addition the sociotechnical pathway has been removed since anything other than a purely theoretical treatment of method engineering was seen to be impossible within the constraints of the programme's operation. This reduces the number of pathways to two: computational intelligence and management of SE. Discussion with students and staff indicated that this was an acceptable compromise for most involved in the programme. However, the programme continues to be monitored and compared against other Masters offerings and student satisfaction to evaluate the wisdom of these choices. Also the availability of both the Guide to the SE Body of Knowledge [7] and the forthcoming SE Volume of Computing Curricula 2001 [2] will aid future modifications of the programme, especially in ensuring that it continues to meet international needs.

References

[1] British Computer Society (BCS), information available at www.bcs.org.uk
[2] CCSE (Computing Curricula Software Engineering), details available at http:/sites.computer.org/ccse/
[3] Edwards, H.M, and Thompson, J.B. Workshop on Developing Graduate and Postgraduate Software Engineering Courses *Thirteenth Conference on Software Engineering Education & Training (CSEE&T 2000)* IEEE Computer Society, Los Alamitos, 2000, pp 187-194.
[4] Modesitt, K, Bagert, D and Werth, L. Where Are We Now? A Status Report on the First Annual Survey for International Academic Software Engineering Programs, 23rd International Conference on Software Engineering, Toronto, CA, May, 2001, pp. 643-652.
[5] Quality Assurance Agency for Higher Education (QAA), The framework for higher education qualifications in England, Wales and Northern Ireland - January 2001 available from www.qaa.ac.uk
[6] Software Engineering Code of Ethics and Professional Practice is available at the following sSites: http://computer.org/tab/seprof/code.htm, and http://computer.org/tab/sweec/SWCEPP
[7] SWEBOK Project Web Site. Available at http://www.swebok.org
[8] Thompson, J.B. and Edwards, H.M. Software Engineering in the UK 2001, *Newsletter of Forum for Advancing Software engineering Education (FASE)*, Volume 11 Number 119 (Issue 141), November 15, 2001, pp 1-18, available at www.cs.ttu.edu/fase/v11n11.txt.
[9] University of Sunderland, *M.Sc in Software Engineering: An Advanced Masters Course. Definitive Documentation*, May 1999, osiris.sunderland.ac.uk/~cs0hed/mscse.htm

Software Engineering Methods 1
(Paper Session F)

Teaching a Software Development Methodology:
The Case of Extreme Programming

Orit Hazzan
Department of Edu in Technology and Science
oritha@tx.technion.ac.il

Yael Dubinsky
Department of Computer Science
yael@cs.technion.ac.il

Technion – Israel Institute of Technology
Haifa 32000, Israel

Abstract

This article focuses on the teaching of software development methodologies. It presents ten principles of teaching such a topic, while examining each from both a pedagogical and an organizational viewpoint. The teaching principles are demonstrated using the methodology of Extreme Programming (XP).

1. Introduction

Calls have been made recently to integrate software development skills into the curriculum of computer science and software engineering programs ([2], [6]). Parallel to this trend, the importance of the product (software) process is being highlighted, and topics such as productivity and quality are gaining increasingly more attention, especially as a result of recent financial circumstances[1]. One way to group the aforementioned topics is under the heading of Software Development Methodologies (hereinafter abbreviated as SDM or SDMs). This article focuses on teaching SDMs to undergraduate students. The article presents ten principles for teaching an SDM and demonstrates them using the teaching of Extreme Programming (XP), an SDM that has been receiving increasingly more attention in industrial and academic discussions in recent years.

Section 2 describes the research background from which the teaching principles, described in section 3, have been derived. We conclude in Section 4.

2. Research background

The principles presented in Section 3 are based on an analysis of the teaching of XP in a course entitled 'Operating Systems Projects'. This course has been taught for the past six years at the Technion's Department of Computer Science by the second author of this article. The Department of Computer Science is considered to be comparable to the ten leading Computer Science departments in the US. Approximately 1,300 undergraduate students and about 200 graduate students are currently studying at the Department. In addition to its general B.Sc. program, the Department offers 4 special undergraduate tracks in Software Engineering, Information Systems Engineering, Computer Engineering, and Bioinformatics. The Technion in general, and the Department of Computer Science in particular, are one the main suppliers of (software) engineers to the Israeli hi-tech industry.

Each year, approximately eighty students attend the 'Operating Systems Projects' course offered in the Winter and Spring semesters, and fifty students take the course in the Summer semester. As a computer-science project-based course ([8], [10]), the main requirement of the course is the development of an operating systems project. Prior to the introduction of XP into the course, projects were performed in teams of 2-3 computer/software engineering students. The students were required to submit documentation, mid-semester and final presentations and to participate in a project fair. The academic staff consisted of two instructors, who

---

[1] Look for example at the National Institute of Standards and Technology (NIST) New Release of June 28, 2002 at http://www.nist.gov/public_affairs/releases/n02-10.htm.

coordinated the teaching and administration of the course, and of several supervisors. If questions or other issues arose, the students could meet with the supervisors during their regular office hours.

Starting in the 2002 Summer semester, XP has been introduced as the SDM used in the 'Operating Systems Projects' course. XP is one SDM of the family of agile SDMs, which includes methodologies such as SCRUM ([7]) and the DSDM (Dynamic System Development Method2). Flower ([3]) explains that "agile methods have some significant changes in emphasis from heavyweight methods." For example, he mentions that "agile methods are people-oriented rather than process-oriented". XP, in specific, is described by Beck ([1]) as being "a lightweight, efficient, low-risk, flexible, predictable, scientific, and fun way to develop software" (p. XVII).

In addition to the introduction of XP into the 'Operating Systems Projects' course, some studio elements were also introduced into the course. The studio is the basic learning method used in architecture schools and it has been adopted by some other design disciplines as a training environment. In such studios, students develop projects with close guidance of a tutor and with on-going reflection, both on what is created and on the creation process. Studio descriptions in Software Engineering education can be found in Tomayko ([9]) and in Kuhn ([5]). Analysis of how the studio can be implemented into software development environments is presented by Hazzan ([4]). Integration of the studio with XP, in the 'Operating Systems Projects' course, creates a conceptual-physical stimulating development environment. For reasons of space limitation, we will not elaborate on this here. We hope that the spirit of this combination is reflected in our examples presented in Section 3.

Hazzan 2002 reflected practice

The introduction of XP into the course consisted of two main phases: In Phase 1, prior to the onset of the course, a team of four supervisors was introduced to XP and trained to teach it. Table 1 presents the timetable for the supervision team training. The second author, who was the instructor in charge of the course, led the supervisor team sessions. All sessions were conducted with a teamwork orientation and all decisions were made jointly by the supervision team. In Phase 2, XP was implemented in the Summer semester in the form of four studios. Each studio worked on a different project, chosen by its supervisor, in teams of 10-12 students. Attendance of all sessions during the semester was compulsory. In the 2003 Winter semester students were required to select one of the following two options: Developing a project in the XP studio as part of a team of 10-12 students; or developing a project as part of a 2-3 student team, with remote guidance of a supervisor, following a traditional SDM like the waterfall model. The option chosen by each student was his or her development framework for the entire semester. Obviously, different projects of different scale were developed in these two formats.

Table 1: Schedule for the Supervision Team Training

Session No.	Agenda – Supervision Team Training
1	Introduction to XP Personal experience with XP practices
2	The studio structure
3	The supervisor's role in the studio Teaching XP practices
4	Student evaluation policy

The principles presented in the following section were derived from an analysis of the data obtained using the following research tools: Video tapes of the XP sessions in one of the studios, observations of students' work and the social interaction in the studio, students'

2 The DSDM Consortium website is http://www.dsdm.org.

weekly reflections, students' homework assignments, supervisors' reflections, and our ongoing reflection on the course progress.

3. Principles for teaching software development methodologies

This section presents ten principles for the teaching of SDMs. Some of these principles are especially suited to situations in which an SDM is introduced into a Computer Science department for the first time. Based on our experience described above, each principle is illustrated through the teaching of XP. We believe, however, that the principles can be implemented in the teaching of other SDMs as well.

Principle I addresses the *course* structure; Principles II-VI address the actual *teaching* of the SDMs; Principles VII-IX address the *people* involved in the educational environment – the students and the supervision team; the last principle – Principle X - is a *meta* principle which suggests action over preaching. Before presenting the principles in depth, we present them briefly in Table 2. In order to facilitate their remembrance, we have given each of them a one-word nickname.

Table 2: 'Teaching SDM' Principles in a Glance

#	Category	Nickname	Single Sentence Description
I	Course	Project-based	Course structure: Project-based team-based course
II	Teaching	Cognition	Teaching an SDM: What aspect to emphasize?
III		Adjustment	Adjustment of the SDM to a university course framework
IV		Projection	Projection of the SDM's notions into the project development environment
V		Connectivity	The SDM in the context of the world of software development
VI	People	Evaluation	Reflection of the SDM orientation in students' evaluation policy
VII		Listening	Listening to students' objections
VIII		Reflection	Students' reflections and progress diaries
IX		Feedback	Supervisors' hesitations and feedback
X	Meta	Inspiration	Inspiring the SDM rather than preaching it

I. Course structure - Project-based team-based course: This principle suggests teaching an SDM in a project-based course. In such a course, students develop, within a single-semester time frame, software projects that are suited for development using the SDM in question. This setting contrasts with the traditional teaching method, in which SDMs (or any other topic) are presented in the lecture hall, with students passively listening to the philosophy of the SDMs, its process, guidelines and practices. We argue that it is important to teach SDMs in environments that imitate real life situations, projects and software development environments, as closely as possible. Indeed, gaining such experience can prepare the students for their future work in the software industry.

This principle stems from the importance attributed to providing learners with the experimental basis needed for learning complex concepts. This stands in line with the constructivist cognitive perspective, the origins of which are rooted in Jean Piaget's studies. The constructivist paradigm examines learners' mental processes that lead to mental constructions of knowledge based upon learners' knowledge and experience. We believe that an SDM is a complex concept, which can be better understood if learners are afforded the opportunity to experience it. We do not claim that no frontal teaching should be used at all; Some aspects of the SDM can be taught by lecturing. However, we believe that the more students experience the SDM and reflect upon it, the more they improve both their understanding of the SDM's essence and orientation and their professional skills. As is described in Section 2, this principle is implemented in our experience of teaching XP. Further details are provided in the next principles.

II. Teaching SDM: While dealing with the teaching of an SDM, a need arises to integrate some teaching/learning modules into the course, which address the essence of the SDM being taught. Since an SDM is, by nature, a complex topic, several questions must be addressed: What aspects of the SDM should be emphasized? Should one teach all of the SDM ideas? Perhaps only part of them? Which ones? In order to answer such questions, we suggest analyzing and mapping the SDM ideas, in such a way that highlights those aspects of the SDM that form its core, and, for each specific SDM idea, reflects the complexity of teaching it. One way to do this is illustrated in the following mapping.

The main ideas of the SDM are mapped along two dimensions: 'Aspect' and 'Cognitive Awareness'. Specifically, on one dimension, the SDM ideas are divided into either a code/technical aspect or a human/social aspect. The second dimension maps the main ideas of the SDM according to the level of cognitive awareness (or cognitive complexity) required to implement each of them throughout the development process. We believe that such a mapping can be suitable for the mapping of the main ideas of any SDM, and can thus assist lecturers in organizing their courses. Clearly, the mapping presented above is not the only mapping possible. If other mappings are appropriate, they should, of course, be implemented.

The case of XP: XP consists of 12 practices that form the core of the methodology. Table 3 presents these practices according to the two-dimensional mapping suggested above. In this mapping, we roughly assume that some of the practices are easily understood (e.g., 40-hours a week), some are hard to understand (e.g., simple design or metaphor), and others are at an intermediate level of cognitive complexity (e.g., coding standards).

We believe that when XP is taught, such a mapping enables the instructor to choose which aspects to focus on, in such a way that students will not be overwhelmed with too many hard-to-grasp concepts in too short a period of time.

Table 3: Mapping of the XP Practices

Cognitive Awareness \ Aspect	Code/Technical Perspective	Human/Social Perspective
High	Refactoring Simple design	Metaphor Collective ownership
Intermediate	Coding standards Testing	Pair programming Planning game
Low	Small releases Contentious integration	Customer on site 40-hour a week

III. Adjustment of the SDM into a university course framework: As far as the desire to teach an SDM in an environment that resembles, as much as possible, real software development environments is concerned, the traditional university course frameworks sometimes require adjustment of the SDM. This is due mainly to the fact that students take other courses in parallel and cannot dedicate the entire week to their work on the course project.

The case of XP: With respect to XP, two of the adjustments made in order to adapt XP to the framework of a university course are presented, as follows:

- The supervision team hypothesized that when playing the planning game (one of the XP practices) students might not add product features, knowing that they will then be required to implement them. Thus, it was made clear to the students that the rules of the planning game were changed slightly for the sake of the course project. Namely, if as a result of the planning game it would become evident that the project requirements became too broad to be implemented within the time frame of a single semester, a subset of the requirements will be chosen and the project's scope will be defined accordingly. The supervisors undertook to keep the scope of the project realistic relative to the given time frame.

- In order to help students stay focused on the project and on track, the supervisor took the role of the XP project coach (one of the roles in XP). In order to enable the students to experience this role at least partially, it was decided to appoint a coach-apprentice to act as the actual coach in between the weekly sessions. This approach also ensures that the students would feel that they are the responsible entity for the project progress.

IV. Projection of several SDM's notions into the project development environment: This principle suggests that the development environment, in which students are supposed to work, should reflect the SDM being taught. For example, if an SDM emphasizes teamwork, the learning environment should support teamwork. As in the case of the evaluation policy (see Principle VI), this principle supports students' feelings that they receive a clear and coherent message.

The case of XP: Two XP practices, for which this principle was implemented in the case described here, are presented:

- **Pair programming:** In order to promote pair programming, the number of computers in each studio is set to be equal to half the number of students in each studio. Thus, students naturally begin programming in pairs. Still, more effort should be invested to ensure pair-exchanging.

- **Continuous integration:** In university courses, in which students do not perform all of the work together, at the same time, a situation can occur by which a student enters the studio in between weekly sessions, integrates his or her code, causes irreversible damage, and leaves the studio (or in the worst case – drops the course altogether). One plausible solution, which might solve this problem, is to enable integration only during the weekly sessions, which are attended by the supervisor. This solution could, however, slow down students' progress in between weekly sessions and may diminish the importance of this XP practice. Thus, it was decided to formulate, together with the students, a set of rules according to which all students would work and which would be posted near the integration machine. In other words, instead of doing away with continuous integration, a solution was found in order to emphasize the importance of this practice.

V. The SDM in the context of the world of software development: The world of software has witnessed relatively many cases in which new terms have emerged and have shortly turned out to be no more than buzzwords. Thus, when teaching a new SDM, it would be preferable to connect the SDM to the world of software development in general, and to other SDMs in particular. This can be done, for example, by presenting students specific problems faced by the software industry, illustrating how the taught SDM may help overcome them. Students will then, hopefully, feel that, on the one hand, they are being introduced to an SDM that is not detached from the software world and is not just a passing fashion, and on the other hand, that the SDM in question has emerged as a timely answer to the needs of the software industry and that it will be useful to them in their future work as software developers. In this way, the message conveyed to the students is that what they are learning is closely related to what they have learnt so far and to what they will be doing after they graduate.

The case of XP: In the case of teaching XP, the need for agility in software development was first explained and some problems with traditional SDMs were outlined. When students raised questions regarding the compatibility of XP with what they have previously learnt, the connection was made between XP and topics that were familiar to the students from other courses, such as UML and CMM. Such a broad perspective enables students to see XP's place in the software industry and to see that SDMs is a field that is still undergoing development.

The connection between the taught SDM and the world of software development can also be made in ad hoc situations. For example, one of the students had expressed his objection to the concept of simplicity (one of the XP values), saying that "It runs against what we have already been taught – that is, to pre-design, to define all the data structures in advance, to get a global view of the software being developed, before getting into the details". The supervisor's reaction was that the global view is not at all ignored or overlooked. On the contrary, the global perspective of the software is inspired by the refactoring practice and it is used for redesigning the software in a continuous process. However, it was emphasized that there are cases, at certain stages of software development, when a mental global picture cannot be conceived, and then simplicity and software development in small releases can be useful tools.

VI. Reflection of the SDM orientation in student evaluation: It is accepted that when a university instructor wishes that his or her students follow specific principles that he or she deems important, these principles must somehow be incorporated into the evaluation policy of the course. This is particularly true when an SDM is used in a project-based course. It is reasonable to assume that students naturally devote more effort to what is valued (and graded), and eventually improve their understanding of the SDM.

The case of XP: This principle was applied in the course described here, by assigning a course grade that was composed of a personal component (35%) and a team component (65%), which was identical for all members of the team. We believe that such an evaluation scheme conveys the message that both teamwork and individual contribution count. It is assumed that, on the one hand, students will be encouraged to contribute to the teamwork, and on the other hand, this method affords those wishing to excel, the opportunity to improve their grade through the personal component of the grade.

Table 4: Grading Policy in the Project-Based XP Course

Team Component (65%)	Individual Component (35%)
15% - Setting up the computerized environment of the studio	45% - Attendance the 8 Studio meetings Written reflections at the end of each meeting
25% - Project documentation	Pair-programming session with the supervisor
60% - For each of the 2 project releases: • Implementation of all customer stories • Complete releases on time (according to students' estimations in the planning game)	Homework assignments about XP practices Presentation of a first-test experience 55% - Performance of a personal role (release presenter, iteration presenter, in charge of continuous integration, customer, tracker, coach assistant, in charge of testing)

Table 4 presents the evaluation model formulated by the supervision team and used in the four studios in the Summer 2002 semester. As can be observed, most of the XP practices appear explicitly in the evaluation model, with special emphasis on the first-test and pair-programming practices. The first-test practice gets its importance from the supervision team's belief in educating students for production of high quality software products. The student-supervisor pair-programming session emerged as a solution to the "free riders" phenomenon, which was evident in previous semesters (when the supervisors did not meet the students on a weekly basis and had no way of knowing just how the project was actually progressing).

VII. Students' objections: If Principle I is applied and if the student-lecturer lecture hall interaction is replaced by intensive student-supervisor communication in a studio or in another development environment, it is reasonable to assume that the change in the teaching approach will affect both students and supervisors. Specifically, since we are dealing with educational institutions in which both students and teachers have learning/teaching belief systems, it is natural that feelings of discomfort will arise when teaching conditions change. This principle addresses the question of how students' reactions should be addressed when such feelings emerge. In Principle IX we address supervisors' concerns. Based on our experience, we propose that instructors and supervisors should try sympathizing with students' feelings towards the new learning environment and be patient with them until students start becoming aware of the benefits that can be gained from the new course setting in general, and from the introduced SDM in particular.

The case of XP: As it happens, in the course described here, student objections disappeared in part after only one week. Thus, it seems that the sympathizing attitude mentioned above was indeed called for. This shift in students' attitudes can be explained by their newly emerged awareness to the advantages of the new approach. First, they were told that if they proceed according to the decisions they made in the planning game, they would complete their projects by the end of the semester. This situation stands in contrast to other project-based courses, in which some students do not complete their project by the end of the semester, dragging it even months later. Second, students began to realize that their team might actually support their work, and not just hinder it, as they originally suspected it would.

In order to illustrate students' concerns with respect to the new course format, we present two issues that were raised by students during the first meeting of the semester:

- *"The main component of the grade is the team component, and I do not know who my team members are. How can I trust them? This is not a real working place"*. It seems that this concern stems from bad experiences students had in other courses, in which they were required to develop projects in teams. It seems that, in some cases, students had had to cope with "free riders". We believe that XP is taught in such a way that avoids such a situation: First, the team works together in the studio and no student would like to be perceived as a "parasite". Second, each student has a very specific task assignment, which is determined during the planning game.

- *"Who is the team leader? Who controls what students do?"*. The instructor explained that in the previous format of the course as well, there was no control over students' work. Furthermore, it was emphasized that the weekly meetings and the coach-apprentice increase the control over the project progress.

VIII. Student reflections and progress diaries: In order to learn about the feelings of students, their working habits and their social interactions with respect to the project development during the course, students should be offered tools and means for self-expression. The ability to express one's impressions gives students the feeling that their thoughts and feelings are of interest to the course instructors and supervisors. In addition, if students wish to complain, this is a good way to encourage them to do so. In this spirit, students should be encouraged to express not only positive ideas, but also negative feelings and suggestions for improvement.

Furthermore, we believe that such means of expression enhance students' reflective skills; skills whose importance in software development processes is acknowledged and which are encouraged by the studio approach. As it is well known in the software industry, a reflective person, who learns both from the successes and failures of previous software projects, is more likely to improve his or her own performance in the field.

The case of XP: The following two means of expression were offered to students in the present XP course, in order to express their reflections and feelings and to describe project progress: A team diary, which is part of the 'project documentation' evaluated as part of the team grade (cf. Principle VI); and personal web-reflections, which are posted on the web at the end of each session and which are to be completed within three hours after the end of each session. The web-reflections were short (requiring no more than 15 minutes) and presented questions that address students' impressions from the session they just attended. As it turns out, these web-reflections provided the supervisors with quite good feedback. For example, the first web-reflection that was posted following the first session, just after the first planning game had been played, revealed the following observation. On the one hand, students admitted that working in a big team (10-12 students) is a new experience for them and some of them were looking forward to working in such teams. On the other hand, this working style was also their main concern: They were worried about how the teamwork would be coordinated and who would lead the team.

IX. Supervisors' hesitations: While Principle VII addresses the students' state of mind at the onset of the course, this principle focuses on the supervisors who are to guide students in the new software development environment. This principle is suited mainly to situations in which a *team* of supervisors guides the students, and, similar to the students, experiences the development environment for the first time. In such cases, not only must the supervisors familiarize themselves with the SDM itself, but also they have to adopt a new way of teaching and a new supervision conception. For example, supervisors must be physically present, alongside the students, during the actual software development stages. This is not something previously experienced in the traditional supervision style, in which meetings are held with the students in between student programming sessions. In addition, the new evaluation model requires the supervisors to evaluate items that were not previously evaluated. Indeed, such a change requires a transformation in the supervisors' conception of teaching and of learning processes.

The principle suggests repeated emphasizing of the novelty of the introduced SDM and legitimizing supervisors' feelings of insecurity. Furthermore, it is suggested that the supervisors state before the students that this experience is new for them as well, and thus relate such a situation to real life software development circumstances, in which uncertainty in general, and not-knowing-everything in particular, are frequent components (Cf. Principle V). In practice, the supervisors' role in the new development environment and other supervisor-students-interaction related issues should be discussed during the supervision team sessions held prior to the course. In order to overcome the supervisors' hesitations (and sometimes resistance), general decisions about the course should be made jointly by all supervision team members, leaving each supervisor the freedom to adjust the particular studio he or she teaches to his or her teaching beliefs.

The case of XP: Since the supervision team of the course described in this article was not familiar with XP prior to this course (neither in practice nor in theory), it was necessary to teach them XP philosophy as well as XP practices. This was accomplished during the 4 training sessions described in the Introduction. The sessions were based on short presentations followed by some activity (such as pair drawing, planning game, reflection). In the course of the training process, the supervisors began feeling comfortable with XP. For example, after the first planning game, one of them said: "This way, I believe, less tension will be experienced by the students towards the end of the semester". Comparing her previous supervision experiences with her current knowledge about XP, this supervisor realized that the planning game may enable students to complete their projects on time, without the stress that, in the traditional course format, characterizes the end-of-the-semester period.

Most of the decisions, regarding the structure of the course (4 studios), the course schedule (2 releases, each consisting of two iterations), and the role of the supervisors in the studio, were made jointly by all supervisor team members. As suggested above, in addition to these general decisions, each supervisor made specific decisions with respect to the studio he or she was intended to teach. For example, each supervisor decided on the software project to be developed by the students in his or her studio. In the 2002 Summer semester (the first semester in which XP has been introduced in the course), it was decided to offer students projects that had already been developed in previous semesters and to adjust the scale of such projects to team sizes of 10-12 students. This way the supervisors could focus on the XP practices without being distracted by technical issues. In the 2003 Winter semester, the supervisors felt more comfortable with XP, and new topics for projects were introduced.

X. Inspiration of the SDM: This is a meta-principle that integrates several of the principles described above. It suggests inspiring the SDM, rather than talking about it. In fact, this principle is supported by all of the previous principles, such as the experimental basis, the projection of some SDM principles into the project development environment, and the reflection of the SDM orientation in the students' evaluation model.

The case of XP: We hope that this principle is mirrored in the way we have described the course on which our article is based. We have tried to convey the message that, throughout the entire course, XP is inspired on all levels: Individual, pair, team, supervisor, and customer.

4. Conclusions

This article addresses the teaching of SDMs. The importance of teaching SDMs in the manner introduced here, stems from our belief that students should be introduced to SDMs in a learning environment that simulates as much as possible environments they are likely to encounter in their future careers.

The main ideas are demonstrated based on our experience in teaching XP in a project-based course. Although this article focuses on the teaching of SDMs in general, we would like to present some concluding remarks with respect to our XP teaching experience. First, as was anticipated, students' projects were completed on time. We believe that this fact, by itself, will dramatically (and perhaps entirely) reduce students' resistance in future semesters. Second, and maybe more important, we observed a strong commitment to the project development on the part of both students and supervisors. Student commitment can easily be explained by the evaluation model (Cf. Principle VI) and the planning game: The evaluation model guided students to personal and team commitment; the planning game assigned each student with specific tasks to be accomplished in a specific estimated time. It is interesting to note the commitment to the entire project observed on the part of the supervisors: The supervisors cared about the implementation of the XP practices, and were concerned about the on-time completion of the projects.

In our future work, we intend to propose a more detailed description of the teaching of SDMs within a single-semester time frame. In addition, we have begun an examination of the adoption of the principles presented in this article in the teaching of other topics, such as programming paradigms. For example, the suitability of the ten principles is examined in an introductory object-oriented course taught in the 2003 Winter semester to 25 graduate students, for whom this is their first programming experience.

References

[1] Beck, K., *Extreme Programming Explained: Embrace Change*. Addison-Wesley, 2000.

[2] P. J. Denning, "Educating a new engineer", *Communications of the ACM* **35** (12), 1992, pp. 82-97.

[3] Fowler, M. ,The New Methodology, published in martinfowler.com, http://www.martinfowler.com/articles/newMethodology.html, 2002.

[4] O. Hazzan, "The reflective practitioner perspective in software engineering education", *The Journal of Systems and Software* **63**(3), 2002, pp. 161-171.

[5] S. Kuhn, "The software design studio: An exploration", *IEEE software* **15**(2), 1998, pp.65-71.

[6] B. Meyer, "Software engineering in the academy", *Computer*, May, 2001, pp. 28-35.

[7] Schwaber, K. and Beedle, M., *Agile Software Development with Scrum*. Prentice Hall, 2001.

[8] M. J. Sebern, "The Software Development Laboratory: Incorporating Industrial Practice in an Academic Environment", *Conference on Software Engineering Education and Training (CSEE&T)*, 2002, pp. 118-127.

[9] J. E. Tomayko, "Carnegie-Mellon's Software development Studio: A five-year retrospective", *SEI Conference on Software Engineering Education*, 1996, http://www.contrib/andrew.cmu.edu/usr/emile/studio/coach.htm.

[10] D. Wilson, "Teaching XP: A Case Study", *XP Universe Conference*, 2001.

Improving Project Planning/Tracking for Student Software Engineering Projects through SOPPTS

Jeff Zhang, Dolores Zage, Wayne Zage
Computer Science Department
Ball State University
Muncie, IN 47306 USA
jzhang@cs.bsu.edu; *dmz@cs.bsu.edu*; *wmz@cs.bsu.edu*

Abstract

The Student Online Project Planning and Tracking System, SOPPTS, is an online system designed and implemented to enhance the communication avenues and the project planning/tracking requirements of student projects for the Ball State University (BSU) software engineering classes. This paper presents the design and assessment of this tool. SOPPTS has been designed and field-tested to provide real-time feedback from faculty on student project progress, to offer online guidance for project planning and to produce automated tracking of student projects. The tool assessment included interviews of both students at the undergraduate and graduate level and faculty. The interview was a set of specific questions chosen to document each participant's experience and impressions of utilizing SOPPTS. Data evaluation consisted of compiling the reoccurring themes during the interview process. The major themes that emerged are the increased efficiency in developing, recording and tracking of student project plans, the visibility and immediate accessibility of this information and the improved and timely communication among the student team members, faculty and client partners.

With the improved access to information and facilitated communication through SOPPTS, the project planning and tracking skills for the software development teams improved. Moreover, the informal aspects of team communication and synergy, factors that can be as important as the technical aspects, were enhanced.

1. Introduction

In order to deliver any project of magnitude successfully and on time, good project management is a necessity. This is especially true in software development. Project planning, scheduling and tracking are important activities of project management [8]. These skills are introduced in the software engineering classes at Ball State University. For these classes, students form software development teams that develop a complete software system starting with the requirements and ending with final delivery, including all documentation, to a customer or client-partner. Not only must these students satisfy the requirements for the course, they must also satisfy the requirements of their client partner.

After the acceptance of a project, each student team composes a list of software development tasks. A team leader assigns tasks to team members. Each student on the team prepares a weekly progress report. The faculty and student teams communicate about the project's progress through these weekly reports and the project deliverables that are handed in at assigned times. The reports and deliverables are reviewed by the faculty mentor and returned to the team members with comments and suggestions. Most importantly, faculty must be sure that teams are meeting their schedule and quality targets.

A critical part of project planning is to itemize the tasks, develop an initial schedule and assign team members as needed to accomplish those tasks. As development progresses it is important to monitor the completion of those tasks, to review the associated products and to determine if changes, alternative plans, or reassignments are required. Since the projects are team-oriented, it is essential that a synergy develop among team members to complete tasks and also between the faculty mentor and student team members for advice and insight into client and project issues.

The issues listed above gave rise to the inception of Student Online Project Planning and Tracking System, SOPPTS. SOPPTS was designed for the online learning environment, which makes it an accessible tool for the educational environment. The use of a web-based system for project management can improve visibility into a project's progress status and provides a timely "management alert" capability [3]. SOPPTS provides students with project planning and guidance technology to help them plan and track their software projects online, and incorporates a feedback mechanism for faculty guidance.

2. Our approach to designing SOPPTS

The purposes of this study were to design and evaluate an online system that enhances the communication and project tracking skills of the computer science students at BSU. This system should be similar to those found in industrial settings that the students may find themselves in after graduation. Even though the first targeted user-group was members from a computer science department, the system was intended not only to address the needs in the software engineering classes, but also to provide BSU with a tool that can be useful in many other disciplines that employ student team projects in the curriculum. Therefore, SOPPTS needed to be flexible to handle the various project scenarios and intuitive to accommodate different user profiles.

3. An overview of SOPPTS technology

For the design of SOPPTS, choices for both the Web server software and the database management system (DBMS) were carefully considered. Microsoft Access 2000 was chosen as the DBMS. Internet Information Server (IIS) and the Active Server Pages (ASP) were selected as the server-based technology.

4. Structure of SOPPTS

From the SOPPTS homepage (http://www.cs.bsu.edu/gwen/soppts), the four main sections, Register, Profile Update, Team Project Management and Forum can be accessed. Each of the sections serves a unique purpose and provides its own functionality. Register and Profile Update are designed for SOPPTS' administration. The Register section allows new users to complete the registration process. The Profile Update section displays the current profile of the logged-in user and the editing of the profile. The Team Project management section is the main portal to the activities and information for team planning and tracking. The Forum section is the electronic SOPPTS project bulletin board. Some of major functionalities in these sections will be discussed below.

4.1 Team Project Management

Two categories of SOPPTS users are first, the student team members plus the client partners and secondly, the faculty mentors. Student team members and client partners are responsible for their team plan and have access to only their team's project information. Faculty mentors are responsible for assigning the SOPPTS users to teams. Faculty also must be able to view all of the team plans and their progress (See Figures 1 and 2). The Team Project Management section allows a SOPPTS registered faculty member to create a team and to update or assign registered SOPPTS users to a team.

4.2 Student Team Project Management

Project planning is a critical activity in the software development process. Wu and Simmons [9] further stress the importance of planning, stating that planning gives the first view of a software project's future. The project plan begins with choosing a software life cycle model. Students are introduced to the various life cycle models in the course lectures. Due dates for the project deliverables are strictly maintained. These deliverables follow very closely to the products produced in the phases of the waterfall model. The classic waterfall model allows the student project to begin swiftly at the start of the semester and requires the students to experience the entire software development methodology. Furthermore, other life cycle models contain the same phases of development. If a selected project lends itself more naturally to another development process, such as iterative prototyping or rapid application development, then students may select a reasonable alternative. Recognizing this, SOPPTS includes templates for class project deliverables and approximate due dates based on the student project schedule.

Following the lifecycle phases, construction of the task list begins. Tasks form the atomic components of the project [4]. Each task should have a name as a form of identification and an expected start and end dates. Using the above templates, registered team-assigned students customize and decompose the tasks in SOPPTS to guide the development of their project. In Figure 1, a basic set of development tasks is displayed, accompanied by a planned start date and a planned end date for each task. A task is also associated with a deliverable to verify progress and finally each task is assigned to one or more members of the team. The interdependencies between tasks are recorded and these tasks are scheduled in order to avoid or minimize delay of the project.

Figure 1. Team project task management

Throughout the semester, the student team members will update these task records as progress on each task proceeds. The actual start and end dates of a task can be entered. During the time frame of completing a task, the percentage completed can be entered and updated as progress on the task is made. Also the interim and final task deliverable can be uploaded and linked to a task. These deliverables can be viewed and downloaded by the team members and client partners or by the faculty mentor.

When working on a complex project, it is important for team members, client partners and faculty to track the project to confirm a team's adherence to the schedule and to detect problems early when there might be time to do something about them. If the students and faculty do not track projects, they cannot control them. And, if a project is not being controlled, it is out of control [6]. Without tracking, students and teachers have no way to monitor potential problems or to know whether the project plans are being carried out correctly or accurately. In the past, it was difficult to find an effective way to track a project except by periodic static reports. With SOPPTS, students and faculty can view the plan through the online task progress chart (Figure 2). When users click the *bar chart button* in Figure 1, SOPPTS dynamically creates this chart from the task records stored in the SOPPTS database.

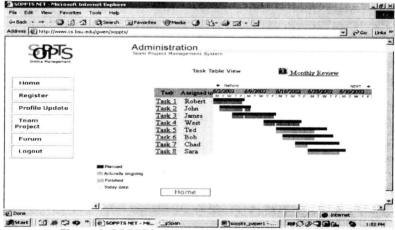

Figure 2. SOPPTS online task progress chart

Figure 2 shows an example of the dynamic online progress chart. Every task will either have one bar or two bars. One bar indicates that only the task and its planned start and end dates have been entered. A second bar indicates the amount of progress made on the task. In Figure 2, the top horizontal dark bars represent eight tasks' planned starting and ending dates. The bottom bar for each task will either be green denoting a finished task or orange indicating a task in progress. The horizontal green bars of Task 1, 2, 3 and 4, indicate that these tasks have been completed. All of these tasks began on their planned start date and all of them finished before their planned end date. The lower orange bars on Task 5, 6, 7 and 8 indicate that work is progressing on these tasks and that they are 80%, 70%, 30% and 90% complete, respectively. The goal is to permit the team members and faculty to determine at a glance the team's resource allocation over time and the progress made on each task. This online progress chart can illustrate gaps in the process and where potential problems may occur. For example, in Figure 2, task 7's deadline is June 29, but the task is only 30% complete and behind schedule. This delay could cause the entire project to be late. Chad should be contacted to determine the cause of the delay. If a problem is discovered early, the team leader or faculty member may have time to resolve this problem and accommodate the delay.

4.3 Faculty Project Management

In a project team, all team members contribute toward one single project. All of the team members must use the necessary skills of analysis, design, coding, verification and documentation. Through SOPPTS, the faculty member can assign the students to teams and monitor individual student participation through the list of tasks, the assignment of team members to these tasks (Figure 2), and the associated task documentation (Section 4.4). For example, SOPPTS can aid a faculty member in spotting slippages in a timetable for a deliverable. In the educational environment, it is important to determine if this slippage is due to the problem in time management or if the task is too complex for the skill level of the team members. These possibilities are important to remedy in a timely manner.

SOPPTS provides a window into the development process of student teams. SOPPTS also forces the students to divide the project into manageable subprojects. Just like an industrial software project manager, the faculty member must insist on a well-defined method with clearly defined deliverables. SOPPTS helps students reach this objective.

4.4 Online Electronic Submission

SOPPTS facilitates communication between faculty, client partners and student team members by providing an online submission function. With SOPPTS, students can submit all of their work electronically. These deliverables or homework assignments are stored in the SOPPTS database. Afterwards, the faculty member can read and evaluate these assignments online. Not only does the faculty member have a permanent record of the submission and an automatic organization of the submission, but also the faculty can use other tools to evaluate these submissions. For example, spell or code checkers or CASE tools that perform reverse engineering techniques can be applied to the appropriate submissions.

4.5 Aiding communication

One of the objectives of SOPPTS is to provide students with project planning and guidance technology for their software projects. An important facet of guidance is the feedback from the faculty and client partners. After the student team members enter their project planning information into SOPPTS, the faculty and client partners can access SOPPTS and review the students' projects. Faculty and client partners require an efficient response method within SOPPTS. The trouble of invoking a mail program and hunting and typing in a correct email address would limit the frequency of responses. By clicking the *feedback* link on the Project Management page, a feedback form is displayed and the reviewer can send email directly to the appropriate team members. The students are sent the reviewer's message immediately. All feedback is stored in the database for review.

The students of BSU and many of the client partners for whom the projects were being developed are located several hours from the campus. Obtaining and submitting the information online was a major advantage for them. Another positive by-product was in the formation of teams. In the past, team members selected each other on the basis of vicinity and their schedules. With the online feature, geographically distributed teams are possible, thus providing the students with an opportunity for a richer team experience.

SOPPTS also contains some self-monitoring mechanisms. When a task that is not 100% complete passes the planned end date, SOPPTS will send an email to the faculty and student members. Upon logging in, project plans that have a past due date, tasks that span more than seven days or unassigned tasks that have passed their start date are flagged. SOPPTS makes it easy to record the progress of project work. Evaluations can be periodically performed to observe modifications, such as changes in end dates, task assignment or tasks that have been deleted or added to a project. This information can be useful for assessments and process improvement.

5. SOPPTS Analysis

The students' individual perceptions and reactions to SOPPTS were perhaps the most critical evaluation element. One advantage of using interviews as a means of assessing SOPPTS' usefulness is that interviews document the actual as opposed to the ideal [1]. Eight months before the interviews were conducted, the consent form and two sets of interview questions, one for faculty and one for students, were developed and submitted to the appropriate university committees for approval. In February 2002, four faculty members and two students were approached to determine their reactions to SOPPTS and provide a source for data analysis. The questions were modified and formal taped interviews occurred from March 2002 to May 2002. Nineteen participants from three different groups were interviewed. Six senior undergraduate computer science majors, six graduate second year computer science majors, six computer science faculty members and one biomechanics faculty member participated.

5.1 Interview Analysis

Content analysis was performed on the nineteen interview transcriptions for the purpose of identifying patterns, themes and biases [10]. The analysis began with the construction of a table that mapped each interview question with an individual's response. There were eighteen columns representing the combined and overlapping set of faculty and student interview questions. The table rows contained the major phrases from the answers supplied by the nineteen interviewees. These phrases were carefully viewed to search for common concepts or reactions. Each identified concept or reaction was placed in a second table. Once the concepts and reactions were extrapolated and placed in the second table, the table was reviewed to determine trends or patterns.

The data were analyzed using the triangulation technique, which is one way of improving the probability that the findings and interpretations uncovered will be credible [5]. Triangulation of data supports research findings by showing that independent measures reveal the same findings, or do not contradict other findings in the study [7]. The earlier informal observations gathered from the six participants (the four faculty and two students) were compared to common themes found in the formal taped interviews. There was no overlap of the participants in the informal observations and formal interviews.

5.2 The Emerging Themes

Numerous phrases from the interviews were examined in the data analysis, which led to the identification of twenty-three main concepts (Table 1). These twenty-three main concepts merged into six general themes forming the columns for the emerging themes table (Table 1). Analysis of the data revealed that SOPPTS furnished students and faculty better access to information, led to improved communication, enhanced the learning environment, facilitated the learning of skill sets and improved time and project management.

Table 1: Emeging themes and trends

Theme 1	Theme 2	Theme 3	Theme 4	Theme 5	Theme 6
Better access to information	Better communication	Enhancement of learning enviroment	Enhancement of learning skills	Time management	Project management
1. Progress was visible	5 Consistent through record keeping	10. Work locations more flexible	14. Public nature of planning task assignments	17. Deliverables	20. Publicly defined task scheduling
2. Organization increased	6. Faculty feedback to students	11. Work submission easier	clears up misunder-standings; public	18. Deadlines	21. better task assignments
3. Team spirit improved	7. Student questions answered more swiftly	12. Records accessible	feedback gets students back on track	19. Dates and times on all submissions	22.better tracking skills
4. Helped faculty evaluate students' work	8. Better than email	13. Documents not lost	15. Public nature rewards hard working students and warns lazy students; also helps instructors predict future problems		23. Monitor tasks better
	9. Forum discussion		16. Instructors can see learning taking place		

Major Trend		Major Trend
Better communication and access to data		**Improvement of skills**

Results
1. Useful tool
2. Enhanced learning
3. Enhanced communication

6. Conclusion

By exposing project information to the different project stakeholders, namely student team members, faculty and client partners, problems seem to be addressed promptly and effectively. This was perhaps the greatest impact using SOPPTS. This motivating property was also experienced at the University of Paderborn and University of Braunschweig through their web delivered project performance table [2]. SOPPTS provided the communication platform through its various interfaces and users supplied the information. SOPPTS enhanced the learning experiences of the student participants, as well as the teaching experiences of the faculty. Students experienced time and task management. Faculty could track the students and projects more completely and, therefore, provide important feedback to the students and produce more in depth evaluations of their work.

In general, all participants thought that SOPPTS was valuable for the student project planning process. Students suggested that all classes require the use of SOPPTS just to use the features of the forum room and the online submission. For our study, only a few teams from the software engineering class used SOPPTS. It was suggested that all teams be required to use it from the start of the semester. Several participants have asked to continue to use SOPPTS for other course group projects. Additional features requested included providing more online information and pull-down help boxes in SOPPTS.

Overall, SOPPTS brings a new dimension to the planning and tracking of student-directed projects for all the project stakeholders. It is seen as a valuable supplement in courses where team project development occurs.

7. Future Enhancements

SOPPTS currently executes on the Microsoft Windows 2000 and utilizes Microsoft Access 2000 for the database support. A future enhancement to this tool would be to extend the number of platforms and database environments on which it executes. Providing additional platforms may increase SOPPTS' use for student-directed projects in other disciplines.

Much needs to be included into the development for a distributed student software project management tool. The inclusion of aspects from software estimation and project risk management are yet to be interfaced into SOPPTS. A future SOPPTS tool will make effective project tracking easier than ever. The positive response that was received from this first prototype is an encouragement that SOPPTS is on the right track.

8. References

[1] Cocklin,B. (1996). Applying Qualitative Research to Adult Education: Reflections Upon the Analytic Processes. Studies in the Education of Adults, 28,88-116.

[2] Gehrke, M., Giese, H., Nickel, U., Niere, J., Tichy, M., Wadsack, J. and Zonforf, A, (2002). "Reporting about Industrial Strength Software Engineering Courses for Undergraduates". ICSE'02, May 19-25, Orlando, Florida.

[3] Hefner, R. (2000). "Managing Projects through a Corporate Repository", Proceedings of the 33rd Hawaii International Conference of System Science.

[4] Lam, H.E. and Maheshwari, P. (2002). "Task and Team Management in The Distributed Software Project Management Tool". Proceedings of the 25th Annual International Computer Software and Applications Conference.

[5] Leedy, P and Ormrod , J. E., (2001). Practical Research, Planning and Design (7th ed.), Upper Saddle River, NJ, Merrill Prentice Hall.

[6] McConnell, S. (1997). "Tool Support for Project Tracking". IEEE Software.Vol. 15, No. 5

[7] Miles, M.B., and Huberman, A.M. (1994). Qualitative Data Analysis: An Expanded Sourcebook (2nd ed). Thousand Oaks, CA: Sage.

[8] Pressman, R. (2001). Software Engineering A practitioner's approach. (5th ed.) Berkeley: McGraw-Hill.

[9] Wu, C. S. and Simmons, D. (2000). "Software Project Planning Associate (SPPA): A Knowledge-Based Approach for Dynamic Software Project Planning and Tracking". Proceedings of the Twenty-Fourth Annual International Computer Software & Application Conference

[10] Zhang, J. (2002). Designing and Implementing the Student Online Project Planning and Tracking System: Students and Faculty Evaluation of the SOPPTS Software. Doctoral dissertation. Ball State University, Muncie, IN.

Together We Stand: Group Projects for Integrating Software Engineering in the Curriculum

Darren Dalcher and Mark Woodman
School of Computing Science e-Centre
Middlesex University,
Trent Park, Bramley Road,
London N14 4YZ, UK.
d.dalcher@mdx.ac.uk; m.woodman@mdx.ac.uk

Abstract

Software engineering is done by individuals within teams and in organisations, with all that those words imply. It is crucial to make this fact, and its implications, concrete to students who aspire to be or work with software engineers. Although frequent collaborations are encouraged throughout degree programmes, final-year group projects remain the favoured mechanism for achieving this goal. This paper describes and reflects on our experience of introducing group projects to balance theory, technology and practice into five different degree programmes. A novel facet of our approach has been to locate these projects in the context of a course on software project management in parallel with the preparation of capstone, individual projects. Hence, the final-year group projects are viewed as essential complements to the individual projects and together they encapsulate the theories and systematic practices of software projects we know as software engineering. We argue that this approach injects realism into what might have been seen by students as abstract – primarily by providing students with experience of working as part of a team and so enabling them to engage with large and significant projects.

1. Background

We begin by describing why we have introduced the type of projects into a new set of degree programmes at Middlesex University. To explain our approach we touch on the (non-) issue of the separation between software engineering education and computer science education and outline the general nature of degrees in the UK and the influence of national bodies on curricula. Later we explore the impact of the new project arrangements on students, staff and the academic provision. Appendices give some detail that should allow the reader to visualise how the projects work in practice.

In the UK, as in much of Europe, software engineering is seen as representing the body of professional, systematic software development practices for all of computing (or informatics). The terms 'software engineering', 'computer science' and 'information systems' are used to distinguish *overlapping* subsets of the discipline, and curriculum, from each other. The terms are used to convey the different emphases in degrees whose titles include the terms or variations of them. In practice, the same departments and often the same people, teach the degrees titled *Software Engineering* or *Computer Science*. Hence arrangements for software engineering education are not seen as being distinctly different from, say, those for computer science education. Furthermore, students' disdain of 'engineering' has forced many departments to sneak the ideas of software engineering into otherwise-labelled parts of the curriculum.

Undergraduate degrees in the UK generally encompass three years of specialist study. This is often augmented by an industrial placement year undertaken before the final year. Students of computing – computer science, software engineering or information systems – thus get three specialised years worth of advanced theoretical material. Many degrees are composed of learning units, often called modules. Depending on the university and its regulations, students select from a limited set or can 'mix and match' from a large set with relatively few constraints. (We offer both.) In general, many of the units/modules that students cover during those three years focus on independent assessment emphasising different aspects of systems development and software engineering. However within six months after graduation many of the students find themselves working on medium to large projects as a part of a team – an experience they may not be prepared for.

Of course, the distribution of software engineering throughout the curriculum means principles and practices are situated where they are most relevant. For example, for students specialising in multimedia development, notions of a requirements analysis and of a lifecycle can be, and arguably should be, taught in the context of designing and managing digital media projects. However, distribution throughout the curriculum of software engineering ideas runs the danger of not being properly linked together into a cohesive and coherent whole. In recently redesigning all our bachelor degrees, we have deliberately taken a distributive approach with mandatory key learning modules – packages of 180 hours of study – to ensure acquisition of crucial knowledge and skills. A pair of these core modules ensures the place of software engineering in all our degrees.

All computing programmes in the UK are now expected to conform to the Computing Benchmark Statement established by the national Quality Assurance Agency for Higher Education (QAA) which defines the standards for the award of honours degree in all areas of computing, including software engineering. Irrespective of the orientation of a degree, it is expected that all degree programmes will entail both underpinning, theoretical principles and their practical application. In particular, graduates are expected to acquire knowledge and skills relevant to problems with possible computer-based solutions such as, the analysis of such problems, the determination of requirements for solutions, and the design and practical implementations of cost-effective solutions. We take the view that whether a degree allows a student to specialise in business information systems or in interactive systems, it must include the software engineering of such systems.

In the UK the needs of industry are represented by the British Computer Society (BCS), a nominated body of the British Engineering Council, that can offer accreditation to educational courses at Chartered Engineer level. The BCS, under its Royal Charter, is required to establish and maintain standards of professional competence, conduct and ethical practice. This duty includes the responsibility to develop and maintain educational standards and professional examinations [1]. The Society undertakes a schedule of inspection visits to UK universities who wish to seek exemptions for appropriate degree programmes to provide an alternative route to professional membership of the society and for accreditation leading to a chartered engineer status. Full exemption is awarded when a programme is deemed to provide breadth and depth influenced by relevant research and industry trends, with adequate theoretical underpinning. Inevitably, the area and extent of projects comes under close scrutiny as part of the BCS exemption and accreditation visit (as well as those from the QAA) as it represents the major 'integration' exercise performed by students prior to graduation. We took this integrative aspect of projects very seriously in the design of our degrees.

The School of Computing Science at Middlesex University is one of the largest in the UK with some 4,000 students from a rich diversity of backgrounds, ages and countries. We are based on three campuses where we offer an internationally recognised range of high quality undergraduate and postgraduate programmes in computing science, information technology, multimedia technology, business information systems, communications systems and networking and telecommunications. The school takes great pride from the use of innovative learning and teaching techniques which enable students to take responsibility for their own learning and develop their ability to argue critically and think independently. During 2000–1 we reviewed and rationalised our programmes following the publication of the national Computing Benchmark Statement [2]. One important purpose of the review was to achieve BCS accreditation for our programmes and BCS professional project exemption for individual undergraduate projects – goals we subsequently met. As a result of our review we refined our vision of our undergraduate curriculum and very carefully placed project work – both group and individual projects – at the heart of the curriculum. In doing so we directly addressed the perception reported by industry colleagues that graduates lack "real-world skills".

2. Projects for Integrating Software Engineering

Following the aforementioned review, the project provision was revamped to maximise the potential benefits to graduates, particularly to make their experience of projects more closely correspond to what they would experience after graduating. Under the new arrangements two major projects are offered in the final year of the degree, the group project and the individual project. Students who complete both will have devoted a minimum of 360 hours to project work. These hours correspond to the credit available for the work, but are naturally enlarged by extending the project period from the beginning of the first semester to near the end of the second, including several weeks with no scheduled teaching (e.g. for vacation periods). Crucially, the group project is carried out and the individual project is initiated *in conjunction with* extensive teaching on software project management. This teaching covers a broad range of methods and tools needed in software engineering projects. Hence, while reaching final-year maturity, students are equipped to reason about and select appropriate methods and tools in the concrete and pressing context of both the group and the individual projects.

Although ultimately students and potential employers perceive individual projects as true indicators of their abilities, it is group projects where software engineering becomes a reality. Indeed, by juxtaposing the study of software processes and project management with all the human complexities of teams, the group and individual projects are integrating software engineering into the curriculum.

The central focus of a group project is a practical, real-world problem, with a group's seminar tutor acting as a sponsor. The objectives of the group project are to give students experience in:

♦ teamwork,

♦ engineering,

♦ prioritising and managing a substantial piece of work,

♦ developing a project portfolio,

♦ fostering a range of project management competencies, and

♦ communicating formally and informally about progress.

These are spelt out in classes that support student learning and in the support materials provided and reinforced by grading criteria published to students.

The group project thus introduces the students to the practical problems associated with team working and managing a large undertaking. Students receive guidance on conduct of team projects by:

- a standard set of guidelines (see the brief extract in Appendix 1);

- regular formal lectures, including several given by local academics who are specialists in related fields;

- interactive group tutor-led seminars;

- guest lectures from industrial speakers; and

- an industrial project clinic.

Group projects are carried out by teams of students studying for the same degree. The projects are generally proposed by academics, but groups may devise alternative proposals, which must be subsequently approved. During weekly seminars, students are expected to approach their tutor, as project sponsor, for clarification of the requirements, which are eventually formalised and signed off. Students are encouraged to consult subject experts available within the school, and make use of an industrial project clinic.

Whereas a group project lasts one semester of the final year, an individual project spans both semesters. It is initiated at the start of the first semester, which allows students to demonstrate their ability to plan, organise, carry out and present a substantial piece of independent work and to complete it in a competent and professional manner. Students are encouraged to develop their own proposal and discuss it with a suitable member of staff introduced by their seminar tutor. These tutors act as temporary supervisors during the first semester while students develop their proposal in consultation with prospective supervisors.

Progression to the second project module depends on the successful completion of all components in the earlier module, including the individual project proposal part. A typical proposal includes aims, objectives, problem definition, evidence of requirements, context description, a limited, but relevant, annotated bibliography, a method rationale, a brief product description, a list of deliverables, an evaluation method, a list of required resources, detailed plans and a completed sample task agreed with the supervisor. During the first semester students present their proposal to allow feedback and peer involvement. Students who progress to the individual project, will therefore have completed a significant amount of the background and planning work and have a refined and agreed proposal. (They will thus be some way into the project.) The second semester is dedicated to the supervision and completion of the individual project.

Grading (i.e. marking) of individual projects is done by the project supervisor and a second marker (i.e. grader). All group projects are double-marked by the seminar tutor and by a second tutor from another group to ensure consistency of grading. To ensure consistency and to simplify administration a Web-based system has been developed for projects (sample screens from the system are given in Appendix 3.)

A wide spectrum of projects is offered to students depending on the specialisms in their degree programme and on the backgrounds and specific interests of staff, so no single prescription is exactly appropriate for all projects. However, it is possible to identify two typical kinds of project:

Engineering (or Development) Projects. These attempt to solve a practical problem through problem analysis (including pertinent literature search), design and practical implementation. This is normally followed by evaluation of project results based on the earlier analysis and review, and reflection on the design issues and the choices made. The tradeoffs are expected to reflect social, legal and ethical aspects in a professional manner. They will also encompass decisions concerning reliability, quality and timeliness. The main purpose of this type of project is to resolve a (reasonably) well-understood problem by proceeding in a well-organised manner and passing through a series of phases, each culminating in a deliverable or document. The student will submit a dissertation encompassing a project report together with the implemented software and appropriate documentation. This type of project is expected to convey professional standards with full justification of choices, tradeoffs and assumptions. Indeed, a student's ability to reflect on their own performance is graded – see Appendix 2.

Research-based projects. These focus on empirical or investigative work into a (possibly) ill-understood problem. These projects also encompass intermediary documents indicating progress, and culminate in a submitted dissertation describing the results and implications of the investigation.

The practical application of software engineering principles is thus learnt by students in doing both a group project and an individual project. Their learning is supported by the teaching on project planning, group working, presentation skills and ethical and professional issues covered during the formal lecture and the seminar sessions in the first semester. The seminars support the application of those skills, highlight ethical dilemmas and inform students about intellectual property and plagiarism in software and system development. For student project modules we have found that most institutions provide little or no teaching, but it is teaching synchronised with deadlines in student projects that make software engineering meaningful and integrate its ideas with the rest of the curriculum. Hence, for example, lectures survey major topics just before students need to apply them and point to additional sources that students need to customise for their project. It is hoped that students will become autonomous learners and utilise their experience on further projects. Tutorials also attempt to anticipate and provide for specific tasks. Industrial project clinics and guest lectures by leading consultants and practitioners offer an industrial perspective on development and project work. Extensive material developed for the two modules provides additional information on projects, research methods, the required format and the requirements for a BCS approved project.

In summary, our approach to student projects, is predicated on the special relationship between the individual project which is now planned in the first semester, the group project completed in the first semester, the formal lectures and seminars, supporting both projects, in the first semester and the individual guidance given by the project supervisor (primarily in the second semester). The net result is that a third of the final year is now largely dedicated to project work that puts software engineering into practice.

3. Educating Graduates Versus Skilling Practitioners

Organisations, and society at large, need software engineering, but its principles and practices tend to be taught to individuals as is if they were aimed at the individual. Inevitably this fallacy, for students especially, makes software engineering somewhat abstract, somewhat disconnected from them. Humphrey's linkage of individual and team processes [3, 4] to organisations' may bridge the gap for experienced practitioners, but if we are to empower students to become effective software engineers and effective members of software teams, we must provide them with meaningful project experience.

We have achieved this by linking group and individual projects to relevant software engineering teaching. While many modules in the various degrees we offer include mini projects and group-work, they are relatively small exercises, rather than what the ACM curriculum terms a *capstone* project. The driving need for such projects stems from the fact that graduating students had little or no experience of group-working on a significant project. Many employers require that graduates understand how to work and deliver products in teams; this is no easy task. In fact, many endeavours can be characterised as multi-author, multi-participant non-trivial development and there appears to be a growing demand for practitioners with a working knowledge of concepts, principles and methods. The challenge for us is to provide something that is small enough to be 'complete-able' within one semester, yet it also needs to be realistic and non-trivial to justify full utilisation of the life cycle and prioritisation to ensure that the final deadlines are met.

The group project provides the students with the opportunity to work together collaboratively and to apply their problem solving skills on a larger and more significant problem. Because the problem is significant it means it needs to be split. The group project enables students to work in a group environment and benefit from the strengths available within their group while maintaining a natural 'support network'. It also enables them to specialise within a larger project. As the project is long, the activities need to be scheduled and their execution carefully monitored. Students are reminded that the project resembles a project in industry, where they will be allocated to a group working on a specific task and are expected to complete that task. The project lasts one full semester and hence time management, planning and monitoring are crucial to successful completion.

The keys to success appear to be the inter-related aspects of co-operation, co-ordination and communication:

Co-operation. Work must be shared among team members and it is in the team's interest to ensure that everyone becomes involved. During the semester students are exposed to team structures, group dynamics and inter-personal working relationships. Deadlines are both realistic and firm. Forming internal support networks ensures that when problems are encountered help is at hand and the group as a unit can continue toward its given target.

Co-ordination. Project work entails division of work, scheduling of time and prioritisation of tasks. This work needs to be monitored consistently. Groups are expected to select the most suitable techniques or methods to complete their tasks. It is crucial therefore to ensure group members deliver what is expected of them and that it is delivered on time and to the agreed specification.

Communication. Presentations and reports underscore the need for care and the importance of communication skills (not just for the purpose of attaining grades). The overall task is concerned with solving a problem and dealing with tradeoffs between different aspects of the problem. Students are encouraged to reason about their choices and document their decisions. A critical part of the completed group portfolio is the explicit recording of the rationale and assumptions and the justification of the choice of methods and approaches. This represents sound professional practice (and enables progress monitoring and on-going risk assessment).

Experience suggests that total reliance on classroom teaching produces graduates, but is insufficient to produce practitioners. Part of the learning experience involves interacting with uncertainty and failure. Indeed, the reflection that ensues as a result of small failures and unworkable paths and options is an essential part of problem solving and a cornerstone of professional practice. Adjusting a course of action and updating plans is an important part of the learning experience. It also provides a great scope for further discussion thereby satisfying the academic part (i.e. the assessment) of the report. Working on real-world problems injects realism into the course. Developing a software engineering competence requires interaction with the essence of design through the application of problem solving approaches to a dynamic and changing problem. As part of dealing with a larger problem, students learn more about the various phases involved in product development and the problems and dilemmas associated with managing that effort (the project). They get to find out about and experience complex software systems. Moreover, they gain useful experience they can start to utilise after graduation, but which should be the underpinning of a developing professional awareness for a full working life. Denning [5] reasoned that computer science and engineering degrees should require the demonstration of accomplishments and competencies. Providing the students with an opportunity to build a problem-driven experience enables students to exercise reflection and problem solving in practice. This reflection sometimes finds its way into the reports in the form of "if I had to do this project over again…" Interestingly, the fact that students are encouraged to reflect, appears to have an impact on the individual projects in the second semester as they attempt to avoid repeating mistakes (plan to throw one away, in a forgiving atmosphere?)

4. Early Results

The module is undertaken by all Single Honours students within the Computing area, as well as by many of the Joint Honours students. To date, some 1110 student have taken the module across the three campuses – with attendant administrative complications due to scale and distribution. The annual figure is likely to rise over the next few years as older degree programmes that do not require projects are replaced by new programmes that do.

Typically a group will contain five students. The idea was that they would all come from the same core programme to enable them to focus on an area that is likely to be relevant to all members of the group and to enable us to allocate a seminar tutor with the same specialism. Due to time-tabling problems across campuses this has been difficult to attain forcing some seminar tutor to extend their areas of specialism.

The seminar tutor is likely to play a number of roles:

♦ a customer who provides a partial version of the requirements with whom the team is expected to interact on an on-going basis and negotiate a common understanding of the problem area;

♦ a mentor capable of helping with technical advice and indicate new directions, avenues or sources worth investigating;

♦ a sponsor who may be able to relax some of the requirements (albeit not the constraints);

♦ a final arbitrator when team members are incapable of resolving dilemmas;

♦ a personal advisor helping with individual or group problems;

On the other hand, the team roles played by students in their group vary considerably and depending on the type of project. Invariably, a team leader emerges. Whether the team decides that one of them should play the role of planner, one should be an administrator, one a designer, etc. depends on the nature of the project. Because of their need to demonstrate their contribution to the team to their tutor and to each other, many roles, such as that of report author, are shared.

The interaction with the seminar tutor is very intensive requiring a great input of time, attention and involvement (and may lead to burnout and requests for 'reflection periods' away from intense group projects).

Another problem we have experienced is with late comers who appear to interfere with the general performance and dynamics of a group. Students who join a group late must be allocated carefully and must be accepted by groups which may have already formed a management structure and started to bond. Indeed, a group's work is likely to broadly follow the 'forming-storming-norming-performing' stages of group development (see Appendix 1). When a late addition is made, Brooks's apposite observation becomes concrete, and not just an assertion in a book [6].

200

On the positive side, student feedback appears to be very supportive of their experiences and the work they have done as part of the group project. However many friendships have been challenged as a result of having to work together on an intensive project.

5. Final Thoughts

Practising on a real project brings software engineering and project management to life. It also provides a link between material the students have already covered on the practice of software development, management, risk and quality. This link is vital as students are expected to integrate all aspects while covering most of the software development process and provide a meaningful (and in many cases memorable) project experience.

The projects linked to relevant teaching of software engineering aim to produce reflective practitioners capable of working in interdisciplinary teams (and hence capable of identifying skill complements and maximising a team's ability to work on a project). Our students experience the fact that real project work is not as well as organised as in textbooks, forcing them to synchronise activities, prioritise and generally make tough, constrained decisions about the management of projects.

Students are required to finish their projects and to do so within the timing constraints imposed by teaching semesters. They can therefore adjust the functionality, quality and effort levels but not overall timing. They learn that they need to allocate mini-delivery cycles to ensure the overall work finishes on time, especially when they are required to synchronise work products with other members of their team. By the end of the project most recognise the triangular relationship between time (which may be fixed by the university or any future client), effort (replacing cost), and the quality and amount of delivered functionality. The quality of the final product, and the resulting grade, are likely to be directly related to the amount of effort and the ability to complete on time.

Projects take the students beyond the theory. They enable students to practise the knowledge, skills and competencies have acquired throughout their degree. They also enable them to obtain new ones. The main focus of the assessment is on the deliverable and the reflection it embodies. We therefore extend the client notion of looking at the product to encompass the lessons the student acquired along the way. In reality the students get to engage with theory and practice, with product and project and thereby to develop their own process for addressing projects, which improves from the first semester to the second. But above all they get to engage with people; with clients and co-developers, with experts, gate keepers, supervisors and monitors.

The project structure described here has been well received by the BCS, leading to full accreditation of our programmes, as well as by employers and our industrial collaborators. From the perspective of the project co-ordinator, planning and launching such a new project programme is a major challenge: Conceiving the new scheme is time-intensive and takes a number of iterations. Supervising projects is resource-intensive. Engendering a new project culture is effort-intensive. So over all what have WE learned? Well, after all this is a project and like our students, we have also learned about the crucial role of working with people (and the need for reflection when we get something wrong!).

6. References

[1] The British Computer Society. Guidelines on Course Exemption & Accreditation. Information for Universities and Colleges, August 2001 (see http://www.bcs.org.uk).

[2] Computing Benchmark Statement, Quality Assurance Agency for Higher Education, Sheffield, England (available via http://www.qaa.ac.uk).

[3] Watts S. Humphrey, Personal Software Process, Addison Wesley, 1999.

[4] Watts S. Humphrey, Introduction to the Team Software Process, Addison Wesley, 1999.

[5] Peter J. Denning. "Educating a New Engineer", Communications of the ACM, Vol. 35, No. 12, Dec. 1992.

[6] Fred P. Brooks, The Mythical Man-Month, Addison Wesley, Reading, Mass., 1975/1995.

Appendix 1: Extract from Student Handbook

The following advice is extracted from the handbook provided to project students.

Group project allocation, organisation and supervision

Students will be allocated to seminar groups according to campus, programme and pathway. Group projects are generally proposed by staff and are posted on the School web site. The projects reflect pathway topics, real-world problems or research problems. The work can thus be implementation-oriented within a specific area, research-centred, revolve around practical/industrial problem or be based on an individual case study. The balance between the production of a set of project management plans and schedules and the production of a real working artefact will be negotiated with the tutor and formalised in a contract. Possible scenarios within a seminar group:

♦ 4 teams working on separate problems

♦ 4 teams working on the same problem using different approaches, methods or tools

♦ 4 teams working on products that will be linked and integrated at the end

♦ One large project with 4 teams focusing on different portions of the work – with constant interaction

♦ On-going incremental development where students build on baselines from previous years.

During seminars students are expected to clarify requirements with the tutor (sponsor). Students may also consult experts in the School and make use of the industrial project clinic. Groups are populated homogeneously, in terms of subject and specialism, in order to assume some common technical knowledge. Their compatibility in terms of team roles will be assessed as part of the team building.

The work of the groups is likely to follow the 'forming-storming-norming-performing' stages of group development. The first stage is emphasised through work designed to exhibit the enhanced power of working in a group, whilst also introducing students to some of the disagreements and disputes that may emerge as a result of teamwork. As the group moves into 'norming' and finally, 'performing' stages, the project portfolio will be developed and completed. A critical part of the portfolio is the explicit recording of the rationale, assumptions and the justification of the choice of methods and approaches. This represents sound professional practice and enables monitoring and on-going risk assessment.

The group project will enable students to work in a group environment and benefit from the strengths available within their group. Groups will complete the project portfolio, which includes a variety of plans, a general design scheme (with implementation where appropriate) and the application of management techniques to their topic. Groups will be expected to select the most suitable method to cover each section required in the project management portfolio (with particular reference to the individual context of their project). The rationale for each selection needs to be made explicit within the documentation.

In each group, one person will be elected as group leader and another as secretary by the members of the group. These two positions entail some additional responsibility which should be taken into account when work is allocated. The group leader resolves conflicts and disputes. Also it is the group leader's responsibility to ensure that group members deliver what is required of them and that they are on time (this may not make the group leader overly popular). Normally the group leader is also in charge of integrating the results of individual efforts into a coherent whole. The secretary is responsible for recording all decisions and any information obtained during the seminar sessions. They will also be expected to keep records of meetings and attendance of members. They are also likely to be in charge of integrating the report itself into a coherent professional looking whole.

Appendix 2: Form for Students to Evaluate their Work

Students add comments against the criteria in the following form and this self-evaluation is assessed towards their grade

Please enter your comments below explaining to your supervisor and second marker how you considered/addressed the following:	
Elucidation of the problem and the objectives of the project	
An in-depth investigation of the context/literature/other similar products.	
A clear definition of the problem	
A clear description of the stages of the life cycle undertaken or the ordering of the project activities. Please note that this refers to a structured, staged approach for deriving a solution. It does not imply a sequential development pattern, but rather refers to a focus on the development process and on multiple identifiable phases.	
A description of the use of appropriate tools and the choice of methods to support the development process, the information gathering and/or the investigation (should also address the range of potential tools/methods and reasons why final selection was made).	
A description of how verification and validation were applied at all stages (with a particular emphasis on test plans and their derivation).	
Consideration of the quality of the solution or findings -- if a product is being developed, it is often expected that it will exhibit the attributes of quality, reliability, timeliness and maintainability	
A critical appraisal of the project, indicating the rationale for design/implementation decisions or other choices and lessons learnt during the course of the project.	
Evaluation (with hindsight) of the product and the process of its production (including a review of the plan and any deviations from it and self evaluation of the work). You may also want to consider future work.	
Use of and organisation of references	
Use of and organisation of Appendices - technical documentation	
The quality of presentation	
The use of language	
The fact that critical appraisal, rationale, justification and lessons derived from the effort in the final evaluation can be applied to both the product (artefact, solution or result) and the process.	

Appendix 3: Screens from Web-based Project System

Figure A3.1 shows a summary of the status of current projects as seen by the academic co-ordinating projects. Figure A3.2 summarises information held on projects an individual academic must supervise or grade. Tools on the left hand frame allow information to be changed (subject to the privileges of the user). Following links on the right hand frame allows various types of query to be made and provides the tools for grading projects.

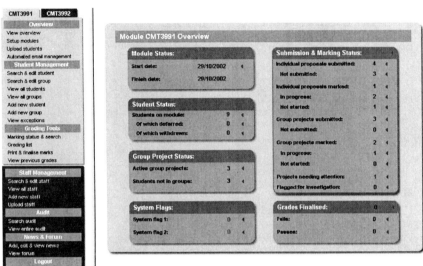

Figure A3.1: Overview of status of group projects

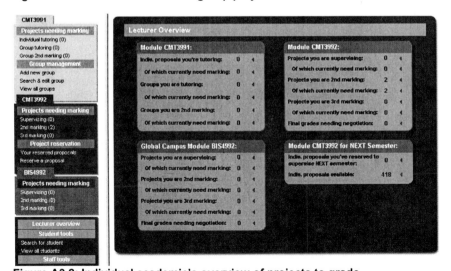

Figure A3.2: Individual academic's overview of projects to grade

Software Engineering Methods 2 (Paper Session G)

Modelling: A Neglected Feature in the Software Engineering Curriculum

A. J. Cowling
Department of Computer Science,
University of Sheffield,
Regent Court, Portobello Street,
Sheffield, S1 4DP, United Kingdom
Email: A.Cowling @ dcs.shef.ac.uk

Abstract

This paper argues that the concept of modelling, and particularly of software system structures, is not being given sufficient attention within current sources that describe aspects of the software engineering curriculum. The paper describes the scope of modelling as a general concept, and explains the role that the modelling of software system structures plays within it. It discusses the treatment of this role within the various sources, and compares this both with the experience of the role that such modelling plays in the undergraduate curriculum at Sheffield University, and with the practice in other branches of engineering. The idea is examined that modelling should be treated as a recurring concept within the curriculum, and it is shown that this gives rise to a matrix structure for the software engineering curriculum. The paper discusses how such a structure can be mapped into a conventional hierarchical curriculum model, and the relationships that need to be made explicit in doing so. It describes the practical implications of these results for the structures of degree programmes in software engineering.

Keywords

Software engineering education, software modelling, software engineering theory, software engineering practice, software processes, curriculum structure, degree programmes.

1. Introduction

As its title suggests, the motivation for this paper is a concern that the process of curriculum development for software engineering (SE from now on) is in danger of neglecting the topic of modelling, and particularly the modelling of the products that SE is concerned with developing. The purpose of the paper is therefore to examine the role that this topic should have, both to demonstrate that there is genuine cause for this concern, and to suggest a remedy for it.

The starting point for this is to define, in section 2, the scope and organisation of the topic of software modelling, and then in section 3 to examine the role that it currently has, as evidenced by various published sources, and in particular the Guidelines for SE Education [1], where it appears as a "recurring concept". Sections 4 and 5 then compare this with the role that it should have, based respectively on the experience gained from the undergraduate degree programme in SE in the department of Computer Science at Sheffield University, and general practice in other branches of engineering. To see how software product modelling can be given an more appropriate degree of emphasis, section 6 reviews the significance of treating it as a recurring concept, while section 7 shows how the conclusions of this might be accommodated within the

1093-0175/03 $17.00 © 2003 IEEE

models that are being developed for the SE curriculum. To bring out the practical relevance of what is otherwise a fairly theoretical discussion, section 8 examines some of the implications of this for SE degree programmes, and section 9 summarises the conclusions of the paper.

2. The Scope of Modelling in SE

As noted in the introduction, the SE Guidelines provide an obvious starting point for defining the scope of the topic of software modelling, in that they identify a set of seven topics that are called "recurring concepts", a term that is borrowed from Computing Curricula 91 [2] (CC91 from now on). One of these seven recurring concepts is entitled "Software Modeling", and the definition for it that is given within the SE Guidelines is as follows. "The Software Modeling component covers principles and methods for modeling software architectures and software development entities. This includes techniques for using abstraction, modularity and hierarchy to model software functionality, data object relationships, behavior models, and formal methods." In practice, this set of topics can be broken down into more detail in a hierarchical fashion, as illustrated in figure 1, where there are two important features to note.

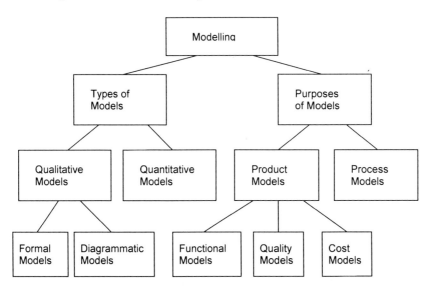

Figure 1: A Hierarchical Structure for Modelling in SE

One feature is that the types and purposes of models are orthogonal, so that both product and process models will each have qualitative and quantitative forms. Of these, the qualitative or structural models are concerned with describing the different kinds of concepts (eg modules, functions or "data objects") that occur in the structure being modeled, and the various relationships between them (such as "hierarchy") that go to make up this structure. Such models can then be expressed either diagrammatically using notations like UML [3] or its predecessors, or formally using notations such as Z [4], VDM [5] or B [6]. By contrast, quantitative models are expressed in terms of equations relating different properties of the objects being modeled, although usually the forms of these equations will then be derived in part from the underlying structures that are described in a qualitative model.

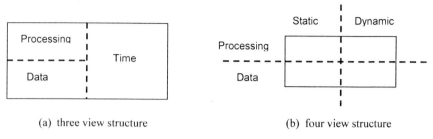

(a) three view structure   (b) four view structure

Figure 2: The three-view and four-view structures for models of system functionality

The other feature is that the product models divide into three main groups, covering the aspects of functionality (where the term is used here to also include the underlying "data object relationships"), quality (which partly relates to the aspect of "behavior"), and the cost of construction. Of these, the qualitative functional models form the basis for the other two groups, and conventionally they are divided either into either three or four groups, as illustrated in figure 2, although an important insight from formal methods is that these are actually not different models, but simply different views of the parts of a single integrated model (represented by the outer rectangles in the figure). The older structured analysis and design methodologies identified just three of these views, as shown in figure 2(a), but they referred to them as separate models, namely data models, processing models and time (or behavioural) models. More recently, many of the object oriented methodologies have recognised that the last of these three effectively splits into two parts, one concerned with the behaviour over time of the data for a system, and the other concerned with the behaviour over time of the processing that it performs. This, therefore, gives a division into four views, in which each of the data and processing aspects are divided into a static part and a dynamic (behavioural) part, as shown in figure 2(b).

3. The Current Role of Modelling in SE

To see the extent to which software product modelling is being neglected within the SE curriculum, one starting point is the set of common introductory textbooks on SE. This is where the project to construct the SE Body of Knowledge [7] (SWEBOK) started, and a check has been made on the index and contents pages of a large part of their sample, plus a few others, to determine what references they make to this topic. With a couple of exceptions (both published in 2001), if there is any mention of modelling in them it is typically referring either to process models, or to modelling non-functional aspects of systems such as cost or reliability. In general there is certainly no suggestion that either modelling itself as a concept, or the application of it to the structures of the products being created, should be treated as a coherent topic within SE. Even in the two newest texts, which do introduce modelling, the coverage focuses primarily on its role within requirements analysis, rather than as a concept that underpins the whole of SE.

To be fair to the authors of the older texts, this could be partly a problem of terminology, since related terms such as abstraction, formal methods or different types of diagrams all appear, and point to material that is essentially about aspects of modelling. Also, it could be argued that at least some of these textbooks were written originally for readers who already had a significant knowledge of basic computer science (CS from now on), and so who might be expected to be familiar already with at least some of these concepts of modelling. Nevertheless, the effect is that the coherent treatment of the concept itself is still missing, and particularly insofar as it relates to activities such as specification, design, construction, validation or verification.

This effect has then carried over into some of the documents that define models for aspects of the SE curriculum. Since the SWEBOK project started with a similar sort of analysis of textbooks, and also of the ISO/IEC standard 12207 [8], it is not surprising that the Strawman version of its guide made little reference to modelling, and this is still the case with the current version [9]. Indeed, the term does not appear anywhere in the chapter headings or sub-headings of the guide, and one has to go down to the overviews of each chapter in the introduction to the guide to find any references to it, and these are only in the context of conceptual modelling within requirements analysis (in the overview of chapter 2), models for software metrics (in the overview of chapter 8) and process models (in the overview of chapter 9).

Similarly, the structure of the SE knowledge area for the CS volume of Computing Curricula 2001 [10] (CC2001 from now on) follows much the same pattern, since it is based on the same set of sources, together with the Guidelines document. This structure did, however, have to reduce the material heavily to fit into a single knowledge area, so that many topics had to be condensed or even omitted. Consequently, modelling does not appear in the titles of any of the twelve knowledge units that make up this knowledge area, although it does appear in some of the topics that, but not with as much importance as activities such as requirements analysis or design, or others of the recurring concepts from the Guidelines document.

Most recently, the first stage in developing the SE volume of CC2001 has involved producing a definition of the model known as SEEK (SE Education Knowledge), and the first public draft of this [11] had just been released at the time that this paper was being written. This has a wider scope than the SWEBOK guide, since it also needs to describe foundational material that is required to support SE, as well as the core SE material. For the latter, though, it follows a very similar structure to the SWEBOK, which it explicitly acknowledges as a key input. The result is that its coverage of modelling is similarly weak, although there are more references to it. Thus, "Modelling" is one of four units in the "Fundamentals" area, "Requirements modelling and analysis" is one of six units in the "Requirements" area, and several other units have aspects of modelling as one of their topics, such as "Metaphors and conceptual models" as one of the topics in the "User interface design" unit, and "Modelling and specification of software processes" as a topic in the "Process concepts" unit. While this is an improvement, it still does not bring modelling up to the level of importance attached to topics such as software processes or software quality, which both form complete knowledge areas.

4. Modelling and the Sheffield SE Programme

This limited coverage of modelling in these sources contrasts with the experience of the author and colleagues in developing and delivering an undergraduate degree programme in SE. This started in 1988, and its early development is described in [12], which emphasises the role of regular reviews of its goals and curriculum. As highlighted in section E.1 of the SE Guidelines, and as discussed in a separate paper [13], these reviews have increasingly focused on the skills that the students should develop within the programme, and particularly the overall skill of being able to develop software systems. The best way of achieving this is through projects involving the development of actual software systems, particularly if these can be real systems for real clients [14]. The most recent major revision of the Sheffield curriculum (its fifth) has therefore been based on the principle that its "spine" should be formed by a sequence of major projects, one in each academic year, with the rest of the curriculum being driven largely by the need to ensure that the students have acquired the knowledge needed for undertaking these projects.

Since this programme follows the standard UK model that full time bachelor's degrees take three years, it is the first year that gives students their basic introduction to SE (rather than the second year, as it might be in the North American model), and hence lays the foundation for their ability to develop software systems. This first year is structured round a project that is carried out in teams, and is based on fairly simple scenarios – typically requiring three to five business classes, and a similar number of relationships – with individual lecturers playing the roles of clients in order to give a variety of approaches to each scenario. The process for these projects is a standard "waterfall" progression through a sequence of five stages: requirements analysis, formal specification, design, implementation and testing. Each stage involves the production of an appropriate deliverable, and a key feature of the projects is that, after each stage, each student team passes its set of deliverables on to another team who have not previously seen that scenario, so that the new team will work on it for the next stage.

From experience of running these projects, it has become apparent that at each stage the primary focus of the teaching has to be on equipping the students to produce the technical content of these deliverables. This technical content largely consists of the models of the systems under development that need to be produced at each stage, which are respectively: a conceptual model (mainly UML use cases and a class diagram), a formal model (in Z), a design model (mainly UML sequence diagrams), the code itself (in Java) and a functional testing model (a set of test cases). Thus, at least in the first year of this programme, the bulk of the curriculum content for core SE consists of various aspects of modelling, and the other topics that are fitted round this are mainly ones which appear in the "Fundamentals" area of the SEEK.

It has also been our experience that progressively less formal teaching time has needed to be spent in this first year on aspects of software development processes, as once the basics have been introduced, the students essentially learn the rest by doing it in the project. Much the same is true of software quality and software tools, and in particular our experience of trying to utilise software tools for these projects has been very mixed. It has given the students valuable insights into the contributions that tools can make, but the difficulties involved in using them have often consumed a disproportionate amount of time compared to the benefits gained from them.

In the subsequent years, though, the emphasis does have to switch more towards processes, since the projects that are carried out in the second year use external clients, and as a result are much more varied, so that the issue of how to adapt the process to suit the constraints of different projects becomes much more important. This has been particularly true in the last year or two, where these projects have also been the subject of pilot studies in the newly-formed Sheffield SE Observatory. The aim of these studies has been to establish the methodology for experiments comparing agile processes (namely extreme programming) with more traditional ones, and so the curriculum has needed to cover a fair amount of material relating to these different approaches to SE processes, in order to set the scene for these experiments [15]. Even so, the more general concepts of product modelling still form a significant element in the second and third years of the curriculum, underpinning as they do the coverage within the relevant modules of topics as varied as design patterns, database structures and software cost estimation, all of which depend to some extent on models of software system structures.

5. Modelling in Other Branches of Engineering

Given this difference between our experience, that modelling of the artefacts to be developed is a key feature of the SE curriculum, and the coverage of this kind of modelling within formal SE curriculum structures, where it plays a much less significant role, it is appropriate to compare this situation with practice in other branches of engineering. In preparing this paper a simple piece of research was done, consisting of a series of keyword searches of the university library catalogue, using the keywords "Introduction", "Engineering", and then the names of different branches of engineering (civil, electrical, mechanical and chemical). From the results of each search, a small set of textbooks were selected which appeared to be representative of that branch of engineering, trying in fairness to avoid ones whose titles suggested that they would in any case be strongly oriented towards particular kinds of models. The contents of these were then examined, looking primarily at chapter headings and the topics that they covered, to see how (if at all) they treated modelling.

The results of this were that ten out of the twelve texts all had the same characteristic, that their early chapters are almost entirely concerned with describing and analysing the fundamental models used in that branch of engineering for the materials, components and systems with which they are concerned. The two exceptions were a text which (despite the title "Introduction to civil engineering construction") actually turned out to be not for engineering students at all, and another (with the title "Civil engineering practice: an introduction") that was essentially about professional issues, which means that neither of them could be regarded as representative.

These conclusions for the importance of modelling were then validated by a series of discussions with colleagues from other engineering departments in the University of Sheffield, who all confirmed that they see the introduction to their branches of engineering as having to centre on the combination of theory (as represented by these models) and practice. Also, they particularly confirmed a feature that had been noted in examining the textbooks, namely how often the phrase "theory and practice" occurs in their chapter headings. This is hardly surprising, since arguably it is the combination of these two aspects that is the most fundamental characteristic of engineering. Despite this, though, one will search almost in vain for any occurrence of the word "theory" in the contents pages of the standard textbooks on SE, or in their indexes either, with the exception of a few references to Boehm's "Theory W" [16], which has only very limited relevance to the issues being discussed here.

6. Modelling as a Recurring Concept

While this clearly confirms that the concept of modelling ought to play a more important role in the SE curriculum than it currently does, it also creates a problem for those trying to develop models of the curriculum, namely that of how this concept should be fitted in to these models. As has already been indicated, the SE Guidelines tried to solve this by adopting from CC91 the idea of recurring concepts, and describing modelling as one of these. Unfortunately, though, this idea of recurring concepts does not seem to have been generally accepted, in that it has not been used in the structure of the SWEBOK, while the CC2001 project seems to have abandoned it altogether, for there is no mention of it as a structural feature in the CS volume, and it has not so far been utilised in the SE volume either.

This is regrettable, as it has been shown elsewhere [17] that the idea of recurring concepts can be valuable in those aspects of a curriculum that are dependent on material from related disciplines. On the other hand, the idea of recurring concepts is not an easy one to work with, because concepts can recur for a variety of reasons, and the fact that these have not previously been analysed may have contributed to the idea falling out of favour. To try to remedy this, the way in which the idea was used in the CC91 model has been reviewed, to analyse how the various recurring concepts can be classified. The definition that it used of a recurring concept was that it should have three characteristics: it should occur throughout the discipline, it should have a variety of instantiations, and it should have a high degree of technological independence. This gave a very mixed set of twelve concepts, and the analysis suggests that these can be classified into four categories, depending on why they possessed these characteristics and hence their impact on the structure of the curriculum. These four categories are defined in table 1.

Table 1. Proposed categories of recurring concepts.

Category and Examples	Structuring Role
Emergent CC91: consistency and completeness, ordering in space, ordering in time.	The concept appears in different forms in different topics, and only serves to integrate the delivery of these topics.
Applicable CC91: complexity of large problems, security, reuse. SE Guidelines: ethics and professionalism, tools and environments, documentation.	The concept forms an identifiable topic, and other topics then apply it.
Structural CC91: binding, levels of abstraction, tradeoffs and consequences. SE Guidelines: software quality, software metrics.	The concept forms an identifiable topic, which shapes the treatment of other topics that apply it.
Foundational CC91: conceptual and formal models. SE Guidelines: software modelling, software processes.	The concept underpins the basics of many other concepts.

The significance of the foundational recurring concepts is that they play nearly as important a role in structuring a curriculum model as do the basic knowledge areas. Indeed, in the case of the "software processes" concept, this role in the SWEBOK, CC2001 CS and SEEK models is that its structure as a set of activities does not merely recur across their sets of knowledge areas, but provides the very basis from which many of them have been identified. By contrast, the foundational role of "software modelling" has not had the same impact on structure, but it is shown by the fact that each of these activities within the process can be described essentially in terms of constructing, transforming or validating product models, so that the structure of this concept (as described in section 2) does not merely recur across topics derived from the concept of software processes, but is orthogonal to them.

7. Modelling and Curriculum Structures

This property of orthogonality means that the underlying structure of the SE curriculum is really a two-dimensional matrix, with dimensions for software modelling and software processes respectively. Indeed, it has been argued elsewhere [18] that there are really three foundational concepts for SE – products, processes and people – which would give a three-dimensional structure. Fortunately, the role of people can be largely separated into two parts, as users of the products and as developers within the processes, so that by factoring out issues of ethics and professionalism the structure can be reduced to a two-dimensional one. This, though, still leaves the problem that the most convenient format in which to document a curriculum model for human readers is the one-dimensional one of a list or set of knowledge areas, each composed of knowledge units and topics. Hence, the challenge is to reduce this matrix structure, based on product models and processes, to the form of such a linear hierarchy, but without losing the essential relationships between these components that derive from this underlying matrix.

Solving the first part of this challenge is straightforward, since it essentially involves selecting one of the dimensions of the matrix and using its decomposition to identify what we might call a primary set of knowledge areas, and then adding to this a secondary set to cover major topics that would otherwise be factored out by this process. This is exactly what all of the curriculum models for SE have done, using the process dimension as their basis for the primary set of knowledge areas. It might be an interesting academic exercise to try to develop an alternative model by starting instead from the product dimension, but such an exercise is outside the scope of this paper. Instead, it is more helpful to focus on the problem that has not been properly solved yet with the current models, which is the second part of this challenge, namely that of representing properly the relationships between their knowledge areas and the orthogonal topics that derive from the software product modelling dimension of the underlying matrix.

In considering how this second part of the challenge might be solved, there is a useful analogy that can be drawn with the two orthogonal topics of data structures and algorithms in CS. This is based on the observation that software product models effectively describe the structures of the data that is created and used in the activities that make up SE processes, while these different activities can then be seen as describing (in a more-or-less algorithmic fashion) how this data is processed. The way in which this orthogonal property of data structures and algorithms is handled in the CS volume of CC2001 is by defining the foundational concepts of each as separate knowledge areas in their own right, namely "Discrete Structures" and "Programming Fundamentals". Then, the material where they inter-relate is formed into a separate area, namely "Algorithms and Complexity".

Scaling this solution up to the orthogonal relationships between software product models and SE processes suggests strongly that the foundational concepts of each should form separate knowledge areas. Then, the material where they inter-relate is, of course, precisely what has been referred to above as the primary set of knowledge areas. Currently the existing models go part way towards adopting this solution, in that they all include a knowledge area for SE processes, reflecting the fact that it is a foundational recurring concept. As yet, however, none of them have included an equivalent knowledge area for software modelling, as the other foundational recurring concept, and the whole argument of this paper leads to the conclusion that such an area should be included.

A further step, which would help to make the relationship between products and processes clearer and more explicit, would be to make a separation between two types of material that might appear in the knowledge areas corresponding to these foundational concepts. In the current models, the knowledge areas for SE processes contain a lot of material that is there in its own right, rather than because it has a foundational role for the primary set of knowledge areas. Similarly, a knowledge area for software modelling would contain much material that was not specifically focused on unifying the areas across which this concept recurs. Hence, the material that is most directly concerned with structuring each of these dimensions should be factored out of these knowledge areas, and instead organised separately. This could be done either as a "foundational" knowledge area for each one, or else as knowledge units within one introductory knowledge area. The latter is probably preferable, since it would then have the explicit role of defining the structure of the rest of the model, and this should include the "people" dimension as well the ones for products and processes. Such a knowledge area would also provide an obvious location for some of the historical background that students need to be given, in order to set in context their study of the technical aspects of the discipline of SE.

8. Modelling in SE Programmes

Underlying these theoretical issues of the meta-modelling of knowledge are some highly practical ones, of what needs to be taught to students on an SE degree programme, and in what order. At the start of an undergraduate degree in SE, it can not be assumed that students will

214

know anything in particular about developing software systems, any more than it can be assumed they will know much basic CS. They may know something about programming, and if not they will need to be taught it, so that they can create algorithms and data structures as required. As well as this, the differences in scale between programs and software systems means that students must also master the structures that are used in creating complete systems. These structures are at the heart of software product modelling, and so this topic covers precisely the concepts that students need in order to understand software systems or create them, which is why it has to be taught right at the start of any undergraduate programme in SE.

Indeed, in the course of learning SE students effectively have to go through two main stages (or three, if one counts learning basic programming as a separate stage zero). Stage one covers the activity that one might call "software development", meaning the production of pieces of software that represent feasible solutions for some basic set of functional requirements. In terms of disciplines this activity lies in the intersection of SE and Information Systems, so that many of the textbooks to support it have titles that refer to systems analysis and design. They also often have a focus on the use of UML, which is now such a well-established notation that, whatever ones view may be of its technical merits, a graduate from a degree programme in SE must need some knowledge of its basic principles to be regarded as properly qualified. Starting off the teaching of SE with such an introduction to software development, particularly if it is strongly based on practical projects, will help to provide this, as well as giving the students a foundation for subsequently taking a more critical view of it.

By comparison with real SE, this topic of software development deliberately takes a very restricted view of many activities. Thus, it pays virtually no attention to issues of process, since typically the teaching has little alternative but to follow a basic waterfall sequence, and the same is likely to be true of any projects that students carry out as part of it. Similarly, virtually no attention is paid to issues of finding optimal solutions, rather than just feasible ones. This means that aspects such as product quality or process quality have to be confined to the practicalities of how basic validation and verification are performed, rather than attempting to quantify these concepts at a point in their education where students are still struggling with the binary problem of whether their systems work at all. Indeed, the benefit of this restricted approach is precisely that it abstracts away from (in other words, avoids the complication of) issues that the students are not really equipped to understand at this stage.

Once students have got within sight of the point where they can develop systems that will actually deliver some basic functionality, it is then realistic to go on to stage two, and actually teach them SE. Of course, it almost certainly is good to mention at least some of the distinctive issues of SE right at the start of stage one, just to set the context, but it is only at stage two that it is actually realistic to expect students to understand and use them. This is because engineering has to be based on theory, and software modelling provides a fundamental part of this, such as the ways in which models are created during requirements analysis, transformed during design, used to generate equivalents (ie code) during construction, and checked for consistency and completeness during validation and verification. Only once these have been properly mastered, as part of the software development stage, will the students be in a position to either appreciate why "real" SE (including its theory) is important, or to do it themselves.

9. Conclusions

The main conclusion of this paper is that software modelling, as described in section 2, is important to the SE curriculum on both theoretical and practical grounds. The theoretical ground is that the structures and properties of the models with which it is concerned capture the basic theory that underpins the whole of SE as an engineering discipline. The practical ground is that students in the early stages of learning SE need to master the use of at least its basic models in order to carry out any of the activities of actually developing software systems, which is the essential purpose of SE.

Unfortunately, by comparison with the central role that modelling has in other engineering disciplines, the current curriculum models do not give this topic its proper emphasis. The main reason for this is the difficulty caused by its status as one of two foundational recurring concepts, the other being the concept of SE processes that has been used to derive the primary set of knowledge areas in each of these models. These two recurring concepts are orthogonal, and the solution that is proposed to the problem of documenting the resultant matrix structure as a linear hierarchy is to create an explicit knowledge area for software modelling, in the same way that ones have been created for SE processes. The elements of these concepts that actually provide the structure for the discipline should then form a separate introductory knowledge area.

Within SE programmes, the importance of modelling should then be reflected in a two-stage approach. Stage one, called software development, covers the basic models and their use in the core activities of SE. Stage two then uses this as a basis for teaching real engineering, drawing as necessary on the underlying theory provided by these models.

References

1   D J Bagert, T B Hilburn, G Hislop, M Lutz, M McCracken, S Mengel, *Guidelines for Software Engineering Education Version 1.0*, Software Engineering Institute, Carnegie Mellon University, Technical Report CMU/SEI-99-TR-032, (August 1999), and also at <http://www.sei.cmu.edu/publications/documents/99.reports/99tr032/99tr032abstract.html>.
2   A B Tucker (ed), *Computing Curricula 1991*, ACM/IEEE Computer Society Joint Curriculum Task Force Report, ACM Press and IEEE Computer Society Press (1991).
3   G Booch, J Rumbaugh & I Jacobson, *The Unified Modeling Language User Guide*, Addison Wesley, 1999.
4   J M Spivey, *The Z Notation: A Reference Manual*, Prentice Hall, 1989.
5   C B Jones, *Systematic Software Development Using VDM*, Prentice Hall, 1986.
6   J B Wordsworth, *Software Engineering with B*, Addison Wesley, 1996.
7   IEEE Computer Society, *Guide to the Software Engineering Body of Knowledge: A Strawman Version*, available at <http://www.lrgl.uqam.ca/publications/pdf/365.pdf>.
8   ISO/IEC, *Information Technology – Software Life Cycle Processes*, International Standard ISO/IEC 12207:1995(E), (1995).
9   IEEE Computer Society, *Guide to the Software Engineering Body of Knowledge: Trial Version (0.95)*, IEEE Computer Society (May 2001), and also at <http://www.swebok.org/stoneman/version095.html>.
10 IEEE-CS and ACM Joint Task Force on Computing Curricula, Approved Final Draft Version of Computing Curricula 2001 (15th December 2001), at <http://computer.org/education/cc2001/final/index.htm>.
11 A. E. K. Sobel (ed), *Computing Curricula – Software Engineering Volume: First Draft of the Software Engineering Education Knowledge (SEEK)*, 28th August 2002, available electronically at <http://sites.computer.org/ccse/artifacts/FirstDraft.pdf>.
12 A. J. Cowling, The first decade of an undergraduate degree programme in software engineering, *Annals of Software Engineering* 6, 61 – 90 (1998).
13 A. J. Cowling, What Should Graduating Software Engineers Be Able To Do?, these proceedings.
14 A Stratton, M Holcombe & P Croll, Improving the Quality of Software Engineering Courses Through University Based Industrial Projects, In M. Holcombe, A Stratton, S Fincher & G Griffiths, *Projects in the Computing Curriculum: Proceedings of the Project 98 Workshop, Sheffield 1998*, Springer Verlag, London, pp 47 – 69 (1998).
15 M Holcombe, M Gheorghe, F Macias, Teaching XP for Real: some initial observations and plans, In *Proceedings of 2nd International Conference on Extreme Programming and Flexible Processes in Software Engineering (XP2001)*, 14 - 17, (2001).
16 B. W. Boehm and R. Ross, Theory W Software Project Management: Principles and Examples, *IEEE Transactions on Software Engineering* 15, 902-916 (July 1989).
17 A. J. Cowling, Structuring the Disciplines Related to Software Engineering: A General Model, In *Proceedings of the 14th Conference on Software Engineering Education and Training*, IEEE Computer Society Press, 231-239 (2001).
18 A J Cowling, A Framework for Developing the Software Engineering Curriculum, *Proc. ACM/IEEE International Workshop on Software Engineering Education*, Sorrento, 1994, pp 111 - 118.

An Experimental Card Game for Teaching Software Engineering

Alex Baker, Emily Oh Navarro, and André van der Hoek
Department of Information and Computer Science
University of California, Irvine
Irvine, CA 92697–3425 USA
abaker@uci.edu, emilyo@ics.uci.edu, andre@ics.uci.edu

Abstract

The typical software engineering course consists of lectures in which concepts and theories are conveyed, along with a small "toy" software engineering project which attempts to give students the opportunity to put this knowledge into practice. Although both of these components are essential, neither one provides students with adequate practical knowledge regarding the process of software engineering. Namely, lectures allow only passive learning and projects are so constrained by the time and scope requirements of the academic environment that they cannot be large enough to exhibit many of the phenomena occurring in real-world software engineering processes. To address this problem, we have developed Problems and Programmers, an educational card game that simulates the software engineering process and is designed to teach those process issues that are not sufficiently highlighted by lectures and projects. We describe how the game is designed, the mechanics of its gameplay, and the results of an experiment we conducted involving students playing the game.

1. Introduction

It is now well known that software engineering professionals working in industry are generally unsatisfied with the level of real-world preparedness possessed by recent university graduates entering the workforce [2, 5, 9, 12]. Their frustration is understandable – in order for these graduates to be productive in an industrial setting, organizations that hire them must supplement their university education with extensive on-the-job training and preparation that provides them with the skills and knowledge they lack [5]. The root of the problem seems to lie in the way software engineering is typically taught: theories and concepts are presented in a series of lectures, and students are required to complete a small, toy project in an attempt to put this newfound knowledge into practice. Although both of these components are necessary and useful parts of educating future software engineers, they lack an adequate treatment of many of the critical issues involved in the overall *process* of software engineering. Specifically, the time and scope constraints inherent in an academic setting prohibit the project from being of a sufficient size to exhibit most of the phenomena present in real-world software engineering processes – those that involve large, complex systems, large teams of people, and other factors such as management, workplace issues, and corporate culture. Although the instructor can explain most of these issues in lectures, students do not have an opportunity to participate in an entire, realistic software engineering process firsthand.

To address this problem, we have developed a unique approach to teaching the software engineering process: Problems and Programmers, an educational card game that simulates the software engineering process from requirements specification to product delivery. Problems and Programmers provides students with an overall, high-level, practical experience of the software engineering process in a rapid enough manner to be feasibly used repeatedly in a limited amount of time (i.e., a quarter or semester). Furthermore, it takes the focus off of actual deliverable artifacts and highlights the overall process by which they are developed.

It is our intention that 1 or 2 class periods in a course would be dedicated to learning and playing the game as a way to supplement the material already learned. Surely, lectures are still needed to teach the fundamental concepts and theories of software engineering, and projects still provide students with useful experience in creating deliverables, but the addition of this game could enrich the curriculum. As an initial evaluation of the game's feasibility and worth as a complementary teaching tool, we recruited a group of students who had passed an introductory software engineering course to play the game, and collected their feedback.

The remainder of this paper is organized as follows: Section 2 outlines the overall objectives of Problems and Programmers, both as a game and as an educational tool. Section 3 details the design and mechanics of the game. Section 4 briefly describes the experiment we performed to evaluate the effectiveness of the game, as well as lessons learned from it. We end in Section 5 with our conclusions and directions for future work.

2. Objectives

Problems and Programmers is a teaching tool, and as such its purpose is to educate. One possible approach to teaching any subject is to create a simulation. In the case of Problems and Programmers, the game simulates the overall software engineering process. This allows students to get a good feel for the process as a whole, but also allows for individual lessons learned about how cards work in the game to be easily translated to real-world lessons.

In general, each event in the game needs to be associated with a corresponding event in the real world. Accomplishing this goal has a twofold benefit. First of all, the connections between the game's rules and lessons learned make the rules more intuitive and easy to remember. Secondly, these associations allow the teachings of the game to be more relevant to the real world, and thus more useful.

When setting up the simulation, it is important that the game reward good software engineering practices and punish persistent deviations from them. After all, if the game were designed such that forgoing all requirements and design specification was consistently successful, the game would either be perceived as unrealistic, or worse yet teach that such a thing was a good idea! Because of this, it is necessary to ensure that the paths to victory in the game represent good software engineering practices.

Clearly, a simulation can take on many forms and must make many tradeoffs between faithfulness to reality, simplicity and fun factors. If the game were to be unrealistic or overly complex, it would lose most of its effectiveness as a teaching tool. Therefore we used the following guidelines in the design of the game:

- *The game should teach both general and specific lessons about the software engineering process.* General lessons include ideas such as the fact that multiple stakeholders will guide a project's direction, or that software engineering is a non-linear process. Specific lessons include that rushing coding often increases the time it takes or that unclear requirements documents can lead to inappropriate designs. These lessons should be taught through intermediate, as well as "end-of-the-game" feedback in the form of visible consequences [1, 8].
- *The game should promote proper software engineering practices.* Misusing resources, cutting corners, or otherwise straying from usual procedures should be, at best, a risky proposition. Unwise actions should be met with negative consequences, with as much visibility as possible as to why the consequences occurred, maximizing the teaching effectiveness of the game [3].

- *The game should be relatively easy to learn and quick to play.* One of the game's main strengths is its ability to give a high-level view of the software engineering process in a condensed timeframe. The simulation's value would be significantly reduced if learning and playing the game took too long [7, 10].
- *The game should be fun.* While this goal will be secondary to some of those above, it is certainly important that the players would want to play the game. The fun of the game will be a large part of what will make the lessons learned more memorable [7].

These goals can be summarized as: the game should be practical and enjoyable and teach good lessons and good practices. We believe that we have succeeded in meeting these goals, and in creating an innovative and effective teaching tool. Our specific approach to creating Problems and Programmers is detailed below.

3. Overall Design

The game is organized as a competitive game, in which students take on the roles of project leaders in the same company. They are both given the same project and are instructed to complete it as quickly as possible. The player who completes the project first will be the winner. However, players must balance several competing concerns as they work, including their budget and the client's demands regarding the reliability of the produced software.

In completing their project, players play cards based on the waterfall lifecycle model, as shown in Figure 1. While we had experimented with allowing players to choose from alternative lifecycle models, the rules required to do so violate our goal of simple gameplay and had to be forgone. As it stands, the waterfall model is the one that most students will be most familiar with and will still demonstrate nearly all of the principles that we were striving for.

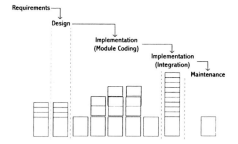

Figure 1: Phases and corresponding play areas in problems and programmers.

While most actions are available at any time, players are encouraged to create their requirements document early on, as working on it later can require reworking of other deliverables. Similarly, other deviations from the lifecycle will have adverse consequences.

As players move through the lifecycle phases, they place cards in areas from left to right, as seen in Figure 1. First, players create a column of requirements cards. Then they play design cards in a column to the right of this, and then have their programmers create code cards during implementation. Finally, all of these code cards are collected into a column of integrated code to the right. In this way, the progress through the phases is indicated in a physical and straightforward manner, and players can easily track their progress.

In the following subsections we will describe the game's play from beginning to end and briefly go over the choices and lessons presented to the players.

3.1 Setup

At the start of the game, a project card is selected (see Figure 2). This gives the attributes of the project that the players will be completing, including its length, complexity, and budget. Then, each player draws five cards from the main deck. Here they will find three types of cards: concepts, programmers and problems. Examples of each of these are also shown in Figure 2. Concept cards represent decisions that a player may make regarding their approach to the project. For example, the Reusable Code concept card allows for a free code card to be added, while a Walkthrough card allows for unclear requirements cards to be re-worked. Programmer cards are the player's workhorses and are necessary to write, inspect and fix code. Finally are problem cards, which are at the heart of Problems and Programmers' gameplay. These are cards that are played by one player against the other. If the receiving player meets the condition on the card, they must suffer the consequences described.

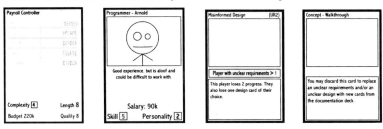

Figure 2: Examples of a project card, programmer card, problem card, and concept card.

3.2 Turn structure

Once each player has their five cards, they begin the game. Each turn players go through the following steps:

1. *Decide whether or not to move to the next phase of the life cycle.*
2. *Draw cards.*
3. *Take actions, as allowed in the respective phase.*
4. *Play any programmer and concept cards.*
5. *Discard any unneeded cards.*

This turn structure keeps cards moving between the decks, into the players' hands and into the play areas. It is also arranged specifically to make the turnover of concepts and program-mers difficult. If players are using up their entire budget, for example, they cannot fire pro-grammers to free up money until the end of their turn. At this point they have missed their chance to hire any new programmers until next turn, and those programmers will not be able to act until the turn following that. This represents that in the real world it takes time for pro-grammers to get used to the environment and the project at hand.

The most important step of each turn is the "take actions" phase. The exact sequence of events in this step will depend on the lifecycle phase that the player is in.

3.3 Requirements

Players are encouraged to stay in the requirements phase early on, and to spend this time to play requirements cards. These are placed in front of the player and used to represent work they have spent making their requirements document thorough and complete. In game terms, the more of these cards the player acquires, the less problem cards they will be vulnerable to. For example, by working on requirements for one turn at the start of the game and acquiring two requirements cards, a player makes themselves immune to any problem cards with the conditions that a player have "less than 2 requirements cards".

While most documentation cards are blank, sometimes players will reveal one that is marked "unclear". Some problem cards will cause problems for players with 1 or more "unclear" requirements cards, their total number of requirements notwithstanding. Players are able to replace these cards, but doing so counts towards their two-card-per-turn limit. This represents to players that there are multiple desirable qualities for the requirements document, but also brings a bit of tactics to the game. Software engineers will sometimes need to spend more time on their requirements than they had planned if things are not going smoothly.

3.4 Design

The design phase is handled in a similar manner, but players instead produce cards that represent the thoroughness of a design document. The procedure of the game is the same as in the requirements to promote learnability. In addition, the same documentation deck is used to keep the play area as uncluttered as possible. As with requirements, players are not forced to spend any time in their design phase. Again however, there are numerous cards that will allow the opponents of reckless players to thwart them.

3.5 Implementation

Once players have decided that they have done enough design, they may move onto their implementation phase. Once they have done so, their programmers are able to take action based on the number of skill points they have. Their options include:

- *Produce Good Code:* Which takes time based on the project's complexity.
- *Produce Rush Code:* Taking half the time of good code.
- *Inspect Code:* For one point, a piece of code can be inspected, and is flipped face-up.
- *Fix Bugs:* For one point a programmer can also work towards fixing one of their bugs. The exact action will depend on the type of bug, which will be discussed below.

By using these actions in different combinations, players are able to use a variety of coding styles. A programmer can methodically produce good code and inspect it, fixing bugs as they are found. Or, a programmer can create a mass of rush code and then inspect it all at the end. However, the rules are set up to encourage strategies with more real-world validity.

One of the primary ways that these types of strategies are encouraged is through the bug system. Each code card that is completed is placed into play above the programmer that created it, with the red "rush" code or the blue "good" code side up as appropriate. Whether this code has bugs or not is hidden on the other side of the card until that code is inspected. When code is inspected, it is flipped over, with its orientation maintained (see Figure 3).

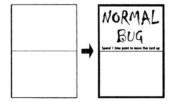

Figure 3: A piece of rush code that is inspected and revealed to have a bug in it.

The "rush" side of the cards is more likely to contain bugs, and these bugs tend to be more severe. There are 3 types of bugs in the game: simple bugs can be replaced with new code fairly quickly. Normal bugs take time to fix, based on how early in the project they are discovered, while nasty bugs can render more recent code obsolete and require it to be redone.

3.6 Implementation (Integration)

Once a player has completed the required number of code cards they can begin to integrate, spending one turn per programmer they had working on the project. Only when the necessary code has been both completed and integrated can the project be considered finished.

3.7 Product delivery

The final phase of a player's turn is product delivery. In this phase, the player shuffles all of his or her code cards and reveals some of them at random. If any are found to have bugs, these bugs must be fixed, and if they are severe enough the game can be lost altogether. Overall, players may be able to get away with submitting slightly faulty code, but usually they will get caught and pay the price.

But, if all of the revealed code cards are-bug free, the customer is satisfied and the game is won! There is some luck at the end, but this not so unrealistic. It is still almost always the more thorough player that wins, and the concepts of the game are certainly still reinforced.

4. Evaluation

4.1 Experiment design

We recruited 28 undergraduate students who had passed the introductory software engineering course at U.C. Irvine. They were matched randomly into groups of 2, received instruction on how to play the game, and then played against each other for approximately 1½ hours, completing 1 to 2 games. Following this, they completed a questionnaire stating their thoughts and feelings about the game in general, their opinions about the pedagogical effectiveness of the game in teaching software engineering process issues, and their educational and professional background in software engineering.

4.2 Experiment results

In general, students' feelings about the game were favorable, as summarized in Table 1. On average, students found the game quite enjoyable to play (4.1 rating out of 5) and relatively easy to play (3.5). They also felt that it was moderately successful in reinforcing software engineering process issues taught in the introductory software engineering course they had taken (3.5) and equally successful in teaching software engineering process issues in general (3.4). For the most part, they agreed that Problems and Programmers would be helpful to teaching software engineering concepts if incorporated into the introductory software engineering course (3.6).

Students' answers to the open-ended questions also reflected their positive feelings about Problems and Programmers. Regarding the enjoyability of the game, some students remarked:
- *"Because this game is fun, I think students will tend to learn more. It's interesting how such a card game can teach one about software engineering concepts."*
- *"[It] makes me think there is hope to make learning fun one day."*

- *"[I like] the various strategies you can employ. I guess this speaks to the depth of the game."*

Regarding how well the game teaches software engineering process issues, students wrote:
- *"Consequences are more drastic than mentioned in class. We could clearly see this in the game."*
- *"It was easy to understand the process because it was a game."*
- *"You need to put the time into earlier phases (design) or else it will come back to get you."*

Table 1: Questionnaire results.

Question	1	2	3	4	5	Avg
How enjoyable is it to play? (1=least enjoyable, 5=most enjoyable)	0	0	6	13	9	**4.1**
How difficult/easy is it to play? (1=most difficult, 5=easiest)	0	3	10	12	3	**3.5**
How well does it reinforce knowledge of SE process taught in class? (1=not at all, 5=definitely)	0	6	9	7	6	**3.5**
How well does it teach new SE process knowledge? (1=not at all, 5=definitely)	7	8	6	3	4	**2.6**
How well does it teach the SE process? (1=not at all, 5=very much so)	1	4	8	12	3	**3.4**
Incorporate it as standard part of SE course? (1=not at all, 5=very much so)	1	6	3	12	6	**3.6**
As an optional part? (1=not at all, 5=very much so)	1	5	4	10	8	**3.7**
As a mandatory part? (1=not at all, 5=very much so)	1	6	8	11	2	**3.3**

Although responses were positive for the most part, it is clear that some aspects of the game need to be improved. For instance, several students felt that the requirements and design phases of the game were boring. Clearly, more breadth needs to be added to this part of the game play, possibly in the form of new types of problems that can be played during these phases. Moreover, many believed that the learning curve for the game was too steep. Perhaps the instruction process can be streamlined or the game made simpler to alleviate this problem. Most importantly, students generally felt that the game was not very successful in teaching new software engineering process knowledge that was not introduced in class. While reinforcing concepts taught in lectures is a useful benefit in and of itself, the tool would be even more valuable if it could also introduce new knowledge. An investigation will be required to determine whether this can be done by incorporating more software engineering process issues into the game (running the risk of adding further difficulty to learning the game), making the existing ones more obvious, or a combination of the two.

5. Conclusions and Future Work

Problems and Programmers represents a first attempt at using a physical card game to teach students about the software engineering process. It addresses many of the weaknesses of more traditional techniques and brings additional benefits in the form of face-to-face learning and enjoyable play. When used in conjunction with lectures and projects, Problems and Programmers allows students to gain a thorough understanding of real-world lessons that might otherwise have been poorly understood or overlooked altogether.

Our card-based approach holds several advantages over existing automated simulations [4, 6, 11]. In comparison, it has a very visual nature, is simple and fun to play, allows for collaborative learning and provides almost immediate feedback to players about the lessons to be learned. The physical nature was difficult at times and occasionally restricted the lessons we could teach, but we feel that the game represents a good balance between our stated objectives.

The results of our experiments show that students will embrace the use of the game, as most of our test subjects felt that playing the game was both a useful lesson and an enjoyable experience. Additionally, most students felt that it would be a valuable addition to a software engineering course's curriculum. We plan to examine this further by introducing the use of the game into several classroom settings. We will be collaborating with 3 other institutions in this matter, giving us a robust test of the game's applicability in educational settings.

More information about Problems and Programmers, as well as a freely downloadable version of the cards, is available at: http://www.problemsandprogrammers.com.

6. Acknowledgements

We thank the other members of our research group for their invaluable suggestions regarding the design and implementation of Problems and Programmers.

This research is supported by the National Science Foundation under Grant Number CCR-0093489. Effort also sponsored by the Defense Advanced Research Projects Agency, Rome Laboratory, Air Force Materiel Command, USAF under agreement numbers F30602-00-2-0599 and F30602-00-2-0608. The U.S. Government is authorized to reproduce and distribute reprints for governmental purposes notwithstanding any copyright annotation thereon. The views and conclusions contained herein are those of the authors and should not be interpreted as necessarily representing official policies or endorsements, either expressed or implied, of the Defense Advanced Research Projects Agency, Rome Laboratory or the U.S. Government.

8. References

1. Anderson, J.R., et al., *Cognitive Tutors: Lessons Learned.* The Journal of the Learning Sciences, 1995. **4**(2): p. 167-207.
2. Callahan, D. and B. Pedigo, *Educating Experienced IT Professionals by Addressing Industry's Needs.* IEEE Software, 2002. **19**(5): p. 57-62.
3. Chi, M.T.H., et al., *Eliciting Self-Explanations Improves Understanding.* Cognitive Science, 1994. **18**: p. 439-477.
4. Collofello, J.S., *University/Industry Collaboration in Developing a Simulation Based Software Project Management Training Course,* in *Proceedings of the Thirteenth Conference on Software Engineering Education and Training,* S. Mengel and P.J. Knoke, Editors. 2000, IEEE Computer Society. p. 161-168.
5. Conn, R., *Developing Software Engineers at the C-130J Software Factory.* IEEE Software, 2002. **19**(5): p. 25-29.
6. Drappa, A. and J. Ludewig, *Simulation in Software Engineering Training,* in *Proceedings of the 22nd International Conference on Software Engineering.* 2000, ACM. p. 199-208.
7. Ferrari, M., R. Taylor, and K. VanLehn, *Adapting Work Simulations for Schools.* The Journal of Educational Computing Research, 1999. **21**(1): p. 25-53.
8. McKendree, J., *Effective Feedback Content for Tutoring Complex Skills.* Human-Computer Interaction, 1990. **5**: p. 381-413.
9. McMillan, W.W. and S. Rajaprabhakaran, *What Leading Practitioners Say Should Be Emphasized in Students' Software Engineering Projects,* in *Proceedings of the Twelfth Conference on Software Engineering Education and Training,* H. Saiedian, Editor. 1999, IEEE Computer Society. p. 177-185.
10. Randel, J.M., et al., *The Effectiveness of Games for Educational Purposes: A Review of Recent Research.* Simulation and Gaming, 1992. **23**(3): p. 261-276.
11. Sharp, H. and P. Hall, *An Interactive Multimedia Software House Simulation for Postgraduate Software Engineers,* in *Proceedings of the 22nd International Conference on Software Engineering.* 2000, ACM. p. 688-691.
12. Wohlin, C. and B. Regnell, *Achieving Industrial Relevance in Software Engineering Education,* in *Proceedings of the Twelfth Conference on Software Engineering Education and Training,* H. Saiedian, Editor. 1999, IEEE Computer Society. p. 16-25.

What Cognitive Activities Are Performed in Student Projects?

Éric Germain and Pierre N. Robillard
École Polytechnique de Montréal
{ eric.germain, pierre-n.robillard @ polymtl.ca }

Abstract

Software processes are being increasingly taught to software engineering students. Previous studies have however shown that actual activities performed in the course of student projects differ widely from what students had been taught. This study defines a new cognitive activity classification scheme that has been used to record effort spent by six student teams producing parallel implementations of a same software requirements specification. Three of the teams used a process based on the UPEDU, a teaching-oriented process derived from the Rational Unified Process. The other three teams used a process built around the principles of the Extreme Programming (XP) methodology. Results show that coding-related activities dominate the effort distribution for all the teams. Also, variations in the relative emphasis put on each activity between processes are low and limited to a small number of activities. The study provides lessons that may be useful when evaluating the importance of specific software processes.

1. Introduction

There seems to be an increasing interest about the teaching of software processes (see for instance [1-4]). But this interest does not translate into the acceptance of a common set of process principles. In particular, two main software development philosophies seem to emerge. The first one promotes the utilization of a very well defined process involving precise definition of roles to be played, activities to be performed and artifacts to be produced. Such an approach generally involves the production of artifacts which purpose is to support early decision making on requirements and design matters, effective communication, knowledge reuse and mutual work inspection. The main principle here is that efforts made in upfront planning activities and in artifact production will result in lower overall cost, timely product delivery and better software quality. The Rational Unified Process (RUP) [5] is an example of a process that fits this approach. The UPEDU [6-8] constitutes the adaptation of the RUP for teaching the software processes in software engineering and computer science programs.

The other philosophy, called "Agile Software Development" [9-10], promotes quick response to changes in requirements as well as extensive and ongoing collaboration between the development team and the customer. The approach specifically downplays the importance of formal processes and comprehensive documentation. It is based on the assumption that one cannot truly anticipate project requirements right at the beginning of a software development project, and that the proper way to deliver timely, quality software in a cost-effective manner is instead to build flexibility within the development activities. The "Manifesto for Agile Software Development [10]" provides the basic values of agile development in detail. Some methodologies derived from this approach include Adaptive Software Development, Scrum, the Crystal family, Feature-Driven Development, Dynamic System Development Method and Extreme Programming.

In addition to such methodological variety, it is reasonable to consider that a generic process will have to be adapted to each organization and project that requires one. There is no such thing as a universal process. For instance, users of the RUP are provided with tools that allow them to build their own subset of the proposed activities and artifacts.

Students enrolled in a software engineering program and who have received training on software processes are expected to be, at the end of the program, more sensitive to issues affecting software quality, cost and lifecycle. This does not mean however that those individuals will apply everything they learned as is. Previous studies [11-13] in the context of the "Software Engineering Studio", a project-oriented course for senior-level students, have shown a significant gap between theory as taught and practice. Those studies were using effort slips as an indicator of relative activity intensity. Analyses performed were however limited by the activity and artifact classification of the UPEDU-based process used, which was reflected in the effort tracking tool used. It was thus rather difficult to determine exactly which cognitive activities had been performed.

Using those studies as a foundation, we defined a set of cognitive activities that aims at accurately recording the various activity states of a software developer in the course of a project. The utilization of such a classification allows us to study the impact of software process notions learned on the cognitive activities actually performed by the students during a project course.

We do not expect our results to be ready for immediate generalization to industrial practices because of the academic nature of the setting and of the impact of the particular project, lifecycle and technology chosen. Meanwhile, repeating such an experiment in an industrial setting would be quite difficult because of the need to record individual cognitive activities at developer level. However, we think that the study presented in this paper provides clues that may be useful when evaluating the importance of a specific software engineering process.

2. The Software Engineering Studio

The Software Engineering Studio is an optional project-oriented course offered to senior-year students in computer engineering at École Polytechnique de Montréal. Its purpose is to allow students to get a practical experience of software development by participating in a small-scale, complete software development project. Teams of students must develop a complete implementation based on software requirements specifications provided by the instructors. They also must use a well-defined software engineering process. Participants thus get an early experience in building an operational software project from A to Z through design, implementation, testing and management activities. This project course teaches them the realities of teamwork and of project completion within schedule. As a secondary objective, students get more familiar with a specific application domain or set of technologies. An earlier version of the Studio has been presented in [14]. The Studio has also served as a testbed for the study of development effort and artifact quality. Some individual studies performed using data generated in the course of a Studio edition have been documented in [2-4].

The Winter 2002 edition of the Studio featured the development of a Web-based meeting management system aimed at organizers of meetings where the number and geographic dispersion of participants make scheduling difficult. The software system to be developed would allow meeting coordinators to send availability requests to a set of individuals so that each one can specify their personal availability periods. The set of availability periods would then be graphically represented using a special calendar tool that would allow a coordinator to visualize the relevant information at a glance, making the scheduling decision easier to take.

The decision would then be transmitted electronically to all participants. The software system would be responsible, among other things, for ensuring proper data storage, update and communication between all participants. All communications would be performed using standard e-mail. Figure 1 shows a screenshot from one of the software products delivered.

Figure 1. Screenshot from one completed product

The main feature of the Winter 2002 edition was the use of two different software engineering processes. One of the goals of the study was to determine the influence of the software process on the participants' behaviour. The instructors therefore chose to assign each half of the class to one of the two software processes selected. Thus, three of the teams were assigned a process based on the Unified Process for EDUcation (UPEDU) [8], which is derived from the Rational Unified Process [5]. The other three teams were assigned a process built around the Extreme Programming methodology (XP) [15]. Figure 2 illustrates the prescribed software lifecycle calendar. The diagram shows the iterations prescribed for each process. Iterations with the form "XP*" relate to the XP-based process, while those with the form "UP*" relate to the UPEDU-based process.

A common release-level framework was used to define the lifecycle for both processes. Thus, for all the teams, an initial specification was provided at the beginning of the semester. A complete implementation of that specification was due after 45 days. Thereafter, a second specification was issued that requested a moderate architectural change to the system. Implementation of that change was due after an additional 15-day period. Iterations XP1 through XP5 and UP1 through UP3 belong to the initial development cycle, while iterations XPM and UPM belong to the end-of-semester maintenance phase.

At the iteration level, the lifecycle was customized for each of the process used. Since iterations in an XP project are usually shorter than in the typical UPEDU project, the lifecycle for the XP process included a greater number of iterations covering the same time

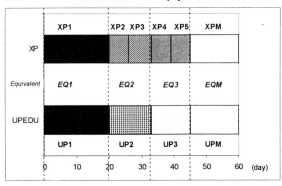

Figure 2. Software lifecycle calendar (in working days)

frame. The iterations targeted by this alteration are those at the middle and at the end of the development cycle. It was however not obvious that the first iteration should be shorter for the XP teams, since this initial iteration is crucial for laying out the skeleton of the system.

Also, the instructors wanted to leave enough time for every participant to get used to the development environment provided and to get minimal comfort with the language and technologies, to which most students had not been exposed previously. The initial iteration has therefore been kept identical in length for both processes. Also, the maintenance cycle has been limited to a single iteration due to general agreement by the students that this would be sufficient considering the limited scope of the changes requested. The remaining iterations have been set out so as to get a ratio of two XP iterations to one UPEDU iteration. The correspondence of UPEDU iteration end dates to XP iteration end-dates was required for the purpose of facilitating the analysis of the resulting data on effort spent. Figure 2 illustrates the equivalent iterations EQ1, EQ2, EQ3, EQM, that have been defined for that matter.

The team and individual evaluation grid for the course is shown at Table 1. 75 points out of 100 were attributed to each team as a whole. 25 points were allowed on an individual basis.

3. Cognitive activity classification

In previous editions of the Studio, students were asked to record effort spent under each process activity. This approach has the benefit of allowing a direct measurement of the process itself. However such a classification can only be used under the assumption that the list of activities defined in the process covers every possible work situation without bringing excessive overlap. Such an assumption has not been confirmed. Indeed, an analysis performed using data from the 2001 edition of the Studio

Table 1. Evaluation grid

Scope	Criterion	Weight
Team-level evaluation	Product quality	25 %
	Artifact quality and timeliness	25 %
	Effort slip quality, completeness and timeliness	25 %
Individual evaluation	Contribution to the team	25 %

showed possible presence of ambiguity and confusion among participants in relation with the process activities as defined by the instructors [11]. Another problem with the approach was that the presence of two separate software processes prevented the utilization of a single process-based scheme that would allow comparison of effort spent for all the teams. An alternative approach was to use a process-independent classification that lead to implicit assignation of effort to the proper activity. A classification based on the evaluation of explicit, mutually exclusive cognitive activities constituted an interesting path to this target.

Table 2 illustrates the classification that was used for the purpose of the study. The classification includes 14 activities that are grouped into four categories. Participants were presented all 14 activities without the category framework, which has been defined strictly for analysis purposes.

Although most activity names are self-explanatory, we provide below a short description of some of them. Category "Preparation" encompasses cognitive

Table 2. Cognitive activity classification

Preparation	Implementation
Think	Code
Read	Code & Test
Browse / Search	Test
Draw	Integrate & Test
Write	
Discuss	
Control	**Support**
Inspect / Review	Tech. Administration
	Training
	Other

activities that are related to activities that may be considered as prerequisites for coding. Activity "Think" refers to the process of self-reflection and thus encompasses every effort spent by a stand-alone participant for which no input nor output was present. Activity "Read" refers to the action of reading a specific document such as a textbook or an article for the purpose of assimilating a well-defined block of information, while activity "Browse / Search" was aimed at the action of reading documents or web pages in a non-specific order, as when searching for documents that will eventually be read. Activities "Draw" and "Write" refer to the respective production of diagrams and text of all kinds. Activity "Discuss" refers to every discussion taking place between a team member and one or more persons that may or not be team members.

Category "Implementation" was aimed at those activities that are central to the coding process. This category was especially important from an experimental point of view since coding-related activities constitute the vast majority of the effort spent under strict implementation of the Extreme Programming methodology. The classification had to reflect the fact that, under XP, coding, integrating and testing often occur as intertwined activities. Activities "Code", "Test" and "Code & Test" have therefore been defined in order to take account of the possible combinations of coding and testing. Activity "Integrate & Test" reflects the fact that, presumably, integration is a short duration activity that leads immediately to testing.

Category "Control" was aimed at the quality assurance actions that were likely to take place after every preparation or implementation step. It encompasses one single activity called "Inspect / Review" which refers to the technical review activities that may be performed after the initial production of any artifact. Category "Support" included other activities which occurrence would be interpreted as merely accidental and weakly linked to fundamental behavioural characteristics of the participants.

4. Analysis of cognitive activities performed

Figure 3 illustrates effort spent on each cognitive activity as a percentage of total effort spent in each of the three following grouping: XP-based projects, UPEDU-based projects, total (sum of the six projects). The three most important contributors to effort are the same for all groupings: "Code", "Code & Test" and "Write". Those activities, along with "Draw", are the most output-oriented of the activity classification. They amount to 57% of total effort spent under the total grouping. Coding-related activities alone amount to nearly half (47%) of total effort under that same grouping. This shows clearly that, beyond central analysis, design and testing skills that are, rightly, promoted within the software engineering community, this discipline remains a coding-intensive one, even when performed by students aware of the importance of software process activities. This finding might provide a part of the answer to the question raised by McConnell: "How important is software construction?" [16] Software construction is indeed a very important matter, at least in terms of its intensity relatively to other disciplines.

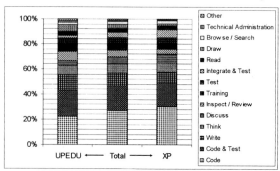

Figure 3. Effort distribution by activity (%)

A Pareto analysis [17] of figure 3 shows that half of

the activities (7 / 14) cover 80% of the total effort spent under the general grouping. Meanwhile, a thorough look at the center of the Pareto distribution shows that 7 activities gather between 3% and 5% each. Support activities encompass only 7% of the total effort, most of it being spent in training.

Figure 4 illustrates the same distribution, but modified to help analysis of the central activities. Coding activities and less relevant support activities have thus been removed from this activity distribution analysis. Activity distribution within this partial set does not follow a typical Pareto distribution. The first 2 activities (starting from the bottom) account for 40% of the effort, instead of an

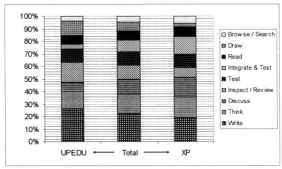

Figure 4. Effort distribution by activity, partial set (%)

expected 80% using the Pareto principle. It is necessary to add up effort spent on the first six activities to reach that 80% level. This is an interesting result since it shows that our classification fills out its purpose of acting as a powerful discriminating criterion for activity classification. Some activity merging would however have to be performed so to help provide a clearer picture of which activities predominate among those performed by the participants.

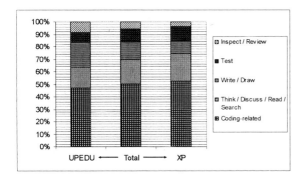

Figure 5. Effort distribution by composite activity, partial set (%)

First, output-producing activities "Write" and "Draw" differ only by the type of output generated. We chose to merge them into a single "Write / Draw" composite activity. Also, activities "Integrate & Test" and "Test" cover essentially the same kind of work. We chose to merge them into one "Test" composite activity, encompassing only testing made outside of a coding task. Finally, activities "Think", "Discuss", "Read" and "Browse / Search" all cover tasks that are performed as preliminary steps to the output of any artifact, while not producing artifacts themselves. We therefore chose to merge them into a single composite activity.

Figure 5 illustrates the results of the merging operation. Under this reclassification, the output-less composite activity becomes the second most effort-intensive one, right after the coding-related activities. It is interesting to note that this particular set of activities amounts to 39% of the total non-coding and non-support effort. Also, coding-related and output-less activities amount to 70% of all effort spent.

5. Concluding remarks

Developing software is an open problem. There can be as many solutions as there are individuals or teams. In this study, all the teams provided acceptable software products in relation to the requirements specification issued. All were also constrained by the common lifecycle and met all deadlines.

Even though the software process used seemed to have an impact on the importance of some cognitive or composite activities, we did not observe any significant relation between the process used and the overall effort magnitude. Effort spent by XP teams as a whole indeed exceeded effort spent by UPEDU teams by a whopping 29%. However, external factors that may have affected this figure are numerous and thus make it highly questionable. The only three-participant team was a UPEDU team and showed the smallest total effort of the six teams. We may interpret this as the expression of the fact that those students had to be more productive than the other teams to reach their objectives, or that they may have benefited from their size in terms of reduced required interactions.

The project required quick learning of the Java Servlet technology by the participants. Since the XP teams had to start coding almost immediately, they faced technological difficulties earlier than the UPEDU teams. We observed significant technology-related knowledge transfers from the XP teams to the UPEDU teams at the time when the latter started producing code. It must be noted that other kinds of knowledge transfers, for instance ones related to architectural decisions, seem not to have occurred on a large scale. Traces of such transfers have not been found in the resulting artifacts, except in the form of common reuse of a few key external components. Total absence of knowledge transfer would have been very difficult to achieve in practice. However, the use of a project definition that is less challenging from a technological point of view than the one actually implemented would possibly have downplayed the importance of this particular factor.

This study illustrates a basic observation of team software development based on two different software engineering processes. In spite of the limited scope of the study, a few general conclusions can be drawn. These conclusions need more experimentation in order to be validated.

The effort spent on core activities within each development project are more or less independent of the software engineering process used. The process will just bring more emphasis on one type of activity rather than another. This shifted emphasis does not have a spectacular effect on the overall distribution of the cognitive activities performed. One possible interpretation is that some core activities will require a minimal effort investment regardless of the software process used.

We observe that a well defined software process such as the UPEDU will put more emphasis on the engineering aspects of the software implementation by stressing the pre-coding activities while the XP-based process will put more emphasis on testing and ad hoc communications. While these observations are totally in line with the definition of the processes involved, what is most interesting is that these differences between processes are simply not as great as one may have expected and do not impact the effort-intensive coding activity family.

6. Acknowledgements

We are grateful to Mihaela Dulipovici who participated in the preparation of the semester, acted as teaching assistant for the course and was deeply involved in artifact and effort slip quality evaluation. Also, this project would not have been possible without the participation of all the students enrolled in the "Software Engineering Studio" course during the Winter 2002 semester. We would also like to thank Alexandre Moïse and Martin Robillard for their insightful comments while we were building the requirements specification for the semester project.

This work was partly supported by the National Sciences and Engineering Research Council of Canada (NSERC) under grant A0141.

7. References

[1] M. Halling, W. Zuser, M. Köhle, and S. Biffl, "Teaching the Unified Process to Undergraduate Students", Proceedings of the 15th Conference on Software Engineering Education and Training (CSEET'02), IEEE Computer Society, 2002, pp. 148-159.

[2] D. Umphress and J.A. Hamilton, Jr., "Software Process as a Foundation for Teaching, Learning, and Accrediting", Proceedings of the 15th Conference on Software Engineering Education and Training (CSEET'02), IEEE Computer Society, 2002, pp. 160-169.

[3] M. Höst, "Introducing Empirical Software Engineering Methods in Education", Proceedings of the 15th Conference on Software Engineering Education and Training (CSEET'02), IEEE Computer Society, 2002, pp. 170-179.

[4] El Emam, K., "Software Engineering Process", SWEBOK – A Project of the Software Engineering Coordinating Committee (trial version 1.00), IEEE, Los Alamitos, CA, 2001, pp. 9-1 – 9-18

[5] Kruchten P., "The Rational Unified Process: An Introduction", Reading, MA, Addison-Wesley, 2000.

[6] Robillard, P.N., and P. Kruchten, "Software Processes with the Unified Process for Education (UP/EDU)", Addison Wesley, Boston, MA, 2002

[7] École Polytechnique de Montréal, « UPEDU », http://www.upedu.org

[8] P.N. Robillard, P. Kruchten, and P. d'Astous, "YOOPEEDOO (UPEDU): A Process for Teaching Software Process", Proceedings of the 14th Conference on Software Engineering Education and Training (CSEET '01), IEEE Computer Society, 2001, pp. 18-26.

[9] Cockburn, A., "Agile Software Development", Addison Wesley, 2002

[10] Agile Alliance web site, http://www.agilealliance.org.

[11] É. Germain, M. Dulipovici, and P.N. Robillard, "Measuring Software Process Activities in Student Settings", Proceedings of the 2nd ASERC Workshop on Quantitative and Soft Computing Based Software Engineering (QSSE 2002), Banff, AB, Canada, 2002, pp. 44-49.

[12] É. Germain, P.N. Robillard, and M. Dulipovici, "Process Activities in a Project Based Course in Software Engineering", Process Activities in a Project Based Course in Software Engineering, IEEE, 2002, pp.S3G-7 – S3G-12.

[13] P.N. Robillard, "Measuring Team Activities in a Process-Oriented Software Engineering Course", Proceedings of the 11th Conference on Software Engineering Education and Training (CSEET '98), IEEE Computer Society, 1998, pp. 90-101.

[14] P.N. Robillard, "Teaching Software Engineering through a Project-Oriented Course", Proceedings of the 9th Conference on Software Engineering Education (CSEE), IEEE Computer Society, 1996, pp. 85-94.

[15] K. Beck, "Embracing Change with Extreme Programming", Computer, 10/1999, pp. 70-77.

[16] S. McConnell, "I Know What I Know", IEEE Software, 05-06/2002, pp. 5-7.

[17] Juran J.M., F.M. Gryna, Jr., and F.M. Bingham, "Quality Control Handbook. Third edition", McGraw Hill, New York, 1979; cited in Fenton, N. and Ohlsson, N., "Quantitative Analysis of Faults and Failures in a Complex Software System", IEEE Transactions on Software Engineering, 08/2000, pp. 797-814.

Software Engineering Methods 3 (Paper Session H)

Reflecting Skills and Personality Internally as Means for Team Performance Improvement

Wolfgang Zuser, Thomas Grechenig

Research Industrial Software Engineering, Vienna University of Technology

{wolfgang.zuser, thomas.grechenig}@rise.tuwien.ac.at

Abstract

Formal evaluation of team performance (e.g. with metrics) is a good and well known instrument for providing feedback about finished projects. If performance was behind expectations a further analysis may include an oral discussion of problems that occured during the project, that have been treated ineffectively or even have been put aside. Such problems may include choice and quality of engineering practices, the appropriateness of role and responsibility assignments and relationships between team members, which have been conductive or obstructive to the team. This feedback improves engineering behaviour and strengthens the problem and conflict solving capabilites for coming projects, but can't affect any more the project of concern, which already has been finished.

This paper proposes the usage of a questionnaire based on skills and personality traits for providing feedback to software projects teams during running projects. The result of the assessment should help to improve the performance of the project team by defining roles adequately and putting responsibilities to the right people: It improves the personal relationships within the team, increases the attitude for personal tasks, increases the understanding and respect for the other team members, shows significant misconception of personal strengths and weaknesses and indicates fit or misfit of engineering practices with skills and personalities.

1. Introduction

The proper composition of software engineering (SE) teams is a widely discussed topic. Many useful hints can be taken from the conventional team management literature (e.g.[8, 9, 13]).

Normally Teams have four phases starting with their composition [19]:

(1) Forming: The roles and responsibilities are not clear within the team. Strengths and weaknesses of team members are not clarified yet.

(2) Storming: Roles become more clear. Power struggle can occur. A first impression of strengths and weaknesses of team members has been gained.

(3) Norming: Roles and power distribution is clear and not further discussed. Norms are developed for improving performance. Conflicts can be resolved quickly.

(4) Performing: Norms have been developed and proven to be good. Performance is at its peak. A commitment about goals and trust between team members has been established.

The first and second phase have significantly lower productivity than the others. Beside the problem of not being used to the other team members, much time is used to stabilize one's own position (formal assignment like project leader or programmer) and role (informal, e.g. Driver, Monitor or Supporter [6]). Such conflicts may be the result of lack of sufficient and qualified information about team colleagues:

1093-0175/03 $17.00 © 2003 IEEE

(1) Unawareness of strengths and weaknesses of team members. A good distribution of roles and an assignment of responsibilities to roles can only be done upon a profound knowledge of strengths and weaknesses of each team member.

(2) Missing feedback about team colleagues perceptions. People like to be confirmed about their own perception of their own personality attributes and skills. This strengtens the self-esteem of team members within the team. Missing affirmations of these self-perceptions can spawn over-casted actions for intentionally originating the desired affirmations. Instead of producing the wanted acknowledgement these actions can continuously influence the perceptions of the team colleagues in a negative way.

(3) Conflicting attraction to roles. In case there are more people attracted to certain positions or roles within the team, conflicts about who occuppies the role may arise. Such conflicts may be resolved quickly by investigating the real goals and abilities (skills and traits) of team members. Discussions about the best fit of goals and abilities will lead to a good role assignment.

As a solution for these information shortcomings in SE teams during its starting time we present a questionnaire for self-evaluation of the team in this paper. We present a process how to use the questionnaire effectively. The questionnaire and the carefully used associated process will reduce time from team buidling to performening software teams substantially. Such feedback and analysis opens the possibility to improve within current and coming projects.

Section 2 explains the major related work, which influenced the work of this paper substantially. Section 3 describes some prerequisites for developing a questionnaire suitable for reflecting skills and personality in a SE team. The second part discusses the questionnaire which was finally used in the experiment, which is introduced in chapter 4. The findings of the experiment and some discussions are presented in chapter 5. A short summary and some remarks on further work conclude the article in chapter 6.

2. Some remarks on skills and personality in SE teams

2.1. General findings about skills and personality

Gathering knowledge about useful skills and personality traits of current or potential employees is the most important task for human resource departments and personnel recruitment agencies. They use various number of skill and personality tests, most of them specialized for the job the test is done for, or assessment centers. Tests have some major disadvantages in common: (1) They do not show the behavior of the candidate in a real life situation, (2) faking of the tests is easy and not preventable, (3) stress caused by the test situation influences the result and (4) in case of the use of standard tests (e.g. 16 PF, Myers-Briggs Type Indicator (MBTI)) they don't give much valuable information as mentioned in [14].

Assessment centers compensate those disadvantages mostly by using diverse instruments (tests, project/task simulations, oral interviews), but the costs to run such assessments are very high. The results of simulations and interviews highly depend on the assessor and are therefore subjective. The result is further influenced by the local performance of few days and tasks.

2.2. Skill and personality in SE

The search for typical skills and personality traits of software engineers and roles in SE has been discussed widely. Competencies of software engineers are analyzed in [20, 11]. Special skills of system analysts are described in [15]. A questionnaire for assessing skills of software practitioners dividing skills into 10 categories (object orientation, client server, software engineering, programming languages concepts and coding, database systems and filed, data structures and algorithms, computer design and computer architecture) is described in [1].

There is some research on personality of software engineers using standard personality tests. Personality profiles for application programmers, application system analysts, technical programmers and data processing managers based on the Sixteen Personality Factor Questionnaire are presented in [16]. Various authors tried to find guidelines for team success depending on personality types of software engineers by using Myers-Briggs Type Indicator [17, 2, 18, 10].

Only a few authors tried to find personality traits of software engineers empirically. An empirical study coming up with 12 personality traits of top performing software developers is presented in [24]. Using these findings they developed a model of 6 traits (creative personality, ideal self, military leadership, low origence - high intellegtence, order, endurance, based on the adjective checklist (ACL) and added one self reported trait (years of IT-experience).

The connection of skills and personality and team building, structure and dynamics is also a well known topic in literature. A survey discovering that there is a connection between skills and personality attributes and team performance is reported in [22].

The importance of the usage of tests for giving feedback to managers as well as team members is stressed in [21]. The use of a questionnaire as an information source for composing student projects teams is suggested in [3]. The questionnaire asks for preferred team mates, skills and working habits.

Peer evaluation in software project teams at college as the best method for getting valid information about team dynamics and individual participation of single team members is shown in [23, 5].

The gathering for typical staff attributes for implementing the People Capability Maturity Model (P-CMM) is suggested in [12]. This helps giving feedback indirectly via the P-CMM instruments. Personal feedback to single participants is not part of the suggestions.

Formal approaches to team building can help to assess skills systematically. Quantitative methods for team composition based on a quantitative model of skills is presented in [4]. Such an approach doesn't seem suitable for giving intuitive feedback to team members. A team building method upon analysis of required and available skills is shown in [25] but does not give insight in how to assess the skills from persons.

3. Designing a questionnaire for skills and personality assessment in SE teams

3.1. Criteria for a suitable questionnaire design

Many questionnaires are designed for different situations. Only a few get a higher attention. Normally these questionnaires have in common, that they are designed with a high insight in the domain, which should be investigated, and a methodologically correct approach of selecting and phrasing the questions. Thus it is important for the questionnaire presented in this paper, that it is designed upon some criteria to guarantee the effectiveness and usability of this instrument:

(1) Skills and personality traits. The questionnaire should assess the skill level and the personality level. Both levels equally have great impact on the performance within the team.

(2) Role and task coverage. The questionnaire must cover all possible roles and tasks within a SE team. Questions have to be designed to affect multiple roles and tasks at once.

Table 1. Question examples

social	organizational	technical
... cares about others abilities	... is timely at meetings	... works at the state of the practice
... talks about private matters	... finishes tasks within time	... is curious about innovations
... is very well in understanding others	... takes over necessary work	... has original, exceptional, useful ideas

(3) Strengths, not weaknesses. It is important to show strengths, which can be applied and improved. The feedback to the team members should be positive by nature and increase the feeling of acceptance in the team.

(4) Comprehensibility. Used phrases should be easy to understand, they should be precise and short. Technical terms should be avoided.

(5) Low costs and ease to use. The questionnaire must be answerable in a reasonable time. Too long questionnaires are exhausting and result in missing answers at the end of the questionnaire.

The fourth criteria limits the number of questions. Calculating one minute per question and assuming that answering all questions should not take more than 50 minutes a total of 50 questions is acceptable.

3.2. Finding the right questions

The initial structure of the questionnaire has been derived from interviews with expert software engineers. All of them have more than 10 years experience in building medium or large software systems. The interview included questions about the kind of projects they had worked in, their personal experiences in teams as a team member as well as a project leader (if applicable). Finally we asked them to name the most important attributes for describing skills and personality of software engineers.

The evaluation of the answers showed that there were three categories where relevant skills and personality traits could be assigned to:

(1) Technical skills. Knowledge about current technologies and the ability to use them in an efficient manner to achieve project goals.

(2) Organizational skills. Experience and methodic background knowledge how to plan and assign roles and tasks.

(3) Social skills. The ability of building and supporting healthy social relationsships within the team and with customers and managements.

Literature research supported the single components sufficiently. We could not find a complete or even partial model of skill categories and personality traits for software engineers. Therefore the specific composition of the skills and personality traits is not contradicted either.

3.3. Description of the questionnaire

The questionnaire contains 12 questions for each category. Further questions deal with the assessment of the attraction to positions (project leader, analyst, designer, programmer, tester) and roles taken from [6] (Investigator, Supporter, Driver,Monitor, Finisher, Implementor, Originator, Coordinator) within the team. Table 1 shows some of the questions used in the final questionnaire.

Each questions offers possible values from 9 to 0. For each question two statements are provided. The first statement should illustrate the value 9, the second statement value 0. The layout of the questions is illustrated in Table 2. Test persons who totally agree to the first statement should tick

Table 2. Questionnaire example

... is a good programmer	9 8 7 6 5	4 3 2 1 0	... creates code that doesn't run
... always really finishes his tasks	9 8 7 6 5	4 3 2 1 0	... tends to deliver incomplete
... is a true coordinator in the team	9 8 7 6 5	4 3 2 1 0	... surely is no coordinator in the team

9 for the person they are currently rating. If they agree with the second statement they should tick 0 for the person under evaluation. The values 5 and 4 should be assigned to people which were just above or just below an average software engineer according to the specific question.

The questionnaire was published via web for ease of questionnaire design, distribution of the questionnaire, data collection and processing of results for creating the feedback for the students.

3.4. How to use the questionnaire properly

Some important issues should be considered when using the questionnaire for providing its total value to SE teams:

(1) The team members must be convinced that their personal results will only be accessible by themselves and nobody else (especially not the project leader or management). It must be prohibited that single team members are forced to show their results to the rest of the team, if they don't want to.

(2) The questionnaire should be answered by all team members at the same time. This should inhibit unwanted influence on the results caused by the knowledge of already given ratings from other team members.

(3) The feedback must be given very quickly. This should prohibit wrong presumptions about the results as a possible cause for conflicts.

(4) Discussion about the feedback should be started shortly after receiving the feedback. Again wrong presumptions should be avoided. The values are no absolute measure for a skill level or personality traits, but show only the skill level and personality traits as they are seen by the colleagues. The provided feedback should only indicate perceptional trends. Discussion and clarification about misunderstandings are desirable and must not be abandoned in favour of the written test result.

(5) The process should be guarded by some authority (e.g. some colleague not part of the team). This should provide the necessary seriousness of the instrument.

4. Using the questionnaire in an undergraduate SE course

4.1. An undergradute SE course

Our department conducts a software engineering course. The course is mandatory for undergraduate computer science students as well as business informatics students. This sample of computer science and business informatics students is representative for a broad variety of skills and personality traits of computer personnel.

It is a two semester course. Students stay within the same team for both semesters. After an initial test, where minimum mandatory skills like object oriented programming or modelling are examined, students are rated into three skill levels (A-C). Each team is composed of two students of each skill level. This spawns equal skilled teams. The teams have to assign the roles (project leader, technical architect, programmers) and tasks within the team themselves. The teams have to finish a predefined project during the remaining first semester of the course. They get a specification document and have to design, code and test a single client of the system. The main objective of the first semester is to get initial experiences about the main goals of the course:(1) Understanding the importance of team work, (2) Learning fundamental practices of project planning, organisation and controlling, (3) Getting used with artifacts in a software development project and (4) Using state-of-the-art technology like object oriented development environments.

During the second semester of the course the teams have to develop a software from scratch on their own. They have to find a customer (usually some short or medium enterprises (SME)), analyze requirements, design the software, code and test it. In many cases the software implemented in the course is actually used by the customers.

4.2. Providing feedback to students

Applying the categories of [19] the teams are within or at the end of the storming phase at the end of the first semester. They have used and produced some artifacts and finished their first part of a software development project. Feedback at this point of time is essential for further development of their team and software engineering skills. We provide as much feedback as possible about team dynamics and the quality of process and artifacts. Feedback about artifacts and process is easy due to the experience of the supervisors and assistants and easy to assess criterions about form and content. Attempts to provide team dynamics feedback by supervisors (have a meeting with the team once a week and few or only some experiences with teams, team structures and processes) or assistants (have a meeting with a team once a month and high experience with teams, team structures and processes) could not discuss as many details as necessary because of lack of time spent with the teams (assistants) or lack of experience (supervisors).

For an improvement of this situation we used the questionnaire described in Section 3.3. The categories found for the questionnaire are very close to the teaching goals of the software engineering course. Therefore the questionnaire design was applicable for the kind of feedback we needed for the students in the described context.

The questionnaire had to be answered by each team member giving ratings for each of his/her colleagues. Furthermore each student had to estimate the mean value which he thought the team would assign to him. Finally each student he had to rate himself as well. The supervisors had to assign values for all team members.

Before the start of the second semester each student got a PDF with his/her personal feedback. For each question we provided the following four values for the students:

(1) Group value: The average value given from the team mates for this question.
(2) Group average: The average of all values assigned to any team members for this question.
(3) Expected value: The value, which the team member expected to get by his colleagues.
(4) Self-assessment: The value, the team member assigned to himself.
Table 3 shows an example feedback for one of the questions.

5. Results and discussion

After finishing the second semester of the course we asked the students in June to give us some feedback about how they used the feedback from January. The feedback was mainly positive and supports the idea of giving feedback:

(1) Most of the students stated that they appreciated getting such feedback and were curious about the results.

Table 3. Feedback example

... is a good programmer; ... is a bad programmer			
Group value	Group average	Expected value	Self-assessment
7.2	6.7	7.0	8.0
... always really finishes the tasks given; ... strongly tends to deliver incomplete			
Group value	Group average	Expected value	Self-assessment
7.8	7.5	7.0	6.0
... is a true coordinator; ... surely is no coordinator			
Group value	Group average	Expected value	Self-assessment
5.2	6.4	8.0	8.0

(2) About half of the students stated that the results were roughly the same as they had expected. They other half stated that they were quite surprised at least by the values of some questions. A short analysis of the data showed that the mean difference of all questions between the value assigned by a student to him- or herself and mean value assigned to the student by his or her colleagues was 1.37. The maximum mean difference for one question was 3.2.

(3) Some of the students were afraid that their team mates would be able to see the ratings of single team members. An extensive oral explanation before using the questionnaire will help to reduce these apprehensions.

(4) Good technical solution. The acceptance of the questionnaire method and the technical solution as a web questionnaire was high. Less than 5 percent of the participating students did not answer the questionnaire or entered useless values (e.g. the same value for all team members at several following questions).

(5) Values from 0 to 4 were used sparely. Most of the questions have a median 7 or 8. This finding is support by [3], where the author reports that students tend to report positive team skills rather than negative ones (8.5:1 times more positive skills).

6. Conclusion

This paper shows a questionnaire as an instrument for giving SE teams internal feedback. The usage of such an instrument can help SE teams to become more productive faster than without such information by shortening the building process of internal structures and accelerating the emerging of trust between the single team members.

Advantages of the questionnaire as a feedback instrument compared to other possibilities of team conflict resolving (team seminars, help by a supervisor, external conflict management by project manager) are:

(1) Happens at work under work conditions: The results of applying this questionnaire come from the most relevant source possible: team mates. They and only they have every day experiences with skills and personality traits of other members in the team. This leads to a well balanced view of skills and personality (not too negative nor too enthusiastic) but also to a deep insight in hidden strengths and weaknesses of team members which can be valuable in critical situations.

(2) Saves money: The instrument is easy to use and feedback is easy to produce. No additional people power or specialized software is necessary for conducting such surveys.

(3) Subjective and relative measures are preferable to absolute scales: Good programmers can be within a team of expert programmers below average programmers (and vice versa). There can be valuable skills, which are above average within the team but below average on a general scale.

241

The important role of catalysts, who can have lower performance than others but help the team in a significant manner by stabilizing team structure and dynamics is mentioned in [7].

Further research will be necessary in the validation of the effects on productivity of SE teams by providing a feedback instrument like the one proposed in this work. A complete and validated skills and personality trait model of software engineers would improve the questionnaire in means of shortness and reliability. The establishment of an widely recognized and proven skills and personality model will be fundamental not only for this special problem.

References

[1] W. G. Al-Khatib, O. Bukhres, and P. Douglas. An empirical study of skills assessment for software practioners. *Information-Sciences Applications*, 4(2):83–118, 1995.

[2] R. P. Bostrom and K. M. Kaiser. Personality differences within systems project teams: Implications for designing solving centers. In *Proceedings of the Eighteenth Annual ACM SIGCPR Conference*, pages 248–85, 1981.

[3] J. Brown and G. Dobbie. Supporting and evaluating team dynamics in group projects. *SIGCSE-Bulletin*, 31(1):281–5, 1999.

[4] G. Burdett and R.-Y. Li. A quantitative approach to the formation of workgroups. In *Proceedings of the 1995 ACM SIGCPR Conference*, pages 202–212, 1995.

[5] C. Chrisman and B. Beccue. Evaluating students in system development group projects. *SIGCSE-Bulletin*, 19(1):366–73, 1987.

[6] L. Constantine. *Constantine on Peopleware*. Yourdon Press, Prentice Hall, 1995.

[7] T. DeMarco and T. Lister. *Peopleware: Productive Projects and Teams*. Dorset House Publ., New York, 1999.

[8] P. S. Goodman. *Designing Effective Workgoups*. Jossey-Bass, 1986.

[9] J. R. Hackman. *Groups that work (and those that dont): creating conditions for effective teamwork*. Jossey-Bass, 1990.

[10] L. T. Hardiman. Personality types and software engineers. *IEEE Computer*, 301(10):10–10, 1997.

[11] G. Hunter. "excellent" system analysts: Key audience perceptions. *Computer Personnel*, 15(1):15–31, 1994.

[12] G. M. Hunter. Managing information systems professionals: Implementing a skill assessment process. In *Proceedings of the 1998 ACM SIGCPR Conference*, pages 19–27, 1998.

[13] J. R. Katzenbach and D. K. Smith. *The Wisdom of Teams: Creating the High-Performance Organization*. Harvard Business School Pr., 1992.

[14] N. L. Kerth, J. Coplien, and G. Weinberg. Call for the rational use of personality indicators. *IEEE Computer*, 31(1):146–7, 1998.

[15] D. Lee, E. Trauth, and D. Farwell. Critical skills and knowledge requirements of is professionals: A joint academic/industry investigation. *MIS Quarterly*, 19(3):313–40, 1995.

[16] E. Moore. Personality characteristics of information systems professionals. *Proceedings of the 1991 conference on SIGCPR*, pages 140–155, 1991.

[17] R. H. Rutherford. Using personality inventories to help form teams for software engineering class projects. *SIGCSE-Bulletin*, 33(3):76–6, 2001.

[18] J. Teague. Personality type, career preference and implications for computer science recruitement and teaching. In *Proceedings of the Third Australasian Conference on Computer Science Education*, pages 155–63, 1998.

[19] B. Tuckman. Developmental sequence in small groups. *Psychological Bulletin*, 63:384–399, 1965.

[20] R. Turley and J. Bieman. Competencies of exceptional and nonexceptional software engineers. *The Journal of Systems and Software*, 28(1):19–38, January 1995.

[21] K. White. Mis project teams: An investigation of cognitive style implications. *MIS Quarterly*, 8(2):95–101, 1984.

[22] K. White and R. Leifer. Information systems development success: Perspectives from project team participants. *MIS Quarterly*, 10(3):215–23, 1986.

[23] D. E. Wilkins and P. B. Lawhead. Evaluating individuals in team projects. *SIGCSE-Bulletin*, 32(1):172–5, 2000.

[24] J. Wynekoop and D. Walz. Investigating traits of top performing software developers. *Infomormation technology & people*, 13(3):186–195, 2000.

[25] A. Zakarian and A. Kusiak. Forming teams: an analytical approach. *IIE Transactions*, 31:85–97, 1999.

Some Experiences with Evolution and Process-Focused Projects

Norman Wilde   Laura J. White   Lorn B. Kerr
nwilde@uwf.edu   lwhite@uwf.edu   lkerr@uwf.edu
University of West Florida, Pensacola, Florida, USA

Darsi D. Ewing   Eischelle A. Krueger
darsi.ewing@tybrin.com   eischelle.krueger@eglin.af.mil
TYBRIN Corporation, Fort Walton Beach, Florida, USA

Abstract

For the last seven years students in the Masters track in Software Engineering at the University of West Florida have focused their capstone course and project work on software process and software evolution. Students initially defined a software maintenance process called GUMP which has been used in all subsequent years. Students use this process in a rolling project in which they maintain and enhance a medium-sized software tool. Simultaneously they improve the process based on their experiences, thus leaving their successors both enhanced software and an enhanced process to use in its evolution. Approximately 50 cycles of software change have been completed following this method, and two years ago a major revision to GUMP was undertaken based on an analysis of this experience. This article, by three of the instructors and two of the participating students, describes the methods used and the experience gained.

1. Introduction

Most Software Engineering Masters programs end with some form of capstone project, intended to pull together the threads of the discipline and give students concrete experience in the application of Computer Science knowledge.

The best form for this capstone work has always been controversial. It is not easy to reproduce all the pressures and constraints of an industrial setting in an academic environment and, in fact, it would probably be counterproductive to do so. Instead a university must try to structure the student's project work, providing a trade-off between realism and organized learning. Not surprisingly, many different trade-offs have been tried almost from the first days of the Software Engineering profession. As early as 1987 Thayer and Endres provided a summary of some of the many approaches that had been tried: individual projects, team projects, canned projects, real-world projects, etc. [11].

A complicating factor is the fact that many of the issues in real-world software development are not evident unless the software is of considerable scale and/or lifetime. The impact of poor design, non-standardized coding, and inadequate configuration management is only seen when a system becomes large and when it needs to be maintained by someone other than the original developers. Accordingly, several universities have tried projects based on maintenance or evolution of an existing software system [2, 6]. Such projects also introduce greater realism since most real projects in industry involve working with somebody else's code. It is rare for a Software Engineer to be assigned a "greenfield" project with all new code. Instead, existing code needs to be enhanced, fixed, adapted or integrated with other code into a new product[1].

A further thread is the recent industrial emphasis on Software Engineering *process*. Since the late eighties it has been realized that a defined process is essential to consistently producing good software. An organization can only improve if it systematically follows the same steps in building software, analyzing collected metrics pertaining to the product and the process, thus learning from that experience, and modifying the process to accommodate that experience.

Learning must progress by stages of planned process improvement. At the Software Engineering Institute, Humphrey defined the Capability Maturity Model (CMM) for software development processes, which established five process levels: initial, repeatable, defined, managed and optimizing [4]. Only at the upper levels is the process stable enough so that the organization can collect meaningful data and achieve statistical process control.

Both software evolution and software process are difficult to teach using lectures. It is very difficult to understand the importance of such evolution tasks as program comprehension, configuration management or regression testing until faced with the need to apply them to a significant software system. Those rare academic courses that focus on evolution inevitably include a large project component [7]. Similarly, while principles of process design, quality assurance, aspects and impacts of team sizes larger than that generally afforded in the academic environment can be expounded in lectures, it is hard to understand the complexities of their application without trying them on a real project.

Accordingly, for the last seven years the University of West Florida has focused project work in its Masters track in Software Engineering on these two themes: *software evolution* and *software process*. The result has been a considerable learning experience, both for the instructors and for the students. In this paper, authored by three of the instructors and two of the students, we present the history of our approach and the lessons learned along the way. While no project strategy is ideal, we believe that the focus on these two themes has been effective in preparing our students for the realities of software professions.

2. Experiences in teaching process

The University of West Florida is a medium-sized institution located in the panhandle of Florida; the Software Engineering track has been offered both at the main Pensacola campus and at the satellite campus in Fort Walton Beach. Both are near military installations, so many of the students have connections to the Air Force, the Navy, defense contractors or to large civil service support organizations. The Software Engineering student population is quite heterogeneous; some students are experienced programmers, but others have written software only in academic environments. Most of the students have full time jobs so the program is offered in the evenings, with most classes meeting once per week.

Two key required courses in the track are *Software Engineering Management* (one semester, 3 credits) and *Software Engineering Project* (two semesters, total 6 credits). Process concepts are presented in the Software Engineering Management course using a seminar and readings format. Up through 1993, the projects in the Software Engineering

---

[1] Changes made to software after its initial release have been traditionally described by the misleading term software maintenance, with its inappropriate connotations of repair. Recently it has been recognized that most projects very quickly begin modifying the software they have produced so that most of the life cycle would be better described as software evolution [8] a term which also connotes planned change as opposed to reaction to events. While the changes made by our students have ranged from minor bug fixes through major planned enhancements we use the term evolution in this paper for simplicity.

Project course involved new software development, with each year's team determining the process that they would follow. Starting in 1994 the focus changed to integrate these two courses more closely and to focus on software evolution.

The 1994 Software Engineering Management class developed the initial version of the process that was to be followed in Software Engineering Project in subsequent semesters. Students have since used this process while enhancing a medium-sized software system, including fixes, new features, and web distribution of the modified system. Each year, the improved system is turned over to the following year's class for further evolution. (This kind of rolling project has recently been recommended by Bertrand Meyer in his proposals for Software Engineering education [5].)

While several systems have been used, most of the work has focused on different components of the Recon toolset for dynamic analysis of software[2]. Recon now has several versions and has grown to about 25,000 lines of C, 6000 lines of Ada, and 8000 lines of Java (raw line counts). It is thus large enough for the students to gain some real experience in dealing with other people's code without being too large to be grasped by relatively inexperienced programmers.

As the software evolves, the students improve the process that they follow. This process is called the *Generic University of West Florida Maintenance Process (GUMP)[3]* and attempts to mirror the typical content of an industrial process at roughly Level 3 (Defined Process) in the Capability Maturity Model. Like most evolution processes, GUMP is driven by software change requests. Change requests are reviewed and, if accepted, become Deficiency Reports (DR's) for the project's job queue. DR's are selected for work in a cycle that goes through analysis, change control, implementation, independent verification and validation and wrap-up (See Figure 1).

There are now two alternative tracks, one for normal code fixes and enhancements and another, called Product Administration (PA), primarily for updates to the documentation and the web pages. The process consists of 14 standards and plans describing everything from the process architecture and organizational structure to specific coding standards. Over the last seven years students have completed nearly 50 cycles through this process, with both the software system and the process benefiting from the experience.

3. Using evolution to teach process

An evolution process such as GUMP offers some notable advantages as a vehicle for teaching software process. In our earlier student development projects there was only a single pass through the process. Students performed analysis, design, coding and testing, leading (hopefully) to the delivery of a product at the end of the semester. The process was heavily constrained by the deadline and thus often degenerated into disguised code-and-test as time ran out.

---

[2] Recon2, and its newer version Recon3, are available free at http://www.cs.uwf.edu/~recon/
[3] Complete GUMP documentation is available on line at http://www.cs.uwf.edu/~wilde/gump

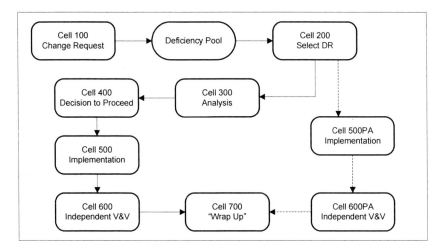

Figure 1 - Overview of the Software Evolution Process
The left path is used for most code changes while the "Product Administration" (PA)
path on the right is used in preparing builds and in modifying the product web site

However, an evolution project allows for several loops through the cycle. To learn the process each year we typically pick a small task, such as a minor bug fix, for the first loop. Then we go on to larger enhancement tasks in subsequent loops. The first time through tends to be fairly chaotic since everybody is new to their area of responsibility. Our students each fulfill one or more roles as defined in GUMP such as, Project Coordinator, Software Engineer, Independent Verification and Validation (IV&V), Software Quality Assurance (SQA), Software Engineering Process Group (SEPG), Software Configuration Management (SCM), etc. In the following loops the process settles down and runs more smoothly. Students thus see the real-world benefits of following a process and not just the initial chaos.

An evolution project also allows us to stress *process improvement*. Each year a different group of students identifies problems and improvements on top of the previous year's improvements. As they work, students suggest changes to the process based on their personal experiences with it. Often we can try out such improvements in one cycle and only introduce them into GUMP after they have gone through such a trial successfully.

GUMP has changed substantially over the years as suggestions have been proposed, tried, integrated into the process, and sometimes discarded. We try to emphasize the idea that an organization's software process represents *codified experience* of what works and what does not for that particular organization. Frequently, students perform an informal self-evaluation of their current level on the CMM and thus generate suggestions for improvements. It would be hard to find time for this kind of evaluative experience except in an evolution-based multi-cycle project.

The evolution process also lets students see the importance and the difficulties of software configuration management. Normally, the entire class consisting of six to twenty students will work as a single team. Some students will work on specific code changes while others are responsible for support areas such as configuration management, quality assurance or metrics. As groups are assigned to work on specific changes to the software, inevitably conflicts arise for access to files and documents when two groups need to change the same work product. The students learn to manage such conflicts by careful planning and by use of the SCCS configuration management tool.

There are, of course, some drawbacks in using software evolution as a teaching aid. Students need to understand the system that they will be working on, including both the problem domain and the architecture of the code. Such learning is both specific and time consuming, and necessarily takes time away from learning more generally applicable Computer Science or Software Engineering topics. Experience has shown that this learning needs to be structured with lectures and exercises. If students are just turned loose to study the code and documentation they tend to get frustrated. On average, we probably spend at least one month out of the two-semester Software Engineering Project just learning the system.

4. Lessons learned - improving the process

Process improvement has been a continuing activity, with each student group introducing major or minor modifications based on its experience. However by the spring of 2000 it was time for a more systematic evaluation of our process. A team of two instructors and two students who had been through the project course undertook a major revision of GUMP over the summer of 2000.

One purpose of the revision was simply to improve consistency and clarity. Over the years many minor inconsistencies had crept into the documents and a systematic review and consistency check was needed. In some areas, such as Configuration Management and Quality Assurance the documentation diverged from the practices that had been found necessary, so a complete rewrite was required.

But a more fundamental goal was to address a feeling that, while GUMP had served its original aims, new issues had arisen that needed to be better addressed. GUMP was originally seen as a process for maintaining code, and the expected activities were traditional bug fixes and enhancements. GUMP had been effective in reducing coding errors; very few new errors had been introduced since its adoption.

However, the Recon tool that the students maintain was now a mature product distributed on the web in several versions. Errors were frequently made in constructing the different builds and deploying them to the web. GUMP did not provide quality control over these activities; in one disastrous case new builds were deployed using code that was six months out of date. Worse, the error was not discovered for almost three months!

The first step of the analysis was to look at the data and documents from 33 completed cycles to see how well GUMP met the needs of the real job mix. The range of activities proved to be very large, with changes ranging from 2 lines modified to thousands of lines modified. Many cycles required no change to the code as such but rather the development and evolution of documentation and web pages, or preparation and deployment of new software builds. Several cycles involved "buy-in" of code developed externally and added to Recon, just as a real software development organization would often buy an off-the-shelf component to be integrated into its products. As can be seen from Figure 2, only about 64 % of our completed cycles were the kind of code changes for which GUMP was originally intended.

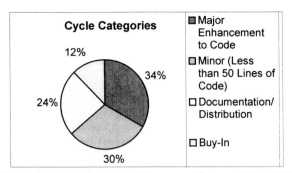

Figure 2 - Classification of Process Cycles, 1994 - 2000

The revised process introduced the two work flows shown in Figure 1. Preparing builds and web site updates does not require extensive analysis or design so such tasks follow the Process Administration (PA) track. This track includes no formal inspections, but the Implementation cell includes an informal walkthrough and the Independent Verification and Validation cell is now required. These controls should catch deployment blunders such as the one mentioned above.

The lesson here for us and for our students is the need to provide flexibility in a process, and to adjust it in accordance with real data from real experience, based on the unique make-up of an organization and its typical product domain.

A continuing frustration and a goal for the future is to improve our collection and use of software metrics data. While timecard data has been collected since 1994, we have found it very difficult to store and analyze that data in ways that would contribute to better cost estimation and management control. Several students have constructed databases with this data and tried different forms of statistical analysis, but the results have shown huge variations in productivity and so have not proven usable for estimation. We seem to be defeated by the diversity of software evolution tasks combined with the wide experience range of our students, not to mention technical glitches that have lost some of the raw data. So far our lesson learned is that getting usable software metrics requires an investment in systematic data collection and analysis that is hard to sustain in a student environment.

5. Lessons learned - using evolution processes in education

Based on our experience we strongly suggest that universities teaching Software Engineering should consider using an evolution process as a significant part of their curriculum. However there are some factors that they should consider.

A single semester is totally insufficient for a rolling, evolution-based project. At least two semesters are needed to provide time for learning the process, learning the software system, doing an initial "shake-down" task so participants learn their roles, and then finally making substantial change to the software system.

Instructor participation is greater in this kind of project than in a conventional one. Since students come and go each year, the instructor has to provide the group memory of both the process and the software system. Even fairly detailed process documentation never is sufficient to let students understand exactly what has to be done at each step. Similarly, written software documentation is never enough to convey the full import of the requirements and design. The instructor needs to make himself an expert in both areas and to spend a lot of time providing this background for the students as they come up to speed in the first semester of the project.

Continuity from one year to the next is essential; frequent changes of instructor will make the project unworkable. Our instructors perform the role of the client and the instructor. This provides interesting opportunities as clients to keep the pressure on the students to deliver the product, while at the same time, as the instructor, keeping the pressure on the students to adhere to the process. Instructors intentionally impose these pressures on our students, in order that they experience first-hand the strong temptations to throw the process out the window "to get the job done", but then since they can't get away with that, they discover that following the process leads to success.

A large group project such as ours also raises issues of grading. Since each student has a different role and each may work on different parts of the code, it is hard to be sure that grading is fair. Our project comes at the end of the students academic work when they have already been examined and assessed in many graduate courses, so we have felt that some imprecision could be tolerated. Generally roughly half the points are assigned as a group grade based on team progress in following the process and producing software, while the remainder is assigned subjectively based on presentations that each student must make in class. In a few years, where the team did not seem to be well integrated, instructors have also used a peer evaluation grade adjustment to identify poor performers. Vernier and Todd describe several alternate models that can be used for grading team projects [12].

With individual students each fulfilling specific roles within the organization, when one student "drops the ball" this has the expected cascading affects on the plan and the deadlines. Instructors emphasize the importance of respect and consideration for teammates, and will sometimes acquire a third role of moderator. Instructors expect that the students hold each other accountable, but insist that this is done in a constructive manner that is conducive to maintaining a cohesive team. For many students, this is their first experience with team dynamics to this extent. Oftentimes, the instructor's greatest challenge is to stand-by and let the students' team interactions play through, rather than jumping in and "rescuing them."

For an evolution-based project it is important to find a good system to work on. It must be of sufficient size so that it presents realistic difficulties in program comprehension, without being so large as to be unmanageable. We have found that a system of 10,000 - 20,000 lines is about right, especially if there are somewhat smaller subsystems that can be worked on independently. It is useful if the problem domain is fairly well known so that students do not need to spend too much time acquiring domain knowledge. We have found software tools to be good systems; Meyer mentions a rolling project at Monash University that uses a graphics simulation package [5].

One problem in using an academic product as we do is that inevitably the project is relieved of some of the time and commercial pressures of "real" software. Students do not need to negotiate with real customers and have more flexibility in delivery dates. Many universities send groups of students to work on real projects suggested by industrial partners [10]. Such projects have a major advantage in reality, but suffer from the difficulties of imposing a uniform process and time scale. As well, it would be difficult to incorporate software evolution into such a project since a company is unlikely to allow outsiders to modify important parts of its key systems. At the University of West Florida, we have abandoned this approach in favor of the more structured process-driven project described here.

6. Current developments

As the internet has created a business need for very rapid development, a recent trend has been the emergence of "lightweight" processes such as eXtreme Programming (XP) that try to provide speed while still preserving reasonable quality standards [1]. The last two sessions of the Software Engineering Management class have included an XP project so that students can be exposed to this new kind of process.

We find that our students often believe that process requires massive amounts of time and paper, two things that they find most distasteful. On the other hand they often believe that XP throws process out the window. However it can reasonably be argued that lightweight processes are not in opposition to the Capability Maturity Model, but rather represent an alternative way of covering most key process areas in environments that require flexible development [3]. It is important for students to recognize and distinguish these kinds of myths. Experience with both CMM and XP projects enables them to go beyond "process is good" or "process is bad" to see that what matters is the right kind of process for any particular project.

We also believe that that the inherent iterative and incremental approach to evolution and the structure of the process defined in GUMP will provide a natural transition to the greater emphasis on a results-based process defined in the CMMI rather than the activities-driven process defined by the CMM [9]. Many of the process areas emphasized in the CMMI are directly related to software evolution so an evolution-based project provides relevant training. We expect that our graduates will easily adapt to an organization that has adopted CMMI or is in the process of transitioning to CMMI.

7. Conclusions

We believe that their experience in these two courses has allowed our students to take a much more professional attitude towards Software Engineering practice. As an example, there is the experience of the very first evolution cycle when the GUMP process was first used in 1994. Although the proposed code change seemed simple, the cycle proved to be traumatic! Requirements were misunderstood, error conditions were poorly defined, and the change failed inspection several times. To the instructor's surprise, the class took a group decision to "fail" the whole cycle and roll back the software to its previous version. Then they proceeded to fix the process problems that had been identified before going on to redo that change, and several others, successfully. We doubt that, in a normal project class focused on development, the students would have been willing to take such a drastic decision with their entire semester's work at stake, and we find the professionalism that they showed to be very encouraging.

In a process-centered project like ours the diverse background experiences of the students can become a benefit. Each student adopts a specific process role, such as programmer, configuration manager, quality assurance leader, and so on. Some students assume roles that they perform on a day-to-day basis in their work, while others take the challenge of assuming a role that they have little knowledge of. In the one case student work experiences enrich the classroom while in the other the role-playing allows exposure to aspects of Software Engineering that a student would not otherwise see.

We feel that students learn much more about the realities of software by engaging in a process driven software evolution project than they would from a more conventional new development project. They are able to experience first-hand the pleasures and pitfalls associated with process and software evolution, preparing them for the most likely environment that they will work in after they graduate. They also inevitably experience the impact of poor group communications or inadequate configuration management control. They are provided with a significant learning experience related to team dynamics, personal integrity and ethics. Our graduates can then appreciate the difficulties of actually distributing and supporting a complete software product, as opposed to simply delivering a program to a professor.

In excess of 120 students have gone through this course cycle since 1994. Unfortunately we do not have any formal way of systematically tracking their future careers but anecdotal evidence indicates that most are working as software professionals, not just as programmers but often in testing, quality assurance, and project management roles. Many have told us that their experience in these two courses was invaluable and was a true capstone to their university education.

8. Acknowledgements

We would like to thank all the students who have gone through the UWF Masters track in Software Engineering and contributed so willingly both to the courses themselves and to teaching their instructors the realities of software process.

9. References

[1]   Kent Beck, "Embracing Change with Extreme Programming", *IEEE Computer*, October, 1999, pp. 70 - 77.

[2]   Gary Ford, "SEI Report on Graduate Software Engineering Education," CMU/SEI-91-TR-002, 1991, Software Engineering Institute, Carnegie Mellon University, Pittsburgh, PA.

[3]   Hillel Glazer, "Dispelling the Process Myth: Having a Process Does Not Mean Sacrificing Agility or Creativity", *CrossTalk: The Journal of Defense Software Engineering*, November 2001, pp. 27 - 30.

[4]   Watts Humphrey, *Managing the Software Process*, Addison-Wesley, Reading, MA, 1989.

[5]   Bertrand Meyer, "Software Engineering in the Academy", *IEEE Computer*, May 2001, pp. 28 - 35.

[6]   Keith Pierce, "Teaching Software Engineering Principles using Maintenance-based Projects", *Proc. 10th Conf. on Software Engineering Education and Training*, April 1997, IEEE Computer Society Press, pp. 53-60.

[7]   Margot Postema, Jan Miller, Martin Dick, "Including Practical Software Evolution in Software Engineering Education", *Proc. 14th Conf. on Software Engineering Education and Training*, February 2001, IEEE Computer Society Press, pp. 127 - 138.

[8]   Vaclav Rajlich and Keith Bennett, "A Staged Model for the Software Life Cycle", *IEEE Computer*, July 2000, pp. 66 - 71.

[9]   Walker Royce, "CMM vs. CMMI: From Conventional to Modern Software Management", *The Rational Edge*, February 2002, URL: http://www.therationaledge.com/content/feb_02/ f_conventionalToModern_wr.jsp (current September, 2002).

[10]   Andrew Stratton, Mike Holcombe, Peter Croll, "Improving the quality of Software Engineering courses through University Based Industrial Projects", in *Projects in the Computing Curriculum, Proc. of the Project 98 Workshop*, Springer-Verlag, Berlin, 1998, pp.47-69.

[11]   Richard Thayer and Leo Endres, "Software Engineering Project Laboratory: The Bridge Between University and Industry", in *Software Engineering Education: The Educational Needs of the Software Community*, Norman Gibbs and Richard Fairley eds., Springer-Verlag, New York, 1987, pp. 263 - 289.

[12]   J. M. Vernier and E. G. Todd, "Experiences with the Organization and Assessment of Group Software Development Projects", *Proc. of the IFIP WG3.4/SEARCC (SRIG on Education and Training) Working Conference*, September 1993, North-Holland, Amsterdam, 1993, pp.309-315.

The Cross-Course Software Engineering Project at the NTNU: Four Years of Experience

Guttorm Sindre[1,2], Tor Stålhane[1,3], Gunnar Brataas[1], Reidar Conradi[1]

[1]*Dept of Computer Systems and Information Science,*
Norwegian University of Science and Technology (NTNU)
[1]{guttors, stalhane, gb, conradi}@idi.ntnu.no

Abstract

Many software engineering courses include all-term projects to convey principles relating to large-scale multi-person development. But even such projects will easily be too small and simple, unless a sufficient amount of study time is allocated to them. This time may be hard to find, especially in strictly programmed profession studies where a lot of general theory courses have to be taken. This paper reports on the experiences from a software engineering project where the solution to the above problem has been to have several courses share one project. This had some advantages. First of all, it allows time for a bigger and more complex project with reasonable sacrifices of "own time" in each of the participating courses. Equally important, it is possible to show connections between the courses. In spite of these advantages, there have also been problems with the project, still leaving room for improvement.

1. Introduction

In software engineering education we are trying to teach methods for building skyscrapers, while all the examples we are able to give in the limited time frame of a lecture are mere camping tents. Practical examples in textbooks also tend to be extremely simple compared to industrial reality. Reading an introductory book on software engineering and following corresponding lectures, plus delivering answers to weekly or bi-weekly exercises, the students may learn *what* the issues in software engineering are, but little about *how* to do it. Since it is the latter they must master in their professional life, this is quite unsatisfactory.

The solution chosen in many SE courses is to expose the students to project work. However, projects can easily fail to be complex enough. Usually, a project must be completed in one term, and often just as part of one of several courses taken during that term. This makes the project limited, both in calendar time and man-hours, and necessitates a low complexity problem, which may not illuminate the core issues of software engineering.

At NTNU's Master of Technology studies, the general requirement is that each term should consist of four courses of equal weight. Hence, a software engineering course would only "own" ¼ of the students' time for a term (=14 weeks of lecturing time). Assuming that a project could spend half of that time (leaving the rest for textbook-reading, lectures etc.), and that an average student works a 40 hour week, this yields 14*40/8 = 70 hours of work per student on the project. Given the limited efficiency of undergraduate students, it will be hard to make a system of much more than 1 KLOC in

---

[2] Dept of Management Science and Information Systems, University of Auckland, New Zealand
[3] School of Computer Science and Engineering, University of New South Wales, Australia

such a project. As warned against in [1]: In a too small project, you do not need a systematic approach with a lot of design documentation, but could more easily code the solution directly. Hence, sound software development processes will feel inhibiting rather than helpful, and this has a negative effect on learning.

Several approaches have been suggested to make complex projects without increasing the workload too much. For instance, the students' work can be part of a bigger system, where much is pre-developed [1], or the students can be organized in large teams, in super-groups with sub-groups [2]. The 2nd year SE project at the NTNU has partly adopted both these approaches, but the ratio of predevelopment is significantly smaller than [1], and the team size (4-6 students) is much smaller than in [2]. However, whereas the projects discussed in [1,2] took place within one course, the project discussed in this paper is shared across several courses of the same term.

The rest of the paper is structured as follows: In section 2 we look at the placement of the project in the study plan. Section 3 describes the four projects that have taken place to date. Section 4 discusses the experiences drawn from the cross-course project. Section 5 makes some conclusions, both in terms of future directions for the project and further research on its strong and weak sides.

2. The Placement of the Cross-Course SE Project in the Study Plan

Table 1 below shows the study plan for the IT students on their way to the degree Master of Technology at the NTNU. All the courses indicated are compulsory for the IT students, and it is not until the fourth year that they get to choose specializations within the IT field. Thus, this is a strictly programmed study plan, inspired by the tradition of German engineering education. Many general courses (e.g., maths, physics, philosophy) are common requirements for all Master of Technology degrees. This ensures a wide platform but reduces the space for courses more relevant for the IT candidates.

Table 1: Current study plan for the degree Master of Technology (IT), NTNU

5th spring	Masters Thesis			
5th autumn	Individual Research Project			
4th spring	Cross-Fac. Proj.			
4th autumn	Customer Driven Project			
3rd spring	Info.sys. (IS)	Prog.Languages	Knowledge Sys.	
3rd autumn	Operating sys.	Math 4	Logic	Techn.Mgt
2nd spring	C R O S S - Sw.eng. (SE)	C O U R S E Databases (DB)	P R O J Comm.tech. (CT)	E C T HCI
2nd autumn	Algorithms	Math 3	Statistics	Physics
1st spring	Programming	Dig./El. Circuits	Computers	Philosophy2
1st autumn	Intro to IT	Math 1	Discrete Math	Philosophy1

The project done in the second spring term is not the only project done by the IT students during the program. There are several others, as indicated by the gray squares: In the 1st spring course *SIF8005 Programming*, there is a small project done by groups of 4 students during the last 6 weeks of the term. The 4th autumn term contains *SIF8080 Customer*

Driven Project, occupying two normal course slots. With a real customer and no textbook/lecture/theory part (covered by the previous course *Information Systems*), this project is even bigger and with a better focus on the requirements phase. This project has been presented in more detail in [8] and later undergone a thorough pedagogical evaluation in [9], with positive conclusions. It will not be elaborated further in this paper.

There are even more projects during the study, but these are not particularly related to software engineering and are therefore not mentioned here.

3. Project Structure

Since RE is well covered by the Customer Driven Project, it is less addressed in the cross-course project. Instead, this project starts with fixed requirements provided by the staff. The overall time plan / deliverables are also set by staff. For the 2002 offering the deliverables were as shown in Table 2:

Table 2: Deliverables, 2002 offering of project (ALL# = common project deliverable, CT/DB/HCI/SE# = deliverables associated with one of the four courses)

Deadline	Label	Contents
Jan 25	ALL1	Project Plan
Feb 1	ALL2	System Test Plan
Feb 8	SE1	Use-Case Diagrams
	HCI1	Conceptual UI Design w/ usability testing
Feb 15	DB1	Conceptual Data Model
	CT1	Class Diagram, description of model
Mar 1	SE2	System Design
	HCI2	Interaction Styles UI Design
Mar 8	DB2	Logical Database Design
Mar 15	SE3	First Increment of System
	CT2	Working XML Protocol
Apr 8	CT3	Java™ Secure Socket Extension (JSSE)
Apr 12	HCI3	Usability Test Report
Apr 19	SE4	Second Increment of System
	DB3	Physical Database Design
Apr 26	ALL3	End Report, including System Test Report and Change Report

As can be seen from the list of deliverables, most of them are associated with one of the four courses. This is practical from a teaching perspective, especially since not all students take all the four courses. From an ideal, "real world" perspective it might be even better if all deliverables were common deliverables, but this would give the teaching staff a much harder job in finding suitable deliverables that covered all the courses equally well. Another possibility could be to have just a final deadline and leave it to each group to find out how to progress in between. But this would probably be too much responsibility on the shoulders of students at this level, except for the best groups. Moreover, such freedom would make it much more difficult for the teaching staff to provide systematic guidance to all groups and particular help to groups with problems. A set progression like the above ensures that all groups are working with the same problems approximately at the same time during the project. For the deliverable ALL1 Project Plan, the students would take the staff-provided deadlines for granted and then add their own more detailed deadlines, make estimates for how many man-hours should be expended on each task, distribute responsibilities within the team, and discuss major risks and how to resolve them.

The problem statement and requirements have varied from year to year, but all revolve around the same high-level architecture: A client-server system, where the server stores data in a relational database. This, of course, is motivated by the selection of courses involved: The database is necessary for the Database course, and the client/server networking aspects necessary for the Communication Technology course. Much of the CT part of the project demands that the students produce UML diagrams and Java code, so this actually increases the amount of typical software engineering work far beyond the SE deliverables of the project (the only notable difference being that the CT deliverables demand knowledge of network communication issues for the students to be able to solve them well).

The project is done in teams. In 2002 there were 391 students taking the project, making up 79 teams. Most teams had 5 members (just a very few exceptions with 4 or 6). The same assignment is given to every team, in the form of set requirements for the system to be developed, and some process requirements in the form of deliverables and deadlines. Using the same assignment for all teams does entail a risk that some students/groups are tempted to copy work off others rather than doing the project themselves. But any other arrangement would put too much work on the staff, given the huge number of students.

The teaching staff compose the teams, after web input from the students about their ambitions and preferences. A key concern is to avoid that, e.g., two good and ambitious students end up in the same group as two poorer students with low ambitions. Such a group constellation yields a clear risk that the good students will do all the work, even willingly, since they perceive it as more time-consuming to try to explain everything to the less clever. Then, the poorer students get through the project with little effort and little learning. The students are not assigned specific roles within the teams by teaching staff, but they are free to assume such roles if there is agreement in the team.

4. History and Experiences

The study plan picture given in Figure 1 is the current one (spring 2002), but has undergone some revision from the first run of the cross-course project in 1999. In 1999, it spanned the courses Software Engineering, Databases, Comm.Tech. (as in 2002) and SIF8015 Logic (using [10-12] as reading material). In 2000 and 2001 it spanned only 3 courses, Software Engineering, Databases, and Comm.Tech., as Logic chose to leave the project and instead have its separate run of compulsory exercises + a smaller in-course project.

There has yet been no formal evaluation of the cross-course project (e.g., in terms of questionnaires, formal interviews with students, etc.), so the following experiences are based on the impressions of the teaching staff. The impressions have mainly come from the following:

- Input from the reference group. At the NTNU, each course is required to have a reference group, consisting of 3-4 students elected by their peers to represent them in meetings with the teacher while the course progresses. These representatives have discussions with their class, for instance in lecture breaks, to decide on issues to be raised with the teacher (both positive and critical comments). Meetings with the lecturer and other members of the course's teaching staff may be held 3-4 times during the term. The idea is that while a single student may be reluctant to approach the teacher with critical comments about the course, the reference group members are able to speak more freely, being persons not afraid to speak up, and because the viewpoints forwarded are not necessarily their own.

- Input from the teaching assistants. These are themselves students, only a year or two ahead of those taking the course, and have been employed part-time by the department to help the students with practical problems in the labs, as well as answering simple course questions that need not be taken all the way to the teacher. By their presence in the lab, the assistants pick up much more quickly any problems in the project, and many students will also be able to air frustrations more freely with the assistants than with the lecturers.

- Students' end reports in the projects, summing up their experiences, including suggestions for improvement of the project. In 2002 the questions related to learning and improvement of the project were made more detailed than before, requesting evaluation and improvement suggestions in several different categories: the nature of the project assignment, the written instructions provided, the lab guidance, the Q&A facility, and the other parts of the project web page.

- Informal conversations between lecturers and students, both during the course and a year or two after.

Although many students have felt moments of crisis during the project, e.g., work burden too big, assignment unclear, poor cooperation within the team, tools not working, pre-developed code not working (!), there have been lots of positive experiences during this period: The project has become so complex that few students have felt that simply coding away from day 1 would have been an option. It has made the students see connections between the courses of that term, in a much better way than what is experienced in other terms (without cross-course projects). And some of the students who have been negative to the learning gains of the project when it took place, have come back more positive after their subsequent summer job in industry, having experienced that much of what they learnt from the project was highly relevant in "real life".

At the same time, there have been some mistakes that the teaching staff has learnt from (described in detail in the sequel), so that the project as of 2001 and 2002 was probably far better pedagogically than the first two runs.

The 1999 run posed the students with the task of developing a client-server system for an ad-financed web news-service. There was little code pre-developed, and many of the students claimed the project was too big – although, to reduce work burden, a limited version of the database was provided midway in the project. The prescribed process was a straight waterfall development. Time ran out in the end, so the project sort of ended with delivering the code, without any emphasis on testing. Each course had its separate deliverables, four for each of the courses. Somewhat unluckily, all these were of a similar size and falling on the same dates (e.g., SE1, DB1, CT1, and Logic1 were due on the same day, similarly SE2, DB2, CT2, Logic2, etc.). Since the number of courses corresponded to the normal team size, this tempted many of the groups to take a very opportunistic approach to work-division, one student doing all the SE deliverables, another doing all the DB deliverables etc. While such a work division could indeed make sense in industry, where project teams are often composed of specialists, it is not a good idea in an educational setting, where all students are supposed to learn all four courses. In the final exam in the database course, one of the exam questions was closely project-related, and here it was observed that about ¼ of the students did well, whereas the remaining ¾ of the candidates were almost blank. This shows that the opportunistic work division did indeed impact the students' learning in a negative manner. The lecturer of the database course was also somewhat unhappy about the limited database that was given out midway in the project, since this meant that the database that each group had made ER-diagrams for in deliverable DB1 and then normalized relational tables for in deliverable DB2, was not used further on in the project but replaced with the standard and limited set of tables provided by the staff. Hence, the students would not suffer onwards in the project if their DB design was bad, and thus not learn from their mistakes.

The 2000 run tried to improve on some of the weaknesses observed in the 1999 run. The assignment was to make a client-server system for a web CD shop. To avoid work-division by course, the deliverables were made different in size and the timing changed so that they were not due on the same date. Moreover, formal requirements were added that each student had to be heavily involved in at least one deliverable related to each course, and had to write at least 15% of the Java code. The 2000 run also put a stronger emphasis on testing, introducing the system test plan as a quite early deliverable and prescribing module tests at a later stage. To ensure that something was finished and tested even if time should run out, an incremental development process was chosen. Moreover, after request from the database teacher, no limited mock up database would be introduced midway, instead each group should use their self-made databases all the way through the project. To make it possible for the students to make a more ambitious system and yet finish in time, more of the code was pre-developed. However, in this respect the project failed. Due to understaffing, the pre-developed code was finished too late and contained errors and unclear issues that hampered the progress of the students. Moreover, the requirements turned out to have been set too ambitiously, so that the students still had to write huge amounts of code themselves. Some of the groups delivered nearly 5 KLOC for the database interface alone (SE deliverable 2). This amount of code may partly have been due to a poor design by those particular groups, but it also clearly reflects that the teaching staff underestimated the size of the deliverable. The database interface code is indeed a tricky deliverable in this cross-course project. To satisfy the learning goals of the DB course, there must be a fairly complex ER-diagram, resulting in a significant number of normalized tables. But the task of writing the necessary Java/JDBC code to interface with a database is normally much more time-consuming than making the database itself. Moreover it is usually fairly monotonous code, not particularly useful for teaching OOD principles. And it cannot be given out as pre-developed, since that would give away the preferred DB design itself.

In 2000, only few groups succeeded in finishing the project with something that was close to running as intended. So, while it did succeed in eliminating the work-division by course and putting a better focus on testing, the overall impression was one of failure.

The 2001 run, where the students built a system for advertising and selling tickets for a group of cinemas, addressed just the problems mentioned above. A PhD student, who would later serve as an adviser to the teaching assistants in the project, developed the entire solution to the 2001 project assignment during the summer and autumn of 2000. Thus it was much easier to estimate the total project workload, and to see what parts could be given out as pre-developed without giving away the solution to the student-developed parts as well. Moreover, the pre-developed parts had already been tested. Finally, it was easier to determine up front that the learning goals of all the participating courses would be sufficiently addressed by the project

This project ran a lot more painlessly than the 2000 run, and all the groups managed to make successful delivery of a running system.

The 2002 run challenged the students with the task of making a multi-user game environment. The choice of making a computer game was inspired by the success that had been experienced in the course SIF8005 Programming, where there had been a smaller project implementing a computer game. This was a somewhat freer task than had been given in previous offerings of the project. Although all groups had to fulfill some set requirements for features that their game had to include, they did not have to – and indeed were not encouraged to – make the same game.

The task gave plenty of freedom, but as a result it was hard to learn from other groups: they had not the same challenges. Some students enjoyed making a game, but for some, developing a game both in the Programming subject and in this project was too much play: They wanted something more realistic. Some groups felt the task had an unrealistically high degree of freedom: In industry requirements are often more fixed.

There was a clear separation between groups that succeeded and groups with less success: The task stimulated creativity for the former groups while for the latter groups, a more controlled project where it had been easier to adjust unwise decisions earlier would have been better.

One problem that had been observed in the earlier runs of this project, was that groups with internal differences in the level of ambition function quite badly when trying to cooperate. Thus, we tried – as far as possible – to compose groups that were homogenous in ambitions. The only extra condition imposed was that all groups had at least two members with good working knowledge of Java. This ensured that no group would be left totally without a chance to succeed, but did of course create a risk that some students that were poor at programming would not learn it through this project either, because the better team members did their share.

As before, a considerable amount of code from the "gold version" of the system was distributed at the start of the project. This helped to get the students started with their work and limits the perceived solution space. The latter point is especially helpful for the student assistants.

The project's home page was enhanced with a Q&A service that became quite popular with the students. During the project, 276 questions were posted – more than 3 questions per group. . We stressed quick responses and most questions were answered the same or the next day. By making the answers public, all groups benefited from the same guidance. Many groups liked the Q & A, but it did not completely make up for the poor guidance. The three topics that received the most questions were databases (23%), communication (20%), and Java code (18%). Since 9% of all questions were pertaining to clarifications of the requirements, it seems that we still have a job to do in this area.

The lessons learnt in the 2002 run of the project will be put into use in the 2003 project, where the students will implement a simple project management system. This project will give the students a more realistic job to do and in addition help them to get more practical experience with project planning and control.

5. Conclusions

This paper has discussed the cross-course project that is shared between the courses Software Engineering, Databases, Communication Technology, and HCI, all taken in the 4th term of study in the IT students' Master of Technology track at the NTNU. The way the project itself is conducted, with students in teams of 4-5, developing a system according to requirements set by staff may not be particularly original. The distinguishing feature of this project, compared to other projects that have been reported e.g. in the CSEE&T conference series [1,2,8,13,14,15], is the way it is shared between four courses taught simultaneously during the project term. While most other educational SE projects are either in-course or own-course, this is thus a cross-course project. This seems to be a smart way of adapting to our university's overall policy that each term should consist of four equally sized courses (especially strongly enforced in the early years of study), which makes it difficult to have sufficiently complex projects within single courses. Not all runs of the cross-course project have been equally successful, but the overall impression is that the project is now well established, and that it does indeed fulfill the goals that were initially set for it, namely that the sharing of a project across the four courses in a term should make the project big and complex enough to illustrate core problems of software engineering, and make it easier for students to see connections between various courses and thus give a more holistic feel of the study program.

Still, further improvement is possible, both in finding good assignments that exercise a satisfactory range of learning goals in all the participating courses without becoming too demanding in man-hours, and in the guidance and tool support provided to the students during the project. Before any significant changes are done to the current project style, however, a natural first step would be to undertake some more formal evaluations of the learning gains associated with the project, as this would give more detailed hints to where it succeeds and not.

References

[1] A.J. Offutt, R.H. Untch, "Integrating Research, Reuse, and Integration into Software Engineering Courses", In: *Proc. 5th SEI Conference on Software Engineering Education (CSEE'92)*, San Diego, CA, Springer Verlag (LNCS 640), 1992.

[2] B. Bruegge, "Teaching an Industry-Oriented Software Engineering Course". In: *Proc. 5th SEI Conference on Software Engineering Education (CSEE'92)*, San Diego, CA. Springer Verlag LNCS 640, 1992.

[3] H. van Vliet, *Software Engineering – Principles and Practice*. 2nd ed., Wiley, 2000.

[4] M. Fowler, K. Scott, *UML Distilled*, 2nd ed., Addison Wesley Longman, 2000.

[5] H. Garcia-Molina, J. D. Ullman, J. Widom, *Database Systems: The Complete Book*, Prentice Hall, 2002.

[6] A. S. Tannenbaum: *Computer Networks*. Prentice-Hall, 1996.

[7] J. Preece et al. Human Computer Interaction. Addison-Wesley 1994.

[8] R. Andersen, R. Conradi, et al.: "Project courses at the NTH: 20 years of experience", In: *Proc. 7th SEI Conference on Software Engineering Education (CSEE'94)*, San Antonio, TX, USA, 1994, Springer Verlag (LNCS 750).

[9] M. Sorge. *Evaluering av prosjektundervisningen ved Institutt for datateknikk og informasjonsvitenskap, NTNU*. Report, PLU (Program for Teacher Education, Section for University Pedagogics), NTNU, 2000. (In Norwegian).

[10] A. G. Hamilton. *Logic for Mathematicians*. Cambridge Univ. Press, 1990.

[11] U. Nilsson, J. Maluszynski. *Logic, Programming and Prolog*. Published on web, checked 17.9.2002, http://www.ida.liu.se/~ulfni/lpp/, 2000.

[12] M. Huth, M. Ryan. *Logic in Computer Science*. Cambridge Univ. Press, 1999.

[13] J. H. Andrews, H. Lutfiyya. "Experience Report: A Software Maintenance Project Course". In *Proc. 13th International Conference on Software Engineering Education and Training, (CSEE&T 2000)*, Austin, TX, USA. IEEE Computer Society Press.

[13] D. Port, B. Boehm. "Experience in Early and Late Software Engineering Project Courses", in: *Proc. 14th International Conference on Software Engineering Education and Training (CSEE&T 2001)*, Charlotte, NC, USA. IEEE Computer Society Press, 2001.

[14] B. Demuth, M. Fischer, H. Hussmann, "Experience in Early and Late Software Engineering Project Courses", in: *Proc. 15th International Conference on Software Engineering Education and Training (CSEE&T 2002)*, Covington, KY, USA, IEEE Computer Society Press, 2002.

[15] M. B. Blake, T. Cornett. "Teaching an Object-Oriented Software Development Lifecycle in Undergraduate Software Engineering Education". In: *Proc. 15th International Conference on Software Engineering Education and Training (CSEE&T 2002)*, Covington, KY, USA, IEEE Computer Society Press, 2002.

Software Engineering Process
Process
(Paper Session I)

Can We Influence Students' Attitudes About Inspections? Can We Measure a Change in Attitude?

Delbert Bailey, Tracey Conn, Brian Hanks, and Linda Werner
Computer Science Department
University of California
Santa Cruz, CA 95064
{dbailey,tconn,brianh,linda}@cs.ucsc.edu

Abstract

As the software industry matures, new development technologies are invented and some of these technologies transition into best practices. Our role as university educators is to teach these best practices and change attitudes so that our students graduate as software engineers who believe in the use of these methodologies. One question that all software engineering educators have is 'Can we measure whether our courses change attitudes about the use of these methodologies?' In this small case study, conventional techniques in psychology for attitude measurement are used to construct scales for measuring software engineering students' attitudes toward the code inspection process. The scales were applied in a pre-pilot survey, a pilot survey, a test survey, and then again in a larger test situation. Our test results suggest that our students improved their intellectual acceptance of code inspections after viewing an inspection video. Students emotionally accepted inspection only after practice. Our work shows that this line of research has the potential to help assess the impact of software engineering teaching methods and materials.

1. Introduction

As the software industry matures, new development methodologies are invented and some of these methodologies transition into best practices. Our role as university educators is to teach these best practices. In addition, we want our graduates to believe in the use of these methodologies. We studied one best practice, software code inspection. Our questions were

- When we teach, do students' attitudes change?
- Can we measure these changes?

It is generally recognized that human factors have a major influence on the software development process and can significantly affect the success of a project and product. People tend to evaluate almost everything they encounter. They see things (e.g., people, objects, activities, or ideas) as likable or unlikable, interesting or boring, attractive or repellent, etc. In general, they tend to be, to varying degrees, positive or negative with respect to things. These evaluations then influence their perception in future experience by filtering out any information that is counter to the evaluation and reinforcing whatever supports it. This takes an extreme form as a self-fulfilling prophecy in cases where an individual has some influence in the outcome of an experience.

Software development methodology is no exception to this phenomenon. New methods are usually introduced with almost religious fervor by energetic, intelligent, and capable advocates. As acceptance begins to take hold, it is nearly impossible for a software engineer not to be for or against the new method. As organizations begin to adopt the new methods, the filtering dynamic of attitude leads rapidly to polarization, since any methodology is bound to have both good and bad characteristics.

For many years psychologists have been interested in how attitudes are formed, changed, and affect behavior. They have developed techniques for measuring attitude. In this study we investigate how it may be possible to measure one particularly important factor: attitude toward the development methodology called code inspection, with the goal of facilitating future studies of to what degree attitude does affect methodology transition into best practice. We found that with more work, our attitude measurement tool has the potential to be more effective at measuring students' attitudes. More importantly, our work shows that this line of research has the potential to help assess the impact of software engineering teaching methods and materials.

2. Background

One of the earliest considerations of human factors in the software development process was Gerald Weinberg's 1971 book on the psychology of programming [14]. Fred Brooks [3] sees human factors as contributing to the problem of managing software development projects in his well known collection of essays. Although human factors have always been known to be important, only recently have software engineering researchers begun to focus on how to handle human factors in their investigations [12].

Thurstone [13] studied how to define and measure attitude as far back as 1927. His methods are still valid today; however, many other useful methods have been developed since then including Likert scaling and adaptations of Osgood's [9] semantic differential. Daniel Mueller's [8] excellent handbook on measuring attitudes explains the different techniques, compares them with each other, and gives practical direction on how to use them and evaluate the results.

Software inspection, as first defined by Fagan [5], is a method for detecting defects. Its aim is to use a group of peers and a formalized reading process to help software engineers detect and locate defects in their code. Defects can then be removed prior to product release. Software inspections have since evolved into what is known as a 'best practice' – a method for accomplishing a task that has been researched, empirically verified, and is considered as one of the most efficient strategies for that task. "Properly applied, software inspections rival testing in defect detection and correction but cost less time and effort" [1].

Redwine and Riddle [11] state that many best practices are not in widespread use even decades after concept formulation. These include automated estimation tools, evolutionary delivery, throwaway user interface prototyping, information hiding, source code control, and inspections – just to name a few. Conceptual integrity, clear recognition of need, prior positive experience, management commitment, and training influence the transitioning of technology into widespread use

The challenge for the software industry is not only to develop good practice but to deploy good practice [6]. Many think that this challenge can be taken up by university level software engineering programs because our programs can provide positive experience in addition to theoretical instruction. Unfortunately, little is known about whether we are successfully modifying students' attitudes about these best practices.

3. Method

For scale construction we used three techniques: self evaluation, semantic differential and Likert scaling. The requirements of the Likert technique were the most demanding and shaped our overall process.

The self evaluation scale consists of one question (What is your attitude toward the code inspection process?) asking the respondents to rank their attitude by selecting one of a sequence of numbers (1-9) which corresponds to strongly oppose, neutral, or strongly favor.

In Likert scaling, respondents are asked to read statements and indicate to what degree they agree or disagree with each statement. The steps in building the scale are: identify the attitudinal object; collect a pool of statements that express attitude about the object; survey a large pilot group; analyze the items based on responses of the pilot group; and edit the survey questions, deleting those that do not work well.

We first developed the collection of statements about code inspection from interviewing, reading the literature, web searching, and just simply inventing them. Recommended guidelines for avoiding poor statements include not using extreme statements or simple statements of non-controversial fact, because these tend to reduce the spread of likely responses. Double-barreled compound statements that create the possibility of agreement with one of the components but not the other should be modified or eliminated. The following are the statements that we used:

- Good programmers would like the code inspection process.
- Code inspection is a waste of time.
- Code inspections are not likely to uncover the significant bugs.
- I do not want anyone looking at my code! Test it! If it works, OK; if not, I will fix it.
- I am uncomfortable with the idea of someone looking at my code.
- Besides finding anomalies, code inspection has other benefits such as education.
- One hour of code inspection will save four hours of regression testing.
- Code inspections can be a powerful tool for finding and preventing problems.
- Since many good products have been produced without code inspections, do not make a time consuming, costly fix to something that isn't broken.
- I do not like to spend my time trying to understand someone else's mess.
- Poor programmers do not like to show their ugly code to others and good programmers would rather spend their time writing good code than preparing for code inspections.
- I would rather write more good code than take the time to bring others up to speed enough to understand the code I already have working.
- Code inspections will find more bugs than individual debugging can.
- Code inspections are a good way to keep programmers on their toes.
- "Given enough eyeballs, all bugs are shallow [10]."
- Code inspection is tedious but necessary.
- I'm reluctant to let anyone see my code because they'll think I'm dumb.
- Code inspection is great because if someone leaves the company, the rest of us will know what's going on.
- Code inspections pinpoint problems before test and save money.
- I don't want to be involved in code inspections with some people because they can find problems with anything I do.
- Code inspections are great because you learn to be a better programmer from the other team members.
- I don't like to show others my code because they will steal my ideas.
- Code inspections are good because when everyone has done their homework and reviewed the code before hand, we are really effective at finding important problems.
- Code inspections are usually stressful; critical rather than supportive.

With semantic differential scaling, respondents are presented with adjective pairs and asked to place a mark between them which best describes the meaning of the attitudinal object for them. The steps in building this scale are similar to the Likert steps except the pool of items is generated by selecting adjective pairs from Osgood's lists that are high in the evaluation dimension of meaning. We used the adjective pairs pleasant/unpleasant, powerful/weak, pleasing/annoying, safe/dangerous, labored/easy, beneficial/harmful, useful/useless, harmonious/dissonant, comfortable/uncomfortable, meaningful/meaningless, good/bad, progressive/regressive, intelligent/unintelligent, interesting/boring, and slow/fast.

The study presented here took place at the University of California, Santa Cruz, a west coast public university, in the winter and spring of 2001. We used a pre-pilot survey with a small group of students and alumni to find some of the expected initial bugs in our process. This survey was done by e-mail and it did highlight difficult items and revealed a double-barreled item. We followed this up with a pilot survey and a two-part test phase.

The pilot survey was given to an undergraduate Java programming class. Fifty-seven completed questionnaires were obtained. A summary of the results is presented below along with the item analysis. Only three items were eliminated.

For the first part of the test phase of the study it was initially planned to survey students in an undergraduate software engineering class just before a video, "Scenes of Software Inspections" [4], was shown and then again afterward. Because we anticipated that there would be a short time between these events, we decided to divide the 24 Likert items into two sets of 12 items, an A set and a B set. That way, respondents on the Likert items would not be faced with considering how they had previously responded. Five of the ten students were given the A set first followed by the B set while the other five received the sets in the opposite order. By doing this, differences in scores between the two administrations of the questionnaire could not be merely attributed to two different sets of Likert items. As it turned out, the before and after events were separated by two days, and there was a lecture on code inspection as well as the video between the two surveys. The questionnaires were then coded so it was possible to match them later by respondent. The results are summarized in the next section.

For the larger test situation, 35 undergraduates (12 females, 23 males) enrolled in a senior software engineering course volunteered to participate in this study. Respondents completed the survey at three points during the course. Unlike the initial test of the scale, we administered the entire set of items each time the scale was given. The scale was first administered at the beginning of the course after the students heard an introduction to software engineering which included a short description of software inspections. The second use was midway into the course after students viewed the video. The third administration was at the end of the course after all students had practiced inspections in class.

4. Results

4.1 Scale construction

The scale construction part of this study produced good results. A summary of the information from the pilot survey and its analysis follows. A detailed discussion of the results of the pilot survey and the first, small test case can be found in Bailey [2]. Some responses were reverse scored so that in all cases, low numbers indicate positive attitude. We got a reasonable spread but positive bias in the scores of the respondents for all three parts of the scale. Most likely the positive bias in the self evaluation section is due to a tendency for most people to want to be positive and to please. Since the semantic differential section is so transparent with respect to how it will score, this may be affecting it also. The Likert section, on the other hand, is less transparent and the items have mixed scaling, so the positive bias for it may indicate something more real. The individual Likert items' correlations with the Likert total scores varied from 0.2916 to 0.6916 and none would be rejected on the basis of having a negative or zero correlation.

For the semantic differential section of the scale, three items were removed before any further use. These items (safe/dangerous, labored/easy, and slow/fast) all have distinctly lower correlations (0.3770, 0.2354, 0.2430) with the total semantic differential score than do the other items and they also have obviously poor correlations with the Likert total scores (0.0768, -0.1469, -0.0550). The remaining items have correlations with the semantic differential total scores that vary from 0.4193 to 0.7762 and correlations with the Likert total scores that vary from 0.2454 to 0.4644.

Table 1 shows how the three sections of the survey correlate with each other.

Table 1. Correlation between scale sections

	Self Eval.	Sem. Diff 12 items.	Likert
Self Eval.	1.0000	0.3300	0.3789
Sem. Diff 12 items.		1.0000	0.5877

Table 2 shows the Cronbach α-reliability coefficients for the different scale types used in the survey questionnaire.

Table 2. Reliability coefficients for scale sections

Scale	α-reliability
Self Eval.	n/a
Sem. Diff. before item analysis	0.8245
Sem. Diff. after item analysis and removal	0.8613
Likert	0.8509
First half	0.7268
Second half	0.7447

These values in Table 2 are high and indicate that the items within the Likert and semantic differential sections are consistent within themselves. The high value for the Likert section made it possible to separate it into two sets. The last two rows of Table 2 also show the change in reliability that occurred. There is a considerable reduction in reliability in going to the smaller sets but they are still useful and the two subsets were self consistent as would be expected from the high reliability for the whole.

4.2 Scale use in two test cases

4.2.1. Small test case (n=10): Table 3 summarizes the results of the scale measurements in the first part of the test. In all 3 sections of the scale there is a favorable increase in attitude. The significance levels are reasonable given that there were a very small number of students (n=10) in the test.

Table 3. First test case statistical parameters

scale type	before	after	Δ	t-value	sig.
self eval.	4.00	3.33	0.67	1.633	<0.1
sem. diff.	38.67	36.00	2.67	1.398	≈0.1
Likert	31.33	29.33	2.00	1.500	<0.1

4.2.2. Larger test case (n=35): Table 4 shows the Cronbach α-reliability coefficients for the scale types used in the second, larger test case (n=35). These values are high and indicate that the items within the Likert and semantic differential sections are self consistent.

Table 4. Second test case reliability coefficients

Scale	α-reliability
Self Eval.	n/a
Sem. Diff.	0.9637
Likert	0.8757

Because of the high reliability values, we did factor analysis on the items in the Likert and semantic differential sections. We found no evidence of groupings of items into factors for the Likert section. In fact, because of our attempts to find factors, we determined that small changes were needed to the items in the Likert section for our future use of this scale. One item was split into two items; the wording of another item was changed to remove a perceived double negative; and the wording of another was clarified. A two-factor solution was found to account for the greatest amount of variance in the items in the semantic differential section (78% of the variance). The first factor (42% of the variance) contained emotional items (e.g., pleasant/unpleasant, powerful/weak, good/bad, pleasing/annoying, harmonious/dissonant, comfortable/uncomfortable, interesting/boring) and the second factor (36% of the variance) contained intellectual items (e.g., beneficial/harmful, meaningful/meaningless, useful/useless, progressive/regressive, intelligent/unintelligent). To review the loading of the items, see Table 5.

Table 5. Factor analysis of semantic differential items

$\chi 2(1) = 60, p < .05$ at time = 1	Emotional	Intellectual
pleasant/unpleasant	.90	.23
powerful/weak	.80	.45
good/bad	.77	.53
pleasing/annoying	.81	.32
beneficial/harmful	.37	.83
harmonious/dissonant	.54	.46
comfortable/uncomfortable	.73	.39
meaningful/meaningless	.55	.64
useful/useless	.34	.92
progressive/regressive	.29	.86
intelligent/unintelligent	.52	.74
interesting/boring	.78	.37

These two factors were used to calculate emotional (EMOT) and intellectual (INTELL) scores for each participant. The obtained alpha coefficients for each construct were .95 and .95. Analysis of Variance (ANOVA) of these factors showed that there were significant differences between their means for the three administrations of the scale. Follow up analysis using Tukey's [7] method for multiple comparisons of the three administrations of the scale (after introduction (time=1), after video (time=2), after practice (time=3)) was done to determine which particular differences were significant. For EMOT, the mean values are significantly (p = .05) different from time 1 to time 3. There is no significant difference from time 1 to time 2, or from time 2 to time 3. For INTELL, the mean values are significantly different from time 1 to time 2, and from time 1 to time 3. There is no significant difference from time 2 to time 3. See Table 6.

Table 6. Multiple Comparisons for semantic differential factors: EMOT and INTELL

Semantic Diff	Time=1	Time=2	Time=3
EMOT mean value	3.85	3.58	3.10
Significant diff from time=1	n/a	no	yes (p=.05)
Significant diff from time=2	no	n/a	no
INTELL mean value	2.88	2.23	2.11
Significant diff from time=1	n/a	yes (p=.05)	yes (p=.05)
Significant diff from time=2	yes (p=.05)	n/a	no

For the Likert portion of the scale (Table 7), the difference between the means at time 1 and time 3 is significant at the p=.05 level. No other pairwise differences are significant.

Table 7. Multiple Comparisons for Likert section

Likert	Time=1	Time=2	Time=3
Mean value	2.37	2.14	2.06
Significant diff from time=1	n/a	no	yes (p=.05)
Significant diff from time=2	no	n/a	no

Regarding the self evaluation section of the scale (Table 8), a multiple comparison of means using the Tukey test indicates that the mean at time 1 significantly differs from the mean at time 2 (p=.05), and the mean at time 1 significantly differs from the mean at time 3 (p=.01).

Table 8. Multiple Comparison for self evaluation section

Self evaluation	Time=1	Time=2	Time=3
Mean value	3.83	2.73	2.53
Significant diff. from time=1	n/a	yes (p=.05)	yes (p=.01)
Significant diff. from time=2	yes (p=.05)	n/a	no

5. Discussion and conclusions

There were some problems in data gathering. A few of the pilot survey questionnaires had a missing response on an item. These were coded for computer processing as neutral. The questionnaires of one of the smaller test case were eliminated from the analysis because the responses were not credible. The questionnaires of some of the larger test class students were missing responses on some of the items.

After item analysis, we have produced a scale consisting of three sections. Each of those sections has excellent α-reliabilities indicating that the scale developed in this study can be useful for additional attitude measurement for inspections.

In the last use of our scale, we had hoped to see a continuous improvement of attitude toward inspection throughout the course. The significant change in the INTELL factor between the first and second administration of the scale and the lack of a significant change in the INTELL factor between the second and third administration of the scale, suggests that students developed their opinions on these practical aspects of inspections from the lecture and video. Practical experience may not have affected these opinions. Given that there is a significant improvement in positive attitude as measured by both the EMOT and INTELL factors toward code inspection from time 1 to time 3, we might be able to say that our students needed both the video and practical experience to see the maximum benefit in changed attitudes. Also, because there is a significant difference in EMOT only from time 1 to time 3 but not from time 1 to time 2, or from time 2 to time 3, it is possible that the students needed to practice inspection before they were able to support the code inspection process emotionally. The fact that our results suggest that our students improved their attitudes toward code inspection regarding their intellectual acceptance after viewing the video but not emotionally until after practicing code inspection, suggests that students should practice code inspection if we want to effectively affect their acceptance of code inspections.

It is possible that this scale and analysis technique can be used for the determination of the effect of education and training programs for other best practices. Of course the choice of items for the Likert section would need to be changed to reflect each different best practice.

Because we did not survey subjects who took this class without viewing the video and/or practicing inspections, we don't know if the change in attitudes toward a more positive position is due to the teaching methods that we used or to the passage of time until the end of the quarter. Or is it due to the survey process itself? It is possible that attitudes would change to reflect a more positive attitude about code inspection even without the use of the video or practice. These are additional questions that we plan to explore during future offerings of software engineering courses. We are in the process of surveying students in the current software engineering class using the scale with the changed Likert items.

Acknowledgements

Heather Bullock and Matthew Berent provided advice on the current state of attitude measurement in psychology. Heather Bullock, Julian Fernald, and Yanfen Chen gave advice on statistical analysis. Charlie McDowell and James Whitehead made their software classes available for testing. Numerous students helped in developing and in taking the survey questionnaires. Some of the Likert items are paraphrases of statements found on the web.

References

[1] A.F. Ackerman, L. Buchwald, and F. Lewski. Software Inspections: An Effective Verification Process. IEEE Software, 6(3):31-36, May 1989.

[2] D. Bailey. Attitude Measurement: Useful Software Engineering Tool? University of California, Santa Cruz Technical report, UCSC-CRL-02-23, May 2002.

[3] F. Brooks. The Mythical Man-Month: Essays on Software Engineering. Addison-Wesley, Reading, MA, 1975.

[4] L. Deimel. Scenes of Software Inspections Video Dramatizations for the Classroom. Software Engineering Institute, Carnegie Melon University, 1991.

[5] M. Fagan. Design and Code Inspections to Reduce Errors in Program Development. IBM Systems Journal, 35(3): 182-211, 1976.

[6] S. McConnell. Closing the Gap. IEEE Software, 19(1):3-5, Jan/Feb 2002.

[7] W. Mendenhall, T. Sincich. A Second Course in Statistics: Regression Analysis, 5th edition. Prentice Hall, Upper Saddle River, New Jersey, 1996.

[8] D. Mueller. Measuring Social Attitudes. Teachers College Press, Columbia University, New York, NY, 1986.

[9] S. Osgood and P. Tannenbaum. The measurement of Meaning. University of Illinois Press, Urbana, Illinois, 1957.

[10] E. Raymond. The Cathedral and the Bazaar: Musings on Linux and Open Source by an Accidental Revolutionary. O'Reilly, Sebastopol, CA, 1999 www.tuxedo.org/~esr/writings/cathedral-bazaar/cathedral-bazaar.

[11] S. Redwine and W. Riddle. Software Technology Maturation. Proceedings of the 8th International Conference on Software Engineering, 189-200, Aug 28-30, 1985, London, England.

[12] C. Seaman. Qualitative Methods in Empirical Studies of Software Engineering. IEEE Transactions on Software Engineering, 25(4):557-572, Jul/Aug 1999.

[13] L. Thurstone and E. Chave. The Measurement of Attitude. University of Chicago Press, Chicago, Illinois, 1929.

[14] G. Weinberg. The Psychology of Computer Programming. Van Nostrand Reinhold, New York, NY, 1971.

Assessing Attitude Towards, Knowledge of, and Ability to Apply, Software Development Process

David Klappholz, Lawrence Bernstein, Daniel Port
Stevens Institute of Technology, University of Hawaii
d.klappholz@ipostoffice.worldnet.att.net, lbernstein@ieee.org, dport@hawaii.edu

Abstract

Software development is one of the most economically critical engineering activities. It is unsettling, therefore, that regularly published analyses reveal that the percentage of projects that fail, by coming in far over budget or far past schedule, or by being cancelled with significant financial loss, is considerably greater in software development than in any other branch of engineering. The reason is that successful software development requires expertise in both State of the Art (software technology) and State of the Practice (software development process). It is widely recognized that failure to follow best practice, rather than technological incompetence, is the cause of most failures. It is critically important, therefore, that (i) computer science departments be able assess the quality of the software development process component of their curricula and that industry be able to assess the efficacy of SPI (Software Process Improvement) efforts.

While assessment instruments/tools exist for knowledge of software technology, none exist for attitude toward, knowledge of, or ability to use, software development process. We have developed instruments for measuring attitude and knowledge, and are working on an instrument to measure ability to use. The current version of ATSE, the instrument for measuring Attitude Toward Software Engineering, is the result of repeated administrations to both students and software development professionals, post-administration focus groups, rewrites, and statistical reliability analyses. In this paper we discuss the development of ATSE, results, both expected an unexpected, of recent administrations of ATSE to students and professionals, the various uses to which ATSE is currently being put and to which it could be put, and ATSE's continuing development and improvement.

1. Introduction

ATSE is a survey instrument for measuring Attitude Toward Software Engineering. ATSE can be used for assessing the outcome of an important aspect of the software development process component of an entire Computer Science degree program. It can also be used in assessing the outcome of a course in Software Engineering, or, as it is currently being used at Stevens Institute, to compare the relative efficacies of different methods of teaching Software Engineering. Finally, it can also be used for assessment of the effectiveness of SPI (Software Process Improvement) efforts in industry.

ATSE's development was begun in connection with work, by Bernstein and Klappholz, on NSF-funded development of novel techniques for overcoming aversion to software development process on the part of technology-oriented Computer Science students. An instrument was required to measure changes in aversion/attitude toward software development process, and ATSE is the result. Instruments for measuring knowledge / understanding of and ability to apply software development process are also being developed, but are not as far along as ATSE, and will not be discussed here.

ATSE is a multiple-choice instrument, with all questions having the same four possible responses: strongly agree, agree, disagree, and strongly disagree. Examples of ATSE questions are:

- Developers of custom software, that is software being developed for a specific customer, should be shielded from the customer by management

- It would be unreasonable for a software developer to be told that s/he must have other team members read his/her code

- When working on a team project, team members should start by coding their own modules and then figure out how to put the modules together

In Section 2 we discuss the way ATSE's development was begun and how it has been improved/refined over a period of close to two years. In Section 3 we discuss ATSE's current and projected uses. In Section 4 we discuss results of recent administrations of ATSE to both software development professionals and to Computer Science Students. Finally, in Section 5 we present our conclusions regarding ATSE, and our plans for further refining it through collaboration with academe and industry, and for making ATSE available for both academic and industrial use.

2. ATSE's Development and Content

In early 2000 authors Klappholz and Bernstein began a collaboration, at Stevens Institute of Technology, directed at improving the content of a required two-semester Senior Project/Software Engineering course in Stevens' Department of Computer Science. Bernstein, a former VP at AT&T, is a veteran of 35 years of managing software development projects, small, medium-sized, and large, commercial and military. Klappholz, having taught Computer Science theory and technology for 26 years, and having himself had a strong aversion to software process, was a recent convert to the importance and intellectual depth of the latter. Together they arrived at the conjecture that the best way to overcome aversion to software development process on the part of technology-oriented computer science students, especially in departments in which many faculty members are themselves cool to the importance of process, is to convince them that without proper appreciation of and attention to process they would fail, not in coursework, but in post-college software development projects in industry. The result was the "Live-Thru" method, currently funded by NSF, for introducing software process [1]-[2].

The need to measure the efficacy of the Live-Thru method led to the initiation of the development of ATSE. Consultation with Gerald Weinberg via e-mail [3] confirmed out impression that no such instrument existed, and promoted the development of ATSE to a first-class research project, for use in assessing the efficacy of Live-Thru's as well as for other uses, both academic and industrial. With CSAB now under ABET, and with ABET's increasing concern with outcomes assessment of degree programs, instruments like ATSE and the other assessment instruments under development by the authors gain in practical importance. Representatives of a number of companies have also inquired about the possibility of using ATSE in conjunction with SPI (Software Process Improvement) activities.

Klappholz and Bernstein began the construction of ATSE by listing various inappropriate, but fairly typical, attitudes held by both (some) Computer Science students and (some) professional software developers. After a very early version of ATSE had been developed, a number software professionals, both academic and industrial, including, notably, Port, contributed additional examples. Individual questions were written by various subsets of Bernstein, Klappholz, Port, and Catherine Kelley, a cognitive psychologist specializing in the use of technology in education. ATSE Version 0 was administered to computer science seniors at Stevens Institute in August 2001; its results were analyzed by Kelley and proved to be statistically unreliable. Post-mortem examinations of the initial questions suggested that a significant problem was that many questions were compound, and, therefore, subject to unintended interpretations. Additional questions, though simple rather than compound, were not worded carefully enough to avoid unintended interpretation.

In Section 2.1 we discuss ATSE Version 1, and in Section 2.2 its vetting for reliability relative to attitudes held by experience software process professionals, and its pruning, into ATSE Version 2, for statistical reliability.

2.1 ATSE's Content

As indicated above, ATSE's developers started by listing what they considered to be bad attitudes toward software development process that they had observed in Computer Science students and software development professionals. Throughout ATSE's development questions have tended to fall into the following hierarchy of topics, though some questions can, arguably, be categorized under more than one heading:

-Attitude Toward Technical/Quantitative Software Development Issues Other Than Writing Code.
-attitude toward technical/quantitative issues typically dealt with in Computer Science programs
-attitude toward technical/quantitative issues typically not dealt with in Computer Science programs; i.e., issues that typically go under the rubric of "software development process."
-attitude toward use of and utility of software metrics
-attitude toward use of and utility of software economics
-attitude toward confronting and dealing with risk:
-Attitude Toward Non-Technical/Non-Quantitative Issues
-attitude toward (inter-)personal issues
-attitude toward issues relating to personal space and introversion
-attitude toward teamwork
-attitude toward the responsibility of software developers with computer science backgrounds
-attitude toward discipline
-other

The forty-three questions constituting ATSE Version 1, categorized under the above headings, may be found in Appendix I.

2.2 ATSE's Vetting for Validity and Reliability

ATSE Version 1 was refined into ATSE Version 2 through the following activities:

-ATSE was administered to approximately 50 attendees at a North Jersey SPIN (Software Process Improvement Network) meeting on January 16, 2002. Immediately after the administration, we ran a focus group on the wording of the questions, possible misinterpretations, and issues concerning bad attitudes toward software development process. As a result, some questions were dropped, others were re-worded, and additional questions were added.

-ATSE was administered to seven members of Xerox Corporation's Software Process Improvement Group at a monthly phone conference on February 11, 2002. Another post-administration focus group was conducted, and ATSE was further refined.

-ATSE was administered to a number of attendees at a CSEE&T 2002 tutorial with a follow-on focus group and an additional iteration of refinement of questions.

-ATSE was administered to approximately fifty students finishing the second semester of Stevens Institute's Senior Project course on April 16, 2002, and the results were again used to refine ATSE.

-ATSE was administered to ninety-eight attendees of the DoD's Software Technology Conference on April 30, 2002. Results of administration of the forty-three questions which, at the time, constituted ATSE, were statistically analyzed and a subset of eighteen were found to constitute a psychologically significant factor with very high reliability.

Almost all STC respondents are software process professionals in the sense that they have had extensive experience as project managers, as process specialists, or as both. Not only do these ninety-eight respondents exhibit statistically reliable patterns of response to the eighteen questions constituting the current version of ATSE, but they also agree with one another to a very large measure on their answers to almost all questions (see Section 4 for more detail). We therefore consider the current version of ATSE to be not only reliable, but also validated in the sense of allowing us to infer "appropriate" or "accepted" or "correct" responses to the eighteen questions..

3. ATSE's Current and Projected Uses

As indicated in Section 1, ATSE's original purpose was to provide a means for determining the efficacy in changing/improving attitude toward software development process in senior computer science majors who had experienced the Live-Thru method of instruction. To determine efficacy of the method, we administer ATSE on entry to the Senior Project course, about six weeks later, shortly after students have undergone the Live-Thru experience, and at the end of the two-semester course.

ABET, which, through CSAC and CSAB, assesses/accredits bachelors' programs in computer science, has begun to focus attention on outcomes assessment rather than just on course content. The desired outcome of most undergraduate computer science programs is successful careers in software development for the majority of their graduates; positive attitude toward, knowledge of, and ability to apply software development process (best practice) are necessities for achieving the desired outcome. ATSE is the first instrument for measuring attitude toward software engineering, and is, as such, a candidate for use in the self-assessment, by computer science departments, of the outcome of the software development process aspects of their undergraduate programs. (We have developed an instrument for measuring knowledge of software development process and are working on one for measuring ability to apply process/best practice; these will be discussed in later papers.)

Through entry and exit administrations, ATSE can also be used for assessing the efficacy of individual courses in Software Engineering and, of course, in comparing different approaches to teaching software engineering. At Stevens Institute we are currently conducting a controlled experiment in which half of the approximately fifty students taking CS461-462, the required Senior Project course are being taught using the Live-Thru method and the other half are being taught using conventional methods. ATSE and our Software

Development Process Knowledge instrument, as well as a standard "teamwork" instrument were administered in August 2002 to all students entering the course. The first two will be re-administered in October 2002, after the end of the Live-Thru period, and again at the end of the academic year, in May 2003. The instrument, under development, for measuring ability to apply software engineering development process/best practice will be applied at appropriate points. Focus groups on all three instruments will be held in May 2003.

In August 2002 ATSE was administered to 124 graduate students in Dr. Barry Boehm's CS577a, Introduction to Software Engineering at the University of Southern California. Interesting results of that administration are reported in Section 4. ATSE is to be administered again at the end of the semester, in December 2002, and plans are currently being developed for performing in-depth interviews of individual students to discuss their interpretations of ATSE questions and their reasons for responding to specific questions the way they did.

We have also started to use ATSE as a means of evaluating the impact of individual, small-scale, educational activities on software engineering understanding and attitude. The pilot experiment involved a homework exercise based upon the man-month model in Fredrick Brooks' Mythical Man Month [4]. Several computer science students who had not yet taken a software engineering course were asked to take the ATSE, read the Brooks book, do the exercise, and, finally, review their answers to ATSE and update their answers. We analyzed changes in answers resulting from reading Mythical Man Month and doing the exercise. The ATSE survey was not discussed with the students until after they submitted their second set of answers. We were pleased to see the students change their attitudes in many of the areas covered by the Brooks material such as importance of software metrics, effort estimation, communications overhead, and responsibility to stakeholders.

4. Results of Recent Administrations

We have already discussed, in Section 2, the areas covered by ATSE. In the current section we discuss interesting patterns of responses to ATSE questions. We begin by discussing questions that the authors thought had clear-cut "correct" or "preferred" responses, but on which STC respondents did not agree with us. All conclusions are, of course, subject to acceptance of the relevant questions as clear and unambiguous, which the reader can judge for him/herself.

The most interesting observation, though it is more a confirmation of our suspicions than a novel revelation, is that the use of software development metrics and other quantitative approaches to software development are not as widely accepted as we would have hoped. This is evidenced by responses to the following questions:

-Programs are sufficiently different from one another that the number of lines of code that a software developer has produced in the past few months is not likely to be a useful predictor of the developer's productivity in the next few months to which only 51% of respondents either disagreed or disagreed strongly

-The number of lines of code a software development team has produced in the past few months is a useful predictor of the team's productivity in the next few months to which only 56% or respondents agreed or strongly agreed

-The removal of bugs from code is a sufficiently "unscientific" process that it's impossible to predict within a factor of two how long a typical software development team will take to get a program sufficiently debugged to release to customers to which only 65% of respondents disagreed or strongly disagreed

-It's unlikely that I'd keep a log/journal of the hours I work on software projects to which only 57% of respondents disagreed or strongly disagreed

Somewhat surprising is the fact that a number of questions, to which respondents strongly agreed with the authors on the appropriate response (either agree or strongly agree for some questions or disagree or strongly disagree for others) did not prove to belong to the statistically significant factor that characterizes questions that made it to ATSE Version 2. A complete list may be found in Appendix II. The following are a number of examples"

-When debugging a program, the first thing a software developer should do after determining the extent of the bug is to find out what is causing the program to perform incorrectly.

-If a team member is not doing his or her part of the work on a team project, it's best for me to ignore the problem and do the best I can on my part of the project.

-It's important for a software developer to be able to write English well.

The desired outcome for most students in most Bachelors and Masters programs in Computer Science is employment in the software development industry and success in that employment. It is, therefore, surprising that, while knowledge/understanding of theory and technology are routinely tested, using such instruments as the Graduate Record Examination subject area test, attitude toward, knowledge of, and ability to apply software engineering development process are not routinely when degree programs are assessed. That such assessment is needed is overwhelming agreed to by software development professionals. In fact, professionals who have participated with the authors in focus groups used to develop ATSE (see above) are appalled at the small role given to software development process in degree programs and to the fact that directors of such programs are unaware of their students' lack of preparation in the field.

As a case in point, Profs. Barry Boehm and Dan Port offer a two-semester graduate Introduction to Software Engineering, CS577a-b, at the University of Southern California. Most USC students pursuing the MS in Computer Science have undergraduate Computer Science degrees, and USC's entrance requirements are quite rigorous. Even among students who opt for CS577, an elective course, not a few enter the course harboring unexpectedly negative attitudes toward important aspects of software development process. ATSE Version 2 was administered to 124 CS577a students. The following are some of the surprising responses relative to responses favored by both the authors and STC respondents:

-Developers of custom software, that is software being developed for a specific customer, should be shielded from the customer by management: 44/124 students either agreed or agreed strongly

-It would be unreasonable for a software developer to be told that s/he must have other team members read his/her code: 25/124 students either agreed or agreed strongly

-If a customer fails to specify everything they need in software being developed for them, then it's the customer's problem if the finished software doesn't work right: 39/124 students agreed or agreed strongly

-Most of the problems given to professional software developers are very clearly defined: 21/124 students agreed or agreed strongly

-When working on a team project, team members should start by coding their own modules and then figure out how to put the modules together: 24 students agreed or agreed strongly

-I would probably get my code debugged and working faster if other people read the code and provided feedback on it: 22/124 students disagreed or disagreed strongly

-On a COTS-based software development project, that is, a project which will use Commercial Off The Shelf software components, it's best for the project manager to assume that each COTS product will perform as specified in its documentation: 43/124 students agreed or agreed strongly

- Software development is a sufficiently uncertain/unscientific activity that schedule overruns of less than 50% should be readily accepted by customers: 38/124 students agreed or agreed strongly

-In a software development project it's usually unproductive for the project/manager to consider problems that might conceivably arise before they actually do arise: 30/124 students agreed or agreed strongly

-In drawing up plans for a software development project, it's best for the project manager to develop schedules based on the assumption that every team member will deliver his/her work product (report, code, etc.) on time: 50/124 students agreed or agreed strongly

-It's most efficient for each member of a software development team to be allowed to write code according his/her own preferred coding style/standard: 32/124 students agreed or agreed strongly

5. Conclusions and further work

ATSE has proved to be of interest to both university faculty and professional software developers. In addition to ATSE's use at Stevens Institute and USC, colleagues at Rutgers University, Monmouth University, and New Jersey Institute of Technology have either used ATSE or agreed to use it in the near future. Software process professionals have asked about then possible use of ATSE in their organizations and we are discussing the possibility, with results going into an anonymous database. The most interesting use of ATSE is, of course, its administration at the beginning of a Software Engineering course or a Software Process Improvement effort, and its re-administration at the end.

The vetting process, for reliability and validity, which reduced the number of questions in ATSE, has left certain topic areas less well covered than we would like. In addition, there are likely to be topics that are relevant to ATSE's purposes but that we have missed entirely. We view ATSE as an evolving instrument. We plan to continue its development with input from and the help of academics and professionals. Administrations of and focus groups on ATSE are currently scheduled at meetings of the Southern California and North Jersey SPIN (Software Process Improvement Network) meetings. We are further proposing to administer ATSE at STC 2003 and to run workshops on ATSE, and on the more general topic of assessing attitude toward, knowledge of, and ability to apply software process at the 2003 meetings of CSEE&T, SIGCSE, and ICSE.

7. References

[1]   Bernstein, Lawrence, David Klappholz, and Catherine Kelley, Live-Thru Case Histories: Eliminating Aversion to Software Process Through Controlled Failure, CSEE&T 2002, Cincinnati, OH, February 2002

[2]   Bernstein, Lawrence, David Klappholz, and Catherine Kelley, Overcoming Aversion to Software Process Through Controlled Failure, DoD Software Technology Conference, Salt Lake City, April, 2002

[3]   Weinberg, Gerald, personal communication

[4]   Boehm, B., Egyed, A., Kwan, J., Port, D., Shah, A., and Madachy, R., "Using the WinWin Spiral Model: A Case Study," July 1999. (PDF)

[5]   Boehm, B., Abi-Antoun, M., Port, D., Kwan, J., and Lynch, A., "Requirements Engineering, Expectations Management, and The Two Cultures", Proceedings, International Conference on Requirements Engineering, June 1999. (PS, PDF)

[6]   Port, D., Boehm, B., "Introducing Risk Management Techniques Within Project Based Software Engineering Courses", Proceedings ICSE 2001

[7]   Majchrzak, A., Beath, C. "Beyond User Participation: A Process Model of Learning and Negotiation During Systems Development," MIS Quarterly. (invited after 2nd round competition to revise as part of a special issue on "New Theory in IS").

[8]   Port, D., Boehm, B., "Using A Model Framework In Developing and Delivering a Family of Software Engineering Project Courses", CSEE&T 2000

[9]   Boehm, B., Egyed, A., Kwan, J., Port, D., Shah, A., and Madachy, R., "Using the WinWin Spiral Model: A Case Study," July 1999.

[10]   B. Boehm, "An Experimental Project Course in Software Engineering," in A. Wasserman and P. Freeman [ed.], Software Engineering Education: Needs and Objectives, Springer Verlag, 1976, pp. 90-102.

[11]   M. Kaatipudi, K. Collier, J. Collofello, and S. Medeiros, "Software Engineering Course Projects: Failures and Recommendations," in C. Sledge (ed.), Software Engineering Education Proceedings 1992, Springer-Verlag, 1992, pp. 324-338.

[12]   B. Bruegge, "Teaching an Industry-Oriented Software Course," in C. Sledge (ed.), Software Engineering Education Proceedings 1992, Springer-Verlag, 1992, pp. 65-87.

[13]   R. Anderson, R. Corradi, J. Krogstie, G. Sindre, and A. Solvberg, "Project Courses at the NTH: 20 Years of Experience," in J. Diaz-Herrera (ed.), Software Engineering Education Proceedings 1994, Springer-Verlag, 1994, pp. 177-188.

[14]   P. Robillard, "Teaching Software Engineering through a Project-Oriented Course," in N. Mead (ed.), Software Engineering Education Proceedings 1996, Springer-Verlag, 1996, pp. 84-94.

Appendix I: ATSE Version 1 Questions Categorized

-Attitude Toward Technical/Quantitative Software Development Issues Other Than Writing Code
  -attitude toward technical/quantitative issues typically dealt with in computer science programs
    -Given the specifications of a program to write, a software developer should be able to figure out, or look up, an appropriate algorithm and an appropriate data structure(s) to use in writing the program.
    -There's no real need for a software developer to understand how sort and search routines work because they're always available as library routines.
    -It's not very useful for a software developer to spend time learning about how to evaluate an algorithm's time and space complexity because memory is cheap these days and chips are very fast.
    -I enjoy designing a program as much as I do coding it.

- It's more important for a software development team/department to know how to get code working right than to know how to get a design right.
- It is unreasonable for a software developer to be given an assignment without being told what data structures and algorithms to use.
- When debugging a program, the first thing a software developer should do after determining the extent of the bug is to find out what is causing the program to perform incorrectly.

-attitude toward technical/quantitative issues typically not dealt with in computer science programs; i.e., issues that typically go under the rubric of "software development process"

-attitude toward use of and utility of software metrics
- Programs are sufficiently different from one another that the number of lines of code that a software developer has produced in the past few months is not likely to be a useful predictor of the developer's productivity in the next few months.
- The number of lines of code a software development team has produced in the past few months is a useful predictor of the team's productivity in the next few months.
- The removal of bugs from code is a sufficiently "unscientific" process that it's impossible to predict within a factor of two how long a typical software development team will take to get a program sufficiently debugged to release to customers.
- When I am given a programming assignment, I rarely start by estimating how long the job will take in order to organize my time.

-attitude toward use of and utility of software economics
- If a 12-month software project falls seriously behind schedule at any time up to the end of the 9th month, it is usually possible to catch up by working nights and weekends.
- Budgets and schedules of software development projects already underway should always be negotiable.
- Software development is a sufficiently uncertain/unscientific activity that schedule overruns of less than about 50% should be readily accepted by customers
- It would be useful for a software developer to learn about Software Economics, that is, the economics of the software business.
- I wouldn't be interested in spending any time to learn about Software Economics.

-attitude toward confronting and dealing with risk:
- On a COTS-based software development project it's best for the project manager to assume that each COTS product will perform as specified in its documentation.
- In a software development project it's usually unproductive for the project/manager to consider problems that might conceivably arise before they actually do arise.
- In drawing up plans for a software development project, it's best for the project manager to develop schedules based on the assumption that every team member will deliver his/her work product (report, code, etc.) on time.
- After holding an initial planning meeting, it's not very useful for a software development team to meet except when a serious problem arises.

-Attitude Toward Non-Technical/Non-Quantitative Issues
-attitude toward (inter-)personal issues
-attitude toward issues relating to personal space and introversion
- It would be unreasonable for a software developer to be told that s/he must have other team members read his/her code. (could be introversion vs. extroversion)
- I'm uncomfortable having other people read my code.

-I would probably get my code debugged and working faster if other people read the code and provided feedback on it.

-I would learn a lot by reading code written by good programmers.

-I have no interest in spending time reading other people's code

-A member of a software development team should be allowed to decide for him/herself what data structures and algorithms to use in his/her code.

-attitude toward teamwork

-If another team member is not doing his or her part of the work on a team project, the best thing to do is to discretely report the other team member to the team leader.

-If a team member is not doing his or her part of the work on a team project, it's best for me to ignore the problem and do the best I can on my part of the project.

-A computer science student is better served, from a future employment point of view, by working on a large one-person software project than by working on a large team project.

-It's most efficient for each member of a software development team to be allowed to write code according his/her own preferred coding style/standard.

-If a team member is not doing his or her part of the work on a team project, it's best for me to ignore the problem and do the best I can on my part of the project.

-attitude toward the responsibility of software developers with computer science backgrounds

-Developers of custom software, that is software being developed for a specific customer, should be shielded from the customer by management.

-If a customer fails to specify everything they need in software being developed for them, then it's the customer's problem if the finished software doesn't work right.

-Most of the problems given to professional software developers are very clearly defined.

-It would be useful for a software developer to learn something about Group Dynamics, that is, the branch of psychology with deals with working in teams.

-I wouldn't be interested in spending any time to learn about Group Dynamics.

-It is unreasonable for a software developer not to be told exactly what the software s/he's being asked to write should do.

-When working on a team project, team members should start by coding their own modules and then figure out how to put the modules together.

-attitude toward discipline

-Most software developers have to at least comment their code for others to be able to debug or modify it effectively.

-Most software developers don't have to document their code at all to be able to debug or modify it themselves.

-I rarely if ever comment my code as much as I should

-If I kept a log/journal of the number of hours I work on my current software assignment(s), it could help me plan my time for future projects. (could also be attitude toward software metrics)

-It's unlikely that I'd keep a log/journal of the hours I work on software projects

-other

It's important for a software developer to be able to write English well.

Appendix II

-I enjoy designing a program as much as I do coding it.

-It's more important for a software development team/department to know how to get code working right than to know how to get a design right.

-*It would be useful for a software developer to learn about Software Economics, that is, the economics of the software business.*

-*I wouldn't be interested in spending any time to learn about Software Economics.*

-*It would be useful for a software developer to learn something about Group Dynamics, that is, the branch of psychology with deals with working in teams.*

-*I wouldn't be interested in spending any time to learn about Group Dynamics.*

-*When debugging a program, the first thing a software developer should do after determining the extent of the bug is to find out what is causing the program to perform incorrectly.*

-*If a team member is not doing his or her part of the work on a team project, it's best for me to ignore the problem and do the best I can on my part of the project.*

-*If a 12-month software project falls seriously behind schedule at any time up to the end of the 9th month, it is usually possible to catch up by working nights and weekends.*

-*It's not very useful for a software developer to spend time learning about how to evaluate an algorithm's time and space complexity because memory is cheap these days and chips are very fast.*

-*It's important for a software developer to be able to write English well.*

Introducing Testing Practices into *Objects and Design* Course

Ellen Francine Barbosa
José Carlos Maldonado
Instituto de Ciências Matemáticas e de Computação
Universidade de São Paulo
{francine, jcmaldon}@icmc.sc.usp.br

Richard LeBlanc
Mark Guzdial
College of Computing
Georgia Institute of Technology
{rich, guzdial}@cc.gatech.edu

Abstract

Though software testing courses are commonly taught as part of Software Engineering curricula, software testing is still a challenging issue in Software Engineering education. Students frequently see testing only as something that happens at the end of the development process. Two challenges can be recognized: "How to make the students recognize the relevance of the testing activity?" and "How to motivate the students on using testing ideas in their projects?". In an attempt to explore the impact of introducing testing practices throughout development, during the past Fall semester we modified the project requirements in a course on object-oriented analysis and design offered to the undergraduate students in Computer Science at Georgia Institute of Technology. Our idea was to require the students to start thinking about testing as early as possible, by including testing-related practices in all phases of the development process. This paper presents the details of the testing approach used in the course and discusses the results we obtained, in terms of the students' attitudes and learning.

Keywords: Software Testing Education, Equivalence Partitioning Testing Criterion, Functional Testing, Object-Oriented Development Process.

1: Introduction

Software testing is one of the most important activities to guarantee the quality and the reliability of the software under development [3, 4, 10, 12, 14]. Thus, the development of students' testing skills should play a fundamental role in meeting the increasing demand for qualified software engineering professionals. However, despite the efforts of the academy to motivate the students regarding its relevance, software testing is not a popular discipline and, in fact, many students seem to believe that testing is only something they have to do to show that their programming assignments work as required.

Traditionally, the testing has been taught according to the classical approach to software development, the waterfall model, where the phases for constructing the system are described in a linear way (from analysis and requirements gathering, to design, to coding, to testing, and to code release) and the tests just take place at the end of the process. Also, the more pragmatic issues of testing are often addressed only in advanced and specific courses on Software Engineering, for seniors or graduate students.

A different strategy for teaching software testing would be to introduce some testing practices as early as possible, during all the phases of the development process, based on a more practical perspective. Modern experience has already suggested that consideration of testing throughout the development phases provides a way to enhance a system's quality and to reduce development costs. The most prominent current example of this thinking is eXtreme Programming (XP) methodology [1] (http://www.xprogramming.com) – a relatively new development approach which proposes, among other core practices, to write tests even before writing code (*"test first, code later"*). Applying this idea in the educational setting can be seen as an interesting way to create new learning opportunities. Besides that, introducing ideas from modern methodologies (like XP) may serve to provide extra motivation to the students.

The work described in this paper was a first attempt at introducing some basic testing practices into an undergraduate course at Georgia Tech on object-oriented design – CS2340: *Objects and design*. The main topic of the course is an object-oriented development process in which students are required to practice the fundamentals of analysis, design and programming by means of a design project assignment, involving a real world situation. During the most recent offering of this course, students were required to incorporate some testing practices from the beginning until the end of their projects. The idea was to provide the students with a more pragmatic view of testing as well as to encourage them to think about testing earlier, during all phases of the development process.

The remainder of the paper is organized as follows. In Section 2, the main aspects of the CS2340 course are discussed. Section 3 describes some ideas to fit testing practices into the scope of the course. Section 4 evaluates the effects of our testing approach on the students' learning. Finally, in Section 5, our conclusions and further plans are presented.

2: CS2340: *Objects and design*

The main goal of the CS2340 course is to explore higher-level issues of analysis and design, with some emphasis on user interface development. It is a one semester course and is offered to the second-year undergraduate students on Computer Science, at Georgia Institute of Technology. Projects are team-oriented, involving the development of a small-to-medium sized object-oriented system, built upon a real world problem. The past Fall semester, for instance, the topic for the course was Genealogy Information (http://coweb.cc.gatech.edu/cs2340). The 160 students had to create a tool that collects genealogical information, notes inconsistencies and flaws in the database, provides some graphical representations, and supports a standard genealogical information format.

As pre-requisites, students taking the CS2340 course have already had:

- one semester on *Introduction to Computing*, focusing on the design, construction, and analysis of algorithms;
- one semester on *Object-Oriented Programming*, in Java; and
- one semester on *Languages and Translation* in C, using tools like LEX and YACC to explore the issues of language implementation, from models of the bare processor up through tokenizing and parsing.

Before or concurrently with the CS2340 classes, students are also required to take one semester *Software Practicum*, where the basics of Software Engineering, including a general view on software testing, are presented.

The design process taught in the CS2340 course encompasses the traditional phases of the object-oriented development, starting from analysis and leading through design and implementation. The process is not linear; students are expected to go back and forth between analysis and design, design and programming, and even analysis and programming phases.

In the analysis phase, students are required to elaborate scenarios and CRC (Class-Responsibility-Collaborator) cards [2]. From a development perspective, "playing" with CRC cards represents a useful way for early capturing the design decisions. They help to define the responsibilities for a given class as well as the interactions between the classes while performing several scenario tasks. Actually, they correspond to an informal approach to object-oriented modeling. From an educational perspective, CRC cards can be easily shared in groups, what is especially useful for the CS2340 team-projects. Besides that, since they are non-technical, there is no language or notation to be learned.

In the design phase, students have to develop UML class diagrams [5] for the system, defining the attributes and services of each class and formally identifying the connections between them. A detailed description of what each service is supposed to do is also required.

In the programming phase, students experience a variant of Smalltalk-80 – the Squeak language – in order to implement the system. In general terms, Squeak (http://www.squeak.org) [7, 11] is an open source and highly portable language, providing a rich multimedia support. By offering a good infrastructure for interesting and complex projects, Squeak is particularly appropriate for teaching Computer Science [8]. In the context of CS2340 classes, it was first used in 1998 and, since then, the experience has suggested that students can complete in a single semester more sophisticated and interesting projects in Squeak than in other languages, such as Java and C++ [8].

Regarding testing activity, despite its relevance in the development process, no systematic method to test the systems was adopted in the previous terms of the CS2340 course. Actually, the past Fall semester was the first time we explored testing practices into the scope of this class. Our testing approach and the results we obtained are described in the next sections.

As a final remark, it is important to notice that the CS2340 course has traditionally been served as a "laboratory" for applying and evaluating new approaches to teaching and learning in Computer Science. Two successful examples on that are the use of CoWeb [6] to promote joint learning; and the introduction of Squeak as a new way to teach user interface design and implementation. In this sense, our attempt to explore a different strategy for teaching software testing follows the established tradition of the course.

3: Testing approach for CS2340

In an attempt to fit testing practices into the scope of the CS2340 course, we chose to work with the Equivalence Partitioning criterion, built upon the functional testing idea. The purpose of functional testing is to find discrepancies between the actual behavior of the implemented system's functions and the desired behavior as described in the system's functional specification [13]. In this sense, there is a general agreement on Equivalence Partitioning as a key criterion for functional testing. Also, the "partitioning idea" can be easily understood even by students who have had little experience with testing. For these reasons, Equivalence Partitioning seemed to be a good starting point for use of testing in the course.

Basically, the criterion consists on dividing the space of possible program inputs into a finite set of partitions, and then selecting test cases from each equivalence class of the partition. An equivalence class defines a set of data values – valid and invalid ones – for which the program will perform the same computation. Every member of an equivalence class is said to be equivalent, with respect to some input condition, to every other member. Accordingly to Ostrand and Balcer [13], the idea behind each equivalence class is that all its elements are essentially the same for the purposes of testing. If the testing's main emphasis is to attempt to show the presence of errors, then the assumption is that any element of a class will expose the error as well as any other one. If the testing's main emphasis is to attempt to give confidence in the software correctness, then the assumption is that correct results for a single element in a class will provide confidence that all elements in the class would be processed correctly.

In the educational setting, the Equivalence Partitioning has generally been taught in terms of small programs, dealing with numerical input values. Using the criterion to test this kind of program is straightforward. However, when the input domain involves more complex types of elements, as in the case of genealogy information, its application may be not so clear. Next we present a small set of directions we established aimed at helping the CS2340 students to apply the Equivalence Partitioning in their projects. Notice we are not suggesting that these directions represent a new method of input space partitioning. Rather, we include them just to provide the details of our approach to guide the students throughout the "partitioning idea" application.

3.1: Directions for applying the equivalence partitioning criterion

Our directions are based on the main activities in the application of Equivalence Partitioning: (1) definition of input conditions; (2) identification of valid and invalid equivalence classes, and (3) definition of test cases to cover the equivalence classes.

Defining input conditions

The definition of input conditions takes place in the OOA phase, at the same time of the development of CRC cards. Based on the idea that input conditions are closely related to the input data provided by the user, we encourage the students to carefully analyze the set of responsibilities related to each CRC card, looking for "hints" on the possible input data items that each class may be handling. It is important to highlight that, although the CRC cards do not explicitly deal with the input data items, analyzing their responsibilities under a macroscopic perspective can provide some insight into that. Additionally, since each class can interact with others, the collaborators should also be investigated in order to find the right class where a specific input item is being treated.

After having identified the input data items, students are required to inspect them in terms of characteristics and interactions. In fact, each input item has specific characteristics related to it, which can directly affect the system's behavior. Furthermore, input items can interact with each other, also resulting on different values in the output domain. Ultimately, the set of characteristics and interactions related to all input data items can be seen as the input conditions for the system.

Our directions for defining input conditions are the following:

1. Analyze each CRC card, looking for "suggestions" on the input data items provided by the user.

    (a) Consider the responsibilities in a macroscopic way. Focus on *what* each class really has to do.

    (b) Analyze the responsibilities of the collaborators too.

    (c) Write down all the input data items related to a specific class.

2. Identify the main characteristics of each input data item.

3. Identify the interactions among the input data items. Think about how a specific input entry can be related to the other input data of the system. Focus on the system's operation (scenarios can help on this).

4. Write down the characteristics and interactions of all input data items related to all classes of the system. They will correspond to the input conditions for the program.

It is worth noting that while CRC cards are helpful to define input conditions, it is also the case that input conditions can be useful in checking the consistency of the CRC cards with respect to the responsibilities and interactions among classes they are covering.

Identifying equivalence classes

The equivalence classes are identified in the OOA phase, after students having defined the input conditions for the system. Actually, the valid and invalid equivalence classes are established by analyzing the input conditions, in terms of the correct and incorrect values needed to cover them. However, before analyzing each input condition separately, it is necessary to consider the entire set of input conditions defined. If two or more conditions are closely related to each other, it can make more sense to join them into a single condition. Conversely, if a condition is too broad, it can be necessary to refine it by creating two or more specific ones.

The directions for identifying equivalence classes are the following:

1. Analyze the set of input conditions for the system.

    (a) Look for related conditions. Try to join them.

    (b) Look for broad conditions. Try to refine them.

2. Analyze each input condition separately.

    (a) Think about the valid values to satisfy the input condition. They will correspond to the elements of a valid equivalence class.

    (b) Think about other possible values associated to the input condition, i.e., the invalid values. They will correspond to the elements of a invalid equivalence class.

3. Enumerate the equivalence classes, assigning a unique number to each class.

It is also important to highlight that the definition of input conditions/equivalence classes in the same context of CRC cards and scenarios, during the analysis phase, can provide to the students a better understanding of the requirements for the system they are developing.

Defining test cases for the equivalence classes

The definition of test cases to cover the equivalence classes requires a more detailed knowledge on the classes (and objects) in terms of structure, attributes, and services that need to be provided. For this reason, it makes sense to define the test cases at the same time as the development of UML class diagrams, in the OOD phase, when the students have to deal with more detailed issues of the design (such as instance variables and methods for the classes).

Still in the OOD phase, students have to elaborate a simple test plan providing information on the test suite they have developed. For instance, they should provide information on the purpose of the test case, the system's class it tests, the equivalence class it covers, the expected result for its execution as well as the obtained result (which should be filled in after the test case execution). Ultimately, test plans are useful mechanisms to the development of well-documented test suites, serving as a basis for the regression tests.

The directions for defining the test cases to cover the equivalence classes are the following:

1. Derive test cases associated with valid classes to cover all of them. A test case can cover a number of valid equivalence classes, as large a set as possible.
2. Derive test cases associated with invalid classes to cover all of them. A test case should be written for each invalid equivalence class.
3. Write a test plan providing information on the test cases.

Since the Equivalence Partitioning application takes place along all phases of the design process, any change in the scenarios, CRC cards or UML class diagrams requires the input conditions, equivalence classes and test cases be reanalyzed. Test plans should also be revisited in order to reflect the eventual changes.

Observe that at the end of the OOD phase a number of test cases have already been written, even before the students have started coding. Actually, the idea is to get the students involved with testing practices as early as possible in the development process. Writing test cases even before writing code forces developers to think about the functionality they are designing. They have to clearly state the context in which the functionality will run, the way it will interact, and the expected results. Although we are not applying the XP methodology, in some sense we are exposing the students to one of its core practices: *"test first, code later"*.

After defining the test cases, students have to execute them against the system under development. Squeak's environment allows to structure, describe the context of test cases and run them automatically by means of a unit testing framework – SUnit [1]. In general terms, S-Unit is a minimal but powerful framework that supports the creation and execution of test cases and test suites. S-Unit can also serve as a mechanism to motivate regression testing: students create a repository of test cases for their classes and, over time, this can yield a growing suite of regression tests that represents the expected functionality of the system at any given time [9].

As a final remark, although our approach focuses on the functional testing ideas, students have also been motivated to keep defining test cases while coding the system, based on its implementation details. However, no specific structural testing criteria have been adopted. This point should be investigated in the future offerings of the CS2340 course.

The testing approach discussed in this section was evaluated in terms of its effects on the students' learning. The results we obtained are analyzed next.

4: Evaluation

The effects of our approach on the students' learning were evaluated by means of a specific question on the final exam and, mainly, by applying a voluntary survey to the students after they had finished their projects (thus, just before the final exam).

The final exam question required the students to construct a test plan for a matching algorithm drawn from the genealogy domain they had worked with in their project. The results on this question were somewhat disappointing. Only about a quarter of the answers earned a score above the average for the whole exam. Most fell in a middle range about 10% below the overall exam average score. The answers indicated that most students had a reasonable idea about what they were supposed to be doing, but many didn't follow through on the details very well.

The survey was composed by four questions, covering the students' attitude toward: (1) the XP idea of starting testing early; (2) using testing criteria; and (3) writing test plans. 105 students answered the survey. On the survey question regarding to the XP testing ideas, we gave the students some statements related to *when* to start thinking about testing during the development process, asking them to choose all the options they agreed with. 12 students indicated that they prefer to deal with testing after coding the system; 53 agreed on applying testing practices through all the phases of the development process; 41 considered that starting thinking about testing in the analysis phase was helpful to better understand the system's functionality; and 23 felt it helpful to design a set of test cases at least before the implementation phase.

Clearly, the students had a positive attitude toward the idea of starting testing activities as early as possible, which suggests that further attempts should be made to integrate this approach into early courses as a way improve student attitudes toward testing and their ability to do it effectively.

On the question about testing criteria, we tried to explore their use related to some aspects of the development process: confidence about test cases; confidence about system's quality; motivation to think about errors; and reduction of the total development effort. Not applying any specific testing criterion was also considered. Again, students were required to select all options they were in agreement. 46 students answered that they would rather test the systems by their "own way", without using a specific testing criterion; 21 felt more confident about the test cases when working with some testing criterion; 36 felt more confident about the system's quality; 29 felt motivated to think about common errors that could be committed during the software development; and 10 agreed with the reduction on the total development effort by applying a testing criterion.

Refining our analysis, we observed that from the 46 students who had a negative attitude toward testing criteria, 35 were strictly "against" the idea of working with them, while 11 students agreed they could be useful in some sense, mainly in terms of thinking about common errors. Actually, from the total of 105 students, 70 agreed on the relevance of applying testing criteria for some aspect of the development process.

In terms of test plans, two questions were applied. In the first question, the students were asked to rate their opinion of having to do a test plan, using a scale from 1 to 5 (1 means "a completely worthless idea" and 5 means "a really valuable part of the development process"). In the second, we provided them with some statements on *how* in the development process the test plans could be valuable; and for *which kind* of systems the test plans would be more useful. They were asked to mark all of the statements with which they agreed. For 62 students, having to elaborate a test plan was a completely worthless or a worthless idea; 31 students presented a neutral position; and only 12 students considered test plans as a valuable or really valuable idea.

Interestingly, from the 62 students who had a negative attitude toward test plans, 40 of them had also a negative attitude toward testing criteria. Our hypothesis is that the negative results about test plans can be related to the application of the Equivalence Partitioning criterion, which is not so suitable for testing systems whose input values are not numerical. This suggests the need to improve our directions for applying the criterion.

It was also notable that 54 students, especially those who had negative (37) and neutral (15) attitudes, agreed with the usefulness of elaborating test plans when developing complex systems. In fact, another reason for the "high rejection" of creating test plans can be related to the kind of system (small-to-medium size) the students had to develop in the CS2340 projects.

Finally, 13 students agreed that test plans could be valuable as a way to keep track of test cases, and 16 pointed out that they could be valuable if changes in the system were required. Maybe, had the students had to work in a project where more changes in the system were required, we had obtained different results. Besides that, we noticed that some of these students were the same who had a negative attitude toward test plans. This suggests that although this specific group of students had been "against" the test plans idea, they were able to recognize its usefulness for some aspects of the development process.

5: Conclusion and further work

In this paper we discussed some ideas regarding the introduction of testing practices in a course on object-oriented analysis and design, required for undergraduate students in Computer Science at Georgia Institute of Technology.

A key point of our work was to encourage the students to use testing practices as early as possible, through all the phases of the development process. In some sense, our approach focused on the idea of a "test-driven development", which is one of the main practices of the XP methodology.

The students' attitudes toward the testing approach were evaluated mainly by means of a survey. In general, although the students have shown a negative attitude on using the Equivalence Partitioning and on having to elaborate test plans, they clearly approved the idea of starting testing early. From this results, we are motivated to continue investigating the approach in future offerings of the course. Especially, we intend to introduce S-Unit early in the development process, as well as to explore the use of other testing criteria in order to produce more significant results.

Acknowledgments

This research has been supported by grants from FAPESP, CNPq and CAPES (Brazilian funding agencies), and from the National Science Foundation (NSF) and the Mellon Foundation.

References

[1] K. Beck. *Extreme Programming Explained: Embrace Change*. Addison Wesley, 1999.

[2] K. Beck and W. Cunningham. A laboratory for teaching object-oriented thinking. In *OOPSLA'89*, New Orleans, Louisiana, October 1989. (Special issue of SIGPLAN Notices, 24(10), October 1989).

[3] B. Beizer. *Software Testing Techniques*. Van Nostrand Reinhold Company, New York, 2nd edition, 1990.

[4] E. Dustin, J. Rashka, and J. Paul. *Automated Software Testing: Introduction, Management, and Performance*. Addison Wesley Longman, 1999.

[5] M. Fowler and K. Scott. *UML Distilled: Applying the Standard Object Modeling Language*. Addison Wesley, 2nd edition, 2000.

[6] M. Guzdial. Teacher and student authoring on the web for shifting agency. In *AERA 99 Session: How can CSCL (Computer Supported Collaborative Learning) change classroom culture and patterns of interaction among participants?*, 1999.

[7] M. Guzdial. *Squeak – Object-Oriented Design with Multimedia Applications*. Prentice Hall, 2001.

[8] M. Guzdial. Using squeak for teaching user interface software. *ACM SIGCSE 2001*, 33(1):219–223, February 2001.

[9] M. Guzdial and K. Rose. *Squeak – Open Personal Computing and Multimedia*. Prentice Hall, 2002.

[10] M. J. Harrold. Testing: A roadmap. In *22th International Conference on Software Engineering*, June 2000.

[11] D. Ingalls, T. Kaehler, J. Maloney, S. Wallace, and A. Kay. Back to the future: The story of squeak, a practical smalltalk written in itself. In *OOPSLA'97*, pages 318–326, Atlanta, GA, 1997.

[12] G. J. Myers. *The Art of Software Testing*. Wiley, New York, 1979.

[13] T. J. Ostrand and M. J. Balcer. The category-partition method for specifying and generating functional tests. *Communications of the ACM*, 31(6):676–686, June 1988.

[14] H. Zhu, P. Hall, and J. May. Software unit test coverage and adequacy. *ACM Computing Surveys*, 29(4):366–427, December 1997.

Software Engineering –
Other Topics
(Paper Session J)

Inspections and Historical Data in Teaching Software Engineering Project Course

Tero Ahtee
Tampere University of Technology
Institute of Software Systems
P.O. Box 553, FIN-33101 Tampere, Finland
tel. +358 3 31153830, fax. +358 3 31152913
tensu@cs.tut.fi

Abstract

At Software Engineering Project Course document inspection data have been collected from meeting minutes. The derived statistics are used in inspections, in project management lectures, and also in software engineering training outside university. The use of historical project data, such as statistics on working hours, and comments from participants in previous courses, have been considered very valuable in teaching; by both the students and course personnel. These are the two specialities that have been used for five years at Institute of Software Systems. This paper gives some hints to project course personnel, for what kind of useful data could be collected easily.

1. Introduction

At almost every university, in information technology or related departments, there are project course(s) whose main goal is teach students the difficulties of software projects. Usually the course personnel changes often, and a longer career by the same course is a rarity. Statistics are not automatically collected, and final reports are not always written. However, in many cases the student groups are really working hard towards a good software product, and their experiences are worth writing down. Such collecting and use of previous projects' data would help future project groups a lot, and naturally guide also the new course personnel.

From inspections only four numbers need to be collected: individual preparation times, inspection time, size of inspection target (document pages or lines of code), and errors found. Historical data collected from finished projects should include encountered risks and problems, comments about methods and tools, statistics about the division of work hours, project management hints and tricks, and discussion about the project. A desirable part in groups' comments would be commentary about the project course itself; pros and cons.

2. General information about project course

At Tampere University of Technology (TUT), Institute of Software Systems, software engineering project matters have been teached over ten years. The writer have been fortunate to be able to concentrate to this project course from 1997. Detailed course statistics have been collected from year 1997.

Students on the *Software Engineering Project Course* [1] are 3rd year students and above; average graduation to MSc takes six years in Finland. Of the students, about two thirds are working either full- or part-time in information technology companies. Attendees have typically studied more than 100 credit units, out of 180 required. Students receive 3-5 credits depending on the project size, equivalent to 4,5-7,5 European credit units. Assigned grades are 0 (fail), 1 to 5 (pass).

The project course at TUT consists of about 20-25 groups of 5-7 students each, they work six months, from September to March, to build a working system from scratch, totalling above 200 work hours per one student. The total project size is usually more than 1000 hours; see Table 1. This course is considered "not the most difficult, but perhaps the most laborious course" at our Institute. This is a hands-on working course, with weekly lectures, but without an examination.

Client may be some individual or organization, or from industry, all of which enhances motivation; most of the course projects are done for some company. The project work may also be a part of a larger project at some company. The projects become real-word assignments with real clients and end-users; end-products are really needed by someone. Some groups may receive a nominal payment from the client at the end of a well-done project. Some students or even a whole group may do their project at work for their employer, this is connecting studies to real-world work. All the projects have succeeded, i.e. completed their work with satisfactory results. This may be partly because of the intensive or rigorous supervision we have set in this course.

Prerequisites are **Software engineering basic course** (requirements document as assignment), **Software engineering methods course** (requirements, and design documents, and a short project plan as assignments) and **Data structures**. Recommended courses are **Testing**, and **Usability**.

The purposes of the course are 1) students make a large whole project themselves; larger than at any other course, 2) to teach documentation and different documents, 3) to teach communication and working in large groups, and 4) to teach good inspection habits and the use of historical project data. It is important that students have already written a requirements specification document twice at prerequisite software engineering courses. Without such a familiarity with the important foundation of the base document the project course may be too difficult.

Table 1: Project size in total working hours (average).

year	project size (average)	course size
1997-98	937 hours	30 groups
1998-99	1248 hours	17 groups
1999-2000	1073 hours	27 groups
2000-01	1054 hours	26 groups
2001-02	1152 hours	25 groups

Groups form up voluntarily; students may find old friends to their project group, or they can look for experts of different skills among other students. Every year a few of attending students are from departments other than information technology.

Participating students have usually not seen a whole project from start to deployment, even if they have worked for several years outside university. They have typically been working just on one life-cycle phase. Also, they have not usually seen project plan, nor have they participated in inspections or reviews. On average, only about one to two persons in a student group have experience on those.

The characteristic requirements of the project course are; one starting meeting, and one final meeting with course personnel, weekly reports are submitted via e-mail, five document inspections with course personnel are kept, two public short presentations are in October and January, and a final presentation (30 min) in March. In addition there are three to four guest lectures, some kind of version control is used both for code and documents, working hours are reported via a fixed-shape working-hour-matrix (see Table 2), and groups make a WWW page about the project and themselves. Slipping from course schedule means naturally a lower grade to students.

The information collected on Table 2 consists of project life-cycle phases and work types. Colums describe the phases; preliminary study and analysis, requirements specification, design, implementation and module testing, integration and system testing, installlation/deployment/maintenance, and other. Rows contain data about different work types; planning, meetings, inspections and reviews, studying and learning, documenting, prototypes and demos, project management, and work.

Table 2: Working hours reporting matrix at project course.

	PREL. ANAL.	REQU- IREM.	DESI- GN	IMPLE- MENT- ATION	TEST.	INST./ DEPL./ MAINT.	OTHER	TOTAL	%
PLAN- NING									
MEET- INGS									
INSP- ECT.									
STUDY									
DOCU- MENT.									
PROT./ DEMO									
PROJ. MAN.									
WORK									
TOTAL									
%									

Document templates are provided by the course personnel. If the client company insists, groups may use the client's document templates, as long as they give the same information as the course templates.

During the course, eleven documents are written by each group;
- feasibility study (preliminary analysis) *1*
- project plan
- requirements specification (functional specification)
- offer *1*
- design document (technical specification)
- (integration or) system test plan
- user manual
- maintenance guide
- test report
- final report *1*
- summary of final report; handouts for final presentation *1*.

(*1* = only one version, not to be updated during project.)

Final presentations are hold on a Friday in March, which is a great "gala day and night" from 08 a.m. to 22 p.m., and a sponsored sauna party after that - sometimes until sunrise. This gives a suitable special and remarkable end to a special course. The best final presentation is voted by the students. The local Information Processing Association *PITKY* can give a scholarship (prize) to a distinguished project group.

During the years many interesting, and also useful, applications has come to daylight; e.g., embedded video graphics card software, a single-user PC application for calculating statistics from stock exchange values, and some multi-user distributed games on the internet. At the 2001-02 course one project group made a configurable web-newsletter for small organizations. They found the product a promising one, so they established a company around the project group. Their company was then accepted to a pre-incubatory programme *Yritystallit*, an IT development group close to the University.

Student feedback is gathered orally during the course at inspections, at the end of the course in a written final report, and orally again at the final meeting after the course in late March. Also, a general feedback and comment WWW-page is open during and after the course, which every student can use once (controlled via student number). At the MSc graduation, the graduates are questioned about useful and difficult courses at our university, and also several other questions by TUT teaching quality assurance group. In the answers, the project course is considered a hard course, but it is also considered the most useful one at our Institute [2]. The main reason for this is that during the course students get a full view of one whole software project, though a small one. They can put into use all they have learnt about software engineering before, at other courses or at work. This project they can use later at their work as a yardstick, a measure of performance.

3. Two specialities at project course

This section explains two specialities used at the project course. First, document inspections, and second, use of historical project data. These two are characteristics that are not found from related course stories [3, 4, 5, 6, 7, 8].

Many companies lack the "good inspections/reviews habit" from their software engineering process even if products have been considered high-quality. It is important to teach inspections well, and familiarize students to the proper use of inspections as a quality assurance aid.

Inspection means formal meeting where errors are detected and diary (minutes) is kept by the secretary, on the course usually the author. All errors found are written to the diary. Review means the less formal session where diary is not necessarily kept, and the whole material is not necessarily discussed through. [9]

The lack on use of history data in companies is evident. Final reports or legacy reports are seldom done after a project, nor special discussions to project plans: what did we learn, what could have been done better and why, and comments about used tools and methods. Such company-specific historical data from previous projects would be a great training aid (and basis) inside company to new project managers, and also software engineers. The use of historical project course data has helped new groups to foresee possible difficulties, and given hints to, e.g., tool selection, application-specific advice, and project management tricks.

3.1 Inspections at project course

Inspections follow the formal method; diary (minutes) is kept during the inspection meeting. Two kinds of forms are used; the *findings log* is filled during inspection, and a *summary* is filled partly before, and partly after the inspection.

The author of the document acts as a secretary; the diary is kept visible to all attendees via overhead projector or data projector. One groupmember acts as a chairman (moderator), all other members are inspectors. The course personnel is an inspector among others. Everybody reads the inspected material beforehand and make comments and remarks to it. At the beginning of the meeting everybody is asked about the number of findings, but that is not marked in log so that nobody considers it as personal evaluation. The inspection is limited to two hours by a downwards-calculating timer used by the moderator. The introduction of this timer has indeed put more power to the inspections.

At the beginning, everybody's preparation (reading) time is asked to the summary sheet. Before start, everybody is asked a positive comment; to mention one good point or technical detail in the document. This is to make everybody say something at the beginning, and break the ice. According to my experience, everybody like the inspections and consider them useful; although the group have all read the document themselves, some new errors always pop up in inspections, that nobody has found him/herself.

Findings (errors) are written to the diary, but not discussed further; the course personnel ensures this. At the end of the meeting, a summary of the findings and the time used are written to the diary. The final task of the chairman is to evaluate the inspection and decide the result of the inspection: is the document accepted, does it need corrections, or is another inspection needed if there have been many severe errors.

As every project group has five inspections, the task of a chairman is circulated among students as much as possible. Every student can see the difference between a difficult document, and an easy one. Also personal differences between chairmen become visible, e.g., if the chairman is slow, all the two-hour inspection time may be needed for even a relatively short document.

Inspections are by far not considered frightening, instead of that students see the meetings as quality assurance events and valuable experiences, although inspections mean some additional work for project groups.

After and during the course, many students have told that they do have inspections or reviews at work, but these are not very useful, mostly because of the lack of time to read the material, and the lack of order and discipline during the discussions, e.g., people may easily slip into coffee-table discussions.

The basic data from the inspections of 1997-2002 include inspection (at most 120 min) and personal preparation times, plus counts of errors found and pages inspected.

The documents inspected at Project course are [Table 3]:
SRS = software requirements specification (functional specification),
PROJECT PLAN = project plan,
DESIGN DOCUM. = design document (technical specification),
TEST PLAN = (integration or) system test plan,
USER MANUAL = user manual/user guide.

Table 3: Size of document (number of pages, average).

	SRS	PROJECT PLAN	DESIGN DOCUM.	TEST PLAN	USER MANUAL
1997-98	32	17	45	26	31
1998-99	39	22	63	39	42
1999-2000	45	25	54	41	35
2000-01	38	26	47	34	29
2001-02	51	30	75	51	55

From the annual inspections data, the following statistics are derived:
- errors (findings) per page [Table 4],
- minutes (inspection time) spent to find one error [Table 5],
- pages scanned through per one hour,
- errors found per one hour [Table 6], and
- time (inspection time) spent per one page.

Table 4: Errors found per document page (average).

	SRS	PROJECT PLAN	DESIGN DOCUM.	TEST PLAN	USER MANUAL
1997-98	1.05	1.21	0.57	1.23	0.93
1998-99	1.07	1.32	0.52	0.87	0.66
1999-2000	0.94	1.17	0.63	0.77	0.97
2000-01	0.95	1.03	0.71	0.67	0.87
2001-02	0.98	1.00	0.52	0.75	0.88

Table 5: Minutes (inspection time) spent to find one error (average).

	SRS	PROJECT PLAN	DESIGN DOCUM.	TEST PLAN	USER MANUAL
1997-98	4.21	4.70	7.41	4.58	4.06
1998-99	3.42	3.71	4.03	3.45	3.96
1999-2000	4.12	4.32	3.78	4.47	3.06
2000-01	3.80	3.72	4.11	4.08	4.64
2001-02	2.95	3.44	3.74	3.70	2.96

Table 6: Errors found per one hour (average).

	SRS	PROJECT PLAN	DESIGN DOCUM.	TEST PLAN	USER MANUAL
1997-98	18	14	14	16	17
1998-99	20	17	17	19	19
1999-2000	17	16	17	15	21
2000-01	18	18	17	17	15
2001-02	23	19	19	18	24

According to student's feedback, inspections help the working groups also in many other ways than just enhancing documents' quality. Inspections bring the group around the same table: everybody is present, also mentally. Understanding of project's subject and technical details deepens, also possibly wrong notions and assumptions are found, and everybody must really read the document before the inspection. Groups also get wished-for feedback from course personnel, and miscellaneous project matters can be asked from course personnel after the inspection.

There is also a guided short discussion after each inspection; how students honestly feel themselves about their document, what were the strengths and weaknesses of the phase product, and how to improve it. This is also to teach students critical thinking.

3.2 Use of historical data at project course

An old saw has that "people learn from their own, smart people from other's mistakes".

The use of historical data from previous projects has helped groups to foresee possible difficulties, and have given practical hints to project management. This data is published on course's additional material WWW page.

The logged matters from final reports are: encountered risks and problems, project management issues, methods and tools, and work statistics; such as lines of code, number of classes, productivity, error correction time. Also comments about the project are collected;

what went well, what did not, and other matters worth mentioning, e.g., humorous incidents during the project. Encountered risks and problems are the most remarkable ones, either predicted or not, which the group did run into during the project. The risks are discussed; their early warning symptoms, means how to avoid them, and cure if the risks became a problem to the project. Project management issues contain different comments about good (or not satisfactory) project management practises during project, e.g., good procedures of keeping weekly meetings, squeezing requirements out of the lazy or busy client, or suitable forms of calendar planning. Groups can give recommendations (or warnings) about methods and tools they have used in their project. Such recommendations can be of great value and good help for the next courses. Work statistics include code size (e.g. LOC or number of classes), productivity (code per hour, documentation per hour), error correction time (percentage and hours of development and total project time). Groups may also write down general comments about the project; what went well, what did not go so well i.e. could have been done better, what procedures to change for next project, and others. The last paragraph in the legacy comments is miscellaneous other matters worth mentioning. Such ones may be great inventions, or even funny incidents during the dark and long winter nights in the project. Typical difficulties inside an inexperienced project group are: estimation of work amount, communication between project members, selection of suitable tools, and risks and handling them. These matters can be helped by searching through the comments from old project courses. The comments are available at WWW pages linked from course's main page. Group's names as well as student's names have been removed from the comments. The only disadvantage is that it takes a lot of time from course personnel to collect the selected comments from groups' reports.

This kind of information available at WWW doesn't harm anyone, and it can't be used to copy a project, because project work subjects are different every year. As all groups use similar-shape working hour table (see Table 2), comparisons can be made easily. However, groups are not evaluated or compared to each other according by working hours. Groups can, if they are interested, compare the percentage of used time in a specific life-cycle phase or work types, e.g., percentage of total project time used in testing, or inspection meetings.

4. Future enhancements

Code inspections. Code inspections have been thought, but not yet implemented; they are not easy to arrange. First, is the code C++ or Java or XML text or some SymbianOS code? Second, the timing of the inspections comparing to course schedule and project work's progress and the target of the code inspection should be chosen very carefully; which modules or part of code. Third, part of the projects are classified as confidential, so involving other students to inspections would be difficult. I have kept code inspections once in past years, but that wasn't very successful mostly because of the second reason.

Individual group schedules. Individual group schedules have not been allowed yet. Nowadays every group have similar deadlines, which makes it easier to course staff to keep track on groups. Naturally, groups can have a faster schedule than the course has, though only four projects have been completed before course deadlines during previous five years. Every now and then individual schedules pop up onto discussion, but course personnel would run into great difficulties while trying to follow each group's different timetable. Some kind of more flexible schedules would be worth considering.

Transferring supervisory work to students. One possibility to reduce the workload of the course personnel, be to transfer some tasks to the student groups themselves. Groups could keep inspections against each other, or at least give some comments about documents. Project groups could be system testers for another groups. I once tried volunteer cross-testing between groups, but it didn't work that time. Once again, confidential projects could deny a wider use of this kind of system.

Collecting more data from projects. It would be interesting to calculate more data from projects, and do research of those, e.g., are there any similarities in the working time, like percentage distribution among tasks of the total hours, between groups.

More emphasis to the use of historical data. It would be a great challenge to introduce such teaching methods and aids, that students takes the advice from previous projects without making themselves similar errors. Also, a proper classification of the collected data would be needed, in order to keep the information easily usable.

More training to project managers. Currently only one student on each group acts as the project manager, so (s)he gets a good view to management issues. It would be very useful to establish a follow-up course considering only the management issues of software projects, to enable more students learn and experience the manager's role. For example students could act as supervisors to project course groups.

Longer multi-term project course. For many years I have been considering of a longer course project, which could last two years or four terms. In such a way the important maintenance phase would be added, about which there is very little teaching in universities, though at TUT we have one course.

Integration to other courses. In the past few years our Institute has put more emphasis on teaching usability issues, and there is currently one collaborative course *Usability in software projects*. More emphasis could be put to integrate this course more closely to project course. Also, more collaboration to current *Testing* course would be interesting and useful to establish. Some other courses' exercise work could include parts of project course's work.

Integration of the client to the course. The client could be integrated more closely to the project work and it's administration, e.g. having evaluation meetings between course personnel and client. Naturally client should have only a consultative role to course credits.

5. Conclusion

This paper explained two specialities used at the project course in 1997-2002 at TUT: document inspections, and use of historical project data. Document inspections data contains four simple but useful variables: individual preparation times, inspection time, size of inspection target, and errors found. Collected historical data from previous projects help both students and course personnel in their tasks; what to avoid, what should be preferred.

Students are encouraged to give reusable comments and ideas from their projects to the final report and at the final presentation. The use of legacy project data is a valuable source of data from the projects made to clients outside university. Data collected from previous courses' projects is available to students at course WWW page, and the results are used in teaching of new groups. Not to collect data from the course as this would be a great waste of opportunity.

The main reason why this course has been considered so useful and valuable at TUT is the amount of work the Institute of Software Systems has allowed me to place in. Teaching this course have been sometimes a hard work beyond weekly working hours, but also very rewarding.

However, there is still a lot of work to do with classification and fine-tuning the collected data, in order to gain more from the huge amounts of work which students put on project course every year.

Acknowledgements

I like to thank professors Ilkka Haikala and Mikko Tiusanen for their help in fine-tuning this article. I also appreciate all the comments from my colleagues at course 8109101. I wish good future projects to all the project course students who have provided the basic data from their projects over all these years.

References

[1] 8102500 Software Engineering Project Course, www.cs.tut.fi/kurssit/8102500/, 11/2002. (In Finnish)
[2] Eila Pajarre: Tutkinnon sisältö, rakenne ja läpäistävyys. 2001, TTKK. 31 p. (In Finnish; Feedback about teaching and courses at TUT, as questioned from graduated masters by the TUT quality group)
[3] Ray Dawson and Ron Newsham: Introducing software engineers to the real world, IEEE Software November/ December 1997, pp. 37-43.
[4] Ray Dawson: Twenty dirty tricks to train software engineers, ICSE 2000, pp. 209-218.
[5] Anke Drappa and Jochen Leduwig: Simulation in software engineering training, ICSE 2000, pp. 199-208.
[6] FASE newsletters (Forum for Advancing Software engineering Education), volume 11 number 06, June 15 2001. www.cs.ttu.edu/fase/
[7] Matthias Gehrke et al.: Reporting about industrial strength software engineering courses for undergraduates, ICSE2002, pp. 395-405.
[8] Bertrand Meyer: Software engineering in the academy, in IEEE Computer May 2001, pp. 28-35.
[9] IEEE Standard Glossary of Software Engineering Terminology (610.12-1990).

A Study Program for Professional Software Engineering

Erika Horn
Institute for Informatics
University of Potsdam
PO Box 90 03 27
14482 Potsdam
ehorn@soft.cs.uni-potsdam.de

Mario Kupries
Department of Mathematical Sciences
University of Alaska – Fairbanks
PO Box 756660
Fairbanks AK 99775-6660
ffmk@uaf.edu

Abstract

A study program for Professional Software Engineering will be introduced, which outlines a philosophy oriented towards software technical requirements in industry and market needs. Important aspects of graduates' profiles will be considered and evaluated concerning their engineering substantiation. According to existing deficits and to software technical demands, a special study program will be specified and explained in detail. To offer high flexibility, lectures of the educational program will be assigned to study complexes. To satisfy the market needs, software and hardware system labs will be proposed and described. The study complexes and labs will be merged into an integrated Professional Software Engineering study program based on international standards. To train M.Sw.E. students, a specialization according to roles, aspects and classes of software products will be recommended.

1. Motivation

A central problem of today's economical development and competitiveness in industry, society and science is the mastering of the complexity of large, software-intensive systems and of the processes of their development and application. The complexity of theses systems is defined by the huge amount and heterogeneity of interacting hardware and software components as well as by the multitude of relations between them, the embedding into technical and organizational environments and the interfaces to humans. The mastering of large software-intensive systems requires a hierarchical, systematic thinking and acting. The success of products and services as well as of enterprises and organizations is increasingly determined by the availability of such adequate software products. Thus, the need of highly qualified specialists being capable to master complex, software-intensive systems as well as to participate in the development and application of software systems adopting different roles throughout the entire process, is the reason for the international movement of establishing the engineering discipline Software Engineering emanciated from Computer Science. Software Engineering becomes a separated engineering discipline focusing on the analysis, construction, test, application, maintenance, evaluation, etc. of software products. Focusing on software products, the following characteristics have to be addressed:

- determination and specification of requirements of large, complex products
- high amount and complexity of software components
- development by division of labor
- undergoing a structured process applying team-based development
- re-use and prefabrication of components and systems
- development, delivery and application units
- embedding and integration into a technical and organizational environment

The orientation towards a product character also includes costs, quality, logistics, security, software management, anthropology, product marketing, etc.

The orientation towards a product character is common for all engineering disciplines and is determining the subjects of teaching as well as of teaching methods This document outlines an educational concept, which addresses product orientation, market needs, rapid technology changes as well as social skills compiled into a Professional Software Engineering study program.

2. Introduction

A study program philosophy for Professional Software Engineers will be outlined oriented towards current deficits and software technical requirements in industry, and considering important aspects of the occupation of future software engineers. In the educational concept the view is taken that the fundamentals of the analysis, modeling, realization and adaptation of software systems are based on the existence of models, technical descriptions and means of expressions. The development of software systems is considered as an overall engineering, model-based process oriented on organizational facts and market needs. Thus by developing software systems a product character is being obtained which has to be reflected in teaching subjects, study programs, technology and knowledge transfer. Since software products cover numerous facets and aspects of complex systems, the training of professional software engineers has to cover overall construction methodologies. To satisfy market needs, professional subjects, software and hardware system labs are defined and described. The concept merges study complexes and labs into an integrated Professional Software Engineering study program based on international standards.

3. Software Engineering as a Professional Engineering Discipline

As an interdisciplinary work and research field Professional Software Engineering (PSE) requires extensive knowledge of various disciplines such as formal semantics, logics, security, software architecture, computer hardware, distributed programming, middleware technology, coordination and planning, decision theory and business organization. In addition to its interdisciplinary character and knowledge from various disciplines, the development of complex modern application systems makes great software technical demands on mobility, adaptability, complex and interoperable interactions, open and human-centered systems. Here it becomes obvious that the practical application of modern technologies is ahead of its engineering substantiation. Examples of existing deficits are:

- non-uniform, non-standardized means of expressions and descriptions
- insufficient technical communication skills
- non-uniform, non-standardized definitions, applications of software building blocks and methodologies
- non-existing, non-standardized order, abstraction layers of building blocks, systems and interactions
- insufficient exploration of approaches and limitations of alternatives for developing systems
- insufficient frame works and platforms for powerful, interoperable and secure application systems
- insufficient development of tools for the intuitive use and handling of modern application systems
- missing concepts of the pre-fabrication and re-use of building blocks, systems and interactions
- no predictability of interactions and dependencies between building blocks, systems and organizations.

The insufficient software technical foundation, a lack of logical levels and substantiated approaches for an engineering analysis, modeling, development, validation and verification of application systems and their building blocks necessitate an engineering treatment and, furthermore, an engineering-based training of future PSE graduates. In analogy to traditional engineering approaches, such a study program has to be based on the teaching of standards, development frameworks and the re-use of pre-fabricated building blocks and partial systems. Thus, the development process of complex software systems has to be taught on the basis of reference architectures and solutions as well as on the basis of experience and abstracted knowledge of developers. This can be achieved by understanding software systems as software products. Software systems are characterized by complexity, openness, diversity, etc. and require substantiated engineering approaches for the modeling, implementation, validation and adaptation. By applying engineering methods, software systems obtain a product character since requirements, models, architectures, specifications and implementation prescriptions are being delivered as parts of the product with every phase of its life cycle. Software products are based and built according to standardized means of expressions and methodologies. This general orientation has strong implications and has to be reflected in the study program by learning engineering approaches and methodologies such as:

- system theoretical and application technical treatment
- abstraction layers, composition and delegation
- allocation of model types to problem space and solutions
- architectural frames and architecture-based development
- paradigms und principles
- team work.

and according to the characteristics of software systems such as:
- huge complexity
- (mass of) people involved
- multi-lingual, -paradigm,
- openness (heterogeneity, distribution, evolution).

The training of Professional Software Engineers has to be oriented towards engineering methodologies and market needs according to the substantiated use of latest software technologies. These requirements are to be integrated into the occupation. Typical practices can be specified for:
- model-based analysis, design, implementation and validation/verification
- team-oriented practicing
- transformation of user-specific technologies
- identification of key solutions to problem space
- product release and marketing plus technology transfer.

4. The PSE study program

The PSE study program outlines a philosophy oriented towards software technical requirements and their engineering substantiation as well as towards the occupation image of future PSE degree holders. It comprises the creation and application of theoretical and engineering fundamentals for models, methodologies, instruments for systematic and team-oriented analysis, development (consisting of construction, implementation, test), application, maintenance, validation and verification of complex software systems.

The program focuses on:

- abstraction layers and model transformation / mapping
- building block methodologies and abstraction levels
- constructive (meaning operational) view of software systems
- architectural frames and patterns for classes of application systems
- aspect-oriented de-composing of software systems
- measurement of couplings, throughput, performance, building block reliability.

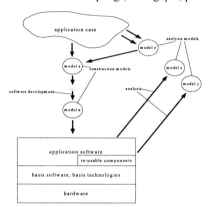

Figure no 1 shows the model-based approach depicting the discourse into abstraction layers and onto different types of models (analysis, construction, implementation, verification / validation). They are interpreted by a development environment. This environment consists of application software (e.g. CASE, word processsor), prefabricated components (e.g. class hierarchies), standard technologies (e.g. databases, operating systems) and hardware.

Figure 1. Model-based methodology

Due to the engineering substantiation of software technical skills based on standards, architectural frames and engineering practice a stringent training concept is formed by the PSE study program.

4.1. Administrative Organization

Since engineering practice is seen as the basis of the concept, the educational program is deeply influenced by model-based, architectural and constructive concerns. To offer high flexibility, the concept's administrative and organizational structure integrates international standards like:

- openness of study program using credit point system
- broad training enabled and enforced by interdisciplinary concepts
- internationally recognized degrees (B.Sw.E., M.Sw.E.)
- stay abroad, multi-lingual study life
- environment of labs, equipment, software, tools, literature, library
- interactions and programs oriented towards market needs.

Interaction with the market is especially beneficial to determine technology developments, trends and future engineering skills applied to system construction. In addition to the orientation towards market needs, practical training is one of the major issues of the concept. Thus, training, internships and projects are integrated dealing with:

- huge complexity and interdependent processes
- passing through all phases of a life cycle
- team work character involving more than 20 members and distributed locations
- industrial representatives and product character.

Next, study complexes [2] of the PSE program are introduced and defined.

4.2. Study complexes and lectures

A study complex is understood as a field of PSE knowledge. Several lectures are allocated to each study complex. Through the planning of study complexes a flexible organization of the study program is achieved. In the first semesters the allocation of lectures to study complexes can be fixed. In higher semesters several lectures can be allocated to one study complex ensuring the freedom of selection within semesters and study complexes. At the same time the open allocation of lectures to study complexes offers the opportunity to:

- adapt the study programs to available resources (instructors, projects, students)
- flexibility according to new research results and lectures
- allocate and recognize study results from abroad
- integrate external specialists (engineers from practice, other universities, …).

Every study complex consists of multiple lectures but is open to numbers and specifications. An exemplary allocation of lectures to study complexes is outlined at next.

Ethics: An introduction to PSE and Computer Science is given based on an overview of subjects, working fields, description of means and instruments, study programs, study forms, communication skills and styles. Ethics is due to enforce the motivation and orientation of students.

Mathematics: Subjects are the partial fields of mathematics related to engineering disciplines in general and to PSE in particular. Examples used in training should cover PSE-relevant content and discourse. To lectures belong:

- common algebra
- algebra and geometry
- discrete mathematics
- logics
- probability theory and statistics
- analysis and numerical mathematics

Fundamentals of theoretical Computer Science: From the point of view of theoretical Computer Science PSE specialists should be able to:

- define a language according to the analyzed context and discourse as well as to implement the language
- read and describe software building blocks using formal specifications
- map formal specifications of software building blocks onto programming elements and structures
- test an implementation according to its specification (validation)
- estimate the complexity of programs und problem space.

To lectures belong:

- formal languages, machine models
- theoretical foundation of software development
- computability and programming language paradigms
- complexity

System technical fundamentals: The description of products and processes using system technical means of expression is commonly used and applied in engineering disciplines. Thus, teaching fundamentals of system techniques is an essential part of the PSE educational program. A system consists of components related to each other and attached to a unit via connectors. Systems are characterized by an external behavior interacting with their environment as well as by an internal structure, which can be analyzed. Different aspects of the structure and behavior of software systems can be described by various system models.

Executing models and simulations of existing or pre-thought (virtual) systems can be examined. To lectures belong:

- fundamentals of system theory
- system modeling, simulation and optimization
- graphs and their application for system modeling
- coding theory and cryptography

Technical fundamentals: Technical fundamentals and practical examples of building blocks of computers, computer architectures and computer networks are taught using system technical models and means of expressions. To lectures belong:

- computer architectures
- models of hardware and hardware description languages
- technical building blocks and building block assemblies
- computer communication and networks

Software basis technologies: Software basis technologies are the partial systems used by PSE specialists to examine and to develop software products. These are operating systems, compiler, interpreter, standard programs for data management, for the representation of data and programs, for computer communication, for searching in networks, for knowledge management, etc. PSE specialists have to choose and to apply standard basis components and to integrate them into development environments. The development of basis components is domain of Computer Science graduates and specialists. To lectures on fundamental techniques belong:

- operating systems
- computer networks and protocols
- languages, compiler, interpreter
- database systems
- expert systems
- information systems

To lectures on complex techniques belong:

- multi-media techniques and tools
- teleconferencing techniques
- workflow modeling and management
- internet and intranet

Analysis of software systems and software artifacts: The aim of this study complex is to impart knowledge of architectures, modes of actions, development processes, operating guidelines of software systems on the basis of existing software products. This education line consists of lectures providing abstracted, ordered and structured knowledge of complex software products and consists of practical sessions held in labs where systems are analyzed by students in teams. To lectures belong:

- concepts of system modeling
- software products grading
- re-engineering of software products
- modeling and simulation
- system optimization

Software architecture: Compared to other technical products, software products consist of building blocks and building block assemblies which can be produced and re-used separately, too. Thus, software development is the composition of building blocks. Generally speaking, software systems are heterogeneous and distributed. According to [5] software architecture describes the building blocks software systems are composed of and the interactions of components using connectors. There are various types of connectors, components and systems. In analogy to other engineering disciplines (e.g. mechanical engineering) software product types can be classified and derived from the point of view of software architecture. They are considered and taught as classes of software systems.

To lectures belong:

- architecture description languages
- construction theory
- frame works and patterns
- technical support and tools
- product lines
- engineering technical fundamentals of software architecture
- basis architecture types
- software building blocks und building block theory

Fundamentals of programming: This study complex contains fundamental concepts of programming techniques, especially for the programming in the small. As subjects are identified:

- algorithms and their design
- data structure and data types
- basics of programming paradigms and languages
- typical, representative data structures and standard algorithms
- basics of algorithm grading
- know-how for testing program fragments.

To lectures belong:

- algorithms, data, programs and standards
- parallel processes and parallel processing
- program tests

Models, methods, paradigms: Theoretical fundamentals, models, methods and tools for the development of complex software products are part of this study complex. It is built upon knowledge acquired in the following lectures:

- basis technologies
- concepts of system modeling
- software architecture
- software project
- software quality assurance
- human computer interaction, ergonomics

As common in all working processes division of labor is necessary for software development. A horizontal as well as vertical division of labor has to be reflected within software development:

- horizontal: according to parts of systems to solve data processing tasks (e.g. data management, user interface, error and exception handling)
- vertical: according to application cases and fields (e.g. planning production systems, materials administration, accounting).

The division of labor is reflected by the study complexes 'software architecture' and 'basis technologies'. To lectures belongs:

- models of software development
- software construction and design
- methods of software development and tools
- software development processes

Software documentation and standards: Principles of software documentation are taught. Students will be introduced into software standards.

Software management: Specific models and methods are taught for the management of software projects. To lectures belong:

- definition and calculation of software projects
- software project organization and management
- software project introduction and acceptance
- technology transfer
- software project coaching and maintenance
- software project and product documentation
- enterprise start-up and leadership
- software marketing

Software quality and quality assurance: Software as a product is characterized by specific quality features. These features have to be specified for the product development in the target specification and to be proven at the product or its pre-released prototype. As common for any other technical product standards are determining and regulating software quality and quality management. These standards have to be implemented and realized in a product-specific manner for the development of the software. To lectures belong:

- software quality and standards
- security and reliability of software systems
- human-computer interaction
- software and system ergonomics

- testing of software systems
- error and exception handling
- measurement and evaluation of software systems
- software quality management

Next, the specified study complexes will be assigned to education lines.

4.3. Allocation of study complexes to education lines

Education lines are oriented towards software products and not towards the partial education fields of Computer Science. Thus, the PSE study program differs substantially from this of Computer Science (compare [4], [3]). As education lines will be introduced:
- theoretical fundamentals of PSE
- system technical fundamentals of PSE and software analysis
- technical fundamentals of PSE
- software basis systems
- software and software development
- software product aspects.

Theoretical fundamentals of PSE: Theoretical fundaments of PSE comprise of mathematical fundamentals of PSE and relevant subjects of theoretical Computer Science.

System technical fundamentals of PSE and software analysis: PSE as well as other engineering disciplines are based on common system techniques and theory. Since these are of great importance, an own education line is being formed. The core of this education line is software analysis, too.

Technical fundamentals of PSE: This education line deals with subjects of technical Computer Science relevant to PSE.

Software basis systems: To realize software products, PSE specialists make use of numerous program systems interpreted by the basis machine of a computer. In contrast to the study program for computer scientists, PSE specialists are not taught to be the developers of such systems, but their users.

Software and software development: An important aim of an engineering discipline is the development of products. This education line teaches knowledge about parts of software products, technical aspects of product development and product development processes.

Software product aspects: This education line deals with knowledge about important aspects of software and software products in social working processes and about the environment of software products.

The study complexes are allocated to the introduced education lines as depicted in figure no 2.

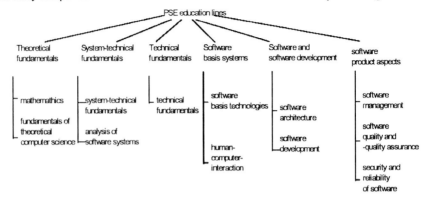

Figure 2. Allocation of study complexes to PSE education lines

To satisfy market needs and to improve the technical skills of future PSE degree holders (compare [1]) practical exercises and laboratories are to be integrated into the concept.

4.4. Enforcing technical skills

To improve technical skills and to enforce the constructive part of the concept, practical training will be held in system laboratories. Labs are specialized according to education lines and thus, are classified into software system and hardware system labs.

4.4.1. Software system lab (software development studio): The software system lab serves the application of acquired knowledge for the analysis, development, adaptation and further development of large software products. By realizing complex practical work requiring the application of knowledge from various study complexes and lectures, an important role is played by the software system lab. It is recommended to have several software system labs established to initialize, fundraise and coach appropriate projects. The concept recommends the establishment of three software system labs:

- Software system lab I: Analysis and re-engineering of software products
- Software system lab II: Development of software products
- Software system lab III: Marketing of software products.

PSE students take part in a one-term software project held in the software system lab II. According to industry's needs all phases of a product life cycle are passed through by developer teams under real market conditions.

Software system lab I: Analysis and re-engineering of software products. The aim is the examination of existing and large software products using various techniques (e.g. techniques of system modeling, software architecture, software ergonomics), the representation of analysis results as well as the re-engineering of system components or partial systems. Partners from industry interested in analyzing and re-engineering their software products and capable to support such projects have to be found. Projects must result in economic benefits.

Software system lab II: Development of software products. The aim is the development of software products using acquired knowledge from study complexes. As a starting point, a task to develop a new software product or to adapt an existing product will be assigned by an industrial principal. All phases of development starting with the compilation of target specification up to releasing the product to the principal have to be passed through by development teams. Issuing documentation is included, too. The software development project has to realize vertical and horizontal division of labor as well as division of roles (e.g. programmer, people involved in quality assurance) in a practice relevant manner.

Software system lab III: Marketing of software products. A marketing concept for a given software product has to be specified and realized. Parts of the concept are:
- product advertising
- product presentation on the net
- preparation of and participation in fairs and exhibitions
- development of exemplary application cases
- compilation of user manual
- selling strategies, contract and license management
- coaching and market introduction/implementation
- hotline organization.

Software system lab III deals with software projects from lab I and II or with given products by an industrial principal.

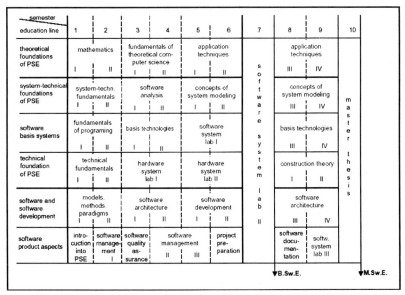

Figure 3: Allocation of study complexes to semesters and education lines

4.4.2. Hardware system lab (hardware performance studio): The hardware system lab serves the application of acquired knowledge of technical aspects of software products. In contrast to software labs, students apply components and partial systems to realize complex and embedded software products.

PSE recommends two hardware system labs:
- Hardware system lab I: Testing, analysis and composition
- Hardware system lab II: Distributed and mobile products.

Hardware system lab I: Testing, analysis and composition. The aim is to impart technical fundamentals by practical training focusing on the application of hardware building blocks and building block assemblies for the realization of software products. Practical work comprises the analysis and testing of hardware components, the composition of components to complex systems and the use of peripherals (e.g. robots).

Hardware system lab II: Distributed and mobile products. The aim is the handling of distributed, heterogeneous and mobile systems (e.g. satellites), practical fundamentals of embedded systems, computer communication, networks, security (e.g. intranet).

The study complexes, software and hardware system labs are allocated to education lines and semesters in figure no. 3.

4.5. Specialization and substantiated experience of future PSE graduates

In addition to study complexes, software projects and labs, the increasing complexity and market needs justify the specialization of future PSE degree holders. The specialization demand is reflected by the concept providing M.Sw.E. students with substantiated experience according to:
- roles in software projects and labs (horizontal, vertical)
- functional and non-functional aspects of software products
- selected classes of software products (e.g. embedded, workflow or multi-media systems).

The specialization of future PSE graduates is not based on the restriction or limitation of study complexes, but is realized by the interpretation of overall fundamentals, methodologies and knowledge for specified project roles, product aspects and classes of software products.

5. Conclusion

Software Engineering deals with the creation and application of engineering fundamentals for the systematic and team-based analysis, development, use, evaluation, etc. of large, software-intensive systems as technical products. The concept for educating Professional Software Engineers described in this document offers subjects, systematic sequences and flexibility to address market needs, industry requirements and rapid technology changes. It is intended to integrate the educational concept into international discussions as well as into standardization and accreditation programs. Having agreed upon study complexes, education lines, software and hardware system labs, the study program has to focus on the application and adaptation of engineering traditions, methodologies and approaches.

References

[1] J. Diaz-Herrera, G. M. Powell, "Educating Industrial Strength Software Engineers", Conference on Software Engineering Education and Training, Atlanta, 1998.
[2] E. Horn, "Classification and delimitation of the study program 'Software Systems Engineering' at University of Potsdam", University of Potsdam, 1998.
[3] S. McConnell, "After the Gold Rush", Microsoft Press, 1999.
[4] D. Parnas, "Software Engineering Programs are not Computer Science Programs", Annuals of Software Engineering, 1998.
[5] M. Shaw, D. Garlan, "Software Architecture. Perspectives on an Emerging Discipline.", Prentice Hall, 1996.

Learning Software Engineering with Group Work

Maria Isabel Alfonso and Francisco Mora
Dept. of Computer Science and Artificial Intelligence. University of Alicante. Spain
eli@dccia.ua.es, mora@dccia.ua.es

Abstract

This paper describes our experience of teaching a Software Engineering course based on the use of group work to teaching and practise theoretical concepts. Our work has three main aims: firstly, for the students to develop a complete software project (from specification to delivery); secondly, to acquire knowledge of the main problems of group work and how to overcome them; and finally, to underline the importance of documenting software projects effectively. The following is the programme that we have developed to achieve these goals.

1. Introduction

Group work is vital for the development of large software engineering projects. Putting together a group that works effectively is therefore a critical management task. There are a number of factors that influence group work [1]: (a) group makeup; (b) group cohesion; (c) group communications; and (d) group organization. Good groups cannot guarantee the success of a project, but bad group work usually results in project failure. So we believe that group work is valuable experience for students, helping them to carry out their future professional work as Software Engineers successfully.

Group work also provides an excellent framework for teaching many Software Engineering topics, in that it allows most of the theoretical issues involved to be practised [2], [3], [4]. So, our efforts focused on teaching some theoretical issues using group work experience with students developing a Software Engineering project.

This paper deals with how we tried to achieve this. In our opinion this is a very difficult task for teachers, due to the fact that a complete large project cannot be developed in a semester, and the real problems associated with this development cannot be experienced. Moreover, we mean each group member to act, not as a specialist focused on a concrete task, (for example, programming, design, or tests), but working in several different tasks instead, and thus learning from all of them. In spite of this very difficult challenge, we developed a course in Software Engineering at the University of Alicante that seems to be extremely satisfactory for both students and teachers.

Large projects are often 'one-off' and suffer from unique problems, but they have in common the need for group work and for effectively documenting the software process. So the course that we developed is based in group work, and has three main objectives:

- To develop a complete project by teamwork
- To show that effective group work is a very difficult task, and learn from this experience, and
- To show the importance of system documentation in the development of a large software project.

We have structured the rest of this paper as follows. Firstly, we present the Software Engineering related courses at the University of Alicante (in Spain), in order to justify the contents of the Software Engineering course that we have developed.

Secondly, we analyse initial questions related to our decisions about the size of the work groups, the methods and tools that we have used, and we give an example of a project proposal that must be developed by the students.

We then explain the life cycle model that we used, and the planning of the tasks that must be carried out, the programme schedule, and the deliverables associated with each milestone defined in the plan.

We show the results obtained from our experience of applying our custom life cycle model, and we finish by explaining some conclusions we have reached from our work.

2. Software engineering at the university of Alicante (in Spain)

At the University of Alicante (http://www.ua.es), students can obtain a five-year graduate degree in computer science called "Computer Engineering". The body of Software Engineering knowledge is mainly obtained from three 60-hour courses. In the first, students learn about requirement specifications, and different methods used to analyse software engineering projects. The second is mainly focused on the study of software project design, and the application of several design methods. The third and last course is the one dealt with in this paper. Instead of analysing a single topic in depth, maintenance or validation for example, we intend to complete students' knowledge of Software Engineering. So we refer to several topics that we integrate with the knowledge that students have already obtained from the first two courses.

We divide the course in 30 hours of theory, and 30 hours of practice. In the theory classes, we summarize the main concepts of the following topics: Planning activities, the testing process, configuration of the management process and the maintenance process.

The course website is at: http://dccia.ua.es/dccia/inf/asignaturas/IS2. The site contains the slides used in the theory room, and other information, such as the bibliography, related papers and links.

The course is taught over four hours per week: two theory hours, and two practical hours, spread over 15 weeks. We explain the concepts in the theory classes and we practice them in the practical classes (except for some of those related to the maintenance process). For each concept, we broadly explain their importance, the methods and tools used to apply it, and how it should be applied depending on several factors, such as the type or the size of project, the resources available, etc. We think that: "A learned concept is much more valuable if we know how to apply it to a real problem". This therefore, is the premise that guides our teaching of software engineering.

3. Preliminary factors

Before we explain our laboratory programme, we would like to present some preliminary factors such as: the size of work groups, the methods and tools used, and the project proposal.

3.1. Group size

We have opted for five member work groups. This number was chosen in order to facilitate organisation of the groups. This organisation is a result of our aiming to involve each member in all tasks, thus learning from all of them. The role of each group member is defined from the beginning, and is explained to the students in the first practical class. Basically, each member plays a twofold role: (1) he/she acts as the configuration manager of a document that must be delivered at the end of course; and (2) he/she acts as a subordinate of the other configuration managers and contributes to create the document that must be delivered. The roles that we have defined are contributes to create the corresponding document that must be delivered. The roles that we have defined are:

- Planning configuration manager (P),
- Design configuration manager (D),
- Source code configuration manager (C),
- Test configuration manager (T), and
- User Manual configuration manager (U)

Each is responsible for developing the corresponding document: planning, design, implementation, test, and user manual. We have created documentation standards in order to control document structure and presentation. We provide templates for all documents, and set the precise contents of each one. Each configuration manager is responsible for the following tasks: (a) allocating and distributing the contents of the documents to the other four group members; (b) integrating the work of group members into the whole document and delivering it to teacher; (c) controlling document changes and quality; (d) writing a final report whose contents depend on the configuration manager type. The final reports contents are as follows (P): makes a real schedule of the project and states the differences with the initial draft schedule; (D): states the match between the design and the source code delivered; (C): reports the correlation between logical and physical design; (T): reports the results of unit testing and the validation testing process; (U): states the match between the requirements and the design. These reports are delivered at the end of the course by each configuration manager (all students).

Besides those described above, each configuration manager must carry out the following tasks: (P) monitor and control the planning project during the development process; (D): monitor and control all design changes during the development process; (C): develop the corresponding implementation standards, and design the integration process; (T): design the drivers and stubs used in tests; (U): monitor and control any changes to the initial specifications during the whole development project process.

The teacher does not set group communications, and each group can decide how to exchange information on the status of their work, the design decisions that have been made, changes to previous decisions and any other information. The group communications implemented are reported in the Planning document.

3.2. Methods and tools

We use an object-oriented approach to develop the proposed project. We have chosen UML (Unified Modelling Language) [5], in order to specify, visualize, construct and document the software artefacts of the project. The reason for this is that this language is widely used by object-oriented developers [6]. The extensive use of UML has led to the creation of CASE tools that use it and generate source code automatically from design. An example of this kind of tool is 'Together', which we have used in order to make students work easier.

It is important to mention that we assume that the students have systems analysis and design knowledge and are therefore familiar with object-oriented design using UML from previous courses. Basically, we use the following diagrams in the Design document: use case, sequence and class diagrams. The use case diagrams provide a means of describing the external view of the system and its interactions with the outside world. The sequence diagram model shows the dynamic aspect of the system while emphasizing the ordering of messages in time. They are used to illustrate the scenarios associated to each case used. The class diagrams show the static structure of the system, the internal structure, and also the relationships between classes and inheritance structure.

We also use Together Control Center v. 6.0. This is a modelling tool developed by TogetherSoft Corporation (http://www.togethersoft.com), which fully synchronises modelling diagrams and source code. This tool also includes all features needed to build enterprise level applications, allowing the entire development team to collaborate using a common language, diagrams and software. We can model the system using UML and generate code automatically in Java. It also provides very useful features such as: a user interface builder, a version control of artefacts created, and a testing framework. The User Interface Builder allows a graphical user interface (GUI) to be designed and built for a Java application. The testing framework allows the development of both unit tests for source code and visual tests for user interface components..

3.3. The project proposal

We now describe an example of a project that we propose to the students. This project has to be developed by each group of students. The project consists of developing an automatic tool to create a calendar from input data related to the type of process model used, and the project activities.

The input data consists of the process model used (waterfall model, incremental model, spiral model), project activities, including their duration, precedence, type of resource and number of units of this resource that each activity requires. It also includes the data from which to construct the calendar and the cost of use of each resource by unit of time.

The output data consists of two possible Gant charts: an activity bar chart and a staff allocation bar chart. For each activity they show the earliest and latest start times, and the earliest and latest finish time. The financial cost of the project is also stated.

We identify the following functionalities: (F1): Choose the process model, this will show a template with the process model chosen; (F2): Introduce the input data, the user can eliminate process model activities or subdivide them into other sub- activities; (F3): Generate the calendar and calculate the financial cost; (F4) Manage data calendars: the user can store the data calendar, restore a previously saved data calendar from another project, or modify it; (F5) Resource manager: the user can add, eliminate or modify resource types used by the project.

This proposal is given in more detail to the students. We allow each work group to make minor changes to these initial specifications.

4. The programme

We have defined a specific process model in order to achieve our objectives of using group work to learn software engineering concepts effectively in the practical hours.

The proposed model has three sequential phases that we have called: user interface centred, basic functionality centred and advanced functionality centred. We will now describe each of them in detail.

4.1. Phase I: user interface centred

The objective of this phase is to obtain a non-functional prototype so as to validate the specifications with the end users. Additionally, as a result of this phase, the students must understand all parts of the system directly related to the user.

Each work group must draw up a Planning document that includes a system specification, the estimated project costs, a project risk analysis and a draft project calendar.

They also draw up a *Design document* centred only in the *user interface* design aspects. This document includes cases and scenarios that will be used to validate the specifications and also to validate the finished product. This document also describes the class diagrams related to user interface design.

Finally, the work group must implement the non-functional prototype, integrating all components designed during this phase and correctly documenting the source code obtained in the corresponding *Implementation document*. This phase lasts 12 hours (6 weeks).

4.2. Phase II: basic functionality centered

The input data is validated during this phase. The group proceed with the design of the data structures that are needed to implement the project. They must also implement the following "basic functionalities": F1, F2, F4, and F5. So, at the end of this phase, the user can input data, which is stored in data structures that will be used to create the calendar. During this phase, the students also acquire more knowledge about the project before implementing the functions that produce the result required by the user.

Each work group must draw up a *Design document* that reflects the program architecture used to support the basic functionalities that are to be implemented. This document contains the new classes created and their relations with: (a) the classes designed in the previous phase referring to the system interface, and (b) the internal data structures created that are used as the basis for implementing the functionalities of the following phase

They also elaborate a black box design of basic functionalities F4 and F5, which will be implemented at the end of this phase, recording possible incidences when carrying out test cases. This black box design and the results obtained are reported in a *Test document* that has to be delivered to the teacher by the corresponding configuration manager.

Finally, the work group has to implement the basic functionalities and integrate them with the prototype obtained in the previous phase. Additionally, the source code must be adequately documented in an *Implementation document* and delivered. This phase lasts 10 hours (5 weeks).

4.3. Phase III: advanced functionality centered

This is the last phase, in which the project must be completed. The group designs the algorithm that implements the functionality F3, which calculates the calendar derived from the input data, and its associated cost.

Each work group must elaborate a *Design document* that includes the possible new classes defined and their relationships with the classes defined in previous phases.

Once F3 is implemented, it must be integrated with the results of phases 1 and 2, and reported in an *Implementation document*.

The functionality F3 must also be white box tested. The test cases obtained are implemented and any possible errors found are debugged. All this information is put into a *Test Doc*ument.

The work group has to create a *User manual document* that reflects the correct use of the program by the possible users. Finally, we can validate the program with the teacher. This phase lasts 8 hours (4 weeks).

5. Evaluation of the proposal

Implementation of the above-mentioned proposal planning for phases I, II and III demands a great effort by the teachers, in that they act as high level managers of the project for each work group. So, they must monitor and control the work carried out by the students at all times.

We have defined three key milestones for the project, associated with the end of each phase. At each milestone, the configuration managers must deliver the corresponding documentation. The teacher then evaluates the work carried out by the group.

The score obtained for each phase depends not only on the quality and contents of documents, but also on other factors such as the attitude of group members, and their ability to overcome problems caused by different personalities in the group.

The teacher scores each phase from 0 to 10 points for each group. Each phase has been weighted differently in order to obtain the final score for the practical hours. Therefore, we have assigned weights of 15%, 20% and 35% for phases I, II and III respectively. The students also have to answer some questions about the development of the project by their work group individually. These questions are weighted as 30% of the final score. So, the final score for the practical hours is:

$(0.15 \cdot PI) + (0.2 \cdot PII) + (0.35 \cdot PIII) + (0.3 \cdot \text{questions})$.

The course score is obtained by calculating the average of the score corresponding to practical hours and the score from the theory hours (a written test). A minimum of 5 points must be obtained in both of them.

6. Analysis of the model proposed

The model proposed for the practical hours in the section 3, as we have previously stated, implies a great effort for the teacher involved, if he has to evaluate several groups. For example, we have experimented with practical sessions (2 hours) with 20 students, meaning four work groups. He has to monitor the work of students continuously and he must mediate if any conflict occurs in a work group. When a milestone is reached, he must evaluate the documentation delivered in a very short time and report the results and the group score to each configuration manager. This means that he has to talk to each configuration manager and explain the errors found and how to solve them, or even recommend that some parts of the work be done again. If the teacher has monitored the work of students correctly before delivery, there is no reason for this evaluation task to be very "hard". This effort will be compensated by the advantages that we feel the model proposed offers.

The evaluation carried out by the teacher allows students to learn actively, in that there is feedback on the work developed by the work group. As each milestone is reached, the students are informed of which parts of their work have to be improved in the next phase, or, if the worst comes to the worst, to be repeated. This allows the student to benefit from this feedback and learn effectively.

Each group suffers from the problems associated with group work, such as poor communication, bad coordination or poor work carried out. They also suffer from a serious problem relating to the different personalities in the group. The teacher leaves it to the students to decide which group they want to belong to. There are groups in which the personalities are complementary, but there are others in which the personalities are totally incompatible. As a result of group makeup, a particular group may not be able to overcome the difficulties that crop up and the group cannot develop the complete project, or some members of the group may decide to leave it, etc. These difficulties have to be borne in mind by the teacher when evaluating them. Although the project cannot be completed due to the factors outlined, we consider that this is a very positive factor for the students, who can learn in spite of having carried out an unsuccessful project.

The students learn gradually, in each phase they focus on one part of the problem and are better able to solve it. Phase I is focused in "what" the problem is, and the students' efforts are focused on understanding the requirements of the end user.

We have noticed that this first phase has a lesser weight associated because the students are beginning to integrate themselves with the group and understand "what" has to be done. The tasks accomplished in each phase are very similar, although they focus on different issues. So, in phase II the students become more familiar with the process model and they can begin to think about "how" to solve the problem. This phase is has a medium weighting. Finally, the third phase has the greatest weighting, in that the students have had overcome two previous milestones and have received the necessary explanations from the teacher about the work carried out. This phase is exclusively focused in "how" obtain the outputs required by the user, and the student are less worried about the process model.

Finally, the students verify the importance of documenting the software project effectively. As a consequence of group work, and the process model proposed, the students must consult documents written in previous phases or written by others members of group. If the document looked up is, for example, bad quality, too extensive or the content is less valuable, this represents a problem that affects the work that must be carried out. As this situation occurs for all group members, they try to create useful and good documents in order to increment their productivity as a result.

7. Analysis of the results obtained

We have applied the model proposed over the last two courses. We have tried several formulas for teaching software engineering with work groups since 1995. We reported three different experiences in 1998 at a national congress [7], and here we propose a new model proposed that we have applied over the last the two courses (2000/01, and 2001/02). We have approximately 140 students per course. This means seven weekly sessions with 20 students each (four work groups). Approximately 98% of the students finish the course successfully. External factors oblige 2% to abandon the course.

Of this 98%, in general the students obtain a high degree of satisfaction due to the fact that they have learned in spite of any problems that may have arisen. They appreciate their experience in that they practice the theoretical issues that they have learned in the theory hours, and other associated software engineering courses. 22 (out of 28) work groups finished the proposed project completely during the 2000/01 course, and 26 during 2001/2002. This is due to the teachers having more experience, in that they also learn from difficulties encountered by students in previous courses and can guide the work of students more effectively. The students were asked to state what were the main difficulties encountered. 90% of them stated that the main problem, which they faced, was coordinating group work appropriately; this was mainly due to the presence of different personalities in the group. 7% of the students considered that the main problem was their lack of experience with the tools used, something that reduces their productivity, and 3% of the students felt the main problem to be the tight schedule.

With respect to the time spent by the students carrying out the proposed project, 65% of the groups needed to work at home two extra hours per week in order to complete the project, 20% of the groups needed to work one extra hour, and 15% stated that they did not need to hold meetings outside the practical hours. 96% of the students appreciated the process model used, in that it clearly defined the tasks that they had to perform, and 93%

considered the documentation standards provided by the teachers to have a positive influence on group productivity.

99% of the students considered that group work turns out to be more difficult than they had imagined initially in the theory hours, and so they consider the practical hours to be a necessary experience. Another interesting fact is that the students appreciated their experience, not only immediately, but also much more so when they started working as software engineers. Students often say to the teacher: "in my job, I have the same problems that I encountered (to a lesser extent) in the practical hours of the software engineering course". So the teachers also experience a high degree of satisfaction.

Finally, we underline the fact that that this high percentage of successful groups is affected by a fact that the teachers have noticed: the students learn that the success or failure of the group depends on the work of all members and on the degree of cohesiveness achieved, favouring "ego-less" programming [8]. Each member can influence the score achieved by the group, and this fact encourages the group members to cooperate actively in order to contribute to the success of the group instead of its failure.

8. Concluding remarks

We have explained our experience of teaching software engineering by using work groups. We have proposed a model for teaching software engineering that includes: (a) a specific group organization, and (b) a specific process model that allows us to achieve three main goals: (1) for each group to develop a complete project, (2) to experience the main problems associated with group work and to learn from them, and (3) to show the importance of documenting software projects effectively.

The model proposed has been applied at the University of Alicante over the past two years. Our experience reveals a high degree of satisfaction among both students and teachers. Among the positive aspects of the model proposed we highlight the fact that it favours: (a) active learning; (b) incremental learning; (c) learning in spite of failure; (d) learning from experience.

10. References

[1] I. Sommerville, *Software Engineering. 6th Edition*. Addison-Wesley. 2001

[2] D.E. Perry et al. *People, Organisations and Process Improvement*. IEEE Software 11(4) 36-45. 1994

[3] P.N. Robillard. *Measuring team activities in a process-oriented software engineering course*. In Proc. of 11 th CSEET, pp. 90-101. Feb. 1998.

[4] O.P. Brereton et al. *Distributed group working in software engineering education*. Inform. Software Technol. 40 (4) 221-227, July, 1998.

[5] "UML Semantics," v 1.1 (1 September 1997), The Object Management Group, doc. no.ad/97-08-04.

[6] J. Rumbaugh, G. Booch et al. , *The unified modelling language reference manual*. MA: Addison-Wesley Longman, 1999.

[7] M.I. Alfonso, F. Mora, F. Martinez, "La programación en grupos de trabajo", JENUI'98, pp. 181-185 , July, 1998.

[8] G. Weinberg. *The psychology of computer programming*. New York: Van Nostrand. 1971.

Panels

Developing an Undergraduate Software Engineering Degree

Software Engineering Retraining — Different Perspectives

Certification for Software Professionals: The IEEE Computer Society's CSDP Program

Developing an Undergraduate Software Engineering Degree

J. Fernando Naveda
(Moderator)
Rochester Institute of
Technology
jfnics@rit.edu

Donald J. Bagert
Rose Hulman Institute
of Technology
Don.Bagert@rose-
hulman.edu

Steve Seidman
New Jersey Institute of
Technology
Stephen.Seidman@njit.edu

Jocelyn Armarego
Murdoch University, Australia
Jocelyn@eng.murdoch.edu.au

Thomas B. Hilburn
Embry-Riddle
Aeronautical University
hilburn@db.erau.edu

Susan Eisenbach
Imperial College London
S.Eisenbach@ic.ac.uk

Keywords: undergraduate software engineering, undergraduate degree, software engineering curriculum, software engineering faculty, accreditation

Panel Summary

As those who have done it can attest, developing an undergraduate degree in software engineering is a daunting and challenging task, and there have been instances where a department has tried, but failed to get its program approved. A strong desire to develop a program in software engineering together with interested faculty may not be enough to build a credible degree, let alone a curriculum that will be approved by all the administrative and State organizations who may have a say in it .This panel brings together a group whose experience in developing software engineering degrees at their respective institutions may be helpful to those thinking about doing so. Each member of the group will describe his/her experiences in developing an undergraduate program in software engineering and address key issues and problems that should be considered in any such effort. There will also be ample opportunity for interaction among the participants.

The following are some of the issues that will be discussed:
- Building a credible program. The difference between paper programs and real programs
- Developing a curriculum. What should the curriculum look like? What sort of support and guidance is available?
- Finding and developing qualified faculty
- Dealing with the politics: Where will the program live? Is the engineering of software real engineering? Is software engineering applied computer science?
- Accreditation issues
- Landmines
- Tactical issues: How can an SE program be built from existing programs of study?

Since it has become clear that software engineering plays a central role in computing, an increasing number of institutions of higher learning are turning their attention to the development of baccalaureate degree programs in software engineering. This trend has been encouraged by the creation of numerous software engineering degrees at masters level, and by the publication of an influential document on undergraduate software engineering education[1] in 1990.

In 1993, the Rochester Institute of Technology (RIT) allowed a core number of its faculty to develop an undergraduate degree in software engineering [2], and in 1996 admitted a group of students to what would become the first baccalaureate degree in software engineering in the United States (interestingly, various Australian and British universities had already been offering such degrees). RIT would not remain alone for long in the US. In 1998 the Milwaukee School of Engineering started its own undergraduate program in software engineering, admitting sophomores from its Computer Engineering program. In 2000, Monmouth University opened its doors to its new program in software engineering. Also in 2000, Georgia's Southern Polytechnic State University's School of Computing and Software Engineering obtained State approval to develop an undergraduate software engineering degree.

These are just a few examples of schools that have successfully implemented software engineering degrees in the US. Many others are sure to follow and it may be just a matter of time before software engineering becomes as popular as computer science. Some actually believe that software engineering could replace computer science as the program of choice for software professionals.

Jocelyn Armarego

Advocates of Software Engineering programs (at either undergraduate or graduate level) agree on one principle at least – SE is different from Computer Science, Computer Engineering and Information Systems, to name a few IT-based disciplines. It is these differences, in goals, focus and approach as well as content that make the development of SE programs necessary. However, that these differences are often not explicitly described makes SE program development problematic.

Developers of SE programs juggle these forces. For example, aligning SE programs within Engineering provides some benefits: the core of engineering practice and professionalism (accreditation, societal considerations, economics, etc) applies to SE as well as more traditional engineering programs. However, consensus on the place of advanced mathematics or the natural sciences may not be so easily achieved (but may be mandated). Hence common goals are in tension with different content needs. Approach and content are also in tension: while there is agreement that CS fundamentals provide some core SE knowledge and skills, software engineering principles and practices should underlie this learning (which implies faculty exists to take this approach). Yet organizational (i.e., university) policy may dictate that content determines who teaches what (e.g., that Computer Science must teach CS fundamentals (probably implying a CS approach).

While the result of this juggling is context-dependent (so what works in Australia may not be viable in other parts, and what are important issues for one group have no bearing on another), the insights we each bring will hopefully help achieve a global perspective on SE program development.

Don Bagert

The development of a proposal for a Bachelor of Science in Software Engineering (BSSE) at Rose-Hulman has been made considerably easier by the fact that there has been general support for the concept of the BSSE by faculty both inside and outside the Department of Computer Science and Software Engineering. However, some of the details were more difficult in gaining consensus and in proposing an actual curriculum model and its implementation. Among those issues were: 1) how the new program would impact the CS curriculum, 2) properly distinguishing the differences between the CS and SE curricula, 3) estimating the impact of the new degree on other departments and 4) dealing with issues involving the culture at Rose-Hulman e.g. the question of whether or not to offer differential equations in an institution where every single existing major did, and desire for the freshman year to be much the same throughout the disciplines.

Tom Hilburn

In the fall of 2002, we formally began offering a B.S. in Software Engineering (BSSE) at Embry-Riddle Aeronautical University. However, the genesis of the degree started much earlier. In early 1990s, we began to make changes in the content and emphasis of our undergraduate computer science program. There were a number of factors that encouraged this path: several of our faculty had software engineering background and experience; the ACM/IEEE-CS *Curriculum 1991* included SE modules and a sample SE curriculum; the employers of our graduates (Boeing, Lockheed-Martin, Raytheon, Rockwell-Collins, Sikorsky, etc.) voiced their need for software developers that were educated as "engineers"; and the university's mission and focus on professional aviation/aerospace programs supported the BSSE. Our approach to developing a BSSE has been evolutionary. We have, through the years, introduced software engineering topics and activities into existing courses, developed new SE courses, encouraged and supported the professional development of our faculty in SE areas, and finally changed the name of our program from computer science to software engineering. Although we face the same problems as others (hiring qualified SE faculty, the lack of exiting SE course material, and the acceptance of SE by the other engineering disciplines), the growing awareness of the criticality of software and its importance in all human-product products is helping us to resolve these difficulties.

Susan Eisenbach

Imperial College Computing has offered a named Software Engineering degree since 1984. It met no opposition either within the Department or within the College, because we were in an Engineering faculty and we've always had an Engineering ethos. We were only a bit concerned that there might not be enough good students who wanted to do it. Although only one of our programmes is named Software Engineering, all our undergraduate degrees are Software Engineering in flavour. The Department has always been in an Engineering Faculty and is funded the same as any other Engineering department. Its degrees are accredited by both the British Computer Society and the Institute of Electrical Engineers for Chartered Engineering status. Intake is highly competitive and we have control over both the number and quality of students who study for all our programmes including our four-year programme MEng Computing (Software

Engineering). Our degrees are extremely popular currently attracting 12 applications for each place.

Within the undergraduate degree, the programme is integrated with substantial components of both theory and practice. Students study 10 courses a year for the first two years almost all required. In their third and fourth years the choice is wide and flexible. There is much practical work. In addition to the integrated lab of the first two years there are group projects every year, a six-month work placement and a substantial final individual project. The students are in great demand upon graduation.

At the Masters level we have two programmes. One is a conversion course that produces Software Engineers. The other is an Advanced course. At this level we feel a more research-based programme is the type of course we wish to run. It's hard to remember when we weren't offering a Software Engineering degree programme.

Steven Seidman

I am the dean of a college of computing sciences (CCS) that currently consists of two departments: computer science (CS) and information systems (IS). CCS is independent of our College of Engineering. One of my primary short-term goals is to develop an undergraduate degree program in software engineering. Each of our departments has faculty members with software engineering research interests: formal methods in the CS department and requirements engineering in the IS department. A software engineering program must therefore cross department boundaries. The path to creating a SE program in this context is far from straightforward.

References

[1] Ford, G. *1990 Report on Undergraduate Software Engineering Education.* (CMU/SEI-90-TR-003). Pittsburgh, Pa.: Software Engineering Institute, Carnegie Mellon University, 1990.
[2] Naveda, J. F. and Lutz, M. J. "Crafting a Baccalaureate Program in Software Engineering," *Tenth Conference on Software Engineering Education & Training*, Virginia Beach, 1997, pp. 74 – 80.

Software Engineering Retraining – Different Perspectives

Mike Murphy (Moderator)
Southern Polytechnic State University
mmurphy@spsu.edu

Jorge Diaz-Herrera
Rochester Institute of Technology
jdiaz@gccis.rit.edu

Dawn Ramsey
Southern Polytechnic StateUniversity
dramsey@spsu.edu

Pam Thompson
Lockheed Martin Aeronautics Company
pam.thompson@lmco.com

Keywords: software engineering retraining, industry-university collaboration, Software Systems Development Certificate, SSDC, Software Engineering Retraining Program, SERP

Panel Summary

This panel looks at software engineering retraining in industry through industry-university collaboration. The particular context for the panel is the Software Systems Development Certificate (SSDC) under the Software Engineering Retraining Program (SERP) that brought together Lockheed Martin Aeronautics Company, Southern Polytechnic State University, and the State of Georgia. This collaboration was previously reported as a work in progress in IEEE Software, vol. 19, no. 5, Sept./Oct. 2002, pp. 30-34 ("A Collaborative Program to Retrain Lockheed Martin Aero Engineers").

The topics addressed include differing perspectives on
- changing industry needs
- curricular responses,
- role of government
- support issues
- the student perspective (before and after)

By the time of this panel presentation, the fourth and last scheduled class in the SSDC program will have graduated. Of particular interest are the administrative and curricular changes that occur over time with such a program.

Certification for Software Professionals:
The IEEE Computer Society's CSDP Program

Stephen B. Seidman
(Moderator)
New Jersey Institute of
Technology
Stephen.seidman@njit.edu

Donald Bagert
Rose-Hulman Institute of
Technology
Don.Bagert@rose-
hulman.edu

Dennis Frailey
Raytheon
d-frailey@raytheon.com

James Mason
SIAC
masonj@verizon.net

Fernando Naveda
Rochester Institute of
Technology
jfnics@rit.edu

Allen Parrish
University of Alabama
parrish@cs.ua.edu

Ann Sobel
Miami University
sobelae@muohio.edu

Keywords: CSDP, certification of software engineers, licensing, IEEE computer society

Panel Summary

For more than twenty years, the IEEE Computer Society has played a leading role in improving the professionalism of software engineers. Its activities include development of a large collection of software engineering standards, publication of many seminal software engineering journals, texts, and reference books, co-sponsorship of undergraduate software engineering curriculum and accreditation activities, and co-sponsorship of the Software Engineering Body of Knowledge (SWEBOK) project.

In 1999, the Society launched an effort to certify the knowledge of practicing software engineers. This effort led to the development of the Society's CSDP certification examination, which was given to a test group in 2001. The examination will be offered to the public through test centers around the world in Spring 2003. The Society has also encouraged the development of face-to-face and online training opportunities for prospective test-takers. These opportunities will also be available in Spring 2003.

Topics that will be covered by the panel include

- the distinction between certification and licensing
- the need for certification of software engineers
- an overview of the CSDP certification program

The panel moderator chairs the IEEE Computer Society's CSDP Training Committee, and is a member of the IEEE CS Professional Practices Committee.

Workshops

Preparing for the IEEE Computer Society
International Design Competition

Software Engineering Course Materials

Tailoring a Successful
Project-Based Course

Tools for Outcomes Assessment of
Education and Training in Software
Development Process

IEEE-CS/ACM Computing Curriculum
Software Engineering Volume Project

SWEBOK

Preparing for the 2004
IEEE Computer Society International Design Competition (CSIDC)

Susan K. Land (Moderator)
Northrop Grumman Information
Technology
susan.land@northropgrumman.com

Alan D. Clements
University of Teesside
a.clements@computer.org

Keywords: Computer Society International Design Competition, CSIDC, design project, multi-disciplinary

Workshop Summary

This workshop aims to promote the annual Computer Society International Design Competition (CSIDC) among academics by providing information on what is required for each team, competition deadlines, how best to prepare, and practical guidance for each phase of the competition. A review of the top five winning teams from the 2002 competition will also be presented, with the characteristics that helped make each of these teams successful.

The IEEE Computer Society challenges undergraduates from around the world to apply their learning to a real-work problem in the annual CSIDC. The goal of the competition is to replicate the type of environment that students might encounter in industry. The CSIDC is a contest in which students are required to work in teams to specify, design, build, test, document, and market a working prototype of a device that could be used to solve a real-world problem. The solution consists of both hardware and software, which typically requires that students assemble multi-disciplinary teams.

CSIDC planners constructed the competition to advance excellence in undergraduate education. By completing the project, students develop competence in planning and managing a large-scale design project, delegating tasks among peers, and working in teams towards a common goal—as well as gaining technical expertise in hardware architecture and software engineering. In CSIDC 2002 approximately 70 teams from countries ranging from the USA to India to Australia competed for the top cash prizes. This workshop provides academics from sponsoring universities, or those interested in finding out more about this international competition, with the information that they will need to help their students compete successfully.

The main goals of the workshop are:

- to promote the CSIDC as an academic incentive to students to participate in interdisciplinary teams
- to promote design as a multi-disciplinary activity
- to promote interdisciplinary teams among educators and perhaps motivate the creation of courses where interdisciplinary teams are the rule as opposed to the exception.

Software Engineering Course Materials Workshop[§]

Thomas B. Hilburn
Embry-Riddle
Aeronautical University
hilburn@erau.edu

Gregory W. Hislop
(Moderator)
Drexel University
Hislop@Drexel.edu

Michael J. Lutz
Rochester Institute of
Technology
mikelutz@mail.rit.edu

Susan A. Mengel
Texas Tech University
mengel@ttu.edu

Mark J. Sebern
Milwaukee School of
Engineering
sebern@msoe.edu

Keywords: software engineering education, web-based community for software engineering education, SWENET, software engineering course materials

Workshop Summary

This workshop will provide participants with an opportunity to discuss and critique software engineering course materials being developed as part of the SWENET project. SWENET is an NSF project designed to create a Web-based community of software engineering education. A key activity in the project is to create, collect, and share software engineering course materials within the context of current accreditation guidelines and curricular models.

Since the introduction of the nation's first baccalaureate program in software engineering at the Rochester Institute of Technology in 1996 [1], a dozen more programs have been fielded and many others are in preparation [2]. ABET has responded to these developments by creating program-specific criteria for software engineering in anticipation that these programs would seek engineering accreditation [3]. Finally, traditional engineering and computing-related programs have begun incorporating software engineering topics into their curricula. In all cases, however, gaps must be bridged in the areas of university infrastructure, faculty development, and supporting educational materials.

SWENET, A Web-based Community for Software Engineering Education, is a project created to address these gaps, most especially the lack of supporting educational materials. The project team consists of experienced software engineering educators from a diverse group of universities across the United States. Each team member has significant experience as a software engineering practitioner, and has actively contributed to the development of software engineering education, including curriculum efforts.

As software engineering educators, we are all too aware of how difficult it is to start from scratch. In particular, the lack of examples, teaching materials, and exercises can significantly impede the

---

[§] The SWENET project is supported by NSF Grant EEC-0080502

328

inclusion of software engineering concepts into undergraduate courses. Our primary goal in developing SWENET is to make it easier for other educators to find materials they can use.

Our initial focus is on four areas: design, process, quality, and requirements. We selected these areas because they are particularly important for an undergraduate education that stresses professional technical competence. Within each area we have defined several modules on specific topics, with each module supplemented by adaptable support materials. The hallmark of a well-defined module is that it is small and self-contained; typically modules will range from one to six lecture hours of material. The supporting resources are key to our approach, as these are exactly the materials that are difficult to create.

This workshop will provide an opportunity for other instructors to learn about SWENET and to evaluate and critique initial SWENET materials.

Workshop Goals

This half-day workshop will:
1. Increase awareness of the SWENET project and of the materials it can provide to software engineering educators and trainers.
2. Identify software engineering educators and trainers who may want to participate in the SWENET Web-based community.
3. Obtain a critique of the content, organization, and structure of the first SWENET software engineering modules.

Workshop Organization

The workshop will be divided into the following activities:
- **SWENET Overview** - A summary presentation to explain the SWENET project history, goals, and status.
- **Module Presentations** - Short presentations of draft software engineering modules. Each module contains material to support software engineering instruction in a particular topical area.
- **Facilitated Review and Discussion** - Small groups will conduct in-depth discussion and critique of the presented modules. The goals for the group will be to identify weaknesses and suggest improvements in content, organization, and packaging of the modules.
- **Summary Presentations** - Each group will provide a summary of group results to the full set of workshop participants.

References

1. J. F. Naveda and M. J. Lutz, "Crafting a Baccalaureate Program in Software Engineering," 10th Conference on Software Education & Training, Virginia Beach, VA, February 1998.
2. K. L. Modesitt, D. Bagert and L. Werth, "Academic Software Engineering: What Is and What Could Be – Results of the First Annual Survey for International SE Programs," 23rd International Conference on Software Engineering, Toronto, CA, May 2001.
3. ABET, Criteria for Accrediting Engineering Programs, Baltimore, MD, November 2001. (http://www.abet.org)

Tailoring a Successful Project-Based Course -- in Which Students Learn to Work in Teams on the Development of Useful Software Products for Real Clients – to the Needs and Resource Constraints of Individual Colleges and Universities

Barry Boehm(Moderator)
USC
boehm@sunset.usc.edu

Dan Port
USC
dport@sunset.usc.edu

David Klappholz
Stevens Institute of
Technology
david@cs.stevens-tech.edu

Keywords: project-based software engineering course, software projects, real clients, USC CS577, team projects

Workshop Summary

The purpose of this workshop is to present an in-depth overview of USC CS577, and to start the processes of:

- *eliciting from faculty at a variety of colleges and universities the different needs and resource constraints to which they would be subject were they to port CS577 to their home institutions*
- *planning the types of adjustments that can be made to CS577 to meet various sets of constraints*

The ultimate preparation for a career in software development is a project-based course in which students learn to work in teams on the development of useful software products for real clients. Published educational materials provide little support for the educator who wishes to teach such an ambitious course. We have embarked on a project whose goal is the development of materials which will enable educators to adapt Barry Boehm and Dan Port's USC CS577, one of the most successful such courses, to their special needs and resources, and to disseminate these materials in the form of a textbook, student and instructor manuals, a web-based course delivery framework, videotapes of USC course lectures, a CD archive of completed student projects, and public training in both adaptation and teaching of the course.

Our starting point is the two-semester project-based Introduction to Software Engineering which Profs. Boehm and Port have developed at USC. The course's effectiveness has been proved and improved over a period of 6 years with over 1000 students, and over 100 real-world customers.

Among the specific issues that will be discussed in the workshop are:

- acquisition of and dealing with clients for student projects -- or training TA's, or oneself, to act as clients in cases in which the possibility of real clients is precluded.
- instructing students in the dynamics of dealing with clients/customers and other stakeholders to arrive at the specification of a software product which will meet stakeholders' business, functional, performance, and other needs and to assess the direction of changes in needs after the product's initial deployment
- instructing students in the preparation of the various documents and software artifacts

necessary for a team to successfully complete a software project and to transition the product to its end users and, ultimately, to those who will maintain and enhance it

- training students in preparing for and conducting various types of review (requirements, architecture/design, code, etc.) so as to detect and correct faults at each stage of the development process
- teaching students how to perform risk analysis, risk assessment, and risk mitigation in order to make choices which arise at each stage of the development process in such way as to maximize the probability of success
- helping students adjust and re-adjust their products' features and details of the software development process over the project's lifetime so as to maximize the probability of producing the most useful possible software product within the allocated time
- helping students identify and deal with problems in team/group dynamics
- selecting teaching assistants, if they are to be available, and training them in helping students with all of the above activities
- determining how to grade intermediate work products, including documents, reviews, and periodic progress reports, in a situation in which it is not the quality of the final software *product*, but rather, learning of the *process* which is the major criterion for success in the course
- helping students relate principles and lessons learned on team projects to software engineering best practices discussed in lectures and readings

Tools for Outcomes Assessment of Education and Training in the Software Development Process

David Klappholz
(Moderator)
Stevens Institute of
Technology
david@cs.stevens-tech.edu

Lawrence Bernstein
Stevens Institute of
Technology
lbernstein@ieee.org

Dan Port
USC
dport@sunset.usc.edu

Peter Dominic
Stevens Institute of Technology
pdominic@cs.stevens-tech.edu

Keywords: attitude toward software engineering, ATSE, student attitude, software process improvement, SPI

Workshop Summary

The purpose of this workshop is to provide university faculty and software development professionals with a background on work already done in developing a tool (ATSE) for measuring students' attitudes to software process, and to involve them in the exploration of its use and further development. The outcome of this workshop will include guidelines for application of ATSE and other instruments within academic computer science programs and in industrial SPI efforts. The workshop will also involve the participant in the evolution of the various instruments.

The use of software is so pervasive that the success of software development projects in a host of application areas is critical to both the USA's economy and its defense. Success in software development efforts requires expertise in both software technology (State of the Art) and software development process (State of the Practice, also referred to as software development "best practice.") It is well understood that a larger fraction of software projects fail than projects in any other branch of engineering. It is further understood that a prime reason for the high failure rate is the lack of acceptance of, even an aversion to, what is perceived by many software developers, particularly those with above-average technology skills, as unnecessarily harsh discipline required by software development process.

It is surprising, therefore, that, while there exist tools for measuring competence in software technology, there exist no tools for measuring competence in software development process. We have embarked on a project directed at producing survey instruments and other tools for use in:

- performing outcomes assessment of the software development process-related aspect of entire undergraduate degree programs in Computer Science
- performing outcomes assessment of industrial SPI (Software ProcessImprovement) efforts
- determining those process-related skills if any, in which a particular Computer Science curriculum is deficient, and suggesting curriculum changes for overcoming specific deficiencies
- performing outcomes assessment of individual courses in software development process (Software Engineering) and of specific pedagogic approaches/techniques used in such courses

332

- assessing individual students' contributions in courses in which students develop software products in teams
- performing outcomes assessment of industry and government SPI (Software Process Improvement) efforts
- determining those process-related skills if any, in which a particular industrial or governmental software development group is deficient, and suggesting specific types of training for overcoming specific deficiencies

Because, as indicated above, it is recognized that a negative attitude toward software process on the part of many software developers is, in large measure, the reason for software development project failures, an especially important part of the proposed work, which we have begun, and made considerable progress on, is the development of a tool – ATSE (Attitude Toward Software Engineering) for measuring students' attitudes toward software process. Other outcomes-related tools will be used for assessing *knowledge of* and *ability to apply* software development best practice. These tools will, thus, cover attitude, knowledge, and behavior.

We have developed a first version of ATSE with input from, and test administrations by, faculty, at USC, Rutgers University, and Monmouth University, and through administrations focus groups, and tutorials at such conferences as CSEE&T 2002. We have begun to validate ATSE with the professional software development community through presentations, administrations, and focus groups at DoD's STC (Software Technology Conference) 2002, and at meetings.of NJSPIN (North Jersey Software Process Improvement Network), LASPIN (Los Angeles Software Process Improvement Network), and Xerox Corporation's Software Engineering Process Group.

IEEE-CS/ACM
Computing Curriculum Software Engineering Volume Project

Rich LeBlanc
Georgia Institute of
Technology
Richard.leblanc@cc.gatech.edu

Susan Mengel (Moderator)
Texas Tech University
mengel@ttu.edu

Ann Sobel
Miami University
sobelae@muohio.edu

Mordechai Ben-Menachem
Ben-Gurion University
quality@acm.org

Timothy C. Lethbridge
University of Ottawa
tcl@site.uottawa.ca

Jorge L. Díaz-Herrera
Rochester Institute of
Technology
jdiaz@gccis.rit.edu

Thomas B. Hilburn
Embry-Riddle Aeronautical
University
hilburn@db.erau.edu

Barrie Thompson
University of Sunderland
barrie.thompson@sunderland.ac.uk

Keywords: computing curriculum, computing curriculum software engineering, CCSE, software engineering education project, SWEEP, software engineering education knowledge, SEEK

Workshop Summary

In this workshop the CCSE Steering Committee members will report on the Volume's progress and the process by which the Volume is being created, and solicit feedback from the session's audience on the Volume's effectiveness.

The Software Engineering Volume is part of the IEEE-CS/ACM Computing Curriculum effort that began in the Fall of 1998 when individuals from the IEEE Computer Society and the ACM formed a Steering Committee and began work on the Computer Science Volume. This Steering Committee came to the conclusion that the area of computing had gone beyond the boundaries of computer science and that one volume could not effectively cover the newer areas that had been developed. It was decided to split the Computing Curriculum effort into several volumes; to cover Computer Engineering, Software Engineering, and Information Systems. The Steering Committee continued to work on the Computer Science Volume and appointed others to work on the other volumes.

Work on the Software Engineering Volume began in 1998 with the Software Engineering Education Project (SWEEP) which produced a draft set of accreditation guidelines for software engineering published in the IEEE-CS Computer April 1998 issue. In the Fall of 2001, SWEEP was replaced by the Steering Committee for the Computing Curriculum Software Engineering (CCSE) Volume and work began on the Volume in earnest in the Spring of 2002 with the assignment of knowledge area volunteers to develop the initial software engineering education knowledge (SEEK): Foundations, Requirements, Design, Construction, Maintenance, Process, Quality, and Management. In March and May 2002, workshops were held at the Conference on Software Engineering Education and Training and the International Conference on Software Engineering. The former produced the initial SEEK and the latter helped to refine it. In June 2002, a workshop was held in Chicago of the knowledge area and other volunteers to help to improve the initial SEEK draft. This led to the addition of Software Testing and Professional Practice to the SEEK. An internal review was conducted of the SEEK by the CCSE Steering Committee and noted software engineering experts. Released for public review in August 2002, the SEEK is undergoing further refinement. In October 2002, the pedagogy volunteers begin their work after having participated in the SEEK public review.

Two of the hallmarks of the CCSE effort by the Steering Committee are the public review process and the inclusion of as many professionals from as many countries as possible. Volunteers from Australia, Brazil, Canada, France, Germany, Hong Kong, Israel, Italy, Japan, Netherlands, New Zealand, Singapore, Spain, Taiwan, Thailand, Turkey, United Kingdom, United States, and Yugoslavia are involved and remain involved as more the Volume is completed. These volunteers represent the sectors of education, commerce, and industry as well as their professional societies.

SWEBOK : Adjustments for Education

Robert Dupuis(Moderator)
University of Quebec-Montreal
dupuis.robert@uqam.ca

Pierre Bourque
ETS Montreal
pbourque@ele.etsmtl.ca

Keywords: Software Engineering Body of Knowledge, SWEBOK, Software Engineering Education Knowledge, SEEK, software engineering education

Workshop Summary

The workshop will present a survey of the current uses of the trial version of the Software Engineering Body of Knowledge (SWEBOK) guide in education. From this survey and from the discussions in other workshops, the participants will be asked to work on the appropriate ways to gather more information from the users, and on how to modify the guide in order for it to play its role in education more appropriately. This will include its relationship with SEEK (Software Engineering Education Knowledge) and the list of topics used as a basis for the curriculum.

Tutorials

**Managing the Performance of
Software Engineering Professionals**

**Training Experts in the Fundamentals:
An Experience in Providing Software
Engineers with the Basis for
Software Process Improvement**

Managing the Performance of Software Engineering Professionals

Lawrence Peters

Software Consultants International Ltd.

lpeters@sci-ltd.net

Keywords: software engineering management, Performance Review Process, software professional performance

Tutorial Summary

This tutorial is directed at Software Engineering Managers and Senior Software Engineers in position of leadership, essentially anyone who is charged with evaluating and improving the performance of Software Professionals (both Software Engineering Managers and Software Engineers). It aims to provide attendees with a method they can employ in their own organizations at whatever level they deem appropriate in order to improve the performance of the high technology professionals reporting to them.

Management science has produced several methods that have improved the ability of corporations to create and achieve strategic goals. At the same time, managers of software professionals are increasingly frustrated by the ineffectiveness of the usual motivational methods in getting software professionals to perform at higher levels. This tutorial demonstrates how to combine our current understanding of the unique psychological and behavioral factors which drive software professionals with an extended form of a popular method for developing and realizing corporate strategy. Via the Performance Review Process, the Software Engineering Manager's focus changes from merely measuring the performance of engineers to truly managing and increasing it. As part of the tutorial, participants will be given a 10 question True/False quiz to help them assess how their knowledge and views match the latest research. By the end of the tutorial, they will be able to correctly address issues raised in the quiz

Participants in this tutorial will come away with:

- A new tool with which to better manage and improve the performance of software teams and individuals
- A better understanding of the unique psychological and behavioral characteristics of software professionals
- What motivational techniques do and do not work on this population
- How to link the corporation's strategy to performance evaluation providing increased performance and motivation
- An understanding of the benefits to the corporation, its Software Engineering Managers and its Software Engineers.

Training Experts in the Fundamentals:
An Experience in Providing Software Engineers with the Basics of Software Process Improvement

Nestor K. Ovalle
Los Alamos National Laboratory
novalle@lanl.gov

Harry W. Egdorf
Los Alamos National Laboratory
hwe@lanl.gov

Keywords: software engineering training, software process improvement, in-house training, Capability Maturity Model

Tutorial Summary

This tutorial presents an in-house software engineering training program used within a software development organization at a large, national, U.S. research laboratory. The program is designed to train experienced software engineers in the requirements and methodology of a software process improvement program being implemented within the software development organization. The software process improvement program being implemented utilizes the framework of the Capability Maturity Model, developed by the Software Engineering Institute at Carnegie Mellon University.

While the software process improvement program within the organization is in an early stage of implementation, the in-house training effort has been underway for a while and is evolving in different stages. The first stage of the training effort focused on introducing and marketing the concepts of software process improvement to the software engineers. The current second stage of training is centered on the implementation of software process improvement within the organization, where the software engineers are introduced to the policies and requirements that have been established for the software process improvement program, their responsibilities for process improvement, and the recommended methods, procedures and guidelines that they can use to effectively implement the process improvement program.

The training program itself has been undergoing process improvement based upon lessons learned from earlier stages of training and based upon the ongoing requirements of the organization's software process improvement program. The presentation will describe the evolution of the training, training content, training methodology, and lessons learned to date. This presentation could provide valuable insight for other organizations undergoing similar training efforts.

Author Index

16ᵗʰ Conference on Software Engineering Education and Training (CSEE&T 2003)

Ahtee, T. 288
Alfonso, M. 309
Bagert, D. 22
Bailey, D. 260
Baker, A. 216
Barbosa, E. 279
Bernstein, L. 268
Brataas, G. 251
Budgen, D. 3
Carrington, D. 36
Conn, T. 260
Conradi, R. 251
Cowling, A. 206
Cowling, A. 88
Crnkovic, I. 140
Dalcher, D. 193
de Oliveira, C. 158
Dubinsky, Y. 176
Duley, R. 99
Edwards, H. 166
Ellis, H. 44
Ewing, D. 242
Germain, E. 224
Gluch, D. 60
Gnatz, M. 120
Grechenig, T. 234
Guzdial, M. 279
Hanks, B. 260
Hazzan, O. 176
Hilburn, T. 99
Hislop, G. 99
Horn, C. 33
Horn, E. 298
Juristo, N. 34
Kameli, N. 60
Kerr, L. 242
Khajenoori, S. 60
Klappholz, D. 268
Kof, L. 120
Kornecki, A. 60
Kramer, J. 32
Krueger, E. 242
Kupries, M. 298
Land, R. 140

Latzina, M. 52
LeBlanc, R. 279
Maldonado, J. 279
Mason, J. 70
McDonald, J. 129
Mead, N. 44
Mora, F. 309
Moreno, A. 44
Navarro, E. 216
Newby, S. 36
Pérez-Martínez, J. 107
Peters, L. 78
Poole, W. 14
Port, D. 268
Prilmeier, F. 120
Robillard, P. 224
Rombach, D. 30
Rosca, D. 129
Rummel, B. 52
Seidman, S. 44
Seifert, T. 120
Sierra-Alonso, A. 107
Sindre, G. 251
Sjögren, A. 140
Sobel, A. 99
Stålhane, T. 251
Stevenson, T. 36
Strooper, P. 36
Teles, V. 158
Tepfenhart, W. 129
Thompson, J. 166
Tomayko, J. 3
Towell, E. 150
van der Hoek, A. 216
Werner, L. 260
White, L. 242
Wilde, N. 242
Woodman, M. 193
Zage, D. 185
Zage, W. 185
Zage, W. 27
Zhang, J. 185
Zuser, W. 234

341

Press Operating Committee

Chair
Mark J. Christensen
Independent Consultant

Editor-in-Chief
Mike Williams
Department of Computer Science
University of Calgary

Board Members

Roger U. Fujii, *Vice President, Logicon Technology Solutions*
Richard Thayer, *Professor Emeritus, California State University, Sacramento*
Sallie Sheppard, *Professor Emeritus, Texas A&M University*
Deborah Plummer, *Group Managing Editor, Press*

IEEE Computer Society Executive Staff
David Hennage, *Executive Director*
Angela Burgess, *Publisher*

Revised 11 March 2002